S0-CFO-606

Managing IMAP

Dianna Mullet & Kevin Mullet

Beijing · Cambridge · Farnham · Köln · Paris · Sebastopol · Taipei · Tokyo

Managing IMAP
by Dianna Mullet and Kevin Mullet

Copyright © 2000 O'Reilly & Associates, Inc. All rights reserved.
Printed in the United States of America.

Published by O'Reilly & Associates, Inc., 101 Morris Street, Sebastopol, CA 95472.

Editor: Mike Loukides

Production Editor: Melanie Wang

Cover Designer: Ellie Volckhausen

Printing History:

    September 2000:   First Edition.

Nutshell Handbook, the Nutshell Handbook logo, and the O'Reilly logo are registered trademarks of O'Reilly & Associates, Inc. Many of the designations used by manufacturers and sellers to distinguish their products are claimed as trademarks. Where those designations appear in this book, and O'Reilly & Associates, Inc. was aware of a trademark claim, the designations have been printed in caps or initial caps. The association between the image of a bushbuck and IMAP is a trademark of O'Reilly & Associates, Inc.

While every precaution has been taken in the preparation of this book, the publisher assumes no responsibility for errors or omissions, or for damages resulting from the use of the information contained herein.

Library of Congress Cataloging-in-Publication Data

Mullet, Dianna
    Managing IMAP/Dianna Mullet & Kevin Mullet.
      p. cm.
    Includes index.
    ISBN 0-596-00012-X
    1. Electronic mail systems 2. Internet programming. I. Mullet, Kevin.

TK5105.73 .M84 2000
005.7'1376--dc21
                                                        00-064970

ISBN: 0-596-00012-X
[M]

Table of Contents

Foreword

For nearly 10 years after I invented IMAP, it was called "the best-kept secret in electronic messaging." Then, around 1995, key electronic messaging software vendors became convinced of its advantages over the older Post Office Protocol (POP), and IMAP's presence in the industry exploded.

Today, IMAP has evolved into a mature, widely deployed protocol. Even longtime proponents of POP have jumped on the IMAP bandwagon. More and more users are demanding IMAP, because IMAP is the only message access protocol that has the flexibility to accommodate their needs.

These users are part of a growing trend to access the Internet from a variety of different computers, appliances, and access paths. In one day, they may use a dialup from home; a wireless link on the bus, train, or ferry; and a super-high-capacity Internet2 link at the office. They may use a laptop while traveling and a desktop at home and work. They may be students using shared machines in a PC lab, with no personal data kept on the PC.

These users have more advanced needs for messaging than a single incoming mailbox that is periodically downloaded to a single computer. They may have a large archive of messages in a multitude of mailboxes that they need to reference at any time and in any place. They may participate in bulletin boards or other shared message collections (e.g., a shared "customer service" mailbox).

It could be any or all of the above. The common thread in these needs is highly diverse mail access patterns and needs. No matter how many different computers, network connections, or mailboxes one uses, IMAP offers the flexibility needed for effective access.

The trend is clear. The word is spreading to those email users who are not yet familiar with IMAP's benefits. Corporate and ISP email providers are feeling the pressure to upgrade their services. Many server administrators, comfortable with a POP-only facility for many years, now find themselves playing catch-up.

Understanding the requirements of the task, much less planning how to do it, can be daunting. Fortunately, the "doing it" part is relatively painless once the way is pointed out.

Kevin and Dianna Mullet have done an outstanding job of presenting practical information on how to install, configure, and manage an IMAP server system. Both major freeware server implementations are covered in detail. I am particularly impressed by how the Mullets have uncovered and fleshed out useful information from mailing list folklore or passing mention in documenting.

A book like this has been needed for a long time. It belongs on every server administrator's bookshelf.

—Mark Crispin
Seattle, Washington
1 July 2000

Preface

This book is both an overview of the IMAP protocol as well as a comprehensive installation and management guide for the two leading Unix-based IMAP servers. The University of Washington IMAP server, written by Mark Crispin, the father of the IMAP protocol, is an easy-to-install server that auto-detects and adapts to numerous mailstore formats on an individual user basis. The Cyrus IMAP server, from Carnegie Mellon University, is a high-performance, scalable server embraced by many larger sites.

As important as IMAP is to the growth of email, we were very surprised to find that a book on IMAP hadn't already been written—at least we couldn't find one. There was a lot of disconnected information out on the Net in various documents in documentation included with source distributions, on web sites, buried inside archives for mailing lists, and in Usenet newsgroups, but there was very little centralized assistance for the system administrator who wanted information on IMAP protocol, server administration, system design, and troubleshooting all in one place.

This book is directed at Unix and email system administrators who are (or might be) using IMAP to get email from their central mailstore to their users' client software. If you have five email users or five hundred thousand, we describe a system in this book that would meet your needs. If your users are all using a common platform like Microsoft Windows, Solaris, or Mac OS, or if none of your users have access to anything but a web browser, we outline ways to provide reliable, robust, manageable, and consistently powerful email service to each of your users.

We're true believers in IMAP because we've found that with a well-designed IMAP system, end-user email frustration is only directed at the content of their email, not at the quality of the service.

How This Book Is Organized

Part I, *IMAP Fundamentals*
> The first three chapters introduce IMAP. They explain what IMAP is, how it fits into the world of email, and how it works. The rest of the book is organized into four parts.

Part II, *IMAP Mail User Agents (MUAs)*
> Chapters 4 and 5 cover IMAP clients and web-based IMAP clients.

Part III, *The Cyrus IMAP Server*
> Chapters 6 through 9 cover the Cyrus IMAP server.

Part IV, *The UW IMAP Server*
> Chapters 10 through 12 cover the University of Washington (UW) IMAP server.

Part V, *Other Topics*
> Chapters 13 through 18 cover miscellaneous important topics that are related to maintaining a robust and reliable IMAP server.

Part VI, *Appendixes*
> We've included three appendixes in the book. Appendix A, *Conversion from Berkeley Mail Format to Cyrus: Tools*, is a list of tools that will aid in the conversion from Berkeley Mail format to Cyrus. Appendix B, *Adding SSL Support to IMAP*, is useful for those readers who want to add SSL support to IMAP. And Appendix C, *IMAP Commands*, is a list of IMAP commands.

Conventions Used in This Book

Italic is used for:

- Email addresses
- Uniform Resource Locators (URLs)
- Program names
- Protocol commands
- Filenames and directory pathnames

`Constant width` is used for:

- Computer output in examples and text
- Source code examples

`Constant width bold` is used for:

- Program invocation commands

Related Books

sendmail, Bryan Costales with Eric Allman (O'Reilly)

Essential System Administration, Æleen Frisch (O'Reilly)

Programming Internet Email, David Wood (O'Reilly)

We'd Like to Hear From You

We have tested and verified the information in this book to the best of our ability, but you may find that features have changed (or even that we have made mistakes!). Please let us know about any errors you find, as well as your suggestions for future editions, by writing to:

> O'Reilly & Associates, Inc.
> 101 Morris Street
> Sebastopol, CA 95472
> 1-800-998-9938 (in the U.S. or Canada)
> 1-707-829-0515 (international/local)
> 1-707-829-0104 (fax)

You can also send us messages electronically. To be put on the mailing list or request a catalog, send email to:

> *info@oreilly.com*

To ask technical questions or comment on the book, send email to:

> *bookquestions@oreilly.com*

We have a web site for the book, where we'll list examples, errata, and any plans for future editions. You can access this page at:

> *http://www.oreilly.com/catalog/mimap/*

For more information about this book and others, see the O'Reilly web site:

> *http://www.oreilly.com*

Acknowledgments

We would like to thank our editor, Mike Loukides, for his enthusiasm, patience, and guidance in taking on this project with a couple of fledgling authors. We would also like to thank Amos Gouaux, Walter Wong, Jon Forrest, and Mark Crispin, the father of IMAP, for their insightful reviews and recommendations. The book would not be complete without their input and astute insight. We'd also like to thank Mark Crispin for offering to write the foreword; we're honored and pleased to have his contribution.

I

IMAP Fundamentals

1

The Internet Mail Model

IMAP stands for Internet Mail Access Protocol. For much of the Internet email system administrator community, it also stands for flexibility, speed, and power. These attributes come from abilities like being able to store all a user's mail centrally, not demand that she store copies of it on each workstation from which she wants to access her mail. IMAP users also store their mail in an arbitrary number of server-side mailboxes, each of which they can move messages into or out of with any IMAP client. When an IMAP user checks her mail, her client need only download some of the header for each message, not the entire message. When she sees messages in her index she wants to retrieve, she can decide which parts of the 13-part message she wants to download, and which she doesn't. These are capabilities that no other standardized mail access protocol permits.

Before we dive into a more detailed discussion of IMAP, though, let's talk about Internet mail in general. Much of this discussion is a definition of terms. In defining those terms, however, we're discussing the language that is the bedrock of Internet electronic mail.

What Is the Internet Mail Model?

The Internet Mail Model, like the Internet itself, is a collection of standardized components all acting with a common goal. In the case of email, the goal is to provide the framework for carrying electronic messages between one user and another. Each of the end users may be on very different platforms. Their respective sites may have vast geographic, technological, and social differences. Those differences demand that the framework be at once both robust and flexible. The Internet's email framework consists of agents, mailstores, and standards. It may help you to reference Figure 1-1 as you read the chapter. The figure shows how the agents, mailstores, and standards work together.

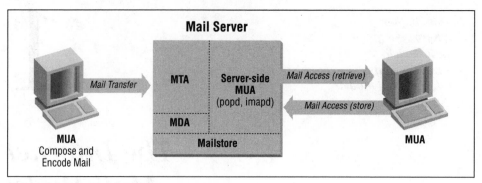

Figure 1-1. Email cycle of life

The Agents (MUA, MTA, MDA)

The software programs that handle Internet messages are called agents. There are three types of Internet messaging agents: the Mail Transport Agent (MTA), Mail Delivery Agent (MDA), and Mail User Agent (MUA).

MTA

An MTA (Figure 1-2) is a program that transmits and receives messages between messaging sites. The sending MTA accepts messages from end user client software and transmits it to a receiving MTA. The receiving MTA receives messages from the sending MTA, determines whether or not the recipient resides locally on the receiving MTA (server) system, and then hands off the message for delivery. If the message is destined for a user on the receiving MTA's system, then the receiving MTA hands the message off to a Message Delivery Agent (MDA) such as */bin/mail*. If the user is not on the local system, then the receiving MTA acts as a sending MTA to pass the message on to the MTA on the remote system.

Figure 1-3 shows typical Internet message headers. Each "Received" header line represents transit through a separate MTA. MTAs do not touch the mailstore. They delegate that work to the MDA.

MDA

The MDA is the trench soldier: the grunt of Internet messaging. All the MDA knows is how to determine which local user the message is destined for and how to put the message in the correct place in the mailstore. Actually, that's not quite *all* the MDA knows. Some super-charged MDAs, such as Procmail, have vast delusions of grandeur, but we'll cover that later in the book. All that's essential to know right now is that the MTA hands the MDA each Internet message destined for a local user and that the MDA is responsible for knowing where to place it in the mailstore.

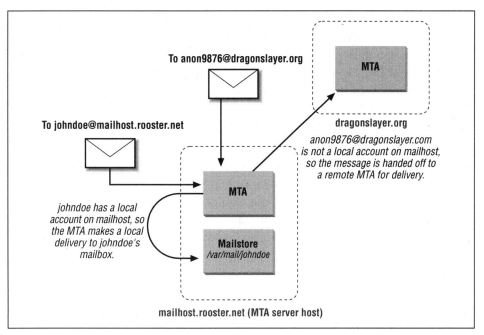

Figure 1-2. The MTA

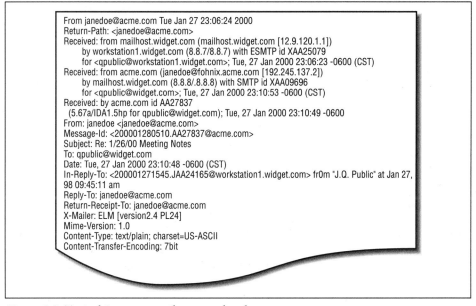

Figure 1-3. Typical Internet email message header

MUA

As we've seen, the MTA, responsible for knowing how to route every conceivable type of legitimate Internet message, is by far the most educated part of the messaging model. The MDA is the hardest-working component. The MUA, on the other hand, is charged with being the most glamorous part of the IMM framework. The MUA is the interface between the MTA and the most unpredictable component of the IMM: the user himself. Strictly speaking, the MUA retrieves mail from the mailstore and sends new messages upstream to the MTA.

The MUA typically retrieves messages from the mailstore in one of three ways: by using a mail access protocol like IMAP or POP, by using a remote file access protocol, or by accessing local files. In the case of IMAP and POP, the MUA function is split between two pieces of software: the mail client and a corresponding server process that mediates between the client and the mailstore using POP or IMAP (see Figure 1-4).

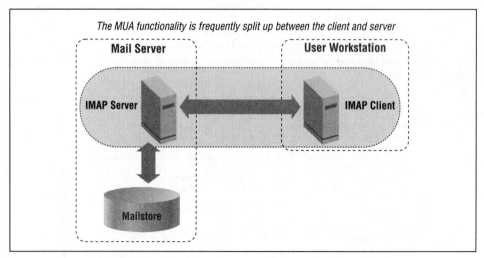

Figure 1-4. MUA function

The Mailstore

The mailstore is the filing cabinet of the mail system. When a user receives a piece of email, it's deposited into his portion of the mailstore. To retrieve his email, he uses an MUA to peer into the mailstore and view his messages. Not too long ago, most mailstores consisted of a single text file per user containing the user's messages concatenated together within that file. Today, mailstores are implemented in a great variety of ways. The volume of email crossing the Internet has grown meteorically, increasing the demand for more efficient and accessible ways of storing mail. Technologies like IMAP that permit hierarchical organization of the user's mail within his part of the server mailstore have resulted in products that abandon the traditional flat file mailstore. Depending on your messaging product, your mailstore may consist of a single file per message, or all the users at your site may share a single high-performance database in which their messages are stored. The Internet standards don't address implementation details of the mailstore—its concern is primarily with transport and format.

The Standards (RFC 822, MIME, SMTP/ESMTP, POP, IMAP)

Internet standards are defined in documents called Requests for Comments (RFCs). The Internet Engineering Task Force (IETF) is a collection of working groups, each of which is a collection of volunteers collaborating to define new RFCs for the Internet or to revise existing ones. RFCs are the deliverable produced by the IETF working groups. All IETF standards are RFCs, but not all RFCs are standards. Some RFCs are experimental protocols, and some are commentaries on existing practices. Some are somewhat transparent attempts to publish proprietary methods and convince the Internet community to embrace them as standards, and some (usually the ones published on April 1st) are wry bits of geek humor.

In this chapter, though, we skim through the standards that are germane to Internet mail. We group these standards into several categories: formatting and encoding mail, mail transfer, and mail access.

Formatting and encoding mail

RFC 822 (Standard)—Standard for the format of Internet text messages
> This is the big kahuna. This RFC lies at the core of all Internet-based messaging. It defines plaintext messages, which themselves consist of a header in a common format, a single blank line, and a body. If ASCII is the DNA of Internet messaging, RFC 822 messages are the chromosomes...or maybe the cells...oh well.

RFC 2076 (Informational)—Common Internet Message Headers
> RFC 822 defines a standard format Internet message header. RFC 2076 goes into greater detail about the specific header lines, their purpose, and their individual contents.

Multi-Purpose Internet Mail Extensions
> The primary motivator for the creation of the working group that created MIME was to support non-ASCII character sets necessary for email in languages other than English. A secondary motivator was a requirement for a standard way to send attachments. Less important, but also a motivating factor, was the need for a standard way to send multimedia content. MIME came about through the realization that a single solution could address all three needs.

Figure 1-5 shows how a graphics file might have been conveyed in days of yore, alongside how it would probably be transported via MIME today. The figure doesn't really do justice to the benefits of MIME. With manual encoding, users were usually stuck to just sending single files in their messages. With MIME, users can send attachments containing any kind of data, of arbitrary length. MIME messages can point to files or other data outside the mail message. The only functional limitation is that the MUA on each end must know how to handle the particular MIME type. If you send an attachment to a colleague of type *application/postscript*, and her mail client doesn't know how to handle that type, you've gained little over manual encoding.

The core of MIME itself is set forth in five RFCs:

- RFC 2045 (Draft standard)—MIME Part 1: Format of Internet Message Bodies

- RFC 2046 (Draft standard)—MIME Part 2: Media Types

- RFC 2047 (Draft standard)—MIME Part 3: Message Header Extensions for Non-ASCII Text

- RFC 2048 (Draft standard)—MIME Part 4: Registration Procedures

- RFC 2049 (Draft standard)—MIME Part 5: Conformance Criteria and Examples

Together, these RFCs define the mail headers, message structure, and data characterization that should permit any computer file or data stream to be conveyed via email without extraordinary demands on the intermediate mail gateways or the receiving client.

MIME appeared on the scene before use of HTTP was widespread. Shortly after MIME began being used, the Web became popular, and suddenly, people needed to send URLs via email. Sending the URL to a file instead of the file itself is popular—instead of sending the file as an attachment, the user sends a pointer to the file instead. Large mail attachments can be problematic. Many ISPs still use only POP service and implement it in such a way that forces users to download all new email without picking and choosing particular messages. Messages with large attachments make downloading POP mail painfully time consuming. SMTP servers often have size limits on messages they'll accept (typically 10–20 MB per message). If a message has a large attachment, it could be rejected by the SMTP server. Sending the URL instead of the file itself gets around those problems. It's no wonder URLs are a popular way of conveying information stored in large files.

A common (much to the consternation of traditionalists) use for MIME nowadays is to send two versions of your message: a *text/plain* version and a *text/html* version with more formatting.

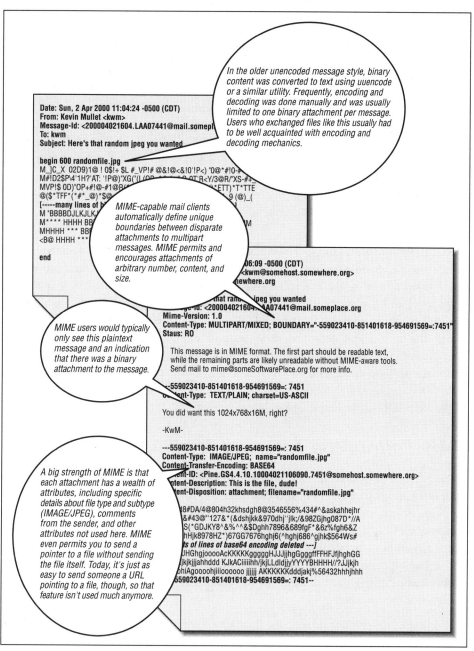

Figure 1-5. Transport using MIME

Mail transfer

The RFCs mentioned in the previous section provide the framework for the construction of an email message. Now we need some standards for describing how that message is conveyed upstream to other hosts on the Internet. The most important of these is RFC 821: Simple Mail Transfer Protocol (SMTP). SMTP defines how mail is transported from one place to another, whether that transport is from your MUA to the MTA or between two MTAs. Figure 1-6 shows an example of a typical SMTP conversation between an MUA and an adjacent MTA. There are additional RFCs that augment SMTP into what is frequently called Extended SMTP, but RFC 821 remains the core standard defining Internet mail transport. A list of additional RFCs may be found at the Internet Mail Consortium site (*http://www.imc.org*).

Mail access

We've looked at standards for conveying mail to a server. We've seen yet other standards specifying how the email should be formatted. It only stands to reason that we now need standards for accessing and managing the mail in a mailstore. POP and IMAP are two of those standards. Later, we'll go into vivid detail about the differences between IMAP and POP. A mail access protocol is a means by which the mail client software may perform operations on messages that have already made it to the mailstore. Note that we don't just say "read" messages that are in the mailstore. Although POP is a "read-heavy" protocol, IMAP permits users to add messages to the mailstore, move them around, and change their attributes or the degree of access other users have to them.

Why Follow the Internet Mail Model?

Unlike closed commercial mail systems, Internet messaging is defined by a series of specifications that are free and open for all. Consequently, an Internet messaging system can be built using a variety of products from several vendors, with assuring that each product will interoperate with all the other products. This is especially important because the open standards defining the Internet itself make for a highly complex environment in which each component of a messaging model must know what to expect of the others. Communication standardization is the soul of the Internet.

The Internet repeatedly proves the fact that there is no problem so large that it cannot be solved by the principle of "divide and conquer." A browse through some of the messaging-related RFCs from the early 1970s shows how early ARPA-net[*] engineers struggled to send email back and forth. Early on, they relied on the

---

[*] Advanced Research Projects Agency network (R.I.P. 1970–1990).

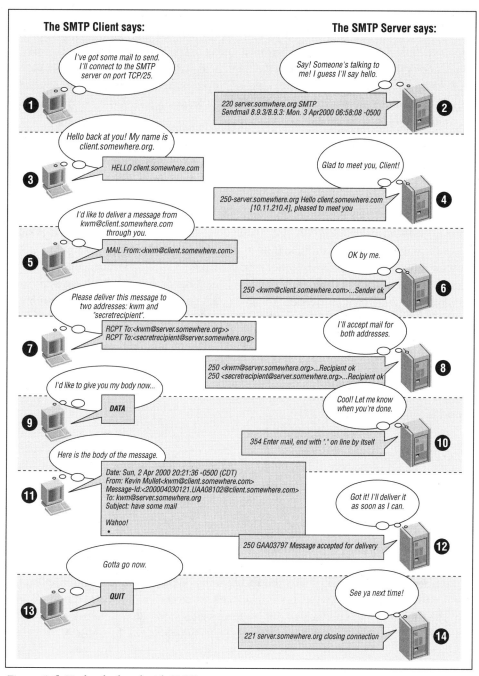

Figure 1-6. Under the hood with SMTP

weak model embraced by many modern-day closed-source solutions: email as a
file-copying program. RFC 469 (circa 1973) kicks around the idea of an email infrastructure based on passing files around using FTP. Even in those early discussions, innovative ideas were alluded to, such as active links to other documents,
redirection to central document repositories,* permanent email archives, and content from arbitrary non-textual sources. Those ideas suggested the need for a hierarchy of standards and protocols.

Before too long, however, the problem of how to best implement email was
divided and conquered. As we've seen, a special-purpose protocol (SMTP) was
developed exclusively for transport of the messages from one place to another.
Other protocols were developed for accessing the mail once it arrived at the destination mailstore (IMAP and POP). Standards were developed for the format of
messages themselves and for encapsulating the payload of those messages
(MIME). With the standards in hand, it was an entirely manageable task for the
various parts that make up Internet email to interoperate, because the means of
doing so was a widely discussed and published set of industry standards. System
administrators no longer needed to worry about whether or not the sendmail,
QMail, and Postfix MTAs would talk to each other. Nor did they need to concern
themselves with whether any IMAP-compliant client would be able to retrieve mail
from their UW IMAP, Cyrus, or proprietary IMAP server.

Now that we have a fair idea of what are the major components of Internet email
and why we have that model in the first place, let's look a bit closer at some real-
world email transactions.

Examples

The stage is set, and now we're ready to introduce the players.

Mail Routing

Think about what happens when mail is sent by a user on a PC using Netscape to
someone who uses the text-mode, Unix-based MUA, PINE. As seen in Figure 1-7,
the sender (Netscape user) sends the message by SMTP to the MTA running on the
sender's ISP's mail server. Once the mail arrives at the mail server, the MTA asks
the MDA to store the message in the local message store. When the recipient reads
his mail, he runs PINE on the mail server itself, which views his INBOX as a local
file. Although in the example, no *network* mail access protocol is involved while
reading the mail, you might think of the mail access protocol in this case as a way

---

* Sixteen years before the Web and 18 years before Gopher!

of converting the mail into something the client can understand. In those terms, the mail access protocol can be thought of as being hardcoded in the client.

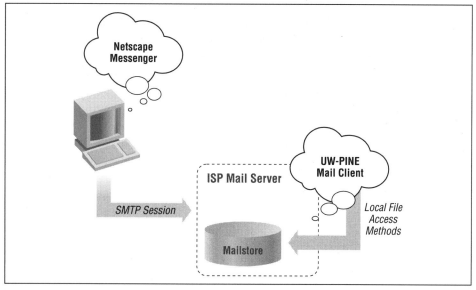

Figure 1-7. Mail routing example

Examples of Agents

An agent is a program that performs a task on behalf of a human user, either directly at the human's behest or indirectly under instruction from another agent. Usually, a chain of agents work in concert to get the information from its point of origin to its intended destination. Unlike the previous examples, Internet email agents perform their duties in the open and usually with the full consent and support of all the participants. Here are some examples of some of the more popular Internet email agents. We'll go into more detail about some of these later, but it's always good to solidify theory with some real-world examples as soon as possible.

MTAs

Any discussion of Internet MTAs could also easily be entitled "Sendmail and some alternatives." The old slogan that "nobody ever got fired for buying IBM" could be adapted equally well to sendmail. Leave it to the Internet community, though, not to leave well enough alone. Recently, viable contenders have come onto the scene, such as Qmail and Postfix.

sendmail is to email what the Internet is to networking. The genesis of sendmail was Eric Allman's Delivermail, which he wrote to connect ARPAnet email to numerous other networks' email. As demands for routing more types of email were made of Delivermail, Allman rewrote it to be much more flexible and user-configurable, and sendmail was born. The ever-increasing flexibility acquired in the twenty-plus-year history of sendmail has come at the price of a complex interface.

Both Qmail and Postfix represent the strategy of performing the MTA mission with many smaller utilities, each of which carries out a narrow part of the MTA function rather than using one larger piece of software. Each has arguably resulted in a system with more straightforward configuration at the expense of a greater degree of process complexity. Both lay claim to being able to transit a bodacious number of messages using a ridiculously small amount of hardware. Which one you're likely to prefer is probably one of those coffee or tea propositions where you'll just have to try each and see which you like better.

We'll go into more detail about MDAs and MUAs later, but let's briefly touch on some of them.

MDAs

As the agent that actually places the email in the user's mailbox, the MDA is probably one of the most often used programs on your mail server. While a single MTA process could handle a large amount of mail bound for one site or a large number of messages from one process, each MDA process usually lives and dies for the processing of a single message.

Examples of MDAs include */bin/mail*, */usr/lib/mail.local*, *procmail*, and Cyrus *deliver*. Each of these programs takes an RFC 822–formatted message on standard input and delivers it to a mailbox. In the case of *procmail*, however, a mailbox could be local or remote, so *procmail* is one of those examples that could be either an MDA, an MUA, or both, depending on the nuances of how it's used.

MUAs

As the frontend to the mail system, the MUA is the highest-profile element in the chain of elements between each Internet email sender and recipient. Ironically, the failure of the MTA or MDA has much greater impact than the failure of a single MUA.

PINE, Eudora, Microsoft Outlook, Netscape Messenger, and Mulberry are all MUAs. Additionally, even sendmail and *imapd* can be considered MUAs. sendmail is frequently used as an MUA to generate messages programmatically. If you were to fire off a sendmail process as shown below, you would be running sendmail as an MTA. The following command starts sendmail running as a daemon and tells it to process the queue every 15 minutes:

```
% /usr/lib/sendmail -bd -q15m
```

If, however, you fired off a sendmail process as follows, you would be using sendsmail as an MUA:

```
% echo "Subject: Hey you!"|/usr/lib/sendmail -v kwmullet@yahoo.com
kwmullet@yahoo.com... Connecting to mx1.mail.yahoo.com. via esmtp...
220 mta220.mail.yahoo.com ESMTP
>>> EHLO security.unt.edu
250-mta220.mail.yahoo.com
250-PIPELINING
250 8BITMIME
>>> MAIL From:<kwm@security.unt.edu>
250 ok
>>> RCPT To:<kwmullet@yahoo.com>
250 ok
>>> DATA
354 go ahead dd
>>> .
250 ok dirdel
kwmullet@yahoo.com... Sent (ok dirdel)
Closing connection to mx1.mail.yahoo.com.
>>> QUIT
221 mta220.mail.yahoo.com
%
```

In addition, each time you use your MUA to connect to an IMAP server, you create an IMAP process on the server exclusively to service the IMAP requests between your MUA and the mailstore. That process is also considered part of the MUA—a server-side MUA. To further distinguish between the server and the client side of the MUA, let's refer to the client side as the MUA and the server side as the Mail Access Agent.

We'll have plenty of details later about MUAs and MDAs. We won't have so much information about MTAs, because they're "SMTP plumbing" in the scope of this book.

2

What Is IMAP?

This chapter looks at what IMAP is and what distinguishes it from other mail access protocols. We discuss briefly where IMAP is now and where it's headed.

IMAP in a Nutshell

IMAP is a way of accessing electronic mail that is stored on a central server.

Certainly, this statement is true, but there's more to it than that. More precisely, IMAP is a way to retrieve messages from one or more mailboxes on a central server, without ever having to download a single message to local hard disk. The messages remain on the server at all times.

By design, IMAP was intended to provide the same level of functionality for mailbox and message access and management that exists with a mailbox located on a local hard drive. Consequently, IMAP has server operations, such as "search for messages matching such-and-such criteria," that are normally associated with mail clients.

You can see the advantages of IMAP very clearly if you work from several computers (e.g., home computer, office computer, and laptop). With IMAP, you don't have to wonder which computer you were on when you downloaded and read a given message. You know it's still on the server.

With the right IMAP client, you can do all of the following:

- Learn when new messages arrive in any of your mailboxes

- Share your mailboxes with anyone or everyone

- Move messages from one mailbox to another

- Mark messages with flags (such as "Important") that are preserved between IMAP sessions

Another distinguishing feature of IMAP is that, not only is your INBOX stored in a central location, but your *mail folders* (mailboxes, in IMAP parlance) are stored in a central location on the IMAP server as well. As long as you've got IMAP client software,* not only can you read your incoming email from just about anywhere on the Net, but you can access all the mail you archived in your mailboxes, too.

One feature that sets IMAP apart is that it supports not one, but *three* interaction models.

IMAP's Three Interaction Models

IMAP has three models for interacting with your mail: offline, online, and disconnected. The three interaction models are at the core of why, on its own merit, IMAP is the most powerful and flexible mail access protocol. The models are formally defined in RFC 1733 (*Distributed Electronic Mail Models in IMAP4*). Let's take look at the three models.

The Online Model

In the online model, messages are left on the mail server and are manipulated remotely by mail client programs. The mail client maintains an open connection to the server for the duration of the session, that is, until the user decides to end the session.

Whether you prefer the online model has much to do with where you think the higher resource burden should be placed: on the client or on the server. If you believe, as we do, that resources are best centralized when possible, then you're likely to prefer the online model. If you believe that centralized resources should be conserved whenever possible, even at the expense of a greater investment on the part of the user, then you're likely to prefer the offline model. Watch out, though, because placing resource demands on the server requires attention and monitoring of system administrators lest things get out of hand. The online model can put a burden on memory and CPU resources if users tend to keep several mailboxes open, or if mail clients are poorly behaved in some way that results in multiple sessions per user.

---

* Actually, you needn't even have IMAP software on your own machine. You can use a web browser to access your IMAP mailstore; web-based clients are discussed in Chapter 5, *Web-Based IMAP Clients*.

In situations where many users share the same PC (such as a kiosk or computer lab), the online model is the only viable alternative. The same holds true in cases where one user reads mail from many different machines.

An advantage of the online model is that it works splendidly over slow or high-latency communication lines. Let's take IMAP operating in online mode as an example. Early IMAP testing was over a 2,400 bps modem,* and a design goal was that it be no less tolerable than running a host-based program over a dialup connection. In fact, IMAP ended up being more tolerable due to client-based caching of data (such as when the message browser redraws locally instead of over the wire). Even over a slow Internet connection, the online model lets a user manage a shockingly large amount of mail. Suppose a user receives a lot of mail and likes to keep all of it. He might easily have thousands of messages spread across hundreds of mailboxes. When that user dials in to his Internet service provider over a 56 Kbps connection, he definitely does not want to download all his mail in order to read just one particular mail message. Using the online model, he would simply connect to the server and select the message he needed. The only time required would be the time it takes the server to access the message and display a copy of the message in his mail client. Furthermore, with IMAP one can usually select to download an attachment *after* reading the message body.

The Offline Model

The offline model can be compared to a post office box. A person goes to the post office, fetches mail from his box, and leaves the box empty. In the offline model, the mail client fetches messages from the server, stores them on the user's machine, then deletes the messages from the server. The user connects to the mail server, checks for new mail, downloads his new messages, and disconnects. Messages can then be filed into mailboxes or otherwise processed, but such actions are done locally, without the participation of the mail server.

There are advantages of the offline model for both users and system managers. First off, the offline model lessens the amount of space mail consumes on the central mail server. Secondly, for users with a modest amount of mail, it minimizes the amount of time spent connected to the server. The offline model is excellent for the user who always uses the same machine to access his mail and prefers keeping the primary copy of his messages on that machine.

The disadvantages of the offline model are equally compelling. Since all of a user's mail is downloaded to her local computer, she's out of luck if she wants to review her mail archives, unless she happens to be at the location where she downloaded her mail.

---

* Radio was also an early design goal of IMAP. Radio users say that IMAP works wonderfully over radio.

Another disadvantage of the offline model is that it suffers from serious problems of scale for users with significant mail volume, especially if those users have slow Internet connections. Of course, this means that there's a burden on each offline user to either buy more disk storage or store less mail. If a user receives 5 or 10 modest-size mail messages a day, then he might not be inconvenienced by having to download them all to read them. If he gets 100 messages a day with sizable attachments, he's going to wish he'd never heard of email by the time he downloads them all, just to be able to read the first 1 or 2. The offline model can also be expensive in terms of storage on the server. Users who maintain multiple copies of mail in multiple locations generally configure the client not to delete mail from the server after download.

As we'll see later in the discussion of the online model, it's much easier on the user when all he really has to download is an index of his mail.

The Disconnected Model

In the disconnected model, the IMAP client connects to the mail server, synchronizes its list of messages and mailboxes with the server, maybe copies the first few messages into a local cache, then disconnects. In this model, the client queues up tasks and plays them later in a single session.

To the casual user, there should be no difference between the online model and the disconnected model, except that occasionally some operations have a slight latency to them. The disconnected model complements the online model, and in fact, most IMAP clients allow the user to alternate between the two models at will. The intent of the disconnected model is to support users who cannot always connect to a server, but still want to handle mail. Disconnected users are the big winners. The disconnected model allows them to process mail when there's no network available. For example, a user might collect her mail at the airport, board the plane, read and respond to her mail in flight, then reconnect to the server at her destination to synchronize her mailbox and deliver her outgoing mail. There are other situations where disconnected mode comes in handy, too. Take wireless applications as an example—especially those where idle connections rack up per-minute charges. Disconnected mode is made-to-order for connections that charge for time.

It all boils down to picking where you want your bottleneck to be. With the offline model, the desktop machine is the bottleneck. With the online model, the mail server is the bottleneck. With the disconnected model, the network could be the bottleneck. It depends on how fast your server can fork all the processes, or how much bandwidth there is to spare in your network.

Why IMAP?

The short answer is that IMAP solves many of the problems inherent in legacy mail systems. Since the earliest days of networking, the best and the brightest in the computer field have looked for successively better ways to corral individual correspondence into threads of dialog that could easily be used online. This section puts IMAP in the context of several legacy mail models and its competing mail access protocol, POP.

Host-Based Email

Host-based email was the original model for email. If you've been using email for many years, you probably started by using this model. In the host-based email model, the MUA, MTA, and mailstore reside on the same physical machine. Figure 2-1 illustrates the host-based email model.

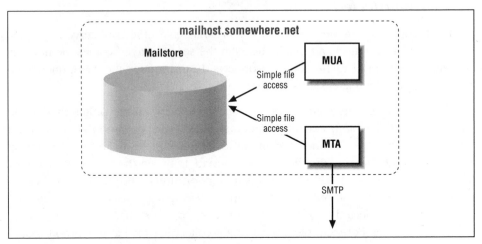

Figure 2-1. Host-based email

Host-based email is a study in single-points-of-failure. Because all functions are carried out by a single system, divisions of responsibility between different parts of the system are unclear. If one part craters, there's a much greater risk that it'll cause the rest of the system to crater. On a host-based email system, the actions of any of the three essential components (MUA, MTA, and mailstore) impact the performance of the others. Host-based email systems are frequently general-purpose compute servers or Internet servers as well. Most enterprise mail systems that have been around for many years began in this model, the shortcomings of which necessitated the development of standardized mail access protocols.

Depending on how you approach it, the host-based email model is either the most or the least secure model around. Some might consider it the most secure because in a single draconian sweep, you clamp down on the security of the mailstore, transport agent, and user agent in one fell swoop. Of course, this is subject to the Primary Firewall Fallacy: a firewall tricks you into believing that everything on the outside is dirty and everything on the inside is clean. Although host-based email may give you a great deal of control over who can get to your mail jewels, from the outside it provides relatively little protection of your users from one another.

Shared Mailstore

In the fledgling days of PC LANs, more often than not email meant an exalted file-copying program like Novell Mail, Quick Mail, or Word Perfect Office. Those programs copied message files hither and yon between directories on a shared filesystem. Checking for new mail amounted to using a remote file-sharing protocol to see if message files had shown up in a given subdirectory, although the mechanics were usually hidden from the user. The mechanics of scaling systems like that presented profound problems.

Nowadays the acronyms have changed, but the relationship between the user agent machines and the mailstore file server remains essentially the same. In host-based email systems, the child lives at home. In the shared mailstore model, the child has gone off to college, but still gets a stipend from the parents every time he asks for it.

Problems with shared mailstores

The shared mailstore model is fraught with problems, including:

File locking

> With this model, we see the introduction of the bane of Internet mail system designers: the dreaded file-locking problem. The problem goes like this. Suppose you have two pieces of software (the MUA and the MTA), both making changes to the same file (user's INBOX). What happens when they both try to change the file at the same time? That problem is easy to manage on host-based email systems, because under the benign dictatorship of the OS, all relatively well written software can play nicely using standard locking mechanisms. When the mailstore is shared between two hosts, and the hosts lack the governance of such a thing as a network kernel, they will invariably make invalid assumptions about when to write to a file.

> As you start engineering your own enterprise mail system, you are likely to find that any model, even host-based mail, is more desirable than the shared mailstore model.

Synchronization

> When one client makes a change to the mailstore, there's no way for other clients to see that change.

Platform dependence

No major operating system shares a file-sharing protocol with every other major operating system. As Lincoln might have said, you can share all of the filesystems some of the time, and some of the filesystems all of the time, but you're never going to share all of them all of the time.

Bandwidth usage

It's clearly inefficient to use a non-client/server database that pulls in the entire database to perform a query. It's equally inefficient to have your mail client pull in your entire mailbox when trying to hunt down a message you received three months ago. Such inefficiencies are multiplied when you pull in your mailbox over the network. That is exactly what happens when you perform an operation on your mailstore, such as a simple search, via a remote file-sharing protocol. It's best to save that kind of bandwidth use for when you truly need to use an entire file, and to instead use client/server mail schemes for routine mail operations.

Mailstore format constraints

While there are plenty of standards to define what that plaintext looks like (such as ASCII, RFC 822, ANSI, and MIME), there are still subtle differences in the way various platforms choose to store such text. A classic example is the difference between the way Microsoft Windows platforms and Unix platforms end physical lines of text. If you've played the cross-platform game before, you've no doubt pulled up files from your Windows file server in *vi*, only to have them peppered with ^M's. Likewise, you may have pulled up a Unix file in a DOS editor only to find that it has become one long, confusing line of text. Such parochial text-formatting problems go away when you replace the remote file-sharing protocol with a standardized mail access protocol.

Proprietary Mail Schemes

Like it or not, proprietary mail schemes are definitely a significant part of the landscape. In these schemes, one vendor provides the entire soup-to-nuts solution. The MUA, the server, and the gateways necessary to make them talk to anything out in the rest of the world are all provided by one vendor. That vendor decides what features you have. That vendor decides how you scale your system. Effectively, that vendor decides the workflow for your enterprise.

The Faustian thing about these messaging-in-a-box solutions is that they're very tempting for decision-makers to put in place, because they offer a variety of features with deceptively low complexity. They also give the decision-maker a single organization to blame if things go wrong.

Another problem is that proprietary schemes lock you in to a solution. Once you have the scheme in place, your users become reliant on its features. Once your users are reliant on its features, it becomes very difficult to move from the proprietary scheme to a standards-based solution that doesn't have those features.

You also become dependent on the vendor. If you ever have to change vendors (for example, because the vendor's solution doesn't scale to match the growth in your usage), you're stuck. On the other hand, a standards-based solution permits you to change vendors as your needs change.

The real problem is that nobody works in a vacuum. Many proprietary solutions do not rely on standard Internet protocols, but instead depend on a proprietary gateway to talk to the Internet. To accomplish your job, be it commerce, education, or research, you need to be able to communicate via email to people outside your particular enterprise. Besides, open source software increasingly duplicates or surpasses the features and performance of proprietary solutions.

Standardized Mail Access Protocols

In this book, what we mean by a standardized mail protocol is a standardized means of communication between an electronic mail client and server. IMAP is one such protocol. Those protocols, although their implementation sometimes gets a little sticky on this point, are agnostic with regard to platform. That is the core of their value. That is, in fact, the core of the Internet's value. IETF-designed standards have a scope and utility beyond that of any vendor's product. Not to get too preachy here, but the functionality of these standards is the reason why the Internet is a contiguous, mostly highly functional network.

The strategy of using standardized mail access protocols is divide-and-conquer. Internet messaging is divided into tasks that are easily managed by straightforward protocols. The variety of implementation available for each of these protocols gives system administrators much more flexibility in choice when providing services to their end users. The openness of the standard-making process and of the distribution process for most highly regarded Internet software guarantees this.

Use of standardized mail access protocols permits a site to restrict mail spool access to the MDA and the mail access protocol. This, in turn, can reduce or eliminate file-locking problems.

In addition to dividing and conquering, standardized mail access protocols are also good at delegation. Because your IMAP client, for example, can delegate to the IMAP server the task of searching through your mailstore for any messages with a given subject line, the search itself has negligible impact on network bandwidth. The cost of that low impact, however, is generally increased processor use on the mail server.

Standardized protocols free each side from having to worry about the minutiae of having to exchange data with the other. Problems such as character type (ASCII or Unicode), end-of-line discipline, or storage format (unified files or separate data and resource forks) are mostly resolved. Continuing irritants include how best to accommodate various internationalized character sets and how best to encode and decode arbitrary binary files and data streams for encapsulation in a mail message. Various ISO, ANSI, and IETF standards go a great distance in resolving those issues. However, the work is not completely done yet.

All things considered, we hope you'll find, as we have, that use of standardized mail access protocols is the path that holds the most promise and is the least fraught with pitfalls.

IMAP and POP: A Comparison

If you look at which mail access protocols have popular market share, there are only two players on the field: POP and IMAP. POP essentially created the market. It also created a need for a protocol with a great many more features. IMAP filled that need.

POP

POP is the granddaddy of standardized mail access protocols. Although recently you could say that there was more POP client software than IMAP client software, now you can say only that there's more well-implemented POP client software than well-implemented IMAP client software. Therein lies the continuing value of POP: its simplicity. POP is a humble protocol. It doesn't keep track of a variety of message states, it doesn't allow the user to search through her mailbox, and it doesn't even facilitate storing messages in a number of mailboxes. It does one thing and one thing only: it makes the messages available to the user to download to her local machine on demand.

For some users, the limitations of POP are just fine. They use one and only one machine to read their mail, and they download all the messages from their mail server to that one machine and subsequently delete them from the server. In the early days of POP, users wanting to read their mail from more than one machine would have found themselves downloading duplicate copies for their email to each machine from which they wanted to view that mail. At some point, when they thought all the various machines had caught up with their new mail, they finally would delete the mail from the server. Fortunately, though, most modern POP server implementations offer the option of leaving mail on the server after it's downloaded.

For POP users, storing mail in mailboxes means storing mail in mailboxes on the local MUA machine. Searching the mailbox likewise means searching on the client machine. Internet Service Providers (ISPs) for the most part have embraced POP as their mail access protocol of choice because of its modest demands on the mail server. POP is undemanding on the mail server because all the real work is done on your local machine. Mail storage, mail searching, and usually address books are all local data on your workstation.

If you use Internet email at home, work, or maybe a few other locations, as a POP user you'll find yourself with numerous duplicate personal mailstores. Having duplicate copies of your mailstore spread over machines is not necessarily a bad thing. Since with POP your mail is not stored on a server and consequently is not backed up as part of an enterprise-wide backup scheme, having duplicate copies is in essence your insurance against disasters such as hard drive crashes or laptop theft.

It's easy to see that POP users must make more of an investment in processor power and storage to accommodate its shortcomings. POP remains, for many ISPs, the most economical way of providing email service to their users. The days of large-margin low-cost ISP POP services are probably numbered, though. As more users become accustomed to the flexibility and power of IMAP in their own enterprise, they're likely to start demanding the same from their ISP.

For further reading, the current version of the protocol (POP3) is described in RFC 1939.

IMAP

Much of the popularity of IMAP is due, ironically, to the frustrations of longtime POP users. Email for most users amounts to much more than simple day-to-day correspondence. It functions as a database of project history, a scrapbook of sorts of personal relationships, and a database of priorities. If so many of the missions to which we put email feel like a database, why not push some of those functions off to the mail server, where disk, processor and backups, and 24-by-7 support are plentiful? With IMAP, clients not only have the option of operating in offline mode (where mail is downloaded and processed locally), but they may also operate in the much more powerful online and disconnected modes. Online and disconnected modes allow storage and searching to take place on the IMAP server.

As an IMAP user, you suddenly have equal access to your email from any Internet-connected machine running IMAP software.* Your local PC—in fact, every

---

* If your site offers a web-based IMAP client (Chapter 7, *Installing the Cyrus IMAP Server*), you can access your IMAP mail from any computer running a web browser.

machine you use from day to day—can crash and burn, and your mail won't suffer a bit. One of the first things you're likely to notice is that you no longer need to download all your messages to see what their subjects are. Because of IMAP-MIME integration, you can now download the email message associated with a 50 MB attachment without downloading the 50 MB attachment itself.

So, great! IMAP has everything an email user might want. But what about ISPs, who worry that their profit margin might evaporate with the substantially larger investment in hardware demanded by the load of IMAP? On the server side, implementation details can cut down on disk usage, such as the "single-store" feature (when a message is delivered to more than one user, only one copy of the message is stored on disk). We'd like to suggest that IMAP is more of an opportunity for revenue than anything else is. Instead of admonishing the users for keeping old mail on the mail server, ISPs now have the opportunity to lease the user as much disk space as he likes to hold his mailstore.

IMAP Culture Versus POP Culture

Because of the rich IMAP feature set, the two protocols are more different than they are alike. However, their similarities are worth mentioning. Both POP and IMAP are standard mail access protocols. Remote access in the room next door to the server makes the same demands as remote access from the other side of the world.* In both protocols, the MUA is physically dissociated from the server host.

A key in deciding which protocol is right for your site is your user constituency. POP is an excellent solution for communities of users that always access mail from a single computer. If POP is used in a community where users access mail from more than one computer, then users keep separate and duplicate mail archives on every machine from which they read their mail. POP has been used in environments where all computers running POP clients share a common filesystem, but that approach introduces all the problems with remote file-sharing protocols that we mentioned earlier in the chapter. IMAP archives, on the other hand, can be accessed from any remote platform with IMAP software. If a webmail gateway is in place, change that to any remote platform with a web browser.

The biggest infrastructure difference between POP- and IMAP-based mail systems is the impact of usage patterns on the mail server. IMAP's appetite for server resources is very different from the laissez-faire management of POP mailboxes. In the world of IMAP, both the user's mail archives and her incoming mail are usually stored on the provider's mail server. That server will be hit every time the user reads a mail message, regardless of whether it's a new or an old message. In practice, a POP mailbox is hit by only a single MUA at a time.

---

* Barring the fact that long-distance users may want to encrypt their traffic.

It's not unusual for an IMAP mailbox to be hit by multiple IMAP clients running on different client machines simultaneously. For example, a user might have a program (like *biff*) that periodically polls her mailbox for new mail every five minutes. At the same time, she might leave herself logged in to the IMAP server via PINE 24 hours a day and check her mail from home using Outlook Express every evening. Not to mention the odd stop at the Internet café where she uses Mulberry to check her mail on her coffee break. Such a barrage of IMAP operations against an IMAP mail server's I/O resources should be considered commonplace.

Why Not Both POP and IMAP?

All the discussion of the relative merits of POP and IMAP and how they are appropriate for different sets of users begs the question: why not do both? This is, in fact, a quite reasonable proposition.

If you run a UW or Cyrus IMAP server, you're in luck—both servers come with a POP server that natively accesses the same mailstore as the IMAP server. Another way to do both is to run a POP-to-IMAP proxy (one comes with the UW server). The POP-to-IMAP proxy never talks directly to your mailstore. It simply translates the POP protocol into an IMAP stream, which is then directed at your IMAP server. In fact, if you have a dug-in POP-ulation that you'd like to convert to IMAP, you could just replace your production POP server with a POP-to-IMAP proxy and tell your users, "By the way, we also offer IMAP if you'd like to try it on for size." That is not an altogether uncommon strategy. The downside of using a POP-to-IMAP proxy is that you end up supporting both POP and IMAP clients.

Fortunately, POP and IMAP clients are increasingly becoming the same software—it's just a matter of configuring them differently.

Advantages of IMAP

Here's the rundown on advantages that are unique to IMAP.

Appending to mailboxes

We implied it earlier in this chapter, but it bears repeating. IMAP may be used not only to retrieve messages from your remote mailbox, but also to add them to your remote mailbox. Again, IMAP operates on email much like a database, with the messages being individual records. Using an IMAP client, a user can freely move messages about between his INBOX and additional remote mailboxes of his own creation.

Multiple mailbox support

The first and most obvious demand of an Internet mail access protocol is a mechanism for storing multiple mailboxes on the server. Many email users use filters to sort incoming mail into several different mailboxes. By allowing the user to have multiple mailboxes on the server, IMAP allows users to access their archived mail from any computer, regardless of location.

Remote mailbox management

POP users are used to accessing their messages in a single, contiguous mailbox. Once they're downloaded, messages can be stored in mailboxes in a single MUA installation. In IMAP, the analog of the POP mailbox is a special mailbox called the INBOX. A user can also perform mailbox operations on more than just his INBOX. A typical IMAP user has a number of mailboxes that he's created on the server, each of which he can rename or delete. He can also change certain aspects of the mailbox, such as modifying the mailbox's access control list (if the server so allows) to permit access to the mailbox by other users.

Support for local mailboxes

A user with a given client, while operating in offline mode, may elect to save messages to mailboxes on her local machine. Another user with the same client, operating in online mode, may elect to save his messages to remote mailboxes. Most IMAP clients support both the offline and online modes. The decision of where to save messages is as much a function of user preference, site administrative decisions, and server resource availability as it is a product of protocol features.

Mailbox hierarchies

Most IMAP servers provide for hierarchical mailboxes, in which one or more mailbox names may be grouped together under another name. This encourages users to organize their mailboxes into more than just a flat list. It's perfectly reasonable to have an arrangement of names at the top level (such as "1999," "2000," "2001," "work," "staff," "private"), with mailboxes underneath them (such as the mailboxes "Jan," "Feb," "Mar," and so forth under the name "2000").

Some servers also permit the higher-level names to be a mailbox; for example, both "2000" and "2000/Jan" contain messages. Other servers restrict the higher-level names to be "non-selectable," that is, they are "directories" of mailboxes and not mailboxes in their own right. This varies from server to server and sometimes between different mailstores in the same server.

Remote mailboxes on multiple servers

IMAP clients typically let you manage mailboxes that live on multiple servers. As well as allowing messages to be moved from one mailbox to another on one server, clients often allow messages to be moved freely between different servers.

Persistent mailbox status flags

One aspect of the IMAP mailbox has no direct analog in POP: the message flag. Like file attributes in a directory, message flags hold status information about that message that lasts beyond any particular session. The flags can be changed freely by the IMAP client. A message can be flagged with a standard flag, such as "important" or "answered," or as a "draft" (i.e., a postponed composition). IMAP also provides for user-defined flags, such as such as "Personal," "Work-related," or "This-would-be-good-for-the-IMAP-book."

Server-initiated mailbox status updates

IMAP assumes that you always want to know when you've received new mail or when another IMAP client changes the flags of a message or removes a message from the mailbox. Any time that you perform an operation on a mailbox, the server can add to its response to the client, "Oh, by the way, you now have N messages" or "Oh, by the way, message M now has such-and-such flags set." In more restricted circumstances, the server can also add, "Oh, by the way, message M has been removed."

Companion configuration protocols

One of two protocols is typically employed for remote storage and location-independent access of IMAP client configuration options: IMSP or ACAP. IMSP (Internet Message Support Protocol), the older of the two, is designed exclusively to store IMAP client configuration and personal address books. ACAP (Application Configuration Access Protocol), the new kid on the block, is designed for storage of Internet application data and configuration. Not only can it store the client configuration and address books, but also other application data, such as bookmarks for your web browser. ACAP's flexibility makes it attractive to use for IMAP, and it can be pressed into service for other missions as well. IMAP and ACAP are discussed in more detail in Chapter 17, *Remote Configuration Storage*.

IMAP extensions

If IMAP had no other features save for this one, it would still have the framework necessary to provide a robust and popular mail access protocol. That framework permits clients to request a list of capabilities of each IMAP server with which it talks. It also ensures that the service life of IMAP will extend far beyond that of POP, because obsolete features can be abandoned and new features can be created on demand.

Performance advantages

IMAP provides a handful of ways to cut down on the amount of time the end user must spend managing her email. Perhaps the most frequent time saver is server-based searching. With IMAP, the performance of a search depends on server resources, not on the communication bandwidth and resources of the client.

Another reason the user experience is streamlined is that the IMAP server sees each message not as a single RFC 822 blob, but as a collection of headers followed by a collection of MIME body parts. Each collection can be listed like a directory, giving the user the ability to download each MIME component as he sees fit. That means that when the user receives an email message in the middle of his workday from Uncle Kevin with 12 MB of digital photos attached, he can read the message and wait until later to download the attachments. The ability to download the message structure independent of the message itself means that IMAP is the traveler's friend. Although John Doe may have a speedy Internet connection at work, the best he can expect while he's on the road is a 56 Kbps modem connection.

IMAP supports non-email data

IMAP can be applied to Usenet News or bulletin board discussions. Many IMAP servers are non-discriminating about where they get their data. That data need not be a product of IMAP or SMTP delivery. Any RFC 822/MIME-compliant message will do.

Shared mailboxes

One of the most productive features IMAP brings to the table is the ability to share read-write access to any given mailbox. This means that the mailbox that receives mail for *help@yourenterprise.net* can be opened by each person in your call center at once, and everyone will be able to keep track dynamically of which messages have been opened.

Another popular use for shared mailboxes is for global announcements. Announcements such as "A huge chlorine cloud is descending on campus" can be added to an enterprise-wide announcements mailbox so that users can read it at their leisure. This feature is frequently combined with IMSP or ACAP storage of client configuration, so users may be subscribed to the announcement mailbox by the administrator.

Mailbox sharing also helps reduce another bane of system administrators: account sharing. If users are able to share mail and other data by just changing an access control list on a mailbox, they have one less reason to give out their password to others to share data.

Finally, mailboxes may also be shared anonymously. Several Internet mailing lists' archives are shared in this manner, providing IMAP users with built-in forwarding, new message notification, and searching capability usually not found in mailing list archives.

Feature Breakdown

Table 2-1 compares POP's and IMAP's features.

Table 2-1. POP and IMAP Feature Inventory

Feature	IMAP	POP
Primary operational model	Online/ disconnected	Offline/ disconnected
Open Internet standard protocol	✓	✓
Free/open source server implementation available	✓	✓
Clients available for a variety of platforms including Mac, PC, and Unix	✓	✓
Supports all three models: online, disconnected, and offline	✓	✗
Natively supports access to a single mailbox from multiple computers	✓	✗
Supports interactive access to multiple mailboxes on different servers	✓	✗
Supports concurrent read/write access to shared mailboxes	✓	✗
Supports access to data other than email messages (e.g., NNTP)	✓	✗
Appending to mailboxes: supports storage, not just retrieval, of messages	✓	✗
Persistent message flags (e.g., "important," "seen," or "answered")	✓	✗
Persistent message IDs	✓	✓
Minimizes server storage	✗	✓
Minimizes connect time	✗	✓
Sends outgoing messages via SMTP	✓	✓

Present and Future of IMAP

In the not-so-recent past, IMAP was largely thought of as an overly complex method for managing email, and POP was considered just fine. However, nearly everyone supports or promises to support IMAP these days. That makes the size of the development investment in IMAP possibly second only to HTTP. You would think this would be a good thing. As you'll read later, however, at least on the MUA side of the house, there's some sloppy implementation going on.

This actually ends up being a *good* thing. In an open-standard marketplace, the more users who reject the one or two large-market-share apps in preference to the plethora of smaller-market apps, the more diversity there is in the market. Some of the best IMAP implementation going on right now is from companies you probably have never heard of before. If the one or two market leaders hadn't given away their market share, the IMAP market would be as locked up as the PC operating system market.

With the added complexity of IMAP comes greater flexibility. With flexibility comes a broader base of technologies on which it can be implemented, ranging from interactive voice response to wireless personal digital assistants (PDAs). In one sense, the success of a standard might be measured by the number of related standards it inspires.

The glory days of IMAP are just beginning. Here's a brief list of where we stand as of this writing:

* Dozens of IMAP implementations exist for nearly every desktop and server platform.

* IMAP is being used as a backend for web-based email interfaces, further adding to its ubiquity.

* The IMAP client market for PDAs, notably Palm OS and Windows CE, is just starting to take off, with a handful of clients for each.

* While users may not be storming the ISP Bastille asking for IMAP by name, the feature list they are demanding fits IMAP to a tee.

* Commercial Internet messaging products now incorporate IMAP support as a core feature.

* University messaging environments now regard IMAP as standard operating procedure.

* IMAP is starting to be offered on architectures like cellular phones, but the jury is still out on how useful IMAP will be in those environments.

Many of the IMAP users in the future will probably have no idea that IMAP is what makes their extended messaging environment possible. Here's where IMAP is headed:

- As universal multi-device connectivity becomes more common, IMAP will surely play a central role in coordinating simultaneous access to users' mail-boxes from many devices at one time. POP simply doesn't scale in that regard.

- An unexpected wrinkle in the story of IMAP has been its growth as a back-office protocol supporting web-based email frontends (see Chapter 5, *Web-Based IMAP Clients*). IMAP's importance will probably be equally split between back office support of web-based frontends and direct interaction with client user interfaces.

- If the activity surrounding the development of extensions to IMAP is any indication, we can look forward to IMAP having a productive life, far exceeding that of POP.

- Finally, as the Internet moves into an age when ever fewer users need to know that such things as IP addresses, netmasks, and mail access protocols exist, IMAP's destiny may be that of the "man behind the curtain."[*]

Open Source Server Implementations

For nearly a decade, there have been only two appreciable open source IMAP servers: the University of Washington's IMAP server and Carnegie Mellon University's Cyrus IMAP server. Both are robust, time- and user-tested servers with an install base to rival any commercial alternative.

We will go into more detail in later chapters about the interesting histories and specific features of each server, but let's take a brief look at them for the time being.

University of Washington IMAP Server

The University of Washington server is the reference implementation of IMAP. It was written by Mark Crispin, the inventor of IMAP. It was started in 1988 at Stanford University as a C rewrite of the original Interlisp client and DEC-20 assembly language server. When Crispin changed jobs for the University of Washington late in 1988, the IMAP project went with him.

The University of Washington IMAP server strives for compatibility with existing Unix systems. If you've stored your mail in a given format on a Unix system over

---

[*] A reference to *The Wizard of Oz.*

the course of the past few decades, chances are that the UW server can read that format out of the box.

The UW server has a number of interesting experimental extensions, such as multiple append and server-based sorting and threading. The UW server also supports an extensive list of international character sets.

The UW server is very modular—it is easy to add support for another mailbox format or SASL authenticator by writing a code module and relinking.

Carnegie Mellon University Cyrus IMAP Server

The CMU Cyrus Server is a component of a project called Project Cyrus.* Started in 1994, the Cyrus project was started because the management overhead of running the existing proprietary system was getting to be too high. CMU was unable to keep up with client development in particular and wanted to use commercial off-the-shelf (COTS) mail clients. Project Cyrus was created to provide a next-generation messaging system that relied heavily on Internet standards and was highly scalable as well as modular, supported disconnected mode, and enabled freedom from legacy architecture. Cyrus was a rejection of the idea of basing an email system on software that just copied files around from place to place in a file-system. Historically, the lack of reliability of such systems has only been exceeded by their lack of scalability.†

Although the core of the Cyrus project is the Cyrus IMAP server, CMU has developed the related protocols IMSP and ACAP, and implementations of those protocols to support their IMAP server, as well. The IMSP and ACAP servers offer a way to store the user's personal client settings remotely. The SASL library provides a way for any Internet standard-based application (client or server) to perform Internet standard authentication. CMU's Cyrus IMAP server also implements the SIEVE server-side filtering language, to boot.

Perhaps its greatest quality is the Cyrus server's feature richness. Given the right client, users benefit from such features as support for IMAP quotas and mailbox access control lists. The University of Washington server is rich with support for differing types of email storage formats. If you've stored your email in a given format on a Unix system over the course of the past few decades, chances are that the UW server can read that format.

The difference between the UW and Cyrus servers can be summarized as follows: UW is a generalist and Cyrus is a specialist.

---

* *http://asg.web.cmu.edu/cyrus/*.

† Not that people learn, however. Many popular LAN-based proprietary email systems are, under the hood, little more than file-copying utilities. Internet email standards rule.

The UW server is engineered to be completely compatible with Unix mail. It assumes the worst case: a site where the mail server also acts as an interactive login server for the general population and where users also access their mail directly with host-based mail clients. The UW server does not add any management overhead—all quota and access control is handled by the kernel (e.g., with Unix file and directory permissions).

Cyrus is engineered to run on so-called "black box" servers, where the user's mail is read by no software other than the Cyrus server. Cyrus offers rich support for IMAP quotas and mailbox access control lists and a great deal of IMAP-specific management control. Cyrus also obtains considerable performance benefit from not having to be compatible with ancient email software.

Midrange-to-large IMAP sites that choose UW generally modify it in various ways to make it more of a specialist, like Cyrus. A number of large IMAP sites do use UW; usually these are large sites that don't want the management overhead of Cyrus.

IMAP-Related Standards and Documents

All the standards and related documents in this section are Request For Comment (RFCs) documents. There is a plethora of IMAP-related Internet Drafts (would-be standards that are still working their way through the approval process), but they change so rapidly that they won't be mentioned here. Everyone has favorite RFC archives. Here are ours. Each of the sites lets you choose the geographically closest archive from which to retrieve your documents:

- Internet RFC documents (*http://www.nexor.com/info/rfc/index/rfc.htm*)
- Internet Drafts (*http://www.nexor.com/info/internet-drafts/id.html*)

A word about these documents—they're the epitome of "hit the ground running" docs. They're meant to be terse and narrow, much like their Unix manpage cousins. Despite their laissez-faire name, RFCs are the canonical standards documents of the Internet. If you have a bet with someone and need an indisputable source to settle the argument, turn to the RFC.

Table 2-2 is a snapshot of the current RFC standards related to IMAP. For a more comprehensive list, you can do a database search on "IMAP" at one of the previously mentioned URLs. In Table 2-2, the most important document is the *Internet Message Access Protocol Version 4rev1*, RFC 2060, by Mark Crispin. Consider it the defining document of the core features of IMAP. Second behind it would be RFC 2683 (*IMAP4 Implementation Recommendations*), which is necessary to read to understand the IMAP "folklore."

Table 2-2. IMAP-Related RFCs and Internet Drafts

RFC Number	Authors	Title
1731	J. Myers	IMAP4 Authentication Mechanisms
1732	M. Crispin	IMAP4 Compatibility with IMAP2 and IMAP2bis
1733	M. Crispin	Distributed Electronic Mail Models in IMAP4
2060	M. Crispin	Internet Message Access Protocol Version 4rev1
2061	M. Crispin	IMAP4 Compatibility with IMAP2bis
2086	J. Myers	IMAP4 ACL extension
2087	J. Myers	IMAP4 QUOTA extension
2088	J. Myers	IMAP4 non-synchronizing literals
2095	J. Klensin, R. Catoe, P. Krumviede	IMAP/POP AUTHorize Extension for Simple Challenge/Response
2177	B. Leiba	IMAP4 IDLE command
2180	M. Gahrns	IMAP4 Multi-Accessed Mailbox Practice
2192	C. Newman	IMAP URL Scheme
2193	M. Gahrns	IMAP4 Mailbox Referrals
2195	J. Klensin, R. Catoe, P. Krumviede	IMAP/POP AUTHorize Extension for Simple Challenge/Response
2221	M. Gahrns	IMAP4 Login Referrals
2342	M. Gahrns, C. Newman	IMAP4 Namespace
2359	J. Myers	IMAP4 UIDPLUS extension
2595	C. Newman	Using TLS with IMAP, POP3, and ACAP
2683	B. Leiba	IMAP4 Implementation Recommendations

3

Anatomy of an IMAP Session

This chapter covers the conceptual middle ground between a layman's understanding of the IMAP protocol and complete coverage, as contained in RFC 2060 (IMAP4rev1). This chapter will provide enough information to arm you to troubleshoot most IMAP problems and evaluate most clients, but not enough to write your own client or troubleshoot some of the stickiest dilemmas. For those situations, you would be much better off using the RFC 2060 documentation and the RFCs for the extensions your server professes to use.

IMAP Session Concepts

This section covers how a client talks to a server, the details of what an IMAP session looks like, and how we captured that information on our network.

IMAP Is Line-Oriented

You may occasionally see IMAP referred to as a "line-oriented" protocol. All this means is that the conversation between the IMAP client and server is transmitted in the form of character strings that end with CRLF. Line-oriented protocol sessions are easy to follow: a command is sent as a line of text to the server, and the server returns its response as a line of text. Line-oriented protocols are easy to learn and understand for the very same reason.

In fact, commands that make up a line-oriented protocol are frequently so understandable that a user can use the commands to masquerade as an IMAP client. As an example, consider just about anyone with access to a version of *telnet* that lets you specify the target port. The Telnet protocol, by definition, uses TCP port 23, but most Telnet software can usually be directed at alternative ports. This means that a user can *telnet* to TCP port 25 and trick an SMTP server into interacting with him as if she were an SMTP client. It's just as easy to for a user to *telnet* to TCP port 143 (IMAP) and interact with an IMAP server as if he were an IMAP client.

Why do we bother telling you this? Line-oriented protocol spoofing, apart from being a common hacking tool, is a helpful troubleshooting tool. If you're having difficulty getting a given client and server to talk, one approach is to take the client out of the equation. If you spoof IMAP from a *telnet* session, you can observe the commands being sent to and from the server and classify problems as either client or server problems.

The primary difference between IMAP and other line-oriented TCP protocols like SMTP, NNTP, and POP3 is that each command from the client is preceded by a short alphanumeric string, called a *tag*. The purpose of the tag is to help the IMAP client keep track of which response goes with which command. Once a connection is opened, all tags generated by the client must be unique until the connection is closed. When the server responds to a command, it attaches the tag that the client sent to its response, as illustrated in Figure 3-1.

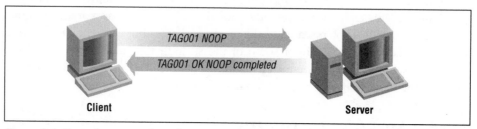

Figure 3-1. Tagged commands and responses

We mentioned that only the server's completion result is tagged. There are actually two classes of server response: *tagged response* and *untagged response*. Untagged responses convey data. They may or may not be in reaction to a command from the client. An untagged response can be thought of as a type of command from the server to the client to update state on the client. An untagged response, like its name implies, is not preceded by a tag. Instead, it is preceded by the "***" character.

Story of an IMAP Session

inetd listens for IMAP requests on TCP port 143.* Strictly speaking, until the first time a client connects to your server on the IMAP port, the IMAP server isn't running at all. An IMAP server daemon (*imapd*) is spawned by *inetd* to respond to each new connection from an IMAP client. *inetd* accepts the client's request for a

---

* The upcoming release, Version 2.0, of the Cyrus IMAP server does not use *inetd*, but instead, runs as a daemon.

connection, then passes the I/O stream off to the IMAP server. The client continues to send commands though port 143 to the IMAP server.

The IMAP server, it should be noted, knows nothing about IP, TCP, or networking. All it knows is how to communicate through STDIN and STDOUT and how to access local mailboxes. From the beginning to the end of each connection, the IMAP server will respond to an arbitrary set of commands. While it may be perfectly legitimate for the client to connect, perform one command, disconnect, connect, perform one command, etc., it's terribly inefficient. We know of no clients that wasteful. Typically (at least during online modes) clients will connect, perform whatever business they need to perform, then disconnect, either when the user shuts down the client or when the server's timeout limit is reached.

Disconnected mode is slightly different. In disconnected mode, the client connects to the server, retrieves new mail that has arrived, moves mail around to various mailboxes if the user so desires, then disconnects as soon as possible, minimizing the amount of time spent online.

IMAP Components

Here we discuss the components of IMAP to prepare us for our blow-by-blow protocol trace later in the chapter.

Modes

As we saw in Chapter 2, *What Is IMAP?,* IMAP clients can operate in one of three modes: *offline* mode, *online* mode, or *disconnected* mode. While you're not likely to see any IMAP operations take place between the client and server that say, "I'm an online session" or "I'm on offline session," these modes are quite an important part of IMAP.

States

First of all, the session can be in one of four states. Commands and responses are, in most cases, valid only in certain states (e.g., you can't issue the command to select a mailbox unless you're in the authenticated state). Although two or more sessions with a given mailbox can each be in different states, no single session can be in more than one state simultaneously. For example, when your client initially connects to the server and you're in the non-authenticated state, you authenticate successfully, leave the non-authenticated state, and enter the authenticated state. Here's a description of the four states. A diagram of the relationship between the states is shown in Figure 3-2.

Non-authenticated state

　　The non-authenticated state begins immediately when a connection starts.

Authenticated state

　　The authenticated state begins when the client authenticates successfully. It
　　may also begin after an error in selecting a mailbox.

Selected state

　　The selected state begins once a mailbox has been selected successfully.

Logout state

　　The logout state begins when the client sends the LOGOUT command or the
　　server unilaterally decides to close the connection (e.g., when the session
　　reaches the inactivity time-out limit). The logout state lasts only long enough
　　for the server to close the TCP connection.

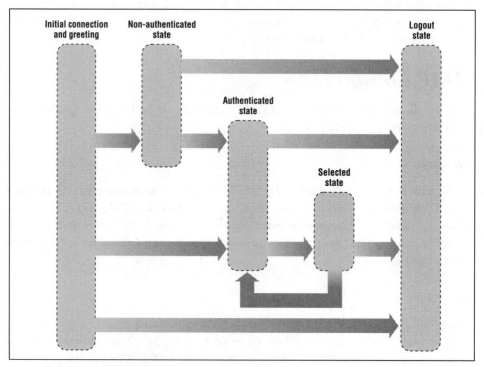

Figure 3-2. IMAP state diagram

Mailboxes

Although there are extensions to provide attributes to mailboxes (such as access
control lists), in the core IMAP protocol all the interesting attributes are associated
with the messages themselves, not the mailboxes.

Messages

There's much more to an email message than the body content. Attributes can range from core values like message numbers and headers to a road map of the MIME contents contained in the message.

Message sequence number

Message sequence numbers begin with 1 and continue sequentially up to the number of messages in the mailbox. Sequence numbers can be reassigned during a session. For example, when a message is deleted and expunged, each message with a higher sequence number than the deleted message is decremented by 1.

UIDs

The UID (Unique Identifier) is a 32-bit message identifier that is guaranteed to be unique within a mailbox. UIDs are preserved across sessions and are used to allow a client that operates in disconnected or offline mode to synchronize its state with the server. Message UIDs are assigned to messages in ascending order, but are different from message sequence numbers in that UIDs do not necessarily ascend contiguously. Although UIDs are mentioned for completeness, message sequence numbers are what you'll actually use when testing and troubleshooting IMAP sessions. You'll see mention of UIDVALIDITY later in this chapter. UIDVALIDITY is the unique identifier associated with a mailbox, not with a message. UID is associated with a message.

Flags

Each message in an IMAP mailbox may have zero or more flags. Flags are tokens that carry information about the message and are usually used to preserve message attributes between IMAP sessions. Several flags are defined. The message flags defined by IMAP are shown in Table 3-1.

Table 3-1. IMAP Message Flags

Flag	Meaning When Flag Is Set
\Answered	The message has been answered.
\Deleted	The message has been marked for deletion.
\Draft	The message is partially composed and being saved for later revision before sending.
\Recent	The message is "recent"—the current session is the first session to see it. It will not be flagged as "recent" in subsequent sessions.
\Flagged	The message has been marked as "important."

Internal date

> The internal date reflects the date and time the message was received by the IMAP server. It is not the same attribute as the date value in the RFC 822 header.

Size

> The message size expressed in number of octets (8-bit bytes) in the message, expressed in RFC 822 format.

Envelope structure

> The envelope structure contains a condensed representation of the RFC 822 header.

Body structure

> The body structure contains a condensed representation of the MIME information contained in the message.

An IMAP Session Play-by-Play

In this section we show and describe an actual IMAP session play-by-play. Our goal is to familiarize you with the most common IMAP operations. Knowing the operations will help you quickly troubleshoot problems independently of the client or server you're working with.

In our examples, we use the *tcpflow* program (see Chapter 18, *IMAP Tools*, for information on where to obtain *tcpflow*) to examine the IMAP client-server interactions. *tcpflow* is a special protocol-analysis program that permits you to watch a conversation take place between a TCP-based client and server. *tcpdump* or your favorite protocol analysis program would work equally well.

Our session was generated in a Telnet session to the IMAP port on the server:

```
% telnet localhost imap
```

Commands are shown in bold, responses from the server are shown in plaintext:

```
A00001 CAPABILITY
* CAPABILITY IMAP4REV1 MAILBOX-REFERRALS LOGIN-REFERRALS AUTH=CRAM-MD5
A00001 OK Completed
```

Each command is preceded by an arbitrary tag. As we mentioned earlier, the tag is an arbitrary string that the server "tags" its responses with. The purpose is to help the client keep track of which response goes with which command. Appendix C, *IMAP Commands*, provides a complete list of IMAP commands. The commands used in the sample session are, for the most part, self-explanatory. In any case, they're discussed in the explanation following Example 3-1, which shows the client/server conversation during an actual IMAP session and discusses each request and response.

Example 3-1. Simple IMAP Session

```
ROOT@Server # tcpflow -c 'host Client and port 143'
tcpflow[3000]: listening on le0
Server: * OK Server Cyrus IMAP4 v1.5.19 server ready

Client: 00000000 CAPABILITY007
Server: * CAPABILITY IMAP4 IMAP4rev1 ACL QUOTA LITERAL+ NAMESPACE UIDPLUS \
        X-NON-HIERARCHICAL-RENAME NO_ATOMIC_RENAME UNSELECT
        00000000 OK Completed

Client: 00000001 LOGIN dianna "xxxxxxxx"
Server: 00000001 OK User logged in

Client: 00000002 SELECT INBOX
Server: * FLAGS (\Answered \Flagged \Draft \Deleted \Seen)
        * OK [PERMANENTFLAGS (\Answered \Flagged \Draft \Deleted \Seen \*)]
        * 1 EXISTS
        * 0 RECENT
        * OK [UNSEEN 1]
        * OK [UIDVALIDITY 929804083]
        00000002 OK Completed

Client: 00000003 NOOP
Server: 00000003 OK Completed

Client: 00000004 FETCH 1 FLAGS
Server: * 1 FETCH (FLAGS ())
        00000004 OK Completed

Client: 00000005 FETCH 1 UID
Server: * 1 FETCH (UID 26888)
        00000005 OK Completed

Client: 00000006 FETCH 1 (ENVELOPE BODY.PEEK[HEADER.FIELDS \
        (Path Message-ID Newsgroups Followup-To References)] INTERNALDATE \
        RFC822.SIZE FLAGS)
Server: * 1 FETCH (FLAGS () INTERNALDATE "5-Mar-2000 10:58:50 -0600" \
        RFC822.SIZE 853 ENVELOPE ("Sun, 5 Mar 2000 11:00:52 -0600 (CST)" \
        "Testing" ((NIL NIL "drm" "nec.unt.edu")) \
        ((NIL NIL "drm" "nec.unt.edu")) ((NIL NIL "drm" "nec.unt.edu")) \
        ((NIL NIL "dianna" "europa.acs.unt.edu")) NIL NIL NIL \
        "<Pine.GS4.4.10.10003051100260.3034-100000@nec.unt.edu>") \
        BODY[HEADER.FIELDS (Path Message-ID Newsgroups Followup-To References)] \
        {70} Message-ID: Pine.GS4.4.10.10003051100260.3034-100000@nec.unt.edu

        )
        00000006 OK Completed

Client: 00000007 FETCH 1 (BODYSTRUCTURE FLAGS)
Server: * 1 FETCH (FLAGS () BODYSTRUCTURE ("TEXT" "PLAIN" \
        ("CHARSET" "US-ASCII") NIL NIL "7BIT" 29 2 NIL NIL NIL))
        00000007 OK Completed
```

Example 3-1. Simple IMAP Session (continued)

```
Client: 00000008 FETCH 1 BODY.PEEK[HEADER.FIELDS (Resent-Date Resent-From \
        Resent-To Resent-cc Resent-Subject)]
Server: * 1 FETCH (BODY[HEADER.FIELDS (Resent-Date Resent-From Resent-To \
        Resent-cc Resent-Subject)] {2}


        )
        00000008 OK Completed

Client: 00000009 FETCH 1 BODY[1]
Server: * 1 FETCH (FLAGS (\Seen) BODY[1] {29}
        This is the message body.

        )
        00000009 OK Completed

Client: 0000000a STORE 1 +Flags (\DELETED)
Server: * 1 FETCH (FLAGS (\Deleted \Seen))
        0000000a OK Completed

Client: 0000000b NOOP
Server: 0000000b OK Completed

Client: 0000000c EXPUNGE
Server: * 1 EXPUNGE
        * 0 EXISTS
        * 0 RECENT
        0000000c OK Completed

Client: 0000000d NOOP
Server: 0000000d OK Completed

Client: 0000000e LOGOUT
Server: * BYE LOGOUT received
        0000000e OK Completed
```

What follows is a description of the play-by-play in the previous example. We'll use the IMAP command tags to refer to different parts of the listing:

Tag 00000000

> The client asks the server for its capabilities using the CAPABILITY command. The server responds with its capabilities.

Tag 00000001

> The client logs in the user "dianna" with plaintext password "xxxxxxxx" using the LOGIN command. The server responds that the user was successfully logged in.

Tag 00000002

> The client selects the INBOX. The server responds with several pieces of information:

— Flags and permanent flags that are defined for the mailbox (*Answered*, *Flagged*, *Draft*, *Deleted, and* *Seen*)

— Number of messages in the mailbox (1)

— Number of messages that have arrived since the session started (0)

— Number of unseen messages (1)

— The UIDVALIDITY (929804083)

Finally, the server returns the command result (OK), indicating that the INBOX was selected successfully and that the mailbox is both read and write.

Tag 00000003

The client sends a NOOP, probably something that it does periodically to ping the server to reset the inactivity timer and make sure the connection doesn't time out.

Tag 00000004

The client uses the FETCH command to request a list of flags that are set on the message that corresponds to sequence number 1. The server answers that there are no flags set.

Tag 00000005

The client uses the FETCH command again, this time to request the UID number of the message corresponding to message sequence number 1.

Tag 00000006

The client asks the server to send some of message number 1's header information (the RFC 822 fields Path, Message-ID, Newsgroups, Followup-To, and References, the message internal date, the RFC 822 size, and the flags that are set on the message).

The server returns, not necessarily in the order requested, the data items requested. Each item is labeled appropriately for consumption by the client.

Tag 00000007

In this sequence, the client is eyeballing the body of the message. Fetching the BODYSTRUCTURE data item, in fact, is one of the more powerful capabilities of IMAP. It permits the client to retrieve the skeletal structure of the message without retrieving the message itself. That capability allows the client to exercise discretion by downloading some parts of a message, such as a short *text/plain* part, and not others, for example a very large *video/mpg2* part.

Tag 00000008

In this sequence, the client is apparently checking to see if the message was "bounced." If so, it would have various "Resent-" header lines. That isn't the case here, so the server returns blank values for the requested header fields.

Tag 00000009

The client requests the body for the message with sequence number [1]. The server complies without a lot of to-do.

Tag 0000000a

The client deletes message number 1, which involves setting the *Deleted* flag on the message. The flag is set using the STORE command. The server responds that the flag was set successfully, and hence, the message is now marked "deleted."

Tag 0000000b

The client sends another NOOP to keep the connection alive and poll the server for new mail.

Tag 0000000c

The client expunges, or permanently removes, all messages marked "deleted" using the EXPUNGE command. The server responds with the message sequence number of each expunged message (in this case, message number 1, the only message in the mailbox). It also responds that the number of messages in the mailbox (EXISTS) is now 0 and that the number of messages that have not been read (UNSEEN) is also 0.

Tag 0000000d

The client sends another NOOP, and the server responds with OK.

Tag 0000000e

Finally, the client sends the LOGOUT command. The server responds by saying "BYE" and closing the connection.

A POP3 Session for Comparison

Veteran Internet messaging techs will recognize Example 3-2 at first glance. Once upon a time, all email was retrieved using POP3. Here's a POP3 session for comparison.

As was mentioned in Chapter 2, POP is much less complex than IMAP, but also has fewer features. Here's a list of differences between POP and IMAP that are evident in comparing the POP3 session (Example 3-2) with the IMAP session (Example 3-1):

- POP operates in offline mode only.
- It has only one mailbox per user, so there is no SELECT command in POP.
- POP has no extensions, such as a Quota or ACL extension.
- It's not possible to determine the structure of a message in POP—all messages are single, contiguous entities. The entire message body must be downloaded.

- POP allows for the selective download of headers and message body separately, and most servers support that option. It's unusual, however, for clients to take advantage of that option. It's not done in our example.

- POP doesn't handle new mail that is received while a POP session is already open. The new mail is unavailable until the current session is closed and a new one open.

Example 3-2. Simple POP3 Session

```
ROOT@Server # tcpflow -c 'host Client and port 110'
tcpflow[3829]: listening on le0
Server: +OK POP3 Server v7.59 server ready

Client: USER drm
Server: +OK User name accepted, password please

Client: PASS XXXXXXXX
Server: +OK Mailbox open, 1 message

Client: STAT
Server: +OK 1 1031

Client: LIST
Server: +OK Mailbox scan listing follows
1 1031
.

Client: RETR 1
Server: +OK 1031 octets
        Received: from Mercury.acs.unt.edu (mercury.acs.unt.edu [129.120.220.1])
        .by security.unt.edu (8.8.8/8.8.8) with ESMTP id FAA03831
        .for <drm@nec.unt.edu>; Sun, 27 Feb 2000 05:57:28 -0600 (CST)
        Received: from venus.acs.unt.edu (venus.acs.unt.edu [129.120.220.72])
        .by Mercury.acs.unt.edu (8.8.8/8.8.8) with ESMTP id FAA25269
        .for <drm@nec.unt.edu>; Sun, 27 Feb 2000 05:55:35 -0600 (CST)
        Received: from SUNFLOWER (rooster.themullets.net [209.223.13.243])
        .by venus.acs.unt.edu (8.8.8/8.8.8) with ESMTP id FAA25103
        .for <drm@nec.unt.edu>; Sun, 27 Feb 2000 05:55:35 -0600 (CST)
        Date: Sun, 27 Feb 2000 05:54:43 -0600
        From: Dianna Mullet <dianna@unt.edu>
        To: drm@nec.unt.edu
        Subject: This is subject.
        Message-ID: <2443111424.951630883@localhost>
        Originator-Info: login-id=; server=
        X-Mailer: Mulberry (Win32) [1.4.4, s/n U-301284]
        MIME-Version: 1.0
        Content-Type: text/plain; charset=us-ascii
        Content-Transfer-Encoding: 7bit
        Content-Disposition: inline
        Content-Length: 28
        Status:
```

Example 3-2. Simple POP3 Session (continued)

```
            This is the message body.

            .

Client: DELE 1
Server: +OK Message deleted

Client: QUIT
Server: +OK Sayonara
```

There are two reasons for diving down to the protocol level. First, when evaluating or comparing IMAP products, nothing is quite as helpful as benchtesting them against one another and watching what happens on the network. When clients, and perhaps servers, first started providing IMAP support, many grafted IMAP functionality on top of their POP engines. Additionally, because IMAP is a protocol that isn't easily grasped in a simple five-minute cruise of the RFC, some vendors will take the short, error-fraught path and try to fake their way to IMAP compliance. You will run into these products, no doubt about it.

The other reason is that once you've chosen your IMAP products and put them into operation, the occasional problem will surface. Often it will be due to a lack of 100% IMAP compliance in either the server or client (usually the client). Unless you care to spend several weeks doing the finger-pointing dance with your vendors, the only way to get the critical smoking gun is to analyze the IMAP traffic on your network. In doing so you will be able to determine whether the problem lies with server or client, and exactly what the problem is.

II

IMAP Mail User Agents (MUAs)

4

IMAP Clients

Having an IMAP server is all fine and good, but it does you little good if you can't actually *read* your mail. That, of course, is where the client comes in.

A microscopic examination of the strengths and weaknesses of each IMAP client on the market is somewhat beyond the scope of this book and beyond the capacity of a book publishing cycle, anyway. We're currently on the threshold of an IMAP explosion in the Internet messaging industry. The features and bugs in any given IMAP client change with the phase of the moon. All that notwithstanding, here's our version of a whirlwind tour of the best freely available (or at least freely demo-able) clients.

Client Features

This section begins by listing and describing a set of features that might be found in the ideal IMAP client. The features are cross-referenced with popular IMAP clients.

Features Reviewed

We cover Windows, Mac, and Unix clients separately; the results of the evaluations are shown in Table 4-1. We looked for the following features in each of the clients. We reviewed only whether the feature exists and actually works or not—not how well it works.

Free
> Is the client available completely free of charge?

LDAP
> Does the client support remote directory lookups via LDAP?

ACAP

Does the client support storage and retrieval of client options via ACAP?

IMSP

Does the client support storage and retrieval of client options via IMSP?

NNTP

Does the client support reading Usenet news via NNTP?

MIME

Does the client handle MIME attachments? In other words, does a MIME attachment show up as a legitimate attachment with some indication of its MIME subtype (*text/plain*, *application/postscript*, or *audio/basic*, for example)?

SSL

Does the client support SSL IMAP sessions? This of course is only useful if you've built SSL support into your IMAP server.

Kerberos v4

Does the client support Kerberos authentication?

CRAM MD5

Does the client support CRAM message digests?

Disconnected

Does the client support disconnected mode? This item should be taken with a grain of salt. Some clients claim to support disconnected mode simply based on allowing a user to read mail while disconnected from the server. They do not, however, allow other basic actions (e.g., deleting messages) to be performed while the user is offline. In these cases, we gave the client a "no" on this point. The criteria that determine whether or not a client truly supports disconnected mode include:

— The user can read messages while disconnected from the IMAP server.

— Changes automatically synchronize when the user goes back online.

— The user can make changes, such as deleting messages or creating folders, while offline.

— The client keeps track of messages that have been replied to or forwarded when it goes offline.

Client-side filtering

Does the client support delivery of incoming mail to folders based on filtering parameters defined within the client?

Local address books

Can the client store email addresses locally?

Remote address books

Can the client store email addresses on a remote server?

Subscribe and unsubscribe

Can the client display or hide a folder by allowing the user to subscribe to or unsubscribe to the folder?

Nested folders

Can the client create folders within folders on the server?

Message threading

Can the client display messages by subject?

Shared folders

Is it possible for the client to create folders on the server and share them to other users, provided that the server supports shared folders?

ACL

Does the client include an ACL viewer and/or editor? This is primarily of interest to sites that use the Cyrus IMAP server.

Alerts

Does the client support RFC 2060–style ALERT response codes, which permit the system admins, through IMAP ALERTs, to notify system users of conditions liked planned outages or other changes in service condition?

Quota report tool

Does the client have a built-in mechanism for checking quota usage? This is primarily of interest to sites that use the Cyrus IMAP server.

Save outgoing mail

Is it possible to configure the client to save a copy of each outgoing message *on the IMAP server* automatically? Some clients save copies of outgoing messages only on the local machine.

Search on message header

Does the client support searching mail headers for a given text string?

Search on folder name

Does the client support searching for a folder name that matches a given text string?

Remote configuration storage

Can client configuration be stored on a remote server?

Table 4-1. Features Supported by IMAP Clients

Features	PINE 4.21	StarMail 5.1	Outlook Express 5.0	Netscape Messenger 4.61	Mulberry 2.0	Eudora 4.3
Windows	✓	✓	✓	✓	✓	✓
Macintosh	✗	✗	✓	✓	✓	✓
Unix	✓	✓	✓	✓	✗	✗
Free	✓	✓	✓	✓	✗	✓
LDAP	✓	✓	✓	✓	✓	✓
ACAP	✗	✗	✗	✗	✓	✓
IMSP	✗	✗	✗	✗	✓	✗
NNTP	✓	✓	✓	✓	✗	✗
MIME	✓	✓	✓	✓	✓	✓
SSL	✗[a]	✓	✓	✓	✗	✗
Kerberos v4	✓	✗	✗	✗	✓	✓
CRAM MD5	✓	✗	✗	✗	✓	✓
Disconnected	✗	✓	✓	✗	✓	✓
Client-side filtering	✓	✓	✓	✓	✓	✓
Local address books	✓	✓	✓	✓	✓	✓
Remote address books	✓	✓	✓	✓	✓	✓
Subscribe and unsubscribe mail folders	✗	✓	✓	✓	✓	✗
Nested folders	✓	✓	✓	✓	✓	✓
Message threading	✓	✓	✓	✓	✓	✓
Shared folders	✓	✗	✗	✗[b]	✓	✗
ACL	✗	✗	✗	✗[c]	✓	✗
Alerts	✓	✗	✓	✓	✓	✗
Quota report tool	✗	✗	✗	✗	✓	✗
Save outgoing mail	✓	✓	✗	✓	✓	✓
Search on message header	✓	✓	✓	✓	✓	✓
Search on folder/mailbox name	✓	✗	✗	✗	✓	✓
Remote configuration storage	✗[d]	✗	✗	✓	✓	✓

[a] SSL is supported in PC PINE only, but will be supported in PINE 4.30 for Unix.
[b] Netscape Messenger allows users to share IMAP folders by setting ACLs on a per folder basis, but the ACL mechanism is proprietary and only works with Netscape's mail server.
[c] ACL viewer only.
[d] Remote configuration storage will be supported in PINE 4.30.

PINE and PC PINE

PINE (Program for Internet News and Email) is a popular character-based IMAP client. PINE was developed at the University of Washington, home of IMAP itself. PINE is available for nearly all Unix platforms. It is also available for Windows machines in a version called PC PINE. PINE was designed to be easy to use. While it has retained its simplicity of operation over many years of development, it has also grown into a very highly configurable, robust client equally suited to both novices and power users. It's worth mentioning that there are other character-based IMAP clients for Unix, but they are not covered here because none even comes close to matching PINE's feature-richness. The Elm mailer was once widely preferred over PINE for its simple interface. Although it supports IMAP, it has come to be considered a holdover from the good old days of "old-school Unix."

The Windows version of PINE, PC PINE, has all the features of Unix PINE, but runs under Windows or DOS. PC PINE has the added benefit of allowing you to attach files that reside on your computer's local disk to email messages without the need to first upload those files to another host. PC PINE, although it doesn't appear to on a first look, does support drag-and-drop attachments (try dragging a document into a Compose window).

The PINE home page is located at *http://www.washington.edu/PINE/*.

Features

PINE supports the following Internet protocols and specifications: IMAP4, SMTP (Simple Mail Transport Protocol), NNTP (Network News Transport Protocol) for reading Usenet news within PINE, and MIME (Multipurpose Internet Mail Extensions). PINE has the option of supporting LDAP and Kerberos, if it's built to include the appropriate libraries. Instructions for integrating LDAP and Kerberos are provided in the PINE online documentation.

PINE offers many features, including:

- Personal address books.
- Context-specific online help.
- A command to grab an address from a message and add it to the address book.
- A message composer with easy-to-use default editor and built-in spell checker. The composer expands addresses as they are entered and provides direct access to the address book.
- Support for both remote and local folders.
- Robust facility for search and selection of messages.
- The ability to perform operations on sets of selected messages at one time.

Version 4.20 and up support client-side mail filtering. PINE does not support "vacation" messages.

Supported Platforms

PC PINE is available for Windows NT, Windows 95, Windows 98, and Windows 2000.

Unix PINE is available in both a binary distribution and source distribution. The binary distribution is available for many flavors of Unix, including AIX, HPUX, Digital Unix, Linux, NeXT, SGI, Solaris, Sun OS, and Ultrix.

In addition to the platforms for which the PINE binary distribution is available, PINE has been ported, built, and tested on many other Unix platforms. Some of those platforms include FreeBSD, NetBSD, SCO, Ultrix, DG/UX, and SVR4. The full list is available at *http://www.washington.edu/PINE/overview/ports.html*.

Configuring PINE for IMAP

PINE's syntax for defining IMAP options is more difficult to handle than most other clients. Examples are provided in this section to make it less confusing.

PINE for Unix

Unix PINE allows the system administrator to exert some control over client options by setting global default options. Any global option can be protected, preventing the option from being overridden by a user's personal options settings.

PINE for Unix has three configuration files:

/usr/local/lib/pine.conf
> The *pine.conf* file contains the system-wide global configuration options (location is configurable). Options in *pine.conf* are overridden by the options in the user's personal *~/.pinerc* file.

/usr/local/lib/pine.conf.fixed
> The *pine.conf.fixed* file contains system-wide options that are essentially "read-only" and cannot be overridden.

~/.pinerc
> *~/.pinerc* is the user's personal configuration file. Options defined in that file override the options set in the system *pine.conf*.

Users can configure PINE either with a menu system through the Setup command, or directly by editing the personal resource file, *~/.pinerc*.

Large sites using PINE and IMAP may want to set site options in the *pine.conf* file to reduce the amount of work their users must go through to configure PINE individually. It's also recommended that large sites "lock down" certain options, such as the outgoing SMTP server, domain name, path to the user's INBOX, and the user's full name.* This procedure not only will make PINE easier to use for the end user, but also will prevent possible problems that could occur if the SMTP server is incorrectly specified or if the user spoofs his personal name. Example 4-1 is a *pine.conf* file that might be used at a large site using IMAP with PINE. Example 4-2 shows the *pine.conf.fixed* file used at that same site.

Example 4-1. pine.conf

```
#       /usr/local/lib/pine.conf -- system-wide PINE configuration

# The following options are set read-only in pine.conf.fixed.

personal-name=
user-domain=
smtp-server=
inbox-path=

# The following options are set but may be overridden by options in .pinerc

nntp-server=newserv.unt.edu
incoming-folders=Announcements {imapserv.unt.edu}user.announce.Internet_News
folder-collections=Folders {imapserv.unt.edu}inbox.[],~/mail/[]
editor=/usr/ucb/vi
speller=/usr/local/bin/ispell
image-viewer=/usr/local/bin/X11/xv
bugs-fullname=Helpdesk
bugs-address=helpdesk@helpserv.unt.edu
suggest-fullname=Helpdesk
suggest-address=helpdesk@helpserv.unt.edu
local-fullname=Helpdesk
local-address=helpdesk@helpserv.unt.edu
forced-abook-entry=help|Helpdesk|helpdesk@helpserv.unt.edu

global-address-book=/data/abook/pine.abook,
    /data/mercury/pine.abook.A-C,
    /data/mercury/pine.abook.D-F,
    /data/mercury/pine.abook.G-I,
    /data/mercury/pine.abook.J-L,
    /data/mercury/pine.abook.M-O,
    /data/mercury/pine.abook.P-R,
    /data/mercury/pine.abook.S-U,
    /data/mercury/pine.abook.V-X,
    /data/mercury/pine.abook.Y-Z

feature-list=enable-8bit-esmtp-negotiation,
    enable-8bit-nntp-posting,
    enable-aggregate-command-set,
```

---

* Locking down the user's full name disables the use of "roles," which some users find useful.

Example 4-1. pine.conf (continued)

```
    enable-alternate-editor-cmd,
    enable-bounce-cmd,
    enable-flag-cmd,
    enable-full-header-cmd,
    enable-goto-in-file-browser,
    enable-jump-shortcut,
    enable-lame-list-mode,
    enable-mail-check-cue,
    enable-tab-completion,
    print-formfeed-between-messages,
    quell-dead-letter-on-cancel,
    save-will-quote-leading-froms,
    signature-at-bottom,
    use-sender-not-X-sender


# Accept PINE's defaults for all options below this line

news-collections=
incoming-archive-folders=
pruned-folders=
default-fcc=
default-saved-msg-folder=
postponed-folder=
mail-directory=
read-message-folder=saved-messages
signature-file=
address-book=
initial-keystroke-list=
default-composer-hdrs=
customized-hdrs=
viewer-hdrs=
saved-msg-name-rule=
fcc-name-rule=
sort-key=
addrbook-sort-rule=
goto-default-rule=
character-set=
composer-wrap-column=
reply-indent-string=
empty-header-message=
use-only-domain-name=no
printer=lp
personal-print-command=
standard-printer=lp
bugs-additional-data=
kblock-passwd-count=
sendmail-path=
operating-dir=
display-filters=
sending-filters=
```

Example 4-1. pine.conf (continued)

```
alt-addresses=
addressbook-formats=
index-format=
viewer-overlap=
scroll-margin=
status-message-delay=
mail-check-interval=
newsrc-path=
news-active-file-path=
news-spool-directory=
upload-command=
upload-command-prefix=
download-command=
download-command-prefix=
mailcap-search-path=
mimetype-search-path=
tcp-open-timeout=
rsh-open-timeout=
new-version-threshold=
```

Options that are not explicitly set, such as **news-collection=**, will take PINE's default value unless a value is defined in *pine.conf.fixed*.

Example 4-2. pine.conf.fixed

```
personal-name=
user-domain=
inbox-path={imapserv.unt.edu}INBOX
smtp-server=smtpserv.unt.edu
use-only-domain-name=
feature-list=enable-lame-list-mode,
    no-use-sender-not-x-sender
```

In the previous example, **personal-name**, **user-domain**, and **use-only-domain-name** are not set—PINE will look up those options and set them at run-time. Forcing those options to be set by PINE helps prevent email spoofing. To enable a feature, include it in the **feature-list**. To disable a feature, prefix it by "no-" (for example, **no-use-sender-not-x-sender**) and include it in the feature list. Features are comma-delimited.

It's worth noting that the syntax for defining IMAP options is identical in the two global configuration files and in the personal PINE configuration file.

A user is free to set options by directly editing her *~/.pinerc* file, but may also set any allowable option from within PINE's configuration menu. Settings that pertain to IMAP incoming mailboxes and folders are set in PINE's Setup Configuration menu. Start up PINE and, from the Main menu, select "Setup" and "Config." You will see a menu that begins something like the one shown in Example 4-3.

Example 4-3. PINE Setup Configuration Menu

```
PINE 4.20   SETUP CONFIGURATION      Folder: INBOX  192 Messages

personal-name            = <Value is Fixed: using "John Doe">
user-domain              = <Value is Fixed>
smtp-server              = <Value is Fixed>
nntp-server              = <No Value Set: using "newserv.unt.edu">
inbox-path               = {imapserv.unt.edu}INBOX
incoming-archive-folders = <No Value Set>
pruned-folders           = <No Value Set>
default-fcc              = <No Value Set: using "sent-mail">
default-saved-msg-folder = <No Value Set: using "saved-messages">
postponed-folder         = <No Value Set: using "postponed-msgs">
read-message-folder      = <No Value Set: using "saved-messages">
form-letter-folder       = <No Value Set>
signature-file           = <No Value Set: using ".signature">
feature-list             =
          Set    Feature Name
          ---    ---------------------
          [ ]    allow-talk
          [ ]    assume-slow-link
          [ ]    auto-move-read-msgs


? Help  E Exit Setup   P Prev   - PrevPage A Add Value  % Print
        C [Change Val] N Next spc NextPage D Delete Val W WhereIs
```

Options that list "Value is Fixed" are read-only options set in the *pine.conf.fixed* file by the system administrator and cannot be changed by the user. In the example, the **personal-name, user-domain**, and **smtp-server** are fixed. The **inbox-path** setting tells PINE to look for the IMAP INBOX on the server *imap.unt.edu*. To change the **inbox-path** or any other option that is not fixed, press C to Change Value, enter the new value, and press Return to make the change. Press E to exit the Setup Configuration menu—you will be prompted by PINE as to whether or not you want to save your changes. Answering Yes will save your changes permanently.

PINE supports multiple IMAP accounts. Setting up multiple accounts is somewhat cumbersome to do via PINE's menu interface, and for that reason we'll show you how to configure multiple accounts by editing the *~/.pinerc*. In the next example, user *johndoe* wants to set up three IMAP accounts. Here is information on the accounts that will be used to configure *johndoe*'s *~/.pinerc*:

Work

The Work account is a collection of IMAP folders that reside in *johndoe*'s IMAP account on the official company IMAP server where he works. The name of that IMAP server is *imap.someplace.org*.

Personal

The Personal folder collection is a collection of folders that reside in *johndoe*'s account on his personal IMAP server, running on his Linux box in his garage at home. That IMAP server's name is *imap.johndoe.net.*

Cyrus archive

johndoe wishes to read mail in CMU's Cyrus mailing list archive, logging in anonymously. The mailing list archive is located on the IMAP server called *cyrus.andrew.cmu.edu*, lives in the *archive* user's mailbox hierarchy, and belongs to the *cyrus* user on that server.

Example 4-4 shows how the `folder-collections` option should be set in *johndoe*'s ~/*.pinerc* to meet his requirements for the three IMAP accounts.

Example 4-4. pinerc folder-collections Settings

```
folder-collections=Work {imap.someplace.org}inbox.[],
                   Personal {imap.johndoe.net}inbox.[],
                   CyrusArchive {cyrus.andrew.cmu.edu/anonymous}archive.[]
```

PC PINE

PC PINE's configuration is identical to that of PINE for Unix. The only difference lies in the filename and location of the user's personal configuration file on the client machine. The name of the user's configuration is either *PINERC* or the value of the environment variable PINERC. PC PINE searches for *PINERC* in the following places, in order of preference:

- $PINERC

- $HOME\PINE\PINERC ($HOME, if not set, defaults to the root of the current drive)

- A file named *PINERC* in the same directory as the PC PINE executable (the file *PINE.EXE*)

The address book is stored in a file named *ADDRBOOK*, and the signature is in a file called *PINE.SIG*. PC PINE expects to find both files in the same directory as the *PINERC* file.

Star Mail

Star Office is a freeware gem. It is an "office suite" of productivity applications, with file formats compatible with Microsoft Office applications. Star Office includes an email client, Star Mail, which supports IMAP. Star Office is free to private, non-commercial users and students. In addition to its native Windows 95/98/NT operating environment, Star Office is also available for other operating systems, including OS/2, Linux, and Solaris.

Star Mail is a component of the Star Office Suite and cannot be installed separately—if you want to use Star Mail, you have to install the whole Star Office Suite.
That could be problematic if you're low in disk space—the Star Office download
for Windows is 80 MB; installed, it requires around 160 MB of disk.

The interface is somewhat non-intuitive to those who are regular users of
Microsoft products. While this is not necessarily a liability, expect some users to
encounter a slight learning curve over the first few times they use the interface.

For more information or to download a free copy of Star Office, visit *http://www.
sun.com/products/staroffice/*.

Features

Client-side filtering

Star Mail is one of the few IMAP clients that, at the time of this writing, provides
client-side filtering.

Import filters

Star Office has tools for importing data from Messenger and Outlook Express.

Remote LDAP searching

Remote address book feature allows you to search Bigfoot, WhoWhere, and
Switchboard, but not your own site's LDAP directory.

Advanced searching

In addition to standard searching of message headers, Star Mail permits searches
through levels of nested folders.

Performance enhancements for slow connections

To avoid wasting time downloading large messages, Star Mail allows the user to
set a threshold on the size of messages and attachments. If the user attempts to
open a message exceeding that threshold, he will be warned and asked whether
to cancel the action or continue.

Configuring Star Mail for IMAP

If you are running Star Office for the first time, it may come up in full-screen
mode. If you prefer to run Star Office in a window, then press Alt-V to bring up
the View menu and unselect "Full Screen."

Star Mail works great with both Cyrus and UW servers and does not require any special configuration, such as specifying the folder path, to support the server namespace.

The configuration required to set up new IMAP accounts is somewhat more complicated than it should be. More steps are required to configure it than are needed to configure the other clients evaluated in this chapter. When we attempted to send mail for the first time after configuring the client, the send failed with an error message that was less than informative. We eventually found out that, in order to send mail out, you must first create an "outbox"—it's not automatically created for you.

Configuring the IMAP options

Follow these steps to set up your IMAP options in Star Mail:

1. Pull down the Tools menu and select the Options. On the Options menu, select Internet (click on the + sign to expand the list of Internet options).

2. Click on Mail/News. You'll see the Mail/News configuration window, shown in Figure 4-1.

3. Enter the full address of your outgoing SMTP host in the Outgoing Mail field.

4. Enter the full address of your IMAP server in the Incoming Mail field.

5. Enter your IMAP username and password in the User ID and Password fields.

The other information is optional to configure for IMAP. Click OK when you're done entering the information.

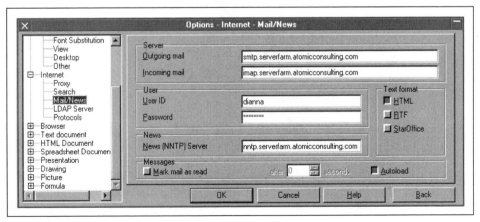

Figure 4-1. Entering IMAP options in Star Office

Reading IMAP mail with Star Mail

At this point, you've done the preliminary configuration, but there's still a bit of configuration to do before you can read your mail. Follow these steps to complete the configuration and read your IMAP mail:

1. Bring up the Star Mail client, which is located in the Star Explorer menu window. To bring up the Star Explorer menu window, pull down the View menu and select "Explorer." If it is already selected (i.e., if it has a check mark next to it on the View menu) but you can't see the Explorer menu window, then the window is minimized. To expand the window, click on the small bar near the top lefthand side of the Star Office window.

2. Next, bring up the Star Mail client by clicking on the E-mail & News bar, as shown in Figure 4-2. The client's menu will be blank if you've never used it before.

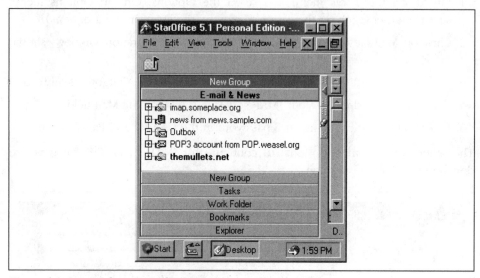

Figure 4-2. Star Explorer E-mail & News

3. You will need to create a new IMAP Account. Begin by right-clicking on the blank background under E-mail & News to bring up the menu.

4. Under the New menu, select IMAP Account... to bring up a window titled Properties of IMAP Account.

5. Click on the Receive tab. You will see a window that looks like Figure 4-3. If you configured your mail options as described in the beginning of this section, then the values should already be filled in. You shouldn't have to change any of the values—just click the OK button to create the IMAP account.

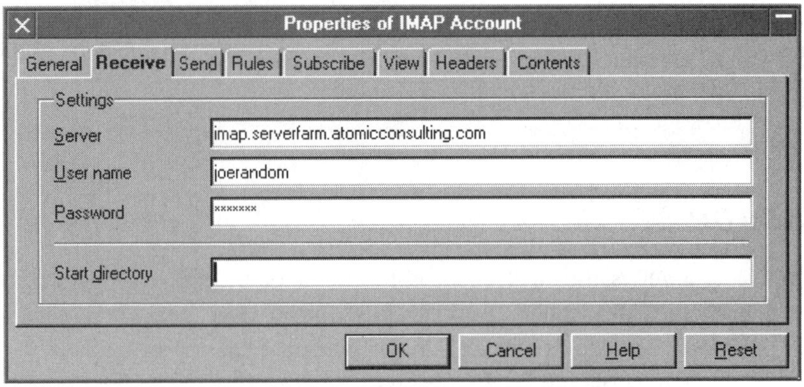

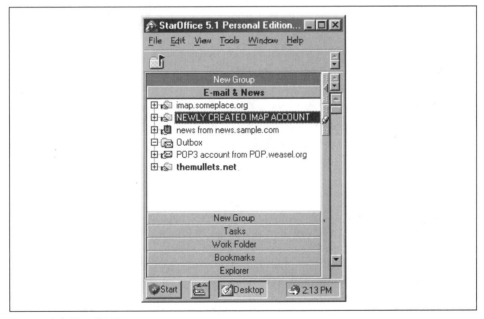

Figure 4-3. Properties of IMAP Account

6. The new IMAP account will appear in the Star Explorer window, as in Figure 4-4. Click on the + sign to connect to your IMAP server and retrieve your messages.

Figure 4-4. New IMAP account

Sending mail out requires that you create an Outbox first. Right-click
on the white background as you did to create a new Email group
and select Outbox from the menu.

Netscape Messenger

Netscape Messenger is the mail client component of the popular Netscape Communicator package. Messenger's popularity is due in large part to the fact that it's
part of the Communicator package—many Netscape users use it out of convenience, rather than for its merits. In any case, it's a widely used client, and for that
reason is mentioned here. All in all, Netscape Messenger is adequate for the majority of users who want a quick, easy, and free way to read their email and manage
addresses. It lacks the functionality that power IMAP users look for in a mail client.

Netscape is available for a variety of platforms, including Windows 95/98/NT, Macintosh, and several flavors of Unix. Complete information and the latest version of
the Communicator package are available at Netscape's download site: *http://
download.netscape.com/*.

Features

Supports SSL

One of the most desirable features of Messenger is that it supports SSL. If your
IMAP server is enhanced to support SSL, Netscape Messenger can be used to avoid
sending passwords in cleartext over your network.

Folders are stored on the IMAP server

Unlike its primary competitor, Outlook Express, Netscape stores all folders on the
IMAP server, including outgoing mail that is automatically saved into a "sent mail"
folder and, also, drafts.

Performs well over slow connections

To improve performance over slow connections, Messenger allows the user to
choose to download only messages that are below a certain message size threshold. Additionally, attachments are downloaded on demand, allowing a message
with a large attachment to be downloaded quickly.

Superior LDAP support

LDAP support is excellent in Messenger. Messenger has a single interface for searching both personal and remote LDAP address books. The address book interface supports search not only by name, but by city, organization, phone number, and, believe it or not, by soundex.* The client also supports integration of custom LDAP schema for searching. The user can drag and drop the results of an LDAP search into her local address book. LDAP directories can be replicated and used in offline mode, and Netscape claims that the local LDAP address book scales to over 200,000 names.

Site customization

The Netscape Communicator Client Customization Kit (CCK) allows sites to customize components of Communicator, including Messenger, and build an installer for distributing Messenger to their users.

Almost-there ACL support

Netscape claims to support ACL modifications and shared folders, but we were not able to make it work with the Cyrus server. It's possible to view the ACL setting on a folder, but modification of the ACL only works with Netscape's mail server.

Configuring Netscape Messenger for IMAP

Netscape is easy to configure and works well with most of its default settings. The only required settings are for your IMAP server, your outgoing SMTP mail server, and your username.

Configuring your preferences

If you're a first-time Messenger user, start up Netscape Communicator, then pull down the Communicator menu and select Messenger. The Mail and Discussion Wizard will guide you through setting your mail preferences.

If you've used Messenger before, or if the Wizard does not pop up to help you, then follow these instructions to configure Messenger:

1. Start Communicator.

2. Pull down the Edit menu and select Preferences....

---

* Soundex is a way of encoding a name (usually surname) that is based on the way the name sounds, rather than the way it's spelled. This is a valuable feature for names that are difficult to spell and are often entered incorrectly into databases. To find the soundex coding of a surname, visit the National Archives and Records Administration's *The Soundex Machine* at *http://www.nara.gov/genealogy/soundex/soundex.html.*

3. Expand the Mail & Newsgroups category.

4. Click on Identity and fill in the information on the Identity form. Don't click OK yet—if you do, you'll close the Preferences window, and you don't want to do that just yet.

5. Click on Mail Servers. Add the fully qualified domain name (FQDN) of your IMAP server under Incoming Mail Servers.

6. Click on your IMAP server under Incoming Mail Servers to highlight it, then click on the Edit button to bring up your IMAP server preferences. There are several options you may want to set, such as whether or not to connect to your IMAP server via SSL (if your server supports SSL), save your password, or empty your Trash folder when you close Messenger.

7. Before you leave the Mail Servers preferences, enter the FQDN of your outgoing SMTP mail host (often the same as your IMAP server) under Outgoing Mail Server. There are other options under Outgoing Mail Server—set them if they're applicable to your site.

8. You now have the bare minimum configuration to allow you to connect to your IMAP server and read and send mail. Click OK to save your preferences.

Reading your mail

To log in to your IMAP server with Messenger, pull down the Communicator menu and select Messenger. Messenger has three panes. The leftmost pane lists your IMAP server and mail folders. The top-right pane lists your mailbox message index, and the lower-right pane lists the contents of each message you select.

Click once on your server name to display your message index. To read a message, click once on the message listing in the index.

Subscribing to folders

Only the mail folders you're subscribed to appear in your mail folder listing. To manage your folder subscriptions, pull down the File menu and select Subscriptions…. Click once on the name of a folder, then click on the Subscribe or Unsubscribe button to subscribe to or unsubscribe from the folder.

Expunging your deleted mail

Messenger's implementation of the IMAP two phase "delete-expunge" model is counterintuitive—you would expect to find two separate buttons or menu items to "delete" and "expunge." Messenger has you "delete" messages as you would in other clients, but to expunge them, you pull down the File menu and select Compact This Folder.

Outlook Express

Outlook Express (OE) comes bundled with Microsoft's Internet Explorer browser. Like Netscape Messenger, OE is popular by virtue of being free.

One drawback is that, in order to install Outlook Express, you'll have to install the entire Internet Explorer (IE) package. That may be daunting to those who don't have copious hard drive space to spare. The "standard" installation, which is the most basic installation you can use and still install OE, requires 72 MB of disk. The disk space required to run IE/OE once it's installed is 47 MB.

Although many people prefer Netscape Messenger over OE, OE generally behaves better with IMAP servers. Overall, OE works well for users who are looking for a bare-bones IMAP client that is quick, intuitive, easy to set up for the first time, and easy to use. Internet Explorer and OE are available for Windows 95/98/NT, Macintosh, and Unix. To download a free copy of Outlook Express, visit *http://www. microsoft.com/ie/.*

Features

Ease of use

Outlook Express is incredibly easy to install, set up, switch to from other email clients, and use. In fact, OE has a facility for importing mail client configurations and address books from other mail clients (the next section, "Configuration," shows you how).

Supports SSL

A great benefit of using Outlook Express is that it supports SSL. You may be concerned about sending passwords in cleartext over your network. Your users can use OE and connect via SSL to your SSL-enabled IMAP server—and passwords will cross the net encrypted.

Advanced searching

OE offers more than just simple searches on message headers. OE allows you to search for a message in a folder and all of its sub-folders. In addition to standard searching by message header fields (sender, recipient, subject line, date), you can also search the message body and certain types of message attachments for a text string.

Performance over slow connections

To improve performance, OE downloads mail in the background, leaving you free to do other tasks while your INBOX is being populated. You also have the option of setting a size threshold on messages to prevent long downloads if you're on a slow connection.

Configuration

If you're running Outlook Express for the first time...

When you launch OE for the first time, a Wizard will automatically appear and prompt you for the information it needs to set up your configuration. If you have not run OE before, then getting started is easy. Simply launch Outlook Express, answer the questions the Wizard asks you—and that's all there is to it!

If you're switching from another client to OE, OE will allow you to import your data from that client to OE. OE will import mail, address books, and configuration settings from the following clients:

- Eudora Light (through Version 3.0)
- Eudora Pro (through Version 3.0)
- Netscape Mail (Version 2.0 or 3.0)
- Netscape Messenger (Communicator)
- Microsoft Exchange Client
- Microsoft Windows Messaging
- Microsoft Internet Mail and News

To import existing data from one of those clients:

1. Select File/Import.
2. Select either address book or messages.
3. Select the application you are importing the mail messages or address book entries from.
4. A Wizard will appear to assist you through the rest of the process.

If you can't conjure up the Wizard...

If you've run OE before with POP and now wish to begin using it to read your IMAP mail, or if the Wizard does not appear when you start it up for the first time for whatever reason:

1. Select Tools/Accounts.
2. Click on the Mail tab.
3. Click on the Add button and select Mail....

The Wizard will appear and ask you for your name, the name of your IMAP server, and the name of your outgoing SMTP server.

Mulberry

Mulberry is a powerful IMAP client for Windows and Macintosh that fully implements the feature set of IMAP and the IMAP extensions. Mulberry is a product of Cyrusoft, Inc., the company co-founded by the former project manager of CMU's Project Cyrus, Matt Wall, and Cyrus Daboo, the original developer of Mulberry. Cyrusoft's philosophy focuses on true adherence to open standards. Cyrusoft seeks to provide a client that provides a full set of features that help the user read mail more productively and efficiently.

Mulberry is popular in the IMAP world, especially at educational institutions. It's been in use at over 1,000 sites since 1995, in 22 countries, with over 300,000 users.

Cyrusoft has been very diligent in providing regular updates for both the Windows and Mac versions of their software simultaneously. They state their commitment to both versions up front, and they have historically stuck with it. You don't have to worry that the Mac client will go away next year. Having both your Mac and Windows users on the same release of the software will make life easier for your end user support staff. Some of the future development plans for Mulberry include Unix clients (Solaris and Linux, initially), Palm OS clients, and Windows CE clients.

Mulberry is a hidden treasure. Mulberry performs well, is stable, and fully implements IMAP. Mulberry's ACL editor is unmatched and is a valuable resource to Cyrus users. Once we got used to Mulberry's interface, we were hooked.

Features

Mulberry's user interface has a different look and feel from your average Windows application, but it's powerful, friendly, and easy to configure. Detailed information on Mulberry is available at Cyrusoft's web site: *http://www.cyrusoft.com/*. Information at that site includes feature lists, free demo for download, FAQ, general information on IMAP, and Mulberry documentation for download.

Performance

Mulberry was designed not only to provide a pleasing user interface, but also to provide high performance. In fact, the folks at Cyrusoft claim that Mulberry is the "fastest IMAP client around," with the fastest connect time, fastest download of MIME attachments, and fastest message display time of any client available. We didn't do any quantitative benchmarks to confirm that claim, but from a strictly qualitative standpoint, Mulberry is definitely the fastest GUI client evaluated in this chapter. Mulberry minimizes memory and disk space requirements by implementing a "plug-in" architecture—users are given the option of discarding features they don't use, thereby claiming back some disk space and memory overhead.

Mulberry does not include a web browser, a news reader, or any other program that has nothing to do with email, which makes Mulberry smaller still in terms of disk space and memory requirements. To avoid wasting time downloading large messages, Mulberry allows the user to set a threshold on the size of messages and attachments. If the user attempts to open a message exceeding that threshold, she will be warned and asked whether to cancel the action or continue.

Support for site customization

A feature of Mulberry that sets it apart from other IMAP clients is its configurable installer. Sites can use the installer to distribute Mulberry preconfigured with customized preferences to their users. Cyrusoft also offers Mulberry Administrator's Toolkit, which can be used to lock down preference settings. The obvious advantage of locking down preferences is to prevent changes to the configuration when Mulberry is used in a multiuser setting, such as in a general access computer lab ACL tool.

Mulberry provides an elegant, outstanding, and very useful Access Control List (ACL) Viewer and Editor to support the IMAP ACL Extension (RFC 2086). Mulberry's ACL Editor is particularly intuitive and easy to use. Each ACL right can be toggled on and off for each user on the ACL list. The ACL editor has a pull-down list of commonly used ACL combinations, such as "read-only bulletin board" and "shared folder." Those predefined ACLs make it easy for users to share folders in the way they intended without making mistakes that could make their mail insecure. The ACL editor is shown in Figure 4-5.

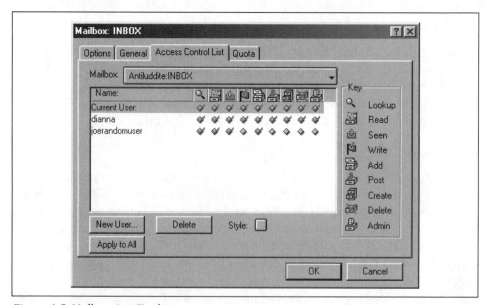

Figure 4-5. Mulberry's ACL editor

Quota viewer

Included in Mulberry is an IMAP quota viewer, which fully supports the IMAP Quota Extension (RFC 2087).

IMSP and ACAP support

Mulberry supports remote storage and retrieval of user options via both IMSP and ACAP.

Encrypted authentication

Mulberry supports two alternatives to cleartext Unix password authentication: Kerberos and CRAM MD5.

Full IMAP support

Mulberry goes beyond the base IMAP protocol and includes full support for IMAP alerts and support for the IMAP Namespace Extension (RFC 2342).

Configuring Mulberry

Mulberry is easy for the end user to configure. The Mulberry documentation includes a one-page QuickStart guide. The interface is intuitive enough to get by without it, but we think it would be the perfect piece of documentation to hand out to users if we were distributing Mulberry at our site.

If you wish to lock down certain preferences at your site, the Mulberry Administrator's Toolkit comes with a program for configuring either the Mulberry installer or the Mulberry itself. The Administrator's Toolkit is packaged separately and is freely available for download, no registration codes required, from *http://www.cyrusoft. com/mulberry/mulbadmins.html.*

Individual user configuration

To configure Mulberry for IMAP, pull down the File menu and select Preferences. You'll see a window like the one in Figure 4-6. Enter your information, and click OK. The preferences take effect immediately.

Site-wide configuration

The Mulberry Administrator's configuration editor allows a system administrator to customize the Mulberry installer or to configure Mulberry itself. An advantage of configuring the installer is that you can distribute the installer without having to unpack the Mulberry distribution, configure Mulberry, and repackage the whole thing.

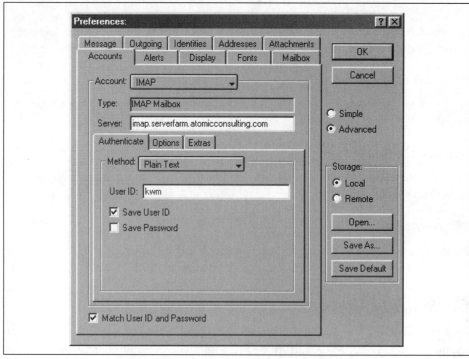

Figure 4-6. Mulberry Preferences

Setting up a site-wide Mulberry configuration is a two-step process: the first step is to set up a configuration file, then run the file through the configuration program to create the configuration. The Administrator's Toolkit comes with a blank configuration file to start with. To get a feel for the types of values that go with the options in the configuration file, you can simply save a local preference file from within Mulberry.

Once you have your blank configuration file, the next step is to run the configuration program. The program will ask you whether you want to configure the Mulberry program or the installer, then will proceed to ask you a series of configuration questions, some of which include questions like:

   Do you want to allow users to save their own preferences?
   Do you want to lock down server addresses and server domains?
   Do you want to lock down the return address?
   Do you want to disallow saving the password in the preferences?
   Do you allow extra header lines?

There are a dozen or so other configuration questions that the configuration program asks, all of which are listed and explained in the Mulberry Administrator's Guide. The format of the configuration file and all possible preferences and values are also listed in the Administrator's Guide.

Once you're done answering the questions, the configuration program will process the answers and carry out the customized configuration.

Eudora

Eudora was originally developed by Steve Dorner at the University of Illinois and began its life as a freeware POP client for the Macintosh. Qualcomm bought the rights to Eudora in 1991 for internal use and developed a version for Windows. Dorner joined the company the same year and is still with Qualcomm today. Eudora was released as a commercial product shortly after Dorner joined Qualcomm. Eudora is popular—there are over 20 million Eudora users worldwide.

There is, as you can imagine, a history behind Eudora's name. The original name, UIUCMail, was something of a tongue-twister. Dorner remembered a story by Eudora Welty about a woman who decides to live at the post office, titled "Why I Live at the P.O." As the story goes, Dorner was processing so much email that he felt as though he lived in the post office. Add to that the fact that the program uses the POP (Post Office Protocol) to fetch mail, and Dorner saw a metaphorical connection. Eudora Welty is flattered by the allusion to her work.

The Eudora 4.3 release offers three user-selectable modes, including a new sponsor-supported mode that provides the full-featured program to consumers free of charge. We evaluated the Sponsored mode version of Eudora. The Sponsored mode of Eudora includes all of the capabilities that were previously available only in the retail version of Eudora. Ads are not keyed to the content of the user's email, nor is personal information sent to advertisers without prior permission from the user. The user has the option of filling out a profile to control the types of ads he'd like to see.

Eudora is also available in Paid mode and Light mode. The Paid mode version is identical in features and capabilities to the Sponsored mode version, but has no ads. Light mode has no advertising, but it does have sponsor logos and is missing some of the features of Paid and Sponsored modes.

Eudora is available for download at *http://www.eudora.com/*.

Features

Enhanced filters

Eudora allows more than just filtering into mail folders. Filter actions include playing sounds, opening the message, printing the message, automatically forwarding the message, bouncing the message, automatically replying to the message, labeling the message with a color, or playing a "speak" message.

Advanced searching

Eudora allows searching on both messages and folder or mailbox names.

Personalities

Eudora handles multiple email accounts very nicely. Personalities can be defined for different IMAP accounts, allowing the user to tie a set of preferences to an account. For example, a user can tie a signature to a particular personality.

Import option

Eudora for Windows allows the user to import settings, mail, and address books from Microsoft Outlook Express or Netscape.

Multitasking

Mail can be composed, received, and sent simultaneously. The user can check and send mail as a background operation.

Message viewing bells and whistles

Graphics, including animated GIF images, and styled text can be displayed inline without opening a separate browser. Eudora's interface has a separate pane below the mailbox window for previewing messages.

Compose options

During composing a message, Eudora automatically completes the name when the user types the first few letters of an address in his address book. The Compose window also includes a spell checker that highlights misspelled words with the click of a button. For fans of HTML mail, Eudora's compose window allows the user to perform HTML formatting, including inserting hyperlinks and embedded graphics.

Other features

Eudora supports vacation-style auto-reply. It has nice, simple documentation and complete online help.

Configuring Eudora

Eudora is very simple to configure. To edit basic options, go to the menu bar, pull down Tools, and select Options. The Options menu is shown in Figure 4-7. Click on the type of options in the left pane. Changes take effect immediately when you click the OK button. The IMAP account you specify will show up as your "Dominant" mailbox or persona. When setting up your IMAP account, leave the "Inbox Prefix" blank—Eudora will query the server and find your Inbox for you.

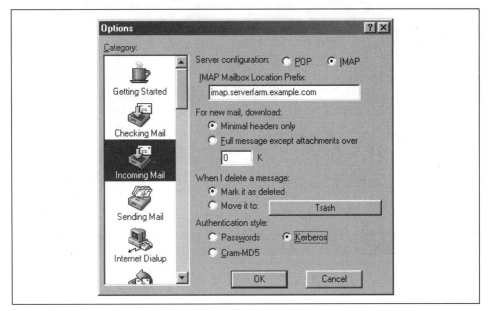

Figure 4-7. Eudora Options menu

To add an another IMAP account, pull down the Tools menu and select Personalities. Click on the Personalities tab. Right-click on the background in the window above the tabs to pop up a menu. Select New from the menu and enter the information about your IMAP account. See Figure 4-8 for an illustration. After you click on the background and select New from the pop-up menu, Eudora will use a Wizard to guide you through the process of adding the new account.

Other Clients

There are dozens of free, shareware, and commercial IMAP clients available for every platform imaginable. A complete and well-maintained list of IMAP client software can be found at *http://www.imap.org/*. Although we evaluated many of the clients on that list, we chose not to mention them here for one or more reasons: incomplete IMAP support, unusually complex installation, support for a single platform only, or a lack of basic features. The list of clients is dynamic—clients are constantly under development and constantly improving, and new clients are being added. It's worth browsing that list for updates from time to time.

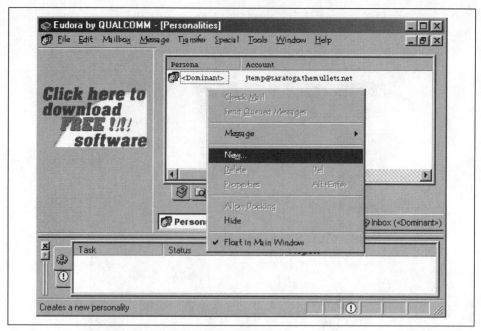

Figure 4-8. Adding another IMAP account to Eudora

5

Web-Based IMAP Clients

One of the major selling points of IMAP, its ability to provide ubiquitous email access, begs an obvious question. If Internet access itself is ubiquitous, but IMAP client installations are not, how do you get to your email? One good answer is to use a web-to-IMAP gateway. Such a gateway presents your IMAP-based mail through a web-based interface, usable with a web browser. IMAP web gateways run the gamut of interface complexity, from interfaces that use standard HTML exclusively to those that generously use JavaScript and Java to present the mail to the user.

Such a gateway permits you to retain the benefits of IMAP when IMAP clients are available, or to use any web browser as an IMAP client when a conventional IMAP client isn't handy. In fact, web-to-email interfaces are used not only by the increasingly popular free email sites, but also by hand-held devices like cellular phones and PDAs, which are using web browsers to connect their owners to their mailboxes.

What's a Web-Based IMAP Client?

A web-based email system is sometimes referred to as a webmail system. Two popular examples of such systems are Yahoo! Mail and Hotmail. A typical webmail system that uses IMAP would consist of the webmail server, on which a web-based IMAP client is run, the IMAP server, and a mailstore.

A web-based IMAP client is software that runs on a web server and enables traditional IMAP email access and functions from within a web browser. Many of the best-known web browsers are bundled closely with IMAP and POP clients for mail reading, but those packages, functioning in that way, are considered full-blown IMAP clients, not web-based IMAP clients.

The "client" in web-based IMAP can be misleading to someone unfamiliar with webmail technology. The "client" in this context is actually the program that runs on the web server, not the web browser itself. A web-based IMAP client can be used from a web browser (Netscape, IE, AOL, Cello, or Mosaic).

Figure 5-1 illustrates a web-based IMAP client. The "client" acts as a broker between both the browser/web-server and web-server/IMAP-server client/server pairs.

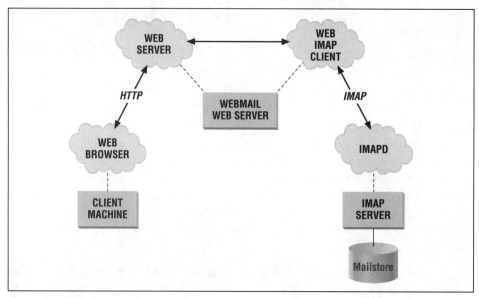

Figure 5-1. Web-based IMAP client

Authors of webmail gateways take a variety of approaches to getting the job done. Some webmail systems run as Common Gateway Interfaces (CGIs), some as Java applets, and others as PHP applications. CGIs are likely to cause a performance hit in situations where execution requires firing up and running another executable image. PHP applications don't cause as many performance problems, because PHP is implemented as a library, not as a wholly separate image. Given the inconsistent levels of Java compliance in different browsers, a good Java IMAP client is understandably hard to find. We looked at clients based on PHP and CGI.

Why Use a Web-Based IMAP Client?

Web-based IMAP clients offer many advantages that are not found in traditional IMAP clients. Let's take a look at what makes web-based IMAP clients so advantageous.

End-User Platform Independence

Suddenly, site managers who support heterogeneous environments of PCs, Macs, Linux, and other platforms no longer have to worry about the support issues involved in supporting mail clients on all those platforms. All machines with access to the Web now run the same mail client. Such platform independence is becoming essential as the work in the network moves from the desktop back to the server.

Global Access

As Internet access becomes more and more of a commodity, the mistaken message that "Web = Internet" is propagating at an unprecedented rate. The fallout of this trend is that nearly every computer on the Internet is bound to have a web browser, regardless of whether it's at an Internet café in Scotland or at an Internet kiosk in the airport. Webmail gateways leverage this reality to deliver universal access to email, regardless of location.

Integration with Existing IMAP Server

Of course, if the only client you'd ever used to access your email were a webmail gateway, it wouldn't matter a hoot what was used on the backend to access your mailstore. In the real world, though, web-based IMAP clients are likely to remain a poor relation of dedicated IMAP MUAs for some time to come. Dedicated clients have a great deal more flexibility and room for individual customization with regard to their interfaces. Given those facts, many of your users are likely to want to continue using their dedicated IMAP clients for much of their email. Picking an IMAP-compliant webmail gateway gives you the best of both worlds: webmail for those that want and need it and conventional IMAP services for users that want or need to go the traditional route.

Centralized Administration

A web-based IMAP client eliminates the need to customize and redistribute an IMAP client every time a new version of the client is released. The process of successive upgrades to new versions of web IMAP clients are transparent to the user, because new servers can be brought up, tested, and put into production with a single atomic action. While individual users can have a great deal more control over a dedicated client, web-based clients are much easier to site-customize from a central authority, like the local IT department. Individual departments, external users, even users of different skill levels can all have their own interface to the webmail system, all residing at the same URL by using existing customization methods. Such methods often include cookies and layer three redirectors, such as the Web Director or Local Director. Cookies are text-based parcels of information that web sites leave with your browser to be able to provide session-oriented services on an essentially sessionless Web. A layer-three redirector intercepts requests for IP-based services and, acting as a proxy, performs the request against an arbitrary number of production servers, thus making any given service more robust than any particular server. Admins may also customize the lead-in page for the web site based on the user's location, host type, or other such elemental information attainable through the CGI API.

Security

The Webmail web server acts, in effect, as a mediator. On one side of it, the user's browser and the web server communicate. On the other, the IMAP web client software and IMAP server talk. Each of the webmail clients evaluated in this chapter rely on SSL to encrypt traffic between the browser and web server. That provides for the security between the user's browser and the web server. That still leaves the issue of the backend traffic between the webmail client running on the web server and the IMAP server.

One popular way of securing this traffic is to run both the IMAP server and web server on the same machine. Users then log on to the web server using SSL. The web server passes the username and password to the IMAP server over the machine's local loopback interface, not the external network. Less secure, but still better than nothing, is to set up a trusted, private network link between the webmail server and the IMAP server.

At the time of publication, security for IMAP web clients concentrated on using SSL between the browser and the web server, not in securing the traffic between the IMAP web client and the IMAP server. System administrators are mostly left to their own devices to secure the latter type of traffic. If you're inclined to run webmail and IMAP on separate servers, you'll probably want to explore setting up a private network for the unencrypted traffic or setting up a VPN between your web and IMAP servers. Hopefully, IMAP web clients will soon support SSL between the IMAP client and server, so you can just slap a third-party SSL wrapper, such as stunnel, into place on your IMAP server and have SSL in place all the way from the browser to the IMAP server.

Another issue for the occasionally paranoid to consider is the risk of entering any sensitive information into an HTML form, like you would be doing when you log in to your mail server using a web-based client. The contents of HTML fields may be visible to JavaScript apps running in other windows of the same browser process. Also, even though your web-based IMAP client is presumably configured to use SSL, there's a slight chance that content caching on your local machine might be happening. If so, an application could conceivably retrieve content from that cache and compromise your email account or the contents thereof. The risk is real, but like so many things in the current state of the Web and Internet security, you must weigh the value of what you're doing against the risk of doing so. If you're genuinely concerned about this particular issue, you could run one browser process for each secure operation (like credit purchases on the Web or checking your email) and another for generic browsing. You might even go so far as to install another browser on your machine to help keep the different processes straight, so you might do secure things in Internet Explorer and other things in Netscape, or the other way around.

Intuitive and Friendly Interface

Users are familiar with web email clients such as Yahoo!, Hotmail (MSN Mail), and other freely available webmail services. Most web-based IMAP clients are very similar in look and feel to the popular free webmail services. They include online help, spell checking, and address books. For many users, a web-based IMAP client eliminates the learning curve involved in using a standard IMAP client.

This is probably a good place to mention that, without exception, these web-based IMAP clients would not be friendly to blind or visually impaired users. We were not able to get them to perform usably in Lynx at all, which left us believing that such users would be better off using a character-based IMAP client on a host system.

Low Cost

Many popular full-fledged GUI IMAP clients typically charge by copy or seat. Either way, the more users you support, the more you pay. Most web-based IMAP clients have one cost, regardless of the number of users—a great benefit for large sites. Better yet, some excellent web-based IMAP clients are available free of charge.

Web IMAP Clients

We evaluated six of the best-known web-based IMAP clients for Unix (Table 5-1).

A Note on PHP

Several of the clients covered in this chapter are PHP applications. When PHP was created, every major web server had its own, proprietary inline scripting language to facilitate easily written, yet non-portable dynamic content. PHP addresses this issue by providing a very powerful, inline scripting language that is usable on many servers and platforms. There are close ties between PHP and various databases, so "databasified" web applications frequently exploit PHP. PHP applications, of course, require a web server that is PHP enabled. For full details on PHP, see *http://www.php.net*.

A Note on Server Platform

There are popular web IMAP clients for NT, including a very successful one from Infinite Technologies (WebMail). A web IMAP client doesn't run in a vacuum, though. It's at the mercy of all the idiosyncrasies of the OS on which it runs, as well as the other systems, such as DNS, LDAP, and the physical host itself, upon which it is dependent. There may be one particular web gateway that has every feature you need. If, however, it's only available for Windows NT and your site doesn't have the desire or expertise to manage a Win NT server farm, then you may find yourself balancing features versus platform.

Table 5-1. Comparison of Web-Based IMAP Clients

Features	IMP 2.0.11	Mailspinner 3.2.5.4	SilkyMail 1.0	EMU 3.0e	WING 0.9
Free	✓	✗	✓	✗[a]	✓
Open source	✓	✗	✓	✗	✓
LDAP search	✓	✓	✓	✓	✗
SSL[b]	✓	✓	✓	✓	✓
IMSP	✗	✗	✓	✗	✗
NNTP	✗	✗	✓	✗	✓
User preferences	✓	✓	✓	✓	✓
Personal address books	✓	✓	✓	✓	✓
Locale support	✓	✓	✓	✓	✗
Customizable interface	✓	✓	✓	✓	✓
Online help	✓	✓	✓	✓	✓
Postpone compose message	✓	✓	✓	✓	✗
Spell check	✓	✓	✓	✓	✓

[a] There is a free version of EMUMail, but it includes banner advertisements that cannot be removed.
[b] Since no one, at publication date, was doing SSL between the IMAP web client and the IMAP server, SSL support in this table implies SSL only between the user's browser and the web server.

IMP

Overview

IMP (*http://www.horde.org*), one of the Horde software projects, is a web-based IMAP client implemented in PHP. IMP is freely available. The latest version is

Version 2.0.11, which is available at *ftp://ftp.horde.org/imp/*. IMP is IMAP4 compliant and works with both the UW and Cyrus servers.

Strengths and Weaknesses

Strengths

IMP is open source and free of cost. It's built based on freely available open source components and open standards. IMP performs better with less overhead than a scripted CGI, because it's implemented in PHP. It includes locale support for several languages, including English, German, Italian, and Brazilian Portuguese.

Weaknesses

IMP was, until recently, somewhat challenging to install on non-Linux platforms because of the variety of packages it required. That's been fixed now, and IMP has very few if any requirements other than the obvious PHP-enabled web server and an IMAP server. There have been several reports, however, that an unmodified IMP server doesn't easily scale larger than 10,000 users or so because of performance problems. Your mileage may vary.

Requirements

IMP can be built on any Unix platform. It has been tested and is known to run on the following platforms:

    AIX 4.3.2
    BSDi
    Digital Unix 4.0d/4.0e
    FreeBSD 3.0 and up
    Linux (Debian 2.1 and 2.2)
    Linux (Red Hat 5.2 and higher)
    Linux (Slackware)
    Solaris 2.6 and higher
    Windows NT 4.0

Horde

The Horde module, the core of all Horde software packages, must be installed on your system as part of your IMP installation. The Horde module source distribution is available at *ftp://ftp.horde.org/horde.org/imp*. The latest version at the time of this writing was 1.0.10.

PHP

PHP 3.0.7 or greater is required by IMP. PHP, which creates most of the dynamic content of your IMP web pages, is a freely available scripting language. PHP is available at *http://www.php.net*. At time of this writing, the latest stable version was 3.0.12. Note that, although PHP 4.x is available, IMP 2.0.11 has not been tested with PHP 4.x.

PHP-supporting web server

IMP requires a web server that supports PHP, such as Apache. Apache 1.3.6, 1.3.9, and IIS 4 will all work with IMP. Once you build IMP to use with an Apache server, you may have to rebuild Apache to support PHP.

Perl

The IMP configuration scripts are written in Perl.

Administration

To store user preferences and address books in a database, you must have a database and must have compiled database support into PHP. Supported databases include MySQL, PostgreSQL, Sybase, Oracle, and Informix.

IMP has the hooks in place to support LDAP searching. For LDAP searching support, you must build PHP with LDAP support. University of Michigan LDAP and Open LDAP have both been used successfully with IMP.

To take advantage of IMP's SSL support, your web server must be SSL capable and enabled.

Site Customization

IMP is highly customizable. Customization is performed either by editing a small set of PHP scripts or by editing text files that define discrete parts of the interface common to all pages, such as page headers and trailers.

Examples

IMP allows the user to change her signature, full name, message header *From:* line, and preferred language. The preferences window is shown in Figure 5-2. The compose message window is shown in Figure 5-3. The message index is shown in Figure 5-4.

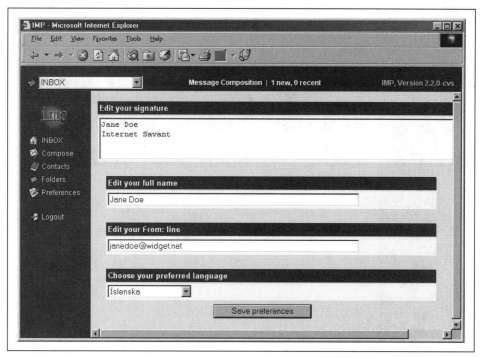

Figure 5-2. IMP preferences

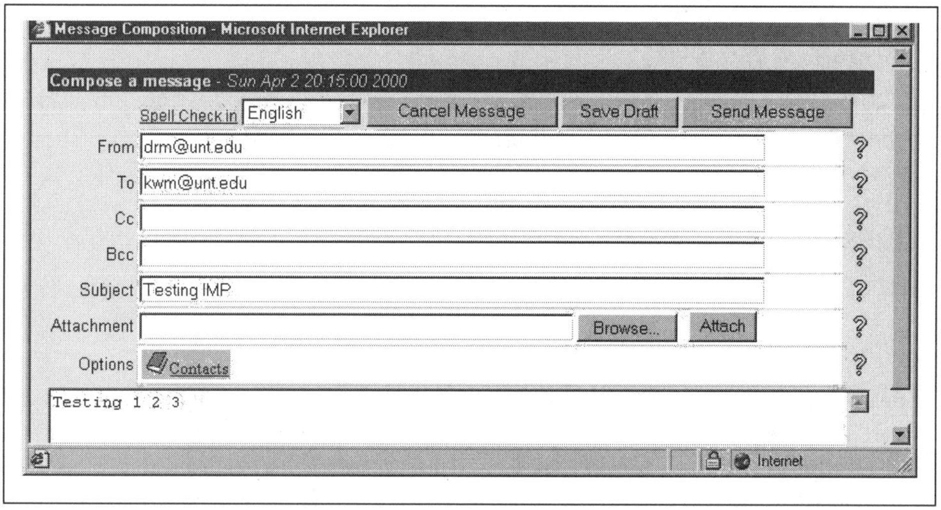

Figure 5-3. IMP compose message

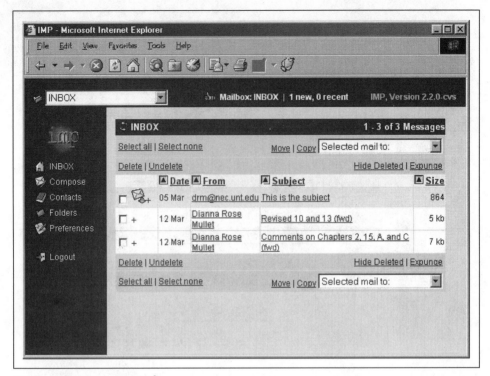

Figure 5-4. IMP message index

For Help with IMP

A good place to start is the IMP portion of the Horde FAQ at *http://faq.horde.org/ cache/1.html*. From there, you can search all the IMP mailing lists in one shot at *http://horde.tdyc.com/*.

IMP web site

The IMP web site is *http://horde.org/imp/*.

Mailing lists

There are two mailing lists for discussion of IMP. The IMP mailing list is directed towards discussion of general IMP issues. To subscribe, send a message with a blank body to *imp-subscribe@horde.org*. The IMP CVS list focuses more on IMP development issues. To subscribe, send a message to *imp-cvs-subscribe@horde.org*. Archives of both mailing lists are available at *http://www.horde.org/mail/imp/* and *http://www.horde.org/mail/cvs/*.

Overall Impressions

IMP gets good marks right out of the gate for being an open source package. Although it leans toward Linux and doesn't have the OS neutrality of many open source packages, that tendency lies mostly in the installation, not in administration. Such factors should be invisible to the end user, so are pretty much just a system administrator concern. Many system administrators who install IMP will find themselves saying, "Now that's how I would have designed it if I were doing it myself!" From the SQL-based user provisioning to the LDAP-enabling for enterprise-wide address books, it's obvious that a great deal of thought and peer review have gone into IMP.

Probably the best feature of IMP is its site customizability. Because of IMP's design, with a combination of straightforward configuration files and PHP scripts, 10 different sites using IMP can each make themselves look nearly completely different. Although a few of the IMAP web clients are somewhat front heavy and present a cluttered interface, the IMP interface is an exercise in KISS.*

Mailspinner

We can easily see users polarizing into those that like IMP and those that prefer Mailspinner. Where IMP is a geek's sandbox full of customizable features and interdependent open source technologies, Mailspinner is a nothing fancy, commercial IMAP web client that just plain works and works well.

Overview

Mailspinner (*http://www.mailspinner.com*) is a high-performance, commercial, closed-source CGI IMAP client. Its interface is quickly embraced even by novice users. Although the system load is lightweight, the price isn't. Mailspinner is one of the most costly commercial clients we've evaluated. For that price, though, you get a system that is designed to scale up to a multiserver, multitier email infrastructure.

There's an online demo available at Mailspinner's web site. Click on "Demo Mailspinner" and fill out the form requesting a username and password for the demo. After obtaining the username and password, you can test-drive the demo, which is a fully enabled installation of Mailspinner. Although there's no free demo for download and evaluation at your own site, we obtained the distribution and a temporary license by calling a sales representative and asking for it.

---

* Keep It Simple, Silly.

Strengths and Weaknesses

Strengths

Users find the interface very intuitive and easy to use with little or no learning curve. It's easy to install and customize.

Weaknesses

Mailspinner is not free. Although its user interface is somewhat customizable, Mailspinner's biggest weakness is that its source code is not available to customers.

Requirements

There are no software prerequistites associated with Mailspinner—everything required to run Mailspinner is self-contained in the binary distribution.

Solaris, Solaris x86, and IRIX are the supported platforms. The product's web site gives the impression that other platforms can be supported, but it does not list them explicitly.

Administration

If it runs on an SSL-enabled web server, Mailspinner uses DES encryption for usernames and passwords.

User preferences can be stored in flat files, in flat files in a hashed directory structure, or in a DBM file. Personal address books are stored as part of the user's preferences.

Site Customization

Mailspinner is customizable to some extent. The Mailspinner installation consists of a daemon, a compiled CGI program, and a set of images—no HTML or CGI source code is provided. It's possible to replace any graphic with your own graphic and to replace any informational or error message with your own message, but you have no direct access to the CGI or HTML code. Supporters of the open source movement will find that aspect of Mailspinner objectionable. Customizing Mailspinner is also somewhat cumbersome. To replace a graphic, you physically move the old GIF file aside and copy the new GIF file into its place. To change an error message, you edit a Unix catalog source file, make the change, and generate a new catalog using the Unix *gencat* utility. This kind of customization precludes adding new features such as a message-of-the-day to the login screen, and forces the system administrator to find a workaround.

Personalization

The user can edit the number of messages displayed on one screen, the time between each mailbox refresh,* and the size of the font.

Examples

Figure 5-5 is an example of the Mailspinner login screen, customized for the University of North Texas.

Figure 5-5. Mailspinner login screen

Mailspinner can be configured to look up addresses in one or more remote LDAP databases. Figure 5-6 is an example of Mailspinner's LDAP lookup, once again customized for the University of North Texas.

Mailspinner's message list is shown in Figure 5-7.

---

* By default, Mailspinner refreshes the mailbox list every 30 seconds. That is just frequent enough to generate complaints from users.

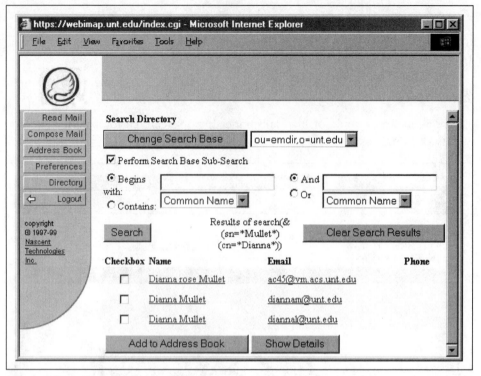

Figure 5-6. Mailspinner LDAP address lookup

To view a message, the user clicks on the message subject. Messages can be sorted on sender, subject, date, or size by clicking on the column heading.

Compose message

Mailspinner allows a user to postpone a message in progress. The postponed message is preserved between login sessions, allowing the user to resume composing the message later. Addresses can be looked up in the user's personal address book or a global LDAP address book while a message is composed, and then selected to be added to either the To: or Cc: fields. Files can be selected from the local machine and added to the message as attachments. The user can spell check the message before sending it.

Locale support

Mailspinner can be customized to support other languages. Mailspinner's default language is English, though, and to support another language appears to require quite a bit of work on the part of the system administrator. The administrator must edit a Unix catalog source file containing informational and error messages and replace each English message with its equivalent in the alternate language.

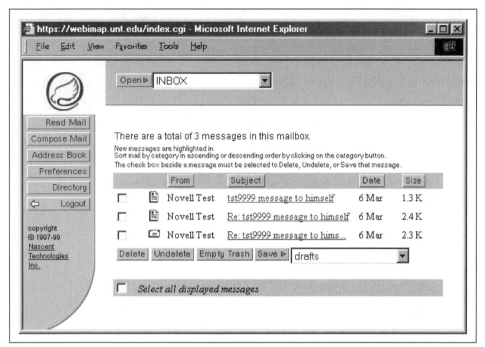

Figure 5-7. Mailspinner message list

Overall Impressions

Mailspinner is a speedy, stripped down client. It doesn't necessarily do everything you'd want a webmail client to do, but what it does, it does well. Unlike IMP, if you look at 10 different Mailspinner sites, they'll look almost exactly alike.

SilkyMail

When we saw the racy opening graphics of the SilkyMail demo, we weren't sure whether we were at the right site. Our anticipation was rewarded with a web-based IMAP client that meets the same high standards as Cyrusoft's MUA, Mulberry (evaluated in Chapter 4, *IMAP Clients*).

Overview

SilkyMail is a PHP application that is based on the IMP client mentioned earlier in this chapter. SilkyMail's added values are IMSP support, an improved user interface, simplified packaging, installation, and improvements in ease of customization. SilkyMail is different from all the other clients we evaluated. It's more like a complete IMAP client that runs within a web browser. In fact, the look and feel of SilkyMail are strikingly similar to the popular Mulberry IMAP client for Windows and Macintosh.

SilkyMail is robust enough to point to any IMAP server containing mailboxes with huge numbers of folders. Like its standard IMAP client cousin, Mulberry, SilkyMail gives you access to all the IMAP state and flag information for each folder. The message indexes can also be selected or sorted on any header field or flag. This is definitely the webmail client that could wean your users off their free email accounts.

Like IMP, SilkyMail relies heavily on the features of PHP. What this means to the user is that SilkyMail is very non-demanding of their particular browser. No Java-Script, Java support, or other whiz-bang features are required.

More information on SilkyMail, including a FAQ, is available at *http://www. cyrusoft.com/silkymail/*.

Strengths and Weaknesses

Strengths

- SilkyMail scales to tens of thousands of users.
- SilkyMail is open source. To those who are familiar with Cyrusoft, it's no sur-prise. Cyrusoft historically has been committed to incorporating open stan-dards in their products.
- It has every feature in the book, including the most complete set of IMAP capabilities in any webmail client (see Table 5-1).
- It's free, and support can be purchased from the vendor.

Weaknesses

SilkyMail opens a separate window to perform certain actions, such as Compose Message. That is definitely not a weakness in itself. Some users, however, do com-plain that having separate windows open can feel sluggish over a slow network connection.

Requirements

- All Unix platforms are supported (source code is provided).
- Nearly everything required is included with the SilkyMail distribution. You will need *autoconf* to build the Configure scripts necessary to install SilkyMail on your system. *autoconf* itself requires m4, so you may need to install m4 first.
- GNU *autoconf* (*ftp://ftp.gnu.org/pub/gnu/autoconf/*).
- GNU *m4* (*ftp://ftp.gnu.org/pub/gnu/m4/*).
- PHP is required by SilkyMail. PHP, which creates most of the dynamic con-tent of your IMP web pages, is a freely available scripting language. PHP is

available at *http://www.php.net*. At time of this writing, the latest stable version was 3.0.12.

Administration

The Apache web server that comes with SilkyMail is already SSL-enabled.

Cyrusoft recommends storing user preferences in a remote IMSP database. However, preferences can be stored on the backend server in a SQL or DBM database.

SilkyMail supports both personal and shared address books. Enterprise and remote LDAP servers can be searched as well, and from the same window.

Site Customization

SilkyMail offers complete visual customization. The login screen can be locked to a specific IMAP server or allow a user to specify any remote IMAP server. Administrators can lock down certain features, such as the IMAP and IMSP server name or any user preference. SilkyMail can be customized to support any language.

Personalization

SilkyMail includes a contact manager for users to store address information. The contact manager includes access the address books stored on an IMSP server.

Examples

The Addressbook Management window is shown in Figure 5-8.

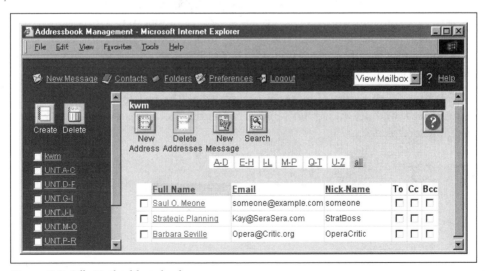

Figure 5-8. SilkyMail address book

The Message Composition window features include auto-address completion, multi-lingual spell checking, auto-quoting on reply. Outgoing messages can be carbon-copied into folders on-the fly. A screen shot of the Message Composition window is shown in Figure 5-9.

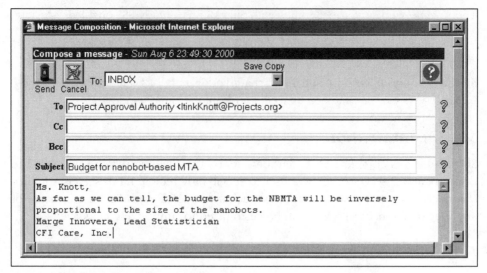

Figure 5-9. SilkyMail compose message

The preferences window is shown in Figure 5-10.

Overall Impressions

Like its standalone counterpart from Cyrusoft, Mulberry, the interface marches to the beat of a different drummer. It makes sense, it's ergonomic, and it works well, but for many people, it just may not be what they're used to and may cause some resistance and a bit of a learning curve. As far as we're concerned, SilkyMail was the most visually pleasing client out-of-the-box.

SilkyMail gets high marks in message presentation. The fact that attachments have separate view and download links makes it friendlier to a greater variety of browsers and client platforms.

EMU 3

We were initially romanced by the jogging emu (his movements are so realistic, you almost expect him to squawk).*

---

* If you have a particularly slow IMAP server or huge mailbox, you'll have plenty of time to dig a hole, build a spit, catch the cute little emu, and cook up some emu burgers. EMU 3 seems to cache an inordinately large amount of information about the mailboxes and messages in order to display the index.

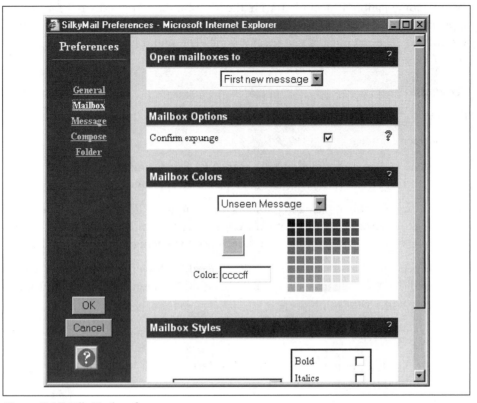

Figure 5-10. SilkyMail preferences

Overview

The version we evaluated was a prerelease version. The demo of the latest version of EMU 3 is available at *http://www.emumail.com/download.html.*

Strengths and Weaknesses

Strengths

EMU 3 comes in a free version, if you don't mind banner advertisements. Some of EMU's strong points include:

- Messages may be postponed while in progress. The postponed message is preserved between sessions, allowing the user to resume composing the message later.
- Client-side mail filtering using user-defined filtering rules.
- Full message header display can be toggled on and off.

EMU documentation is included with the distribution. Appendix B, *Adding SSL Support to IMAP*, of the installation guide contains very useful troubleshooting information. The interface is very neatly done. The menu bars at the top and bottom of message index have clearly labeled buttons.

Weaknesses

The free version has banner advertisements that cannot be removed.

It's not open source.

IMAP flags are not handled 100% correctly; for example, messages flagged "\Answered," don't show up in EMU 3 as answered messages.

There is some difficulty creating folders on a remote IMAP server. The client accepts the input and returns with no errors, but the folder is not created. This may require configuration tuning, but there's no documentation at this point.

Performance when loading a mailbox is noticeably slower than the other clients we looked at in this chapter. Without looking at the source code, it's difficult to say exactly why that is so.

Requirements

The Unix version of EMU 3 runs on most varieties of Unix, including Linux, Solaris, BSDi, IRIX, Digital Unix, AIX, and Free BSD.

GDBM is required.

Perl 5.005_03 and the CPAN module are required to install EMU 3 using the *emuinstall* script. The *emuinstall* script downloads a set of Perl modules required by EMU 3 from a CPAN mirror site, then builds and installs the modules.

If the *emuinstall* script fails, the Perl modules can be installed manually. There's a fair number of them, and they're all listed in the install docs.

Administration

In spite of all the software requirements, EMU 3 is easy to install. The EMU documentation, available on EMU's web site, is excellent and includes a troubleshooting FAQ.

Technical support is available via email to *emu3@emumail.com*.

Site Customization

EMU is customized through use of a proprietary, but well-documented, language called EMUcode. HTML template files with embedded EMUcode are pumped through the EMU engine to produce the EMU experience.*

It may be easier to define multiple user interfaces (customizations that apply to different groups of users) in EMU 3, but it could also be done in some of the open source clients without a major undertaking.

The EMU 3 interface has been translated successfully into Spanish, Portuguese, German, Swedish, and Arabic.

Personalization

The Options window lets the user edit the following options to personalize EMU 3:

> Full name
> E-mail address
> Organization
> IMAP prefix
> Number of messages to display per page
> Number of seconds between reloads of the message index
> Enable/disable real-time SPAM detection
> Personal signature
> Enable/disable autoloading of attached images

Filtering rules are included in the Options window. The user selects the filter Type (e.g., From:, To:, or Cc:), the data to match (literal text or regex), and the destination folder.

Examples

Each of the examples in this section are screen shots of an out-of-the-box installation of the free version of EMU 3, which includes banner advertisements.

The EMU 3 Message Index is shown in Figure 5-11.

The personal address book manager is shown in Figure 5-12.

Figure 5-13 is a screen shot of the Message Composition window.

---

* After seeing other products in this category that were customizable using open source and standards-based tools, we were left wondering why EMU 3 required reinventing the wheel.

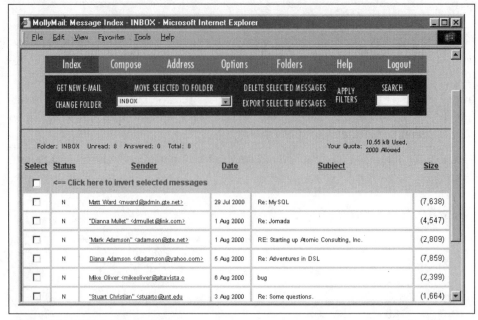

Figure 5-11. EMU 3 Message Index

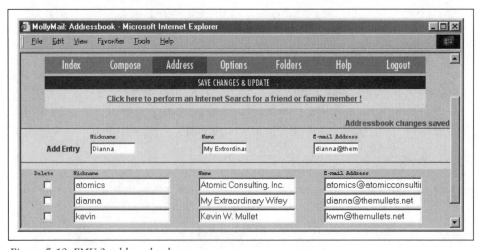

Figure 5-12. EMU 3 address book

Overall Impressions

Other than the fact that performance was less than stellar under real-world loads, EMU 3 has a good feature set and a clean interface. The performance deficiencies, folder behavior, and a few difficulties in message display made us wish we could look at the source code to see how IMAP is implemented.

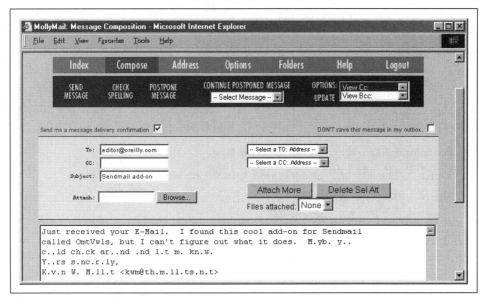

Figure 5-13. EMU 3 Message Composition

WING

WING (Web IMAP and News Gateway) is an open source Apache/mod_perl system that allows users to access email held on an IMAP server using any web browser. WING is reliable and secure, and it scales. It's built completely on open standards and open source components.

Overview

WING was designed and written by Malcolm Beattie at Oxford University to provide webmail services to all 30,000 of their users. Postscript slides describing Oxford University's Herald mail cluster, which uses WING, are available at *http://users.ox.ac.uk/~mbeattie/wing/*.

WING is not trivial to set up. In its current state, it requires many other pieces of software to function and some familiarity with Apache/mod_perl, Perl and SQL. WING was developed primarily for Linux. Other platforms will have to go to extra work to install WING, and modifications of the source code might be necessary to obtain the full functionality experienced on Linux installations.

The software itself is well designed and written, but it is still a work in progress and there are a few rough edges. The interface in particular is somewhat spartan, which may be problematic for users used to glamorous webmail sites like Hotmail. In its favor, though, the software is easy to extend in functionality.

There are no major bottlenecks in large WING implementations, but the central database could potentially become a problem if the underlying system is not well optimized (see Chapter 16, *Server Performance Tuning*, before planning your WING installation). Even so, the database is not accessed on every web hit. It is used only during login and logout and when looking up options and addresses.

Wing is available from any CPAN site: *modules/by-authors/Malcolm_Beattie/ wing-0.9.tar.gz*. It is also available from its home site in several forms:

- Tar archive (*ftp://ftp.ox.ac.uk/pub/perl/Wing-0.9.tar.gz*)

- Source RPM (*ftp://ftp.ox.ac.uk/pub/linux/SRPMS/wing-0.9-1.src.rpm*)

- Binary RPM form for Red Hat 5.x Linux (*ftp://ftp.ox.ac.uk/pub/linux/RPMS/ noarch/wing-0.9-1.noarch.rpm*)

The *wing-admin* mailing list is available for discussions of topics such as WING features, installation and setup, and usage. The author of WING monitors the list and occasionally responds to questions. To subscribe, send a message containing the body "subscribe wing-admin" to *majordomo@maillist.ox.ac.uk*. An archive of the list is available at *http://users.ox.ac.uk/~mbeattie/wing/archive/maillist.html*.

Strengths and Weaknesses

Strengths

Above all, WING is free and it's open source. It scales up to tens of thousands of users (currently used by 30,000 users at Oxford University). Here are some of its other strengths:

- Users can create mailbox hierarchies and move messages between them.

- Messages with MIME attachments can be displayed nicely. Files local to the client browser can be included in a composed message or MIME-attached to it.

- Users can create and store their own bookmarks. The bookmarks appear in the left pane of the browser if the user selects the frames version ("portal view") of the client.

- WING supports import of PINE address books by uploading them via the browser.

- User preferences can be set and saved between sessions.

- Arbitrary headers, with the exception of the From: header, can be added to composed messages.

- Users can manage aspects of their IMAP accounts, such as passwords, setting mail forwarding, and viewing quota usage, via the WING interface.

- Users can create address books, which can be shared with other users and groups using ACLs.

- Users can manage aspects of their account, such as setting the password, editing mail forwarding, and checking disk quota usage.

Weaknesses

WING is very difficult to install. It has many dependencies on other software packages, and it's geared toward Linux more than other platforms. Although WING is difficult to manage, problems are easy to trace and repair because all components are open source. There's also a good support network where help can be found if the going gets tough.

Requirements

- Apache (the latest version of Apache is available from *http://www.apache.org*)
- mod_perl (the latest mod_perl Apache module and integration instructions are available at *http://perl.apache.org*)
- PostgreSQL
- Perl 5.004_04 or later
- The following Perl modules:

DBD-Pg	libnet
DBI	IO-stringy
Data-Dumper	CrackLib
Net-Telnet	Mail Cclient
Apache-DBI	libwww
MD5	MailTools
MIME-Base64	MIME-tools
Term-ReadKey	Net-DNS
HTML-Parser	SQL
Term-ReadLine-Perl	

The CrackLib and SQL modules have not been released to CPAN yet. Both CrackLib and SQL are available as source RPMs at *ftp://ftp.ox.ac.uk/pub/linux/SRPMS/* and as binary RPMs for Red Hat Linux 5.x at *ftp://ftp.ox.ac.uk/pub/linux/RPMS/ i386/*. Non-Linux sites will have to use *rpm2cpio*[*] to convert the RPM source to a cpio archive, then build the modules for themselves.

---

[*] *rpm2cpio* is available at *http://www.iagora.com/~espel/hacks.html*.

III

The Cyrus IMAP Server

6

Introduction to the Cyrus IMAP Server

This chapter provides a technical overview of the features and design concepts that make up the Cyrus IMAP server. The Cyrus server wasn't the first IMAP server, nor was it written by the author of the IMAP standard. True believers in the Cyrus server and its derivatives are likely to tell you, though, that once you've deployed the Cyrus server, you're unlikely to switch to another server. Cyrus boasts a very attractive feature set. It offers robust administration, scalability, and leading-edge IMAP extensions, such as mailbox quotas, plug-in authentication mechanisms, and support for server-side filtering. Detractors are likely to say that UW can be deployed more easily and that Cyrus may not make much sense for a small or medium-size user base.

The Cyrus IMAP server is based on IETF standard protocols, including IMAP4, IMSP, SMTP, RFC 822, MIME, and SASL. IMAP2bis is also supported for backward compatibility with earlier IMAP clients. POP3 is included to support POP users while they're going through the process of selecting an IMAP client.

The Cyrus server is feature-rich, and implements several IMAP protocol extensions, including the IMAP QUOTA and the IMAP ACL extensions. Cyrus is normally run as a "black box" server—users are not meant to access the system by any means other than the IMAP protocol. Mailboxes are stored in a central location and in parts of the filesystem that are private to the Cyrus server. Cyrus was designed with centralized mail storage in mind to make the system easier for administrators to manage. The centralized mailstore also allows such features as mailstore partitioning (discussed later in this chapter). The ability to partition the mailstore makes the server very scalable—as the mailstore grows, the system administrator may add new partitions to the mailstore to accommodate new growth, without affecting the operation of the server. Cyrus shared folders are very flexible—the server not only allows concurrent read connections to the same mail-box, but also supports concurrent write connections.

The Cyrus server differs from other IMAP server implementations in that it is meant to run on sealed, or black box, servers, where normal users are not permitted to log in. Users access their mail strictly via IMAP. Even if a user were allowed to log on to the server where Cyrus runs, she would not be able to do things like "grep" her mail folders for someone's username or compress her folders. That is because the Cyrus mailstore is private to the Cyrus IMAP system. The private mailbox design can be difficult for users to get used to, especially if in the past they've logged in to a Unix shell account and had direct access to mail. Cyrus's black box design, however, gives the server large advantages in efficiency, scalability, and ease of administration.

Cyrus did not turn out to be fantastically scalable by accident. An original goal of Project Cyrus was to produce a mail system that scaled to tens of thousands of active mail readers.* The number of large† sites using Cyrus (Carnegie Mellon University, the University of North Texas, North Carolina State University, the University of Florida, Ohio University, the University of Otago in New Zealand, for example) are examples of Cyrus's scalability. There are even three IMAP server products released commercially—by Netscape, Mirapoint, and MessagingDirect—which are built on the original Cyrus distribution. Although Cyrus is suitable for large organizations, it can be used equally well in small organizations. Although not as simple to deploy as the UW server, it is capable of being installed, configured, and maintained by small computing departments.

History of Cyrus

The Cyrus IMAP server traces its roots back to CMU's Andrew Messaging System (AMS). AMS, the world's first large-scale multimedia mail and bulletin board system, was a very successful proprietary system developed and used at CMU to support the electronic communication needs of the university community. Project Cyrus began in 1992 in an effort to develop a replacement for AMS, which by then was reaching its end-of-life. The first Cyrus IMAP4 server was released in late 1995, one year after IMAP4 was approved as a Proposed Internet Standard. The Cyrus server retained many of the same features that made AMS a success.

---

* Project Cyrus was named after Cyrus the Great of Persia (599–530 BC), who initiated one of the first known postal systems.

† A large site is a site with more than 20,000 active users.

AMS used a file access protocol, Andrew File System (AFS) to access mail. By the time AMS comprised 9,000 users, accessing mail from a mix of Macintosh, PC, and Unix machines, it was painfully clear that a mail system using a filesystem protocol for mail access does not scale well. AFS was not implemented for Macs and PCs. To make mail stored on the AFS servers available to those machines, it had to be served from a "translator" machine. The "translator" was an AFS client set up as a server that acted as sort of a middleman and made mail available to the Macs and PCs. As it turned out, limitations in the AFS client resulted in more translator machines than there were actual AFS servers serving up mail. If that wasn't bad enough, the translator machines were plagued with performance problems. A goal of Project Cyrus was to serve mail using a network protocol that was explicitly designed for mail—IMAP.

An important feature of AMS was its integration of email and bulletin boards. AMS supported controlled access to bulletin boards by allowing a system administrator to apply an access control list to the bulletin board. AMS also provided an addressing scheme that allowed authorized users to post messages directly to bulletin boards via email. Bulletin boards were an essential feature of AMS and were widely used by the user community at CMU. Project Cyrus continued support for bulletin boards, including all the bulletin board features offered in AMS, in the Cyrus IMAP server. AMS, however, did not allow users to make their personal mail folders available to other users. The lack of support for shared personal folders was problematic. There were individuals and small groups who wished to set up private forums, but could not do so without administrative intervention. Project Cyrus addressed the limitation by extending bulletin board support to allow users to share their own folders with other users on the system.

Kerberos was the authentication method used at CMU at the time that AMS was in production. Even in the early 1990s, there was a movement within the IETF to discourage network protocols that relied on cleartext passwords from making it through the standards process. Kerberos support in the Cyrus server (and in the SASL RFC) is a carryover from AMS. Challenge-Response Authentication Mechanism (CRAM) was added to accommodate sites that need encrypted authentication but do not have a Kerberos framework in place. The latest versions of Cyrus support Simple Authentication and Security Layer (SASL), which is a way of adding authentication support to IMAP and other connection-based protocols.

AMS supported MIME, which was a standard that was quickly becoming the accepted way of interchanging multimedia documents via email. The project Cyrus developers included MIME support in the Cyrus server for its growing popularity, but also because it would make for a smooth transition from AMS to Cyrus.

A Late-Breaking Note

Cyrus IMAP 2.0 was in the pre-release stage when we went to press. Cyrus 2.0 represents a major architectural overhaul over previous versions. One of the largest changes is that it no longer runs out of a separate "superdaemon" like *inetd*. The Cyrus IMAP server now runs as a standalone daemon. Here's an overview of the new features in Cyrus 2.0:

- **Improved mailboxes file structure.** The mailboxes file is now a Berkeley-style transaction-protected database. This greatly streamlines the contention between different *imapd* processes for read/write access to the mailboxes file and, by extension, streamlines overall operation.

- **Support for LMTP.** Delivery to the mailboxes from the MTA is now accomplished with Local Mail Transport Protocol (LMTP). LMTP can be used either from one process to another on the same host with Unix sockets, or via Internet sockets. By using LMTP for delivery, an MTA can receive a reliable confirmation or denial of the success of delivery to each local mailbox. This often wasn't possible with other delivery methods. Because this same feature could be used to confirm or deny the existence of specific mailboxes, some system administrators highly restrict the access to LMTP over Internet sockets, especially from remote hosts. The Cyrus *deliver* program is now simply a wrapper to the LMTP delivery agent.

- **Clustering support.** Cyrus Murder: The IMAP Aggregator, provides support for IMAP server clustering.

- **Sieve support.** Server-side filtering through Sieve is enhanced by the addition of regular expression, notification, and IMAP flag features.

- **Simple Network Management Protocol hooks.** You can now roll your Cyrus server into your SNMP managed network scheme. Cyrus now comes with an SNMP agent daemon called *tug-o-war*.

- **Administration via Perl.** Brandon Allbery's Perl-based version of *cyradm* is now included with Cyrus IMAP. Eventually, it will replace the Tcl-based version.

- **MULTIAPPEND extension.** The MULTIAPPEND extension is implemented. Clients may now append an arbitrary number of messages to a mailbox in a single atomic action.

- **LIBWRAP.** Since it's not possible to launch the server(s) out of *inetd*, *libwrap*, which comes with TCP Wrappers, is presented as an alternative way to do IP-based access control.

- **Hierarchical RENAME.** The IMAP RENAME command now works hierarchically.

Cyrus Concepts and Features

This section explains the basic concepts of the Cyrus server design and discusses Cyrus's feature set.

The Cyrus Mailbox Namespace

The Cyrus IMAP server uses a hierarchical mailbox naming convention similar to the naming scheme used in Usenet for naming newsgroups. The mailbox namespace is described in this section from the server's point-of-view. As we will see later in the section, the mailbox names that the user sees in his IMAP client are not necessarily what the system administrator sees when she lists the mailbox names on the server.

Let's take a look at a mailbox hierarchy. Our mailbox belongs to a user whose username is *johndoe* and contains a mailbox for incoming mail and three folders* named *drafts*, *saved-messages*, and *sent-mail*. On a Cyrus server, the incoming mailbox and the three folders would be named:

> *user.johndoe*
> *user.johndoe.drafts*
> *user.johndoe.saved-messages*
> *user.johndoe.sent-mail*

There are several restrictions on mailbox names. Only ASCII characters are allowed; shell metacharacters, /, a leading or trailing period, and two periods in a row are not allowed. Additionally, mailbox names are case-sensitive.

A Word on a Special IMAP Mailbox: INBOX

Although no two mailbox names are the same from the Cyrus server's point of view, that is not necessarily true from the point of view of the IMAP client. RFC 2060 (IMAP) allows for a special mailbox name, *INBOX*. *INBOX* is case-insensitive and refers to the authenticated user's primary mailbox on the server. When an IMAP client communicates with a Cyrus IMAP server, the user's top-level mailbox may be referred to as either *user.username* or as the name *INBOX*. When configuring an IMAP client, it is more common to define the incoming mailbox or incoming mail folder as *INBOX*, and in fact, many clients come preconfigured that way.

---

* Mailboxes other than the incoming mailbox are sometimes also referred to as "folders."

The Cyrus Mailstore

On a Cyrus IMAP server, a filesystem is allocated for the sole purpose of mail storage (under ideal circumstances, this filesystem also resides on its own physical media, but we'll discuss that in a later chapter). Each user's mailbox is represented by a directory on the mailstore's filesystem. Cyrus stores mail in a format that is similar to MH format—instead of storing many messages in a single file as in standard Unix mail (sometimes known as *mbox* or *Berkeley format*), each message is stored in an individual file. Each individual file is in RFC 822 format, like Berkeley mail, the only difference being that the Cyrus mail file terminates each line with CRLF.[*]

Each user has his or her own subdirectory in the Cyrus mailstore directory. The subdirectory and all files within it are owned by the Cyrus user. As mentioned earlier in this chapter, the mailstore is private to the owner of the Cyrus server (usually user *cyrus*), and all other users are restricted from direct access to the mailstore. Incoming mail is written to the user's top-level directory, one message per file. Folders consist of subdirectories below the user's top-level directory. Like the top-level directory, the folder contains individual files, each of which contains a single mail message. Both the top-level directory (incoming mail) and subdirectories (folders) are referred to as "mailboxes." The filename of each mail message within a mailbox is a numeral[†] appended with a period. The numerals are strictly ascending in the order that the message was added to the mailbox.

Each mailbox contains four additional binary files that the Cyrus server uses to manage the mailbox on a per-session basis:

cyrus.index

> This file contains a header of information that applies to the whole mailbox, and one fixed-length record per message. The information stored in the header includes the number of times the mailbox has been expunged (i.e., messages marked for deletion have been permanently removed); the unique identifier (UID) of the last message that was added to the mailbox; the number of messages in the mailbox; the mailbox's quota usage; and the time a message was last inserted into the mailbox. The per-message records contain the UID of the message, the Date: header, the date of last modification, and the size of the mail message.

cyrus.header

> This file contains a magic number, the name of the mailbox's quota root, a copy of the mailbox's ACL, and the names of user-defined flags.

---

[*] This is important to keep in mind when converting other mailbox formats to Cyrus mailboxes.

[†] The numbers are mapped to UIDs in the *cyrus.index* file. Although they are strictly ascending, they are not necessarily contiguous.

cyrus.cache

This file is a performance enhancement. It contains cached headers of every message that the client requests, so that the server doesn't have to go back and peek in the message for the headers. The file contains a counter that keeps track of the number of times *cyrus.cache* has been rewritten by an expunge operation. Each record in *cyrus.cache* contains an IMAP envelope; an IMAP body structure and body; and the size, offsets, character sets, and encodings of the MIME sections of the message. The IMAP envelope, body, and body structure are in a format that the IMAP FETCH command can use.

cyrus.seen

This file contains the username, the time the mailbox was last opened, the sequence of numbers of messages that have been seen, and the message number of the last message that is not recent.*

One caveat to keep in mind is that, once mail is stored in Cyrus format, it can be challenging to extract the mail and revert to the standard Unix mail format. Scripts to tackle this task are provided in Chapter 9, *Cyrus System Administration*.

Cyrus Features

Cyrus IMAP server is feature rich and implements several protocol extensions, including Quota (RFC 2087) and ACL (RFC 2086). In this section we'll talk about how Cyrus implements those extensions. We'll also look at some implementation-dependent "bonus" features that are derived from the Cyrus server design, such as mailstore partitioning and shared folders.

Access control

Permission to access a mailbox is defined in an Access Control List (ACL) on the Cyrus server. An ACL specifies the users or groups who have permission to access the mailbox. Each mailbox on a Cyrus server has an associated ACL. The ACL contains one or more entries that consist of a user or group that the ACL applies to and a list of access rights. Two special groups, *anonymous* and *anyone*, are defined on every Cyrus server by default. The *anonymous* group refers to all unauthenticated users and is most commonly used to provide public access to a shared folder. CMU provides access to their Cyrus Mailing List archives in this manner. The *anyone* group is made up of all users, including the *anonymous* users.

---

* A recent message is one that has recently arrived in the mailbox. The current session is the first IMAP session to have been notified about the message.

ACLs are discussed in detail in Chapter 9. ACLs are very flexible and allow a fine granularity of control over access to a mailbox. It is possible using ACLs to allow different levels of access to different users on the same mailbox.

Shared folders and bulletin boards

Cyrus allows users to share private mail folders with other users on the system without requiring the intervention of a system administrator or any person with special privileges. Shared folders are simply mailboxes with ACLs that allow more than one user to access the mailbox via an IMAP client. Cyrus also supports multiple concurrent read/write connections by different users to the same shared folder.

Bulletin boards are shared mail folders that have the specific feature of allowing many users not only to read, but also to post messages directly to the folder. Users post a message to the board by mailing a message to the submission address of the bulletin board. Bulletin boards are reminiscent of Usenet newsgroups. Many sites manage their own Usenet news server specifically so that the site can provide site-specific, private news groups to their users. For those sites, Cyrus bulletin boards could replace the site-specific newsgroups and make it possible to outsource the public newsgroups. The details of setting up shared folders and bulletin boards are covered in Chapter 9.

Mailstore partitioning

The Cyrus server supports distribution of the mailstore across physical disks. Each mailbox hierarchy is known as a partition. Mailstore partitioning allows the mailstore to be expanded as needed. If the mailstore approaches the capacity of the filesystem it resides on, the system administrator has the option of expanding the mailstore onto another filesystem by adding a new Cyrus partition to that filesystem. He would then either move a subset of existing mailboxes to the new partition or perhaps create any new mailboxes on the new partition.

A mailbox is assigned to a partition at the time the mailbox is either created or renamed (moved). Although a user's hierarchy of mailboxes is usually kept together on one partition, a mailbox need not reside in the same partition as its parent mailbox.* As an example, *user.johndoe* and *user.johndoe.sent-mail* may reside on separate partitions. Mailstore partitioning is invisible to the end user. How to partition the mailstore and assign mailboxes to partitions is described in Chapter 9.

---

* The authors recommend keeping an individual user's mailbox hierarchy contained on one partition for ease of management unless there is a compelling reason not to.

Storage quotas

Storage quotas allow the system administrator to set limits on mail storage for both incoming mail and mail stored in folders. Cyrus IMAP storage quotas are not related to Unix quotas and apply to the Cyrus server only. Cyrus quotas do not apply to a specific mailstore partition—a quota can apply to more than one mailbox on more than one mailstore partition. Mailbox index and cache files are not counted against the quota—only mail message files count.

Quotas on the Cyrus server are hierarchical and very flexible. Quotas can be set at any level of a mailbox hierarchy. The level at which the quota is set is known as a *quota root*. A mailbox hierarchy may have more than one quota root at any level of the hierarchy. The quota set on a quota root applies to the mailbox at that level and all mailboxes below it. As an example, recall that *johndoe* has four mailboxes in his hierarchy:

> *user.johndoe*
> *user.johndoe.drafts*
> *user.johndoe.saved-messages*
> *user.johndoe.sent-mail*

The following quota roots have been set on *johndoe*'s mailboxes:

> *user.johndoe*
> *user.johndoe.saved-messages*

The quota root *user.johndoe* applies to the *user.johndoe, user.johndoe.drafts*, and *user.johndoe.sent-mail* mailboxes. The quota root *user.johndoe.saved-messages* applies only to the mailbox *user.johndoe.saved-messages*. If the quota root on *user.johndoe.saved-messages* didn't exist, then the quota root on *user.johndoe* would cover *user.johndoe.saved-messages*.

Because quotas on the Cyrus server are hierarchical, it's possible to set quotas on folders without setting a quota on incoming mail. However, it is not possible to do the reverse and set quotas on incoming mail without implicitly setting quotas on folders. This is so because of the hierarchical nature of mailboxes on the Cyrus server. The quota applies to a mailbox and all mailboxes below it in the hierarchy, unless quotas are explicitly applied to mailboxes lower in the hierarchy.

Quota limits and usage are stored in a separate file per user in the Cyrus configuration directory, described later in this chapter.

Quota warnings. Cyrus provides a means of specifying a soft quota limit by setting the `quotawarn` option in */etc/imapd.conf.* The value of `quotawarn` is expressed as a percent usage of the quota. When a user selects a mailbox, the server will send an ALERT warning the user that she's exceeded the soft limit if two conditions are met:

1. The user's usage in the selected mailbox exceeds the **quotawarn** threshold.

2. The user has delete rights on the selected mailbox.

Although many IMAP clients claim to be fully IMAP4 compliant, the truth of the matter is that many of them do not handle quotas cleanly. For example, in some clients, if mailbox usage exceeds the soft limit while an IMAP session is open, the client will not handle the alert message when the mailbox is selected. In that case the IMAP session must be closed and reopened and the mailbox selected before the user will see the alert.

Quotas and mail delivery. When mail storage in a given mailbox exceeds the quota limit, mail delivery fails. Delivery attempts to the mailbox in question are deferred and handled in whatever way you choose to make the MTA handle it. Usually, such mail is kept in a local queue and delivery is re-attempted with each queue run for three days or so before it's either delivered successfully, or bounced back to the sender with an error.

If the usage is over the soft limit but has not reached the hard quota limit, however, a message of any size will be delivered, regardless of whether or not it would result in usage that exceeds the hard limit. One may argue that this behavior would open the doors to denial of service (DOS) attacks, but that is not a strong argument against the design. DOS attacks can be prevented by setting a limit on the size of messages in your MTA configuration.* Besides, on the traditional Unix mail systems that use */var/spool/mail* or */var/mail* for incoming mail, system administrators rarely, if ever, set UFS quotas on the mail spool partition. It is considered poor practice because when a user's usage exceeds the quota, mail bounces without the user ever knowing that she is unable to receive mail. Cyrus IMAP quotas are a different story. The Cyrus server alerts the user when usage approaches or exceeds the quota limit. By allowing one message to be delivered to the mailbox and bringing the user over quota, the effect is that the next time the user selects the mailbox, she receives the alert immediately and can begin to correct the problem.

---

* Generally, 10 to 15 MB is considered an adequate maximum message size limit. The greatest benefit of setting such a limit is to disable denial-of-service attacks originating from software that's designed to flood your server with an endless stream of content for a single message until the server fills a filesystem and croaks. Good MTA tuning will prevent such attempts before the message is ever handed off to Cyrus to deliver.

Usenet news integration

The Cyrus server supports exporting Usenet newsgroups as mailboxes. The Cyrus distribution includes programs that interface with an *inn* server to collect news articles and add pointers to them to the appropriate mailboxes on the IMAP server, to remove pointers to expired and canceled articles from the IMAP mailboxes, and to synchronize the IMAP news mailboxes with the news active file. Version 2.0 has much easier news integration than earlier versions of Cyrus. News is discussed in further detail in Chapter 9.

Authentication

With Cyrus, your users need never send their passwords over the network in cleartext. Cyrus natively supports Kerberos 4. The latest version releases of Cyrus (1.6 and higher) include support for the SASL library. SASL makes it possible to authenticate your users with any of the additional encrypted authentication methods supported by SASL, including CRAM-MD5, DIGEST-MD5, and GSSAPI (MIT Kerberos 5). However, not all IMAP clients support Kerberos.

Cyrus IMAP also supports Unix authentication. Unix authentication permits a user to log in to the server using her plaintext Unix password, provided that she appears in */etc/passwd* (or is a member of a netgroup that is included in */etc/passwd*). Unfortunately Cyrus does not provide a way of supporting both Kerberos and plaintext login on the server side—it's either one or the other.

Anonymous login is supported regardless of which authentication method is used, as long as `allowanonymouslogin` is defined in */etc/imapd.conf.*

Many sites that do not implement Kerberos would still prefer not to send plaintext passwords over the network. For these sites, SSL is an option. The Cyrus IMAP server does not support SSL, but SSL support can be added to Cyrus by wrapping *imapd* with the free SSLeay library and *stunnel* and using clients (web browsers, for example) that support SSL. *stunnel* creates an SSL pipe between the web browser and *stunnel* server over the network, then sends the password in plaintext over the loopback interface to *imapd*. The 2.0 release of Cyrus is SSL enabled—it has built-in SSL-enabled IMAP and POP daemons that make an SSL wrapper like *stunnel* unnecessary. For sites using an older version of the Cyrus server, instruction on how to add SSL support to IMAP is provided in Appendix B, *Adding SSL Support to IMAP.*

With the growing popularity of LDAP, many sites that implement both IMAP and LDAP may be interested in using LDAP as an authentication mechanism. Although LDAP authentication is not supported officially in the Cyrus release, there is at least one freely available drop-in LDAP authentication module for the Cyrus server.

The module replaces Cyrus's external authentication daemon (*pwcheck*) with another daemon (*pwcheck_ldap*) that uses an LDAP directory for authentication.*

CMU has also developed an implementation of RFC 2222 (Simple Authentication and Security Layer), the Cyrus (SASL) API, which is integrated into Cyrus releases later than 1.6. The SASL API can be used to provide authentication from either the client or server side. Cyrus SASL includes support for anonymous, DIGEST-MD5, CRAM-MD5, Kerberos Version 4, MIT Kerberos Version 5 or Heimdal Kerberos Version 5, and plaintext.

Selecting an authentication method is beyond the scope of this book, but instructions on how to set up Cyrus to use the both the supported and not-yet-supported authentication methods are outlined in Chapter 8, *Configuring the Cyrus Server*, and Chapter 9.

Cyrus Server Configuration

The parts that make up the server configuration, what each part does, and where to find each part, are described in this chapter. Details on setting up the configuration are given in Chapter 9.

The imapd Server Configuration File

The *imapd* daemon reads its configuration options from the file */etc/imapd.conf*. The location of the configuration file itself is not configurable. Examples of the options specified in this file include:

umask
> The default permissions used by the various Cyrus programs

allowanonymouslogin
> Whether to allow anonymous login to the server

configdirectory
> The location of the Cyrus server configuration directory

quotawarn
> The threshold for over quota warning messages

The `plaintextloginpause` option sets the number of seconds to pause after a successful plaintext login. This option allows users to perceive the cost of using plaintext passwords on systems that support strong authentication. The complete list of options is discussed in Chapter 9 and listed in the *imapd*(5) online manual page.

---

* The source and installation instructions for *pwcheck_ldap* are available from *http://www.linc-dev.com/*.

Server Configuration Directory

The server configuration directory contains databases that describe the server's dynamic configuration in terms of content, status, processes, quotas, and mailbox subscriptions. By default, the server configuration is installed in */var/imap*.

Special files

configdirectory/msg/shutdown

> If *configdirectory/msg/shutdown* exists, then *imapd* will send the first line in the file to the client in the form of an IMAP ALERT* message and shut down the connection. New connections will be denied until the file is removed.

configdirectory/msg/motd

> If *configdirectory/msg/motd* exists under the *config* directory, *imapd* sends the first line in the file to the client as an ALERT message when a connection is made. Many clients handle ALERTs poorly (by connecting more frequently than is necessary and thus displaying the alert for each connection and annoying the user) or not at all.

Mailboxes file

configdirectory/mailboxes is a text file that lists every mailbox name, the mailbox's quota root, and the mailbox's ACL. *mailboxes* is critical to the operation of the Cyrus server. In releases 1.6.22 and earlier, the *mailboxes* file is a plaintext file. The 2.0 release replaces the text file with a transactional Berkeley DB database file. The *mailboxes* file is updated frequently. It can also grow very large as the number of users on the system increases. CMU warns that the *mailboxes* file should never reside on an NFS-mounted partition due to locking problems with NFS.

In Cyrus 1.6.22 and earlier, although the Cyrus system is well-engineered and has proven to be robust, the *mailboxes* file is perhaps its weak link. If the file is corrupted, the road to recovery is not a simple matter of restoring the file from tape. A very recent copy of *mailboxes* is required to avoid a long and laborious reconstruction process. Chapter 9 describes that recovery process in detail. In practice, the text format *mailboxes* file is not necessarily a bad thing—our personal experience has shown that even on large systems (30,000+ users), the *mailboxes* file does not create any noticeable degradation in performance. Cyrus Version 2.0 replaces the *mailboxes* file with a Berkeley DB database that has transactional updates.

---

* ALERT is a server status response that IMAP-compliant clients are required to display to the user in a way that calls the user's attention to the response.

Logging and process information

Cyrus IMAP logs messages to the *local6* facility of *syslog* with severity levels of *crit, err, warning, notice* and *info*. Errors requiring the system administrator's attention are logged to *crit*. I/O errors, including the specific file and Unix error, are logged with severity level *err*. Client timeouts and authentication failures are logged with severity level *warning*. Successful and unsuccessful authentications are logged with severity level *notice*. Mailbox openings and closings and suppression of duplicate deliveries are logged with severity level *info*.

The server also supports per-user telemetry logging. Telemetry logging is very useful in troubleshooting problems, especially in determining whether a bug resides in the server or in the client. Telemetry logging becomes active for a user when the system administrator creates a subdirectory with the user's name under the *configdirectory/log*. The server keeps a protocol level log of sessions that are authenticated as the user in a file named after the server process identification number. The Cyrus user must have write access to *configdirectory/log*. Files created in that directory match the PID of the IMAP process.

A file per active server process is stored in the *configdirectory/proc* subdirectory under the configuration directory. The name of the file is the process identification number of the process. Each file contains the client's hostname; the username, if the user is logged in; and, if a mailbox is selected, the mailbox name.

Quota root

Each quota root has a corresponding file, named after the quota root, under *configdirectory/quota*. The quota root file contains the quota limit in kilobytes and the current usage in bytes. For example, user *johndoe* has a quota limit of 20 MB on his top-level mailbox (*user.johndoe*) with a usage of 13,194 bytes. *johndoe* also has a quota limit of 10 MB one of his folders, *user.johndoe.sent-mail*, and has a current usage of 4,336 bytes. To use the Cyrus terminology, *johndoe* has two *quota roots*, and those quota roots are *user.johndoe* and *user.johndoe.sent-mail*. If we list the contents of the directory *configdirectory/quota*, we see two files named after *johndoe*'s quota roots:

```
$ ls /var/imap/quota | grep johndoe
user.johndoe        user.johndoe.sent-mail
```

This is what we see inside each of the files:

```
$ cat user.johndoe
13194
20480
$ cat user.johndoe.sent-mail
4336
10240
```

The delivered database

When the Cyrus *deliver* program is invoked with duplicate delivery suppression turned on, Cyrus keeps a database of delivered messages, used to suppress duplicate deliveries. The database contains the mailbox name, the message-ID, and the delivery time. Versions through 1.5.24 store the information in DBM format, in *configdirectory/delivered.dir* and *configdirectory/delivered.pag*. Versions 1.6 and up store a database file for each letter of the alphabet. File locking is accomplished by the *configdirectory/deliver.lock* file, which the server locks before updating the DBM database.

Mailbox subscriptions

Mailbox subscriptions are kept under *configdirectory/user*. Each user on the system has a file named *username.sub*. The file contains a list of the mailboxes the user is subscribed to. When migrating from another mail system to Cyrus, it may be possible to collect subscription information, parse it, and write it directly to the users' subscription files before bringing Cyrus up.

The Future of Cyrus

Cyrus is a popular IMAP server. The Cyrus server distribution is downloaded over 3,500 times a month, and there are dozens of sites running Cyrus on a large scale. Three commercial IMAP solutions are based on Cyrus. There is a very active Cyrus mailing list that uses Cyrus as a context for discussing implementation of enterprise messaging systems. Cyrus is here to stay.

Version 2.0a is the latest release. Version 1.6.22 is still considered the stable version at the time of this writing, but a large number of sites still run Version 1.5.19 in their production environments.

Versions of Cyrus later than 1.5.19 have begun to move away from cleartext authentication to methods supported by SASL. Project Cyrus needed to offer more authentication methods for people to use. It's possible to configure Cyrus 1.6.22 to work with cleartext authentication, but it requires some extra work (e.g., you must either configure SASL or PAM appropriately or change the ownership on your shadow password file). The introduction of completely new code into the previously comfortingly consistent Cyrus code base has turned a population of easygoing mail system administrators into a curmudgeon collective.

Many sites have held back from upgrading to newer versions of Cyrus because changing a site's authentication mechanism has serious implications to the infrastructure. Sites that are not ready to replace shadow password authentication with another mechanism may not want to open a security hole by changing permissions on the shadow password file. Solaris sites in particular have found it challenging to make SASL work with PAM. The original 1.6 release excluded support for *pwcheck*,* and some sites complain that 1.6 "force-fed" new features by making that exclusion. However, 1.6.22 does include support for *pwcheck* with the SASL PLAIN mechanism, allowing sites to deal with that as they will. The latest version of the SASL library also includes support for *pwcheck*, so sites can once again pass around cleartext passwords if they so desire. It appears that Cyrus project management is doing its best to accommodate current Cyrus sites, while keeping development right on track with the IETF, which no longer ratifies protocols that rely on cleartext authentication.

Project Cyrus is planning to recommend that sites use CRAM-MD5 and */etc/sasldb* for local authentication instead of PAM. Users in */etc/sasldb* do not have to be listed in */etc/passwd* in order to authenticate. Because they're not listed in */etc/passwd*, nothing special need be done to keep them from logging in to system.

Strengths and Weaknesses of Cyrus

Although you can bring up the UW IMAP server on a multipurpose Unix box with little or no forethought, the same cannot be said of Cyrus. Even under the best of circumstances, putting Cyrus on your machine is a major challenge. The only way to know if you want to "go there" is to weigh the strengths and weaknesses of Cyrus within the context of your own needs and resources.

The strengths of the Cyrus server are that it's popular, scalable, and secure. Here are the strengths in detail:

Popular

> Cyrus is very popular. The community of Cyrus administrators communicates and cooperates via the *info-cyrus* mailing list, which has over 400 subscribers. The Cyrus server is downloaded over 3,500 times every month. In other words, if you operate a Cyrus site, you're in good company. The attitude of other Cyrus sites towards questions and problems posted to the list is always helpful and cooperative. The Cyrus developers often contribute helpful advice and tips to the list, as well.

Scalable

> Cyrus supports quotas on mailboxes—your */var/mail* partition will never fill up unexpectedly. Growth of your mailstore can be controlled using quotas and IMAP partitions.

Secure

> Cyrus natively implements the Kerberos v4 SASL mechanism.

---

* *pwcheck* is a daemon that allows the Cyrus IMAP server to check the shadow password file without requiring the permissions or ownership on the shadow file to be modified.

Supports shared mailboxes

Cyrus supports shared folders by way of ACLs and allows concurrent read-write connections from more than one user.

Here are some of the weaknesses of the Cyrus server:

Cyrus doesn't use Unix mail format

Cyrus's private mailstore and mail storage format make it non-trivial to convert to other mail formats, such as standard Unix format.

Users may feel locked out

What you consider a strength, your users may consider a weakness: users accustomed to directly accessing their mail folders can no longer do so—they must use an IMAP client to get at their mail on a Cyrus server.

Server-side filtering is green

Server-side filtering is still in the early stages. Cyrus does not easily support popular add-on filtering programs like Procmail. Sieve, built into versions of Cyrus later than 1.6, is in development, but there is no practical mechanism or clients available yet that allow users to edit their filters.

Recent changes in direction

Development of authentication methods in the very latest releases of Cyrus (1.6 and later) has not stabilized yet.

I/O intensive

Like other IMAP systems, Cyrus is I/O intensive and requires careful choice of an operating system and hardware configured to handle a heavy I/O load.

Learning curve

There's more of a learning curve involved in managing a Cyrus system.

When Is Cyrus the Right Choice?

The Cyrus server's design is a quite different approach to IMAP than the UW server. The UW server emphasizes personal mailboxes, while Cyrus supports both personal mailboxes and shared mailboxes equally. The Cyrus server's closed, or black box, design makes access to the Cyrus mailstore faster than access through the UW server. There is, however, a trade-off for that performance improvement, such as the inability of users to log in to the server. If there's a need to move mail from a Cyrus server to a traditional Unix mail system or UW server, then there's more to moving it than a simple file copy. The mail must either be translated back through the IMAP protocol or suitably munged using a translating script that copies the mail back into the appropriate format via a filesystem protocol (such a script is provided in Chapter 9).

Here are some criteria that a site can use to determine whether the Cyrus server is a good match:

- Do users need to share private mail folders with other users?

- Is there a per-user limit on the amount of space the user can occupy in the mailstore?

- Does the site need to provide public forums with controlled access (i.e., bulletin boards)?

- Does the site require encrypted authentication?

- Does the site anticipate fast growth in the number of users on the system?

If a site answers yes to the above criteria, then Cyrus is the best choice.

7

Installing the Cyrus IMAP Server

Smooth is the name of the game when it comes to installing the Cyrus server. Aside from the fact that there are several dependencies on other packages, code hacking and Makefile mangling should not be necessary. Cyrus is a very good example of platform-independent open source software that makes no broad assumptions about the technical or psychic ability of the person installing it.

Software Prerequisites

Cyrus *imapd* requires a modest complement of additional freely available software. You need only Tool Command Language (Tcl) Version 7.5 or later and sendmail* 8.7.1 or later. If you're installing Cyrus Version 1.6 or later, Cyrus SASL is also required.

If your site has Kerberos, you can compile Cyrus with Kerberos support to add additional security to your IMAP infrastructure. Although your install might go marginally smoother or faster if you have *makedepend* installed, you can also use the dummy shell script included with the package as a workaround for not having *makedepend*.

---

* Although sendmail enjoys wild popularity as an MTA, you could use any reasonable MTA that permits you to choose Cyrus *deliver* as your delivery agent.

Hardware Note

As with any other service, the hardware demands of Cyrus IMAP can be grouped into demands that are general to any IMAP server and those that are specific to Cyrus IMAP. A good rule is not to just throw hardware, and therefore time and money, at your IMAP server. Find out what kind of appetites your server will have *before* you feed it.

IMAP servers have an appetite for disk I/O, memory, and network bandwidth, in that order. More specifically, Cyrus IMAP has a ravenous appetite for disk I/O bandwidth. The bigger highway you have between your CPU, memory, and disk, the better. To that end, a good Cyrus IMAP machine is one in which user mailboxes are equally split by load between two or more storage channels. The ideal Cyrus IMAP server has two network interfaces and siphons off all non-IMAP overhead traffic (such as networked tape backups) to one interface, leaving the other free to handle IMAP traffic. It also has more than enough memory to handle peak loads.

Chapter 16, *Server Performance Tuning*, covers the details of optimizing an IMAP system, but let's talk briefly about each of these general requirements now. As with any Internet service, memory is of paramount importance. The less paging your system has to do, the better. A good rule of thumb is that your machine should have a bare minimum of 1 MB[*] of physical memory for each active IMAP process. If you assume one process per user and an overhead of about 20 to 30 housekeeping processes on a black box single-purpose IMAP server, then gauging your memory needs becomes a matter of determining how many users will be online at one time. A good starting point might be to figure that 20 to 30% of ISP customers might be connected at any given time, whereas far more, maybe 80%, of business users will be running IMAP processes simultaneously.

Spreading the load across I/O channels is a straightforward proposition. Typically, mail servers begin their life with all users on a single disk partition that, presumably, is serviced by a single controller. Spreading users' mailboxes out to different partitions served by different controllers permits your disk storage to service more users at once. The Cyrus server's built-in support for a partitioned mailstore simplifies partitioning.

The only system requirement unique to the Cyrus IMAP server is the large *mailboxes* file. One way to accommodate this file would be to hang a solid-state disk

---

[*] A Cyrus *imapd* process consumes roughly 400–800 KB of private memory and 1,400–1,600 KB of shared memory. The shared memory usage is counted towards system overhead, and the private memory usage is used to estimate the size of the *imapd* process in terms of capacity planning.

off your mail server and use it exclusively for the *mailboxes* file. Because solid-state disks tend to be more expensive than conventional storage, it might be more prudent to dedicate a partition of RAID storage or just a nothing-fancy disk to the *mailboxes* file. Barring that, anything you can do to isolate the load of constant multiprocess access to the *mailboxes* file from the rest of the system would help. Maybe you can't partition your users' mailboxes into separate storage channels or split your traffic across several network interfaces. You could still put your *mailboxes* file on a dedicated disk with its own I/O channel to increase the load your server can handle.

Where to Get the Software

The canonical source of information on where to obtain the Cyrus IMAP server is the Cyrus IMAP Server Home Page at *http://asg.web.cmu.edu/cyrus/download/*. Toward the top of the first page of that site is a link to download the current distribution. You can also go to *ftp://ftp.andrew.cmu.edu/pub/cyrus-mail/* and select the latest version, or an earlier stable release, such as 1.5.19, if you so desire.

As we mentioned earlier, you will need a few other pieces of software, namely sendmail and Tcl, and for Versions 1.6 and higher,* you will need Cyrus SASL (Simple Authentication and Security Layer). Cyrus IMAP has hooks for Kerberos and Sieve, a server-side filtering language, but both are optional.

The current version of sendmail is always available from the Sendmail Current Release web page located at *http://www.sendmail.org/current-release.html*. Do yourself and your users a favor and don't even think about using the version of sendmail that comes with your OS.† Not only is it practically guaranteed not to include desirable new features, but it's an almost sure bet that there are undocumented security problems that are likely to bait any less-than-ethical folks whose talent outstrips their self-restraint.

The canonical source for Tcl is the web site for Scriptics, the company formed by John Ousterhout, the original author of Tcl: *http://www.scriptics.com/*.

---

* As we mentioned in Chapter 6, *Introduction to the Cyrus IMAP Server*, Versions 1.6 and higher require some extra work to use cleartext or shadow password authentication, forcing some sites to stick with 1.5.19 until they can replace cleartext authentication with something else.

† Never, ever, ever use sendmail 8.6. Here's a quote from *ftp://ftp.sendmail.org/pub/sendmail/.message*: "There is NO 8.6.* patch for CA-96.20. 8.6 is not supported, not secure, and should not be run on any network-connected machine." CA-96.20 refers to a CERT Advisory (*http://www.cert.org/advisories/CA-96.20.sendmail_vul.html*) that documents resource starvation and buffer overflow attacks. By now, such attacks are well known and could be used to give arbitrary levels of access to your mail server to unauthorized people with a bit of easily obtainable code.

SASL is required only for Versions 1.6 and later of Cyrus IMAP. If you've opted to stick with Version 1.5.19, then you won't need SASL. Cyrus SASL is available from CMU's FTP site: *ftp://ftp.andrew.cmu.edu/pub/cyrus-mail/cyrus-sasl-1.5.11.tar.gz* (be sure and check for a later version—SASL is being updated every month or so).

If you need to build Kerberos, and United States export laws permit you to do so, you can get the current revision of Kerberos by using the MIT Kerberos Distribution Authorization Form at *http://web.mit.edu/network/kerberos-form.html.*

Supported Platforms

As an open source product, Cyrus runs on any platform you can build it on. You can bet that Cyrus is more easily built on systems that are somewhat commonly used in the industry. Forget about using that ancient PDP-11 you found in the basement.

Because of its resource demands, choose a machine that can:

* Support the amount of memory your Cyrus user base requires
* Reliably support the fastest network media available on your network
* Support robust disk storage and fast I/O

Installing Cyrus

Installing the Cyrus server is literally as easy as 1-2-3. Configuring the server is quite a bit more complicated, but we'll address that in Chapter 8, *Configuring the Cyrus Server.* First, download and unpack the distribution. Second, decide what build-time configuration options you'll use. Finally, compile the software and do your final install.

Versions 1.6 and Up and SASL

As mentioned earlier, the Cyrus SASL library is a prerequisite for Versions 1.6 and up of Cyrus IMAP. Make sure SASL is installed and configured before compiling Cyrus IMAP Version 1.6 or higher. SASL requires some configuration of its own. CMU recommends configuring SASL to use CRAM-MD5 on a single server, or GSSAPI for use on more than one server. You can also configure SASL to use the *pwcheck* daemon for cleartext Unix password authentication.

Unpack the Distribution

Assuming you've already downloaded Cyrus using a command similar in effect to:

```
% lynx -dump ftp://ftp.andrew.cmu.edu/pub/cyrus-mail/cyrus-imapd-v1.5.19.tar.gz \
  > cyrus-imapd-v1.5.19.tar.gz
```

uncompress it, untar it, and you've got your source tree for Cyrus:

```
% ls -Fs
total 1048                        1048 cyrus-imapd-v1.5.19.tar.gz
% gunzip cyrus-imapd-v1.5.19.tar.gz
% ls -s
total 4688                        4688 cyrus-imapd-v1.5.19.tar
% tar xf cyrus-imapd-v1.5.19.tar
% ls -FaCs
total 4694                           2 cyrus-imapd-v1.5.19
   2 ./                            4688 cyrus-imapd-v1.5.19.tar
   2 ../
```

Setting Up Build-Time Configuration Options

Your first task is to decide on what options to use with the *configure* script. *configure*'s options are shown in Table 7-1. If you have a somewhat commonly configured host that uses shadow passwords, has Tcl installed, and doesn't use Kerberos, you might be able to get away with something like:

```
% ./configure --with-login=unix_pwcheck --without-krb
```

That instructs *configure* to prepare an appropriate *Makefile* for a host that isn't Kerberized, uses shadow passwords, and has Tcl somewhere under */usr/local* or in the compiler's default link path.

Table 7-1. configure Options

Option	Purpose
--help	Dump a list of configure options.
--quiet, --silent, --q	Omit status messages listing what checks are being made.
--version	Show what version of Autoconf is being used.
--prefix=*path*	Install architecture-dependent files in *path* (*/usr/local* is default).
--with-cyrus-prefix=*path*	Set the Cyrus install directory to *path*. Try to leave this alone. It defaults to */usr/cyrus* and Cyrus troubleshooting becomes much more difficult if non-default values are used in the install without a very compelling reason.
--cache-file=*file*	Set an alternate configure cache file *file*. Defaults to *config.cache*. Not necessary under most circumstances.

Table 7-1. configure Options (continued)

Option	Purpose
`--srcdir=dir`	Set the source directory to *dir*. Almost never necessary. Don't use unless there's good reason to suspect that Autoconf can't find your sources or you're working from multiple source trees with one copy of configure and Autoconf.
`--with-cyrus-user=user`	Set an alternate Cyrus *user*. The default is the user *cyrus*. Using other than *cyrus* is not a good idea, especially if sendmail is your MTA. The Cyrus *m4* prototype used in creating the *sendmail.cf* doesn't react well to *userid:group* combinations other than *cyrus:mail*. As with the Cyrus prefix, don't change this unless you've got a compelling reason to do so.
`--with-cyrus-group=group`	Set an alternate cyrus *group*. The default is the group *mail*. See `--with-cyrus-user`.
`--with-statedir=path`	Set an alternate server runtime state directory to *path*. Defaults to */var/cyrus*.
`--with-login=method`	How should Cyrus authenticate users? For Version 1.5.x, use *unix* for cleartext local passwd authentication, *unix_pwcheck* for shadow passwd authentication, and *krb* or *krb_pwcheck* for Kerberos. Versions 1.6.x have the option of *unix* (local passwd) or *krb* (Kerberos).
`--with-pwcheck=method`	(Version 1.5.x only) What method should the *pwcheck* daemon use to authenticate? This option is only used if the `--with-login` option value ended in *_pwcheck*. *pwcheck* figures it out on its own, so this option is probably unnecessary for you. Default is *getpsnam* if *getpsnam* exists; otherwise, it is *getpwnam*.
`--with-auth=method`	Authorization method used by the login method. Defaults to the authentication method with the same name as the login method. Usually not necessary to specify anything other than the default unless you're using Kerberos.
`--with-inn=path`	Path to INN for Usenet news integration.
`--with-krb=path` `--without-krb`	Path to Kerberos V4 libraries. This support requires the DES library and is subject to US export laws. If you don't have Kerberos, use the `--without-krb` switch.
`--with-lock=lock-method`	Force the use of *lock-method*. *lock-method* is either `fcntl` or `flock`.
`--with-tcl=path` `--without-tcl`	Path to the Tcl library and header files. Looks in */usr/local/* and your compiler's default link path by default. Usually not necessary to set this option.
`--disable-cyradm`	If you don't have Tcl, don't have time to build it, or simply don't like it, you can use this option to disable the Cyrus administrative client and use alternative methods like IMAP scripting to accomplish the same goals.

Table 7-1. configure Options (continued)

Option	Purpose
`--with-notify=method` `--without-notify`	This looks like an encouraging hook to pull in an arbitrary notification method, but currently really only specifies if Zephyr notification is to be used for new mail notification or not. Defaults to *zephyr* if the *zephyr* libraries are found, or to *no* (no new mail notification) if they're not found. *configure* can determine the default from the libraries in the search path. The vast majority of sites will want to accept the default.
`--with-zephyr=path` `--without-zephyr`	Zephyr is an instant messaging protocol (*ftp://athena-dist.mit.edu/pub/ATHENA/zephyr/*). Because most sites will configure Cyrus `--without-notify`, those sites will set this option to `--without-zephyr`.
`--disable-privacy`	If you are using Kerberos and want just authentication but not content to be encrypted, use this switch.
`--disable-sieve`	(Version 1.6.x only) Disable support for the Sieve server-side filtering language.[a]

[a] See Chapter 15, *Server-Side Mail Filtering*, for more information on Sieve.

Depending on the version of Cyrus you're building, the *configure* script may accept options in addition to those listed in Table 7-1 (use the command *configure* *–help* for a complete listing). Your system may require unusual options that are not defined in the *configure* script. In that case, you can set the options in your environment before running *make all*. Options set in the environment override options set by *configure*. The options most commonly set in the environment are listed in Table 7-2.

Table 7-2. Options Commonly Set in the Environment

Option	Defines
CC	C compiler program. Defaults to *gcc* if *gcc* is found in the PATH; otherwise, defaults to *cc*.
CFLAGS	C compiler options.
CPPFLAGS	Extra directories to search for header files. The default is none.
DEFS	Miscellaneous options, such as platform options (–DSVR4).
LIBS	Libraries to link with (e.g., –lposix).
LDFLAGS	Linker options. Defaults to none.

To set an option in the environment, run *configure* as shown in the following examples:

```
$ CC=gcc CFLAGS=-O2 LIBS=-lsocket ./configure   (Bourne shell variants)
% env CPPFLAGS=-I/usr/local/lib ./configure     (C shell variants)
```

You can also override the make variables CFLAGS and LDFLAGS after *configure* has been run when you run *make all*; for example:

```
% make all CFLAGS=-O LDFLAGS=-s
```

Now that you've selected a (hopefully modest) number of switches to use with *configure*, your *configure* run should look something like this:

```
% ./configure --with-login=unix_pwcheck --without-krb
loading cache ./config.cache
checking for makedepend... makedepend
checking for gcc... gcc
checking whether the C compiler (gcc  ) works... yes
checking whether the C compiler (gcc  ) is a cross-compiler... no
checking whether we are using GNU C... yes
checking whether gcc accepts -g... yes
(Many lines skipped...)
updating cache ./config.cache
creating ./config.status
creating Makefile
creating man/Makefile
creating lib/Makefile
creating imap/Makefile
creating imap/feedcyrus
creating imtest/Makefile
creating pwcheck/Makefile
creating cyradm/Makefile
creating et/Makefile
%
```

Compile and Install the Software

Configure has now built your *Makefile*. We're going to assume that you don't have *makedepend*, because the included dummy *makedepend* script works just fine—it makes things so easy that you needn't worry about installing *makedepend*. Should you have problems using the dummy *makedepend* script, Cyrus also includes its own *makedepend* in the *makedepend* subdirectory of the source distribution.

When using the dummy script, you should always run *make clean* before you run *makedepend* and *make all*:

```
% make clean
### Making clean in /usr/local/cyrus/cyrus-imapd-v1.5.19/man
rm -f *.o Makefile.bak
### Done with /usr/local/cyrus/cyrus-imapd-v1.5.19/man
### Making clean in /usr/local/cyrus/cyrus-imapd-v1.5.19/et
rm -f compile_et compile_et.o error_table.o
rm -f libcom_err.a
(Many lines deleted...)
### Making clean in /usr/local/cyrus/cyrus-imapd-v1.5.19/pwcheck
rm -f *.o Makefile.bak pwcheck
### Done with /usr/local/cyrus/cyrus-imapd-v1.5.19/pwcheck
```

Next, run *makedepend* followed by *make all*. Your output should be similar to this:

```
% make depend
### Making depend in /usr/local/cyrus/cyrus-imapd-v1.5.19/man
### Making depend in /usr/local/cyrus/cyrus-imapd-v1.5.19/et
./config_script ./compile_et.sh nawk sed > compile_et
ed -s Makefile < eddep
rm eddep
echo '' >> Makefile
echo '# IF YOU PUT STUFF HERE IT WILL GO AWAY' >> Makefile
echo '# see makedepend above' >> Makefile
```

Run *make all* to build the executables:

```
% make all CFLAGS=-O
```

As your *make all* sputters out rather uneventfully, hopefully with no error messages, you can move on to the next step and create the *cyrus* account and add the account to the *mail* group. The procedure for doing so varies somewhat from system to system, depending on the OS and where your users live (NIS, DCE, */etc/ passwd*, LDAP, etc.).

Once you've ensured that the *cyrus* account exists and that it has been added to the mail group, log in as *root* and do a *make install* to complete the install process and prepare your system for configuration. Your *make install* output should look something like this:

```
# make install
./install-sh -d /usr/local/bin
./install-sh -d /usr/local/lib
(Many lines skipped ...)
### Making install in /usr/local/cyrus/cyrus-imapd-v1.5.19/imtest
.././install-sh -c -s -m 755 imtest /usr/local/bin
### Making install in /usr/local/cyrus/cyrus-imapd-v1.5.19/cyradm
.././install-sh -c -s -m 755 cyradm /usr/local/bin
### Making install in /usr/local/cyrus/cyrus-imapd-v1.5.19/pwcheck
.././install-sh -c -s -m 755 pwcheck /usr/cyrus/bin
```

Upgrading from Previous Versions of Cyrus IMAP

Fresh installation of Cyrus may be all well trodden territory for you. If you're upgrading from a previous version of Cyrus IMAP, however, there are a few cleanup tasks to take care of after your upgrade. In addition to the notes that follow, be sure to read the contents of the *doc* directory carefully, with particular attention to the notes on upgrading.

- If you're upgrading from Version 1.5.2 or earlier, delete your *delivered* database and your PTS cache database (if you use the AFS filesystem), if they exist. If you've previously enabled duplicate delivery suppression, the delivered database (*delivered.db*) is in your configuration directory. If you use AFS PTS group support, the PTS cache is in */var/ptclient*. Deleting both these files has no deleterious effects except that, in the case of the delivered database, some duplicate messages may be delivered.

- If you're upgrading from Version 1.4 or earlier, you must run *reconstruct −r* after installing the software and before putting it into production, so that the indexes for all your system's mailboxes are rebuilt.

- If you're upgrading from Version 1.3 or earlier, you'll also have to run a *reconstruct −m* to rebuild your mailboxes file.

- Finally, if you run *imspd* and *imapd* on the same machine and use AFS ACLs, you'll need to be running at least Version 1.5a5 of the IMSP server, because the format of the PTS cache for IMSP has changed.

Components of Cyrus and What They Do

Once you've built Cyrus, you'll have the following programs.

imapd(8)

This is the IMAP server itself. It is invoked by *inetd*(8). In the next chapter, we'll cover how to set up *inetd* to run *imapd*, and ensure that it functions correctly.

deliver(8)

This is the Cyrus mail delivery agent. *deliver* takes mail on standard input and delivers it to one or more Cyrus format mailboxes. It is also the pruning utility for the duplicate delivery database.

reconstruct(8)

The *reconstruct* utility rebuilds the indexes of any number of Cyrus mailboxes and reconstructs the global mailboxes database. *reconstruct* is at the core of any conversion system from other mailbox formats to Cyrus, as well as most disaster recovery strategies. Once you've rebuilt a quota-restricted mailbox with *reconstruct*, it's a good idea to run *quota −f* to repair the appropriate quota root files.

cyradm(1)

This is Cyrus's Tcl-based administrative control and scripting language. The interactive and scripting commands are different, and much if not all of what you can do in *cyradm* is also possible by spoofing the IMAP protocol from other languages if Tcl isn't your cup of tea.

pwcheck(8)

Cyrus *imapd* runs as user *cyrus*, so authentication using shadow passwords isn't directly available. *pwcheck* allows you to use shadow passwords on a non-Kerberized Cyrus system. *pwcheck* is a fairly robust hack that creates a for-*cyrus*-use-only named pipe that the root-owned *pwcheck* daemon uses to check username/password pairs.

quota(8)

This utility reports on the quota root limits and usage of given mailbox prefixes. Given with the *–f* switch, it also fixes quota inconsistencies before doing so.

fud(8)

fud is an experimental workaround to permit remote users with certain finger clients to display information about when a targeted user last read their mail, when mail last arrived at their mailbox, and how many messages are recent for that user. If you're not sure if your finger client supports the *fud* service, then it probably does not. LDAP and ACAP capabilities will likely supersede *fud* in the long run.

pop3d(8)

This daemon presents the Cyrus mailstore, or at least the inboxes, using the POP3 protocol. Good for sites transitioning from POP3 to IMAP4, so you can change the backend more or less transparently, then announce sometime later that IMAP is also available to your users.

rmnews(8)

Coordinates Usenet news article deletion between INN and IMAP.

syncnews(8)

Synchronizes IMAP's and INN's ideas about which newsgroups are active. Groups showing up as IMAP mailboxes but not in the *active* file are deleted. Groups showing up in the Usenet *active* file but not as IMAP mailboxes are created on the IMAP side.

arbitron(8)

Reports on mailbox readership statistics. Of negligible use with private mailboxes, but could be quite useful for sites that make use of shared mailboxes and want to determine who has read which mailboxes and when.

collectnews(8)

Used by INN to update the appropriate IMAP mailboxes when Usenet news arrives.

Common Problems

A number of common installation problems and their solutions are described in the Cyrus Installation FAQ (*http://asg.web.cmu.edu/cyrus/imapd/install-FAQ.html*). We cannot encourage you enough to visit that site if you run into problems during your installation! It has ceased to be a surprise when the same installation question comes up repeatedly on the list, even though the answer is available on the Installation FAQ.

Significant Bugs

- In Versions up to 1.5.19, duplicate delivery suppression displays misleading errors in the *imapd.log* that might cause you to believe a message wasn't delivered at all, when it actually was. This is fixed in 1.5.19 and later.

- There were a number of bugs that are fixed in Version 1.5.14. It is highly recommended that you upgrade if you're running a version older than 1.5.14.

- The IMAP RENAME command doesn't behave hierarchically in Cyrus releases prior to 2.0, so it's been temporarily advertised in the "capability" output as "X-NON-HIERARCHICAL-RENAME" in the interim before it's fixed. Hierarchical rename is fixed in Cyrus 2.0.

- *deliver* has a minor standard I/O problem in which text between a NUL and the end of line of a message will be lost. No fix is available as of the 1.5.19 release.

So much for building Cyrus. Let's move on to the next chapter and the configuration of your Cyrus server.

8

Configuring the Cyrus Server

Now that the none-too-exciting work of building Cyrus IMAP is over, let's get down to business and configure it.

IMAP Configuration File and Directory

The Cyrus IMAP server has a single configuration file: */etc/imapd.conf.* No messing about with the source code or the *Makefile* is necessary. Once you've used the appropriate options to make a build of Cyrus that's appropriate for your site, any configuration is done simply by editing *imapd.conf.*

The Server Configuration File: imapd.conf

First, let's create the */etc/imapd.conf* file, which holds all the defining configuration parameters for *imapd.* Each line of *imapd.conf* contains an option and a value for the option, separated by a colon:

```
option: value
```

Blank lines and lines beginning with # are treated as comments and are ignored. Boolean options take the values **yes**, **1**, **t**, or **on** to turn the option on, and **no**, **0**, **f**, or **off** to turn the option off.

For the time being, it's best to minimize the number of entries in this file to make debugging your installation easier. The barebones IMAP configuration file must contain at least the following entries:

```
configdirectory: /var/imap
partition-default: /var/spool/imap
admins: cyrus johndoe2
```

See Table 8-1 for the purpose of each of the three options.

A user listed in *admins* should never use her administrative account to read mail!

Users listed as *admins* should never log in to the IMAP server to read mail. *admins* have special privileges that may lead to problems if they open a mailbox using certain IMAP clients. For example, *admins* are able to write to parts of the Cyrus system to which non-privileged users cannot write. Notably, if an administrative user reads mail, he might accidentally create top-level mailboxes (e.g., "Trash" or "Outbox") that other users would see as "public" mailboxes. To be on the safe side, do not even create IMAP mailboxes for your *admins*.

The complete set of options is listed in Table 8-1, and is also documented in the *imapd.conf*(5) manual page. Options that list a default value of "No default" have no default value. Options that list a default value of "None" default to an empty value.

Table 8-1. imapd.conf Options

Option	Default Value	Value
`configdirectory`	No default	Required. The pathname to the IMAP configuration directory. The widely used convention is `/var/imap`.
`defaultpartition`	`default`	The default partition (by partition-name, not path) on which new mailboxes are created.

`partition-name`	No default	Required. The full path of the partition *name*. At least one `partition-name` definition is required for the partition specified in the *defaultpartition* option. For example, if the *defaultpartition* is set as follows:
		`defaultpartition: default`
		then the required option is:
		`partition-default: /some/path`

`admins`	None	A list of users, delimited by whitespace, that have administrative rights. *admins* do not have the ability to change the server configuration. Any user can be listed in *admins*, including *cyrus*, but *admins* should never read IMAP mail using the account listed in *admins*.
`srvtab`	`/etc/srvtab`	Kerberos only. The full path of the *srvtab* file containing the IMAP server's private key. This option is only used if the server was compiled with Kerberos authentication.

Table 8-1. imapd.conf Options (continued)

Option	Default Value	Value
umask	077	Umask value used by programs under */usr/cyrus/bin*. By default, when those programs create files, the files have ownership (*cyrus: mail*) permissions: `-rw-------` If you want your *admins* to be able to read the files without becoming root, then set the value of umask to 027 and add your *admins* to group *mail*.
allowanonymouslogin	no	When set, permits the user *anonymous* to log in with any password. If you plan to provide anonymous access to public mail folders, set this option to **yes**.
quotawarn	90	Percent of quota usage over which the server sends a warning message to the user. You'll want to set this so that the user receives a warning when he is within 1 MB or so of his quota limit. Ninety percent is a good value for sites with quotas between 10 and 20 MB.
timeout	30	A value is required for this option. The length of inactivity, in minutes, after which the server logs the session out automatically. If you have large numbers of users logging in over dialups, keep the default—dialup users tend not to log out gracefully. Corporate sites whose users are on the LAN, on the other hand, would probably set the timeout much higher.
imspservers	None	List of hostnames of IMSP servers. This feature was never implemented and has been removed from Versions 1.6 and higher.
defaultacl	anyone lrs	The ACL to set by default on new mailboxes that do not have a parent mailbox. If the mailbox has a parent, it inherits the parent's ACL.
newsspool	No default	The pathname of the news spool directory. The **newsspool** option is used only if the option **partition-news** is defined.
newsprefix	None	The prefix added to the beginning of a newsgroup name to form the corresponding IMAP mailbox name.

Table 8-1. imapd.conf Options (continued)

Option	Default Value	Value
autocreatequota	0	The name of this option doesn't describe the option well—autocreatequota is dual purpose: the value determines whether or not a user can create his INBOX (and hence, his IMAP account) the first time he attempts to log in to the server. If the value is zero, the user cannot create his own account; if non-zero, the user can create his account. If the value is non-zero and positive, the user's quota is set to the value. If the value is non-zero and negative, the user is given an unlimited quota. Sites that have enterprise-wide usernames could save some work by enabling this option. Sites that want more control over the mailbox environment (such as pre-defined folders with per-folder quotas) should accept the default.
logtimestamps	no	When set, the server will log the number of seconds since the last command or response in the protocol telemetry logs.
cleartextloginpause	0	Specifies the number of seconds to wait after a successful cleartext authentication before opening the session. The purpose of this option is mainly to train users to associate a cost with using cleartext authentication. A pause after each login also substantially increases the amount of time it would take to crack any given password with a dictionary attack.
loginrealms	None	Kerberos only. List of remote realms whose users may log in using cross-realm authentication. The realms should be delimited by whitespace.
loginuseacl	no	Kerberos only. When set, an identity that has rights on an INBOX may log in as the owner of the INBOX.
reject8bit	no	When set, the *deliver* program rejects messages with 8-bit characters in their headers. If not set, then 8-bit characters are changed to the letter X.
netscapeurl	http:// andrew2. andrew.cmu. edu/cyrus/ imapd	Specifies the site to contact when Netscape queries the IMAP server for the location of the administration HTTP server. This option must be enabled at compile time. The default site provides only an informational message.

The Configuration Directory

The configuration directory is the repository for information on all components and user data that make up the Cyrus system. The popular convention is to name the configuration directory */var/imap* (that is the convention we will use in our examples). Access to the configuration directory should be restricted to the *cyrus* user and group only. The following commands create the configuration directory and set the correct permissions and ownership:

```
# cd /var
# mkdir imap
# chown cyrus:mail imap
# chmod 0750 imap
```

 The Cyrus server is finicky about file permissions and ownership. Be sure the ownership and permissions are set correctly to prevent problems from happening later.

Odds and Ends

Create the supporting files in the configuration directory with the permissions shown. Create an empty *mailboxes* file and the directories that Cyrus will use to store its configuration information:

```
# cd /var/imap
# touch mailboxes
# mkdir user quota proc log msg
# chown cyrus:mail *
```

Create the directory that was defined in *imapd.conf* as `defaultpartition`. The `defaultpartition` directory is where users' mailboxes are stored. Recall that the `defaultpartition` was defined as */var/spool/imap* in the sample *imapd.conf* shown earlier in this chapter.

```
# cd /var/spool
# mkdir imap
# chown cyrus:mail imap
# chmod 750 imap
```

Configuring the Authentication Mechanism

This section shows you how to configure the IMAP server to perform cleartext shadow password and Kerberos authentication. Cleartext authentication without shadow passwords does not require special configuration. The mechanism for

If You're Configuring Cyrus on a Linux System . . .

You would be well served to set the configuration directory, mailstore, user, quota, and mailstore directory for synchronous updates.

```
# cd /var/imap
# chattr +S . user quota
# chattr +S /var/spool/imap
# chattr +S /var/spool/mqueue
```

Doing so allows you to purchase a slightly higher amount of robustness in exchange for a degree of performance (although if your system has more than 5,000 mailboxes, the performance trade-off has been shown to be too high to support synchronous updates). If a file is updated asynchronously, then the cache associated with that file is flushed to disk some time later. If it's set to update synchronously, its cache is flushed immediately. When the cache is flushed immediately, there's less risk of damage to your system if, for example, it were to halt inadvertently.

Note that this advice applies only to *ext2* filesystems. If you're not sure what type of filesystem you have, use the *mount*(8) command.

authenticating users to the Cyrus server is external to the server itself and eliminates the need for users to have Unix accounts on the server. It's possible to authenticate against an LDAP directory or SQL database, for example. Alternative authentication mechanisms and their associated tools are described in Chapter 18, *IMAP Tools*.

Cleartext Authentication with Shadow Passwords

Cleartext authentication is nothing more than a check against your local *passwd* file. Some flavors of Unix store encrypted passwords right along with usernames and other account information in the local password file. Others store the username and account information in one file and the encrypted passwords in another, separate file (the shadow file). The shadow file has strict access rights—it's owned by root and is readable only by root—and thus protects encrypted passwords from prying eyes.

Cyrus IMAP authentication support changed significantly between the 1.5.19 and the 1.6.22 releases. Versions 1.6 and higher support the *pwcheck* daemon for shadow password authentication from within SASL. There are slight differences in configuring the authentication in Versions 1.5.19 and 1.6.22, which we'll mention later in this section.

Setting up cleartext authentication in Cyrus Version 1.5.19

The *pwcheck* program was introduced in Chapter 7, *Installing the Cyrus IMAP Server*—it is a daemon that the Cyrus server uses to check passwords against the Unix shadow password file. *pwcheck* is required because the Cyrus IMAP server runs as user *cyrus*, and hence does not have read access to the shadow password file (it's readable only by *root*). *pwcheck* creates a named pipe under the directory */var/pwcheck* that the Cyrus server uses to communicate with the *pwcheck* daemon. If you configured your Cyrus server to use *pwcheck*, then you must create that directory and set the permissions appropriately:

```
# mkdir /var/pwcheck
# chown cyrus /var/pwcheck
# chmod 0700 /var/pwcheck
```

pwcheck is meant to be started at system boot time and run as a background process. To start it, create an initialization script for *pwcheck* and arrange for that script to be run at boot time. On a Solaris system, create the file */etc/init.d/pwcheck* shown in Example 8-1.

Example 8-1. pwcheck Startup Script

```
#!/sbin/sh
#
#     Start CMU Cyrus pwcheck daemon

case "$1" in
'start')
        if [ -f /usr/cyrus/bin/pwcheck ]; then
                /usr/cyrus/bin/pwcheck &
        fi
        ;;

'stop')
        pid=`/usr/bin/ps -eo pid,comm | /usr/bin/awk '{ \
            if ($2 == "/usr/cyrus/bin/pwcheck") print $1 }'`
        if test "$pid"
        then
            /usr/bin/kill $pid
        fi
        ;;
*)
        echo "Usage: $0 { start | stop }"
        exit 1
        ;;
esac
exit 0
```

Once */etc/init.d/pwcheck* is in place, arrange for *pwcheck* to be started or stopped when the system is booted or shut down by creating a link from */etc/rc3.d* to the initialization script you created:

```
# cd /etc/rc3.d
# ln -s /etc/init.d/pwcheck S98pwcheck
# cd /etc/rc2.d
# ln -s /etc/init.d/pwcheck K20pwcheck
```

The names of the links to the *pwcheck* script depend on what's already in */etc/rc3.d* and when you want it run in the startup process—any more detail than that is beyond the scope of this book.

Setting up cleartext authentication in Version 1.6.22

Cyrus 1.6.22 uses the SASL framework for authentication. Cyrus SASL 1.5.15 is a separate package that is a prerequisite for Cyrus 1.6.22. Its installation was covered in Chapter 7. On most systems, no special configuration is required. SASL uses the authentication that you specified when you ran the Cyrus configure script. If none is specified, it defaults to the most secure level of authentication available. If you're using cleartext passwords, you should have configured Cyrus with the configure option `--with-auth-unix`.

If you use plain passwords with no shadow, there is no special configuration required. On most systems, SASL will use PAM to authenticate using the plain password. If you do use shadow passwords, there may be some extra work involved. On Linux systems, for example, the permissions on the shadow file have to be changed to allow the *cyrus* user to read it. On Solaris systems, some tweaking of PAM is necessary. Most sites that depend on shadow passwords have opted to either stick with Cyrus 1.5.19 or use *pwcheck* in its most simplistic form with Cyrus 1.6.22.

Kerberos Authentication

If you compiled Cyrus to support Kerberos, you'll need to create a Kerberos key for the Cyrus IMAP server and add the key to the *srvtab* file.

The following example creates a key for the hostname *rooster*. *rooster*'s Kerberos realm is *THEMULLETS.NET*.

```
# ksrvutil -f /etc/srvtab add
Name: imap
Instance: rooster
Realm: THEMULLETS.NET
Version number: <Return>
New principal: imap.rooster@THEMULLETS.NET; version 0
Is this correct? (y/n) [y] y
Password: xxxxxxxx
```

```
Verifying, please re-enter Password: xxxxxxxx
Key successfully added.
Would you like to add another key? (y/n) [y] n
```

Finally, give ownership of */etc/srvtab* to the *cyrus* user:

```
# chown cyrus /etc/srvtab
```

Configuring syslog

The Cyrus server uses the BSD 4.3 variant of *syslog*. BSD 4.3 *syslog* separates log messages into both facilities and severity levels. Before configuring *syslog* on your system to log messages from the Cyrus server, you will need to determine whether your *syslog* is the BSD 4.3 variant. Run the command:

```
% man syslog
```

Look at the definition of the **openlog()** function in the synopsis:

```
void openlog(const char *ident, int logopt, int facility);
```

The **openlog()** function takes either two or three arguments. If the **openlog()** function takes three arguments, then your *syslog* is a BSD 4.3 variant and is compatible with Cyrus *syslog* function calls. To configure *syslog*, edit */etc/syslog.conf* to include a line similar to the following line, which tells *syslog* to log debug level messages to the *local6* facility and write them to the log file */var/log/imapd.log*:

```
local6.debug                    /var/log/imapd.log
```

Then create an empty *imapd.log* file and restart *syslog*:

```
# touch /var/log/imapd.log
# /etc/init.d/syslog stop; /etc/init.d/syslog start
```

If your system's **openlog()** function takes only two arguments, then it's not the BSD 4.3 variant and you must use the *syslogd* and *syslog.conf* that are provided with the Cyrus distribution. Make backup copies of your system's *syslogd* and *syslog.conf,* then change directory to the top level of your Cyrus source distribution:

```
(Stop syslog)
# cd syslog
# cp syslogd /etc/syslogd
# cp syslog.conf /etc/syslog.conf
(Start syslog)
```

Configuring the MTA

Unlike the UW server, Cyrus IMAP's mailstore format ties it intrinsically to the local mail transport agent or, more accurately, to the local mail delivery agent. In this book, we're presuming that you've chosen *sendmail* as your MTA. *sendmail* can serve just about any size user base. If, however, you elect to use another MTA, be mindful of the fact that you'll have to configure it to use the Cyrus *deliver* program as a delivery agent, and use this section as a rough guide.

The deliver MDA

The Cyrus *deliver* program is the mail delivery agent that drops mail messages into users' mailboxes. *deliver* takes a mail message on standard input and delivers it to the specified mailboxes. *deliver*'s configuration options are set in */etc/imapd.conf.*

deliver uses the options listed in Table 8-2 when invoked to deliver mail. Other options are described in the *deliver*(8) manual page.

Table 8-2. deliver Options

Option	Description

-m *mailbox*	Deliver a message to the Cyrus mailbox *mailbox*.
	To deliver to a specific mailbox, for example *user.johndoe.lists*, use
	`deliver -m user.johndoe.lists`
	You must have *p* access rights on the specified mailbox; if you don't, then delivery fails and returns the message:[a]
	`user.johndoe.lists: Mailbox does not exist`
	If a mailbox is specified with the –m argument and a username argument is given, then *deliver* will attempt delivery to the specified mailbox under the mailbox hierarchy belonging to the username. For example, the command:
	`/usr/cyrus/bin/deliver -m lists johndoe`
	delivers a message to *user.johndoe.lists*. Again, the user invoking *deliver* must have *p* access rights (access rights are described in Chapter 9, *Cyrus System Administration*) on the specified mailbox.
	If a mailbox and list of usernames are specified, *deliver* will attempt to deliver the message to the mailbox for each username. For example, the command:
	`/usr/cyrus/bin/deliver –m lists johndoe msmith kjones`
	delivers a message to *user.johndoe.lists*, *user.msmith.lists*, and *user.kjones.lists*.

-e	Enable duplicate delivery suppression.
-q	Force delivery of a message when the specified mailbox is over quota.
-F *flag*	Set the flag *flag* on the delivered message. *flag* can take the values \seen, \answered, \flagged, \draft, or \deleted.
-a *authID*	Specify the authorization ID *authID* of the sender. If no value for *authID* is given, defaults to anonymous. *authID* is a way that person A could allow person B to use his authorized privileges without sharing his password (person B would use her own password).
-r *address*	Insert a *Return-Path:* header containing *address* at the top of the message.
-f *address*	Identical to –*r* argument.

[a] The error message is misinformational—it is returned whether or not the mailbox actually exists if you do not have *p* rights on the mailbox.

To manually deliver the message contained in the file *39.* to *johndoe*'s mailbox from the Unix shell prompt, use the command:

```
% /usr/cyrus/bin/deliver -m user.johndoe johndoe < 39.
```

You must specify both the mailbox name (*user.johndoe*) using the *−m* argument, and the username that the mailbox belongs to (*johndoe*). If you do not specify the username, *deliver* will assume that you want to deliver the mail to the mailbox belonging to the user running the program from the command line. For example, if you are logged in as *smith* and you run the previous example command from your shell prompt, *deliver* will attempt to find a mailbox called *user.johndoe* in your (*smith*'s) mailbox hierarchy, and will fail. If you specify the username of the recipient but not the mailbox name, then *deliver* will attempt to deliver the message to the mailbox *user.username* by default.

Some delivery agents are configured to generate a Unix-style *From** header. *deliver* does not handle the *From* header. If you try to use *deliver* on the command line to deliver a message that contains a *From* header, *deliver* will fail. For example, if the file *39.* contains the line:

```
>From johndoe@localhost Fri Jul 16 11:31:13 1999
```

The *deliver* command will return the message:

```
johndoe: Message contains invalid header
```

As we'll see in the next section, *deliver* should be configured in your *sendmail* configuration *not* to generate the *From* header. The message should minimally contain *To:*, *From:*, *Subject:*, and *Date:* headers. If those headers are missing, the message will be delivered, but it is difficult to say what the corresponding fields in the mail client will contain when the recipient reads his mail. *deliver* will deliver a message that contains no header at all if the message begins with a blank line.

The sendmail Configuration File

sendmail versions newer than 8.7 include support for Cyrus and include a prototype M4 macro file that can be used to build a basic *sendmail.cf* configuration file. This section provides basic instructions for building a *sendmail.cf* file to support Cyrus. The instructions assume that *sendmail* is already installed and that the source distribution is available.

---

* Not to be confused with the RFC 822 *From:* header, we are referring here to the "MTA" *From* header, which has no colon delimiter and is appended to the message by the MTA (*sendmail*).

Build the sendmail configuration file

Change directory to the top level of the *sendmail* source tree. An *ls* should show most or all of the following files:

```
% ls -CF
FAQ              RELEASE_NOTES  doc/          makemap/       smrsh/
KNOWNBUGS        cf/            mail.local/   praliases/     src/
READ_ME          contrib/       mailstats/    rmail/         test/
```

The M4 macros are located in the *cf/cf* subdirectory. Under that directory, you will see a file named *cyrusproto.mc*:

```
% cd cf/cf
% ls cyrusproto.mc
cyrusproto.mc
```

cyrusproto.mc is an M4 macro script used to build a *sendmail* configuration file. Before building your configuration file, you'll need to edit the macro script to specify your operating system version. If you have a domain-specific *sendmail* configuration, you should also include a statement to define your domain. The OSTYPE variable is used to specify the operating system type. The supported values of OSTYPE can be found in the *cf/ostype* directory in the *sendmail* source distribution. For a Solaris 2.x system in the *unt.edu* domain, the following lines would have to be added to *cyrusproto.mc*:

```
OSTYPE(solaris2.ml)
DOMAIN('UNT.EDU')
```

To build a bare-bones configuration file that supports Cyrus, use *m4*:

```
% m4 ../m4/cf.m4 cyrusproto.mc > cyrusproto.cf
```

The *cyrusproto.cf* is a modified version of the *sendmail.cf* that uses Cyrus deliver as the MDA. The MDA specification, as it appears in *cyrusproto.cf*, is shown in Example 8-2.

Example 8-2. Cyrus Mailer Specification

```
##################################################
###    Cyrus Mailer specification            ###
##################################################

#####  @(#)cyrus.m4    8.4 (Carnegie Mellon) 9/2/96  #####

Mcyrus,    P=/usr/cyrus/bin/deliver, F=lsDFMnPqA5@W, S=10, R=20/40,
           U=cyrus:mail,
           A=deliver -m $h -- $u
```

The specification translates as follows (consult the sendmail[*] book for a more detailed understanding):

`Mcyrus`

The name of this mailer definition is "cyrus."

`P=/usr/cyrus/bin/deliver`

Path to the *deliver* program.

`F=lsDFMnPqA5@W`

The list of delivery flags that tell *deliver* how to behave. In particular, the *n* flag tells the mailer not to include the Unix-style *From* header.

`S=10`

Use ruleset 10 to process both the envelope and header sender addresses.

`R=20/40`

Use ruleset 20 to process the envelope recipient address and ruleset 40 to process the header recipient address.

`U=cyrus:mail`

The user and group to become when running the cyrus mailer. *deliver* must always run as user *cyrus*.

`A=deliver-m $h -- $u`

The *deliver* program and its arguments, as described in Table 8-2.

Copy the *cyrusproto.cf* file you just created into the directory where you normally keep your *sendmail* configuration file (usually */etc/mail*), then restart *sendmail*:

```
% su -
# cp /etc/mail/sendmail.cf /etc/mail/sendmail.cf.bak
# cp cyrusproto.cf /etc/mail/sendmail.cf
```

The Cyrus installation document tells you to add the user *daemon* to the mail group in */etc/group*, but that is unnecessary if you're running a modern incarnation of *sendmail* (i.e., the recommended Version 8.7.1 or better). *sendmail* runs as *root*, so the groups it belongs to are irrelevant as far as *deliver* is concerned:

```
# /etc/init.d/sendmail stop; /etc/init.d/sendmail start
```

---

[*] *sendmail*, by Bryan Costales with Eric Allman (O'Reilly).

Testing the sendmail configuration

First and most important: you must set up a Cyrus test account to which mail can be delivered. Use the commands below to set up a basic test account called "debug." If you're using Unix authentication, be sure to put the user in the local password file:

```
% cyradm -user cyrus localhost imap
localhost password:
localhost> cm user.debug
```

Next, use *sendmail* on the command line to deliver a test message to the test account:

```
% su - debug
Password: xxxxxxxx
Sun Microsystems Inc.   SunOS 5.7      Generic October 1998
$ echo "Subject: Testing 1 2 3" | /usr/lib/sendmail -v debug
debug... Connecting to cyrus...
debug... Sent
```

The message should appear in the *debug* user's mailbox. You can check this without using a mail client by looking at the contents of debug's top level mailbox:

```
$ cd /var/spool/cyrus/user/debug
$ ls -ltr
total 18
-rw-------  1 cyrus    mail         135 Jun 19 09:54 cyrus.header
-rw-------  1 cyrus    mail          53 Jul 17 12:19 cyrus.seen
-rw-------  1 cyrus    mail          96 Jul 17 20:08 cyrus.index
-rw-------  1 cyrus    mail         488 Jul 17 20:08 cyrus.cache
-rw-------  1 cyrus    mail         289 Jul 17 20:08 1.
$ cat 1.
Return-Path: <debug>
Received: (from debug@localhost)
        by localhost (8.9.1/8.9.1) id UAA25991
        for debug; Sat, 17 Jul 1999 20:08:36 -0500 (CDT)
Date: Sat, 17 Jul 1999 20:08:36 -0500 (CDT)
From: debug
Message-Id: <199907180108.UAA25991@localhost>

Testing 1 2 3
```

Duplicate delivery suppression and the delivered database maintenance

deliver can be invoked by *sendmail* with the *−e* option enabled. The *−e* option suppresses delivery of messages that have a *Message-ID:* header identical to a message that has already been delivered to a given mailbox. Information on mail deliveries is maintained in the *delivered* database (see Chapter 6, *Introduction to the Cyrus IMAP Server*, for a description). The *delivered* database should be pruned periodically to keep it from growing too large. To keep the *delivered* database clean, run *deliver* with the *−E* argument every day or so. Create a *crontab* entry to run as the *cyrus* user.* The *crontab* entry would look like this:

```
0 2 * * * /usr/cyrus/bin/deliver -E 3
```

The *−E 3* argument, for example, tells *deliver* to prune the *delivered* database of entries older than 3 days. If the database is small, you may decide to prune it less often. There is a cost, albeit a small one, in using duplicate delivery suppression— when it's turned on, every delivery accesses the *delivered* database. The *delivered* database may also be problematic during Cyrus upgrades; depending on the new version of Cyrus being installed, there may be a rebuild required of the *delivered* database. Some sites opt out of suppressing duplicate deliveries at all. The *delivered* database is really only required in Versions 1.6 and higher to support Sieve filtering.

Getting Cyrus Up and Running

Edit */etc/services*, if necessary, to contain the following line:

```
imap    143/tcp
```

Edit */etc/inetd.conf* to include the line:

```
imap stream tcp nowait cyrus /usr/cyrus/bin/imapd imapd
```

Once the files have been edited, restart *inetd*. On most Unix systems, find the process ID, then send a HUP signal to the process using the *kill* command:

```
# ps -ef | grep inetd
root 13005    1  0 22:50:57 ? 0.00    0:00 /usr/sbin/inetd -s
# kill -HUP 13005
```

If your Unix supports the *pkill* command, then you can save a step by using the command:

```
# /usr/bin/pkill -HUP -x inetd
```

Testing Your Server

You've configured your server, in time to just tell everyone it's in production and leave on your vacation for the Bahamas. On second thought, maybe it would be a good idea to test it first.

---

* It is imperative that the *crontab* entry belong to the *cyrus* user, *not* to *root* or some other user listed under *admins* in the IMAP configuration file.

Testing a Cyrus Installation on the Same Machine as Your Production Server

If you are currently running an IMAP server and wish to test a Cyrus installation without disabling the current IMAP server, specify an alternate name and port in */etc/services*, such as:

```
imaptest 243/tcp
```

Add the following line to */etc/inetd.conf*:

```
imaptest stream tcp nowait cyrus /usr/cyrus/bin/imapd imapd
```

After restarting *inetd*, the *imaptest* server will be running on port 243. Switching from the old to the new server is a simple matter of changing the name of the *imaptest* service *in /etc/inetd.conf* to *imap* and restarting *inetd*.

Caution is advised: the test server should never modify files that belong to the production server. Configure your test server's *imapd.conf* to use a different set of configuration files and a different mailstore than your production server uses.

Check That the Server Is Running

Most simple test first. Let's check to see if the IMAP listen is being serviced on the right port and if the Cyrus server is on the other end of that listen. As a normal (i.e., non-administrative) user, *telnet* to the IMAP port on your machine:

```
% telnet localhost imap
Trying 127.0.0.1...
Connected to localhost.
Escape character is '^]'.
* OK localhost Cyrus IMAP4 v1.5.19 server ready
. logout
* BYE LOGOUT received
. OK Completed
Connection closed by foreign host.
```

The command . *logout* closes the connection. If you see a message that begins with . *OK*, then the server is running. Any other message, or no message at all, indicates a problem.

Testing Cleartext Password Authentication

If you use cleartext password authentication, take advantage of the *imtest* program to test authentication.[*] Run the *imtest* program as user *cyrus* or another existing

---

[*] You could *telnet* to the IMAP port and log in using your cleartext password, but some people are (rightfully) nervous about seeing passwords in cleartext on their display. *imtest* does not echo the password.

IMAP account on your system (at this point you probably have not created user accounts yet and have only the *cyrus* account). The following example is run from the *cyrus* account:

```
% /usr/local/bin/imtest -p localhost imap
* OK localhost Cyrus IMAP4 v1.5.19 server ready
Password:
. LOGIN cyrus {L+}
X
. OK User logged in
. logout
```

The reply message *. OK User logged in* indicates that authentication is working. The message *. NO Login incorrect* can indicate any of the following problems:

- The password entered was incorrect.

- The user running *imtest* does not have an IMAP account on the system.

- *pwcheck* should be running and is not.

- There is an error in permissions or ownership somewhere, and it needs correction.

Type the command *. logout* to close the connection and quit.

Testing Kerberos Authentication

If your server uses Kerberos authentication, you can also use the *imtest* command to make sure Kerberos authentication is working. As *cyrus* or another existing user on your system, enter the command:

```
% /usr/local/bin/imtest -k localhost imap
```

If the output ends with the message:

```
. OK User logged in (no protection)
```

then Kerberos authentication is working. Any other message indicates a failure. More specific error messages are logged to the *imapd.log* file—check there for hints about what the source of the problem might be. To end the test and close the connection, type the command *. logout.*

9

Cyrus System Administration

Now that you've installed and configured the Cyrus server, you're faced with maintaining it. This chapter covers the basics of managing a Cyrus system on a day-to-day basis. We will walk through examples of how to create, delete, and list the properties of mailboxes using *cyradm*, the Cyrus administration tool. We will also see examples of how to use *cyradm* to manage existing mailboxes. Cyrus administrators are often faced with the task of creating, deleting, or modifying a batch of accounts. Examples of batch *cyradm* scripts are shown. We will also see examples of how to add and remove partitions to and from the Cyrus mailstore. Shared folders and bulletin boards are valuable features of the Cyrus server. We will see examples of how to set up and manage both.

Cyrus System Administration with cyradm

cyradm is a Tcl-based client for performing system administration on the Cyrus server. *cyradm* can be run in either interactive mode or batch mode. We will look at interactive mode first, and cover batch operations later in the chapter. Note that the information contained in this chapter is not intended to be a comprehensive account of *cyradm*—there are *cyradm* command options that are rarely used. See the manual page, *cyradm*(1), or Appendix A, *Conversion from Berkeley Mail Format to Cyrus: Tools*, for the nitty-gritty details. The objective here is to cover the most common tasks that Cyrus administrators encounter.

To start *cyradm* in interactive mode, simply enter the command:

```
$ cyradm -user username hostname port
```

username is a Cyrus administrative user defined in */etc/imapd.conf. hostname* is the hostname of the Cyrus server. *port* defaults to port 143, the standard IMAP port. Here is an example interactive session:

```
$ cyradm -user cyrus localhost
localhost password: XXXXXXXX
localhost>
```

If you need help, type *help* at the prompt. When you want to quit, use one of the commands *quit* or *exit*.

cyradm has a set of commands for performing common tasks on a Cyrus system, such as creating accounts and listing users' quotas. Table 9-1 lists the commands and gives a brief description of the purpose of each. *cyradm* commands can be abbreviated to cut down on keystrokes—the abbreviations are also shown in Table 9-1.

Table 9-1. cyradm Commands

Command	Abbreviation	Purpose
listmailbox	*lm*	Lists the names of all mailboxes that match a given pattern.
createmailbox	*cm*	Creates a new top-level mailbox.
deletemailbox	*dm*	Deletes a mailbox and all mailboxes below it in its hierarchy.
renamemailbox	*renm*	Renames a mailbox.
setaclmailbox	*sam*	Adds an entry to a maibox's ACL.
deleteaclmailbox	*dam*	Deletes an entry from a mailbox's ACL.
listaclmailbox	*lam*	Lists a mailbox's ACL.
setquota	*sq*	Sets a quota limit on a quota root.
listquota	*lq*	Lists the quotas on a quota root.
listquotaroot	*lqr* or *lqm*	Lists the quota roots on a mailbox.

The *renamemailbox* command is more complicated than meets the eye—it renames a single mailbox only and ignores all other mailboxes in the hierarchy. A workaround for renaming complete mailbox hierarchies is provided later in this chapter.

The .cyradmrc File

If the file *.cyradmrc* exists in *user*'s home directory, *cyradm* will evaluate the file as a Tcl script after connecting and authenticating to *server* and just before reading the first command from standard input.

Common Tasks

This section shows examples of common tasks you'll perform every day using *cyradm*: listing, creating, and deleting mailboxes; setting quotas; and setting ACLs.

Listing Mailboxes

The *listmailbox* (or *lm*) command returns a list of mailbox names that match the pattern given as an argument. The pattern can contain one of the wildcard characters asterisk (*) or percent (%). The * wildcard matches zero or more characters. The % wildcard is like the * wildcard, except that it only matches mailboxes at a single level in the mailbox hierarchy.

You can list all the users on the system by listing their top-level mailboxes (remember, a top-level mailbox is essentially the same as a username in the Cyrus namespace):

```
localhost> listmailbox user.%
```

To list all mailboxes one level below *abt0003*'s top-level mailbox, you would use the % wildcard character to restrict output to include only that level:

```
localhost> listmailbox user.abt0003.%
user.abt0003.drafts     user.abt0003.sent-mail
```

To list all users whose usernames begin with the letters *abt*, you would again use the % wildcard to restrict output to only top-level mailboxes:

```
localhost> listmailbox user.abt%
user.abt0003  user.abt0008
```

The next example shows how the * wildcard character returns mailboxes that match the pattern at all levels of the mailbox hierarchy:

```
localhost> listmailbox user.abt*
user.abt0003            user.abt0003.sent-mail  user.abt0008.drafts
user.abt0003.drafts     user.abt0008
```

Creating a Mailbox or Adding a User

The *createmailbox* (*cm*) command creates a new mailbox, *mailbox*. There is an optional *partition* argument that specifies the name of the partition on which to create the mailbox. If no partition is specified, the mailbox is created on the partition named *default* (it is defined in */etc/imapd.conf* as the `defaultpartition` option).

On production Cyrus systems, users are usually added to the system in batches by running a script, but on occasion, you might have to add a new user manually. Once a top-level mailbox is created for a user, the user is officially "on the system" and can begin receiving email. To add a new user, *abt0010*, you would issue the command:

```
localhost> createmailbox user.abt0010
localhost> listmailbox user.abt0010
user.abt0010
```

abt0010's top-level mailbox would be created on the *defaultpartition.*

A top-level mailbox is essentially the same as an IMAP account—once a user has a top-level mailbox and some means to authenticate to the server, he or she has an account on the Cyrus server.

If the user does not already have authentication credentials, then you should set them up now—see Chapter 8, *Configuring the Cyrus Server,* for details on setting up authentication.

You may also create mailboxes below a user's top-level mailbox. Many sites create a few default mailboxes for each new user added to the system, such as a *Trash* mailbox (*user.username.Trash*) or a *Drafts* mailbox (*user.username.Drafts*), for the convenience of the user.

Mailbox Access Control

Cyrus has an Internet standards-compliant way of organizing access to each mailbox. That method is known as an access control list (ACL). Simply speaking, an ACL is like a security guard with a clipboard sitting at the entrance to each and every mailbox, checking all who would presume to enter against an administrative list of who's allowed to do what. A more familiar example of an access control system may be Unix file ownership and permissions. We don't want to launch into a full-fledged description of Unix access control—it's been done well in other books. Unix files and directories have an owner, and access to other users can be granted with different combinations of group ownership and permission settings on the file.

A Cyrus mailbox also has an owner, and as with a Unix file, access to the mailbox can be granted to other users. Cyrus access control is more granular, though, than the Unix access control model. In the Cyrus model, it's possible to grant more than one group of users access to the mailbox without nesting groups, as you would have to do when dealing with Unix groups. Instead of just the read, write, and execute permissions that are granted on Unix files, a Cyrus user can be granted nine different levels of access (see Table 9-2).

When a new mailbox is created in the Cyrus system, it is created with a default set of access rights that are defined in the IMAP configuration file, */etc/imapd.conf.* That default ACL applies only to newly created top-level mailboxes—mailboxes that are created in an existing hierarchy inherit the ACL of their nearest parent mailbox. That's a bit different from what you would expect if you're familiar with Unix permissions. In the Unix system, permissions on subdirectories are not inherited from the parent directory in a filesystem.*

The question is, then, "when are ACLs used?" They are primarily used to allow users other than the mailbox owner to access a mailbox. This might be desirable when:

- You want to allow a colleague to read mail in a mailbox where you store mail related to a project you're collaborating on.

- A group of users, such as a technical support group, need to share a mailbox and keep track of the status of messages in that mailbox.

- You want to make a mailing list archive publicly accessible to the Internet.†

Read on to find out how to set the ACL for each of those three situations.

The setaclmailbox command

setaclmailbox is the *cyradm* command to modify a mailbox's ACL. The usage is:

```
setaclmailbox mailbox identifier rights
```

identifier refers to a user, group (a group is an entity specific to your authentication mechanism; e.g., a group in */etc/group* if you use Unix authentication—refer to Chapter 8 for information on setting up groups), or one of the predefined special identifiers, *anonymous* or *anyone*, which were described in Chapter 6, *Introduction to the Cyrus IMAP Server.* Rights are shown in Table 9-2.

---

* Subdirectories in a Unix filesystem can be forced to inherit the ownership of the parent directory by setting the appropriate "special" bits on the file.

† CMU makes the *info-cyrus* mailing list archive publicly available as a Cyrus shared folder. It's available through a web interface at *http://asg.web.cmu.edu/archive/mailbox.php3?mailbox=archive.info-cyrus.*

Table 9-2. Mailbox Access Rights

Access Right	Purpose
l	Look up the name of the mailbox (but not its contents).
r	Read the contents of the mailbox.
s	Preserve the "seen" and "recent" status of messages across IMAP sessions.
w	Write (change message flags such as "recent," "answered," and "draft").
i	Insert (move or copy) a message into the mailbox.
p	Post a message in the mailbox by sending the message to the mailbox's submission address (for example, post a message in the *cyrushelp* mailbox by sending a message to *sysadmin+cyrushelp@somewhere.net*).
c	Create a new mailbox below the top-level mailbox (ordinary users cannot create top-level mailboxes).
d	Delete a message and/or the mailbox itself.
a	Administer the mailbox (change the mailbox's ACL).

There are abbreviations describing the more common sets of rights that make it easier to set the more common ACLs. The abbreviations are listed in Table 9-3.

Table 9-3. Abbreviations for Common Access Rights

Abbreviation	Access Rights	Result
none	Blank	The user has no rights whatsoever.
read	*lrs*	Allows a user to read the contents of the mailbox.
post	*lrps*	Allows a user to read the mailbox and post to it through the delivery system by sending mail to the mailbox's submission address.
append	*lrsip*	Allows a user to read the mailbox and append messages to it, either via IMAP or through the delivery system.
write	*lrswipcd*	Allows a user to read the maibox, post to it, append messages to it, and delete messages or the mailbox itself. The only right not given is the right to change the mailbox's ACL.
all	*lrswipcda*	The user has all possible rights on the mailbox. This is usually granted to users only on the mailboxes they own.

Cyrus administrators (those users defined as *admins* in */etc/imapd.conf*) have *l* and *a* rights on all mailboxes by default. When a new user is added to the system, the user is first assigned all rights on her top-level mailbox. In all other cases, when a new mailbox is created, the new mailbox inherits the ACL of the closest parent mailbox. Non-user mailboxes (such as those used to export Usenet news groups) with no parent are assigned the ACL defined in the `defaultacl` option in */etc/imapd.conf*.

To compute a user's or group's mailbox access rights, the server takes the union of the user's rights and the rights of all groups the user is a member of. In the following example ACL, user *mary* is a member of group *helpdesk*, so she inherits *p* rights from the *helpdesk* group and, as a result, has *l*, *r*, *s*, and *p* rights:

```
mary lrs
group:helpdesk lrsp
```

It is also possible to assign a user negative rights by prefixing the identifier (not the access right) with a dash (-) character. The result is that the access rights are removed from the mailbox for the user or group that comprise the identifier. For example:

```
anyone read
-anonymous s
```

This ACL allows *anyone l*, *r*, and *s* rights, while *anonymous* is allowed only *l* and *r* rights. After computing a user's access rights, the server computes the user's negative rights by taking the union of all negative rights assigned to the user and all groups the user is a member of, and removes those rights.

Common examples

Earlier, we promised to illustrate how to set up ACLs for three common uses of shared folders. The first example involves sharing a mailbox with one other user. Suppose *johndoe* has a mailbox, *user.johndoe.grant-proposal*, and he wishes to give his colleague, *annsmith*, read-only access to the messages in that mailbox. *johndoe* would set the ACL on the mailbox as follows:

```
localhost> listaclmailbox user.johndoe.grant-proposal
johndoe lrswipcda
localhost> setaclmailbox user.johndoe.grant-proposal annsmith read
localhost> listaclmailbox user.johndoe.grant-proposal
johndoe lrswipcda
annsmith lrs
```

The second example involves sharing a mailbox with both read and write access to a group of users that needs to preserve the state of the mailbox between access by different users. Such a group might be a Helpdesk. In the example that follows, the group *helpdesk* (defined in */etc/group*) is given write access to the mailbox *user.help*. One member of the *helpdesk* group, *boss*, is granted administrative access—somebody has to maintain the mailbox's ACL, and *boss*, the Helpdesk coordinator, seems to be the best candidate:

```
localhost> listaclmailbox user.help
help lrswipcda
localhost> setaclmailbox user.help group:helpdesk write
localhost> setaclmailbox user.help boss all
```

```
localhost> listaclmailbox user.help
help lrswipcda
group:helpdesk lrswipcd
boss lrswipcda
```

In the final example, a site maintains a mailing list archive and wants to make it accessible to anyone on the Internet. The archive is stored in the mailbox *user.lists.security-l.archive.* To open up access to anyone on the Internet, the access rights would be set to allow anyone to read the mailbox:

```
localhost> listaclmailbox user.lists.security-l.archive
lists lrswipcda
localhost> setaclmailbox user.lists.security-l.archive anonymous read
help lrswipcda
anonymous lrs
```

Deleting a Mailbox or Removing a User

The *deletemailbox* (*dm*) command deletes a top-level mailbox, its contents, and all mailboxes below it in the hierarchy, essentially removing the user from the Cyrus system.

 Administrators do not have delete rights on mailboxes by default.

Before you attempt to delete a mailbox, be sure to use the *setaclmailbox* command to give yourself explicit *d* (delete) rights before deleting a mailbox, as in the following example:

```
localhost> setaclmailbox user.johndoe cyrusadm d
localhost> deletemailbox user.johndoe
```

Managing Quotas

setquota sets the quota limit on a quota root to a given value. Quotas on the Cyrus system are always expressed in kilobytes. Typically, the quota root is a user's top-level mailbox:

```
localhost> setquota user.johndoe 15000
```

The *listquotaroot* (or *lqr*) command lists the usage and limit on the given quota root. In the following example, the user *johndoe* has a quota limit of 15,000 kilobytes on his top-level mailbox and has used 1,363 kilobytes:

```
localhost> listquotaroot user.johndoe
user.dianna STORAGE 1363/15000 (9%)
```

cyradm does not offer a facility for removing a user's quota—quotas have to be removed manually by deleting the quota file associated with the user, then rebuilding the Cyrus quota database. The details are explained later in this chapter.

Renaming a User's Account

The *renamemailbox* command:

```
renamemailbox mailbox newmailbox partition
```

renames *mailbox* to *newmailbox*. The optional *partition* argument is used if you want to move the *newmailbox* to a different partition.

renamemailbox does exactly what its name implies, and that's all it does—it renames a single mailbox. The command has an important limitation, though: it cannot be used to rename a top-level mailbox. Here is what happens when we attempt to rename a top-level mailbox:

```
localhost> renamemailbox user.diannal user.diannam
command failed: Operation is not supported on mailbox
```

Top-level mailboxes cannot be renamed because of a Cyrus architectural issue. Renaming a top-level mailbox requires changes in other parts of the system, such as the mailboxes file, the quota subsystem, the mailbox subscription database, and the names of all mailboxes below the top level in the hierarchy. This can be a problem—many sites allow users to change their account names at some time after the account is initially created. It is also important to note that *renamemailbox* does not hierarchically rename mailboxes—it only renames the mailbox that it is given as an argument. All other mailboxes below that mailbox in the hierarchy are left untouched. CMU will provide a hierarchical *renamemailbox* command in Cyrus 2.0, but it does not yet appear in any release up through Version 1.6.22. Until *cyradm* supports hierarchical renaming, it will be of limited use on its own. Fortunately, as with many limitations, there is a usually a workaround. The workaround, which is implemented as a Tcl script in Example 9-2 in the next section of this chapter, involves these steps (in the order given):

1. Create a new top-level mailbox named for the new username (for example, *user.newname*).

2. Create new sub-mailboxes for all the mailboxes in the user's old hierarchy (*user.newname.sent-mail*).

3. Replace the new, empty mailbox hierarchy with the old mailbox hierarchy.

4. Delete the old account.

5. Reconstruct the new account using the Cyrus *reconstruct* utility.

6. Set a quota root on the new account.

 Note that although you may read about other workarounds that involved direct editing of the mailboxes file, we caution you never to edit the mailboxes file directly! It's an unnecessary risk—the tools exist for working within the system; it's just a matter of stringing them together in the right way to do the job.

Batch Account Maintenance with cyradm

cyradm can be invoked in a script to read and evaluate a series of Tcl commands. In batch mode, *cyradm* command names cannot be abbreviated as they can be in interactive mode (e.g., *setaclmailbox* cannot be invoked as *sam*). When running *cyradm* in non-interactive mode, you will always use one Tcl command that has not been mentioned yet: the command *cyradm connect*. The *cyradm connect* command opens an IMAP connection to the server, and it is always the first command you execute in a batch *cyradm* script.

The usage of the *cyradm connect* command is:

```
cyradm connect connectionname
```

where *connectionname* is an arbitrary handle that denotes the connection to the IMAP server. Once a connection is established, other *cyradm* commands are issued as:

```
connectionname command
```

The command *command* is any one of the *cyradm* commands discussed earlier in the chapter. It may also be one of the following commands that have not yet been introduced:

connectionname servername

Returns the hostname of the server the connection is connected to.

connectionname authenticate

Authenticates the connection. *connection authenticate* has two command switches, shown in Table 9-4.

Table 9-4. connection authenticate Command Switches

Switch	Function
-user *username*	Log in to the Cyrus server as *username*.
-pwcommand *script*	Perform a plaintext password login. *script* must consist of Tcl commands that return the username and password, for example:

```
cyr_conn authenticate -pwcommand {
    set adminid "cyrusadm"
    set adminpw "xxxxxxxx"
    list $adminid $adminpw
}
```

Add New Users

Example 9-1, *addusers*, is a Tcl script that uses *cyradm* to create a batch of new IMAP user accounts and set a quota root on each account. To run the script, type the command:

```
$ addusers filename
```

where *filename* is a plain file containing one username per line.

Example 9-1. The addusers Script

```
#!/usr/local/bin/cyradm -file

# Batch Cyrus user creation script. Usage: addusers filename

set inputfile [lindex $argv 0]   # Name of file containing users
set quotalimit 15360             # Quota limit in Kbytes

eval cyradm connect cyr_conn venus 143
puts stdout "Connected to IMAP server. Authenticating..."

if [catch {eval cyr_conn authenticate -pwcommand {{
    set hostname "localhost"
    set adminid "cyrusadm"
    set adminpw "xxxxxxxx"
    list $adminid $adminpw
}} } result ] {
    puts stderr "$result (cleartext)"
    return -code error $result
} else {
    puts "Authentication successful."
}
```

The script opens a connection to the Cyrus server called *venus* and logs in as user *cyrusadm* with password *xxxxxxxx*. Once the connection is established and authenticated, the input file is opened. The script loops through each line of input, assigns the contents of the line to the variable *user*, and creates a new top-level mailbox for *user*. After the mailbox is created, the quota defined in the variable *quotalimit* at the start of the script is applied to the new mailbox:

```
if [catch {open $inputfile r} fileId] {
    puts stderr "Error: cannot open $inputfile"
} else {

    while {[gets $fileId user] >= 0} {

        ## Create the INBOX

        if [catch {cyr_conn createmailbox user.$user} result] {
            puts stderr $result
        } else {
            puts "Created mailbox user.$user"
        }

        ## Create the default mailboxes

        if [catch {cyr_conn createmailbox user.$user.drafts} result] {
            puts stderr $result
        } else {
            puts "  Created mailbox user.$user.drafts"
        }

        if [catch {cyr_conn createmailbox user.$user.sent-mail} result] {
            puts stderr $result
        } else {
            puts "  Created mailbox user.$user.sent-mail"
        }

        ## Set the quota

        puts "  Setting quota $quotalimit on user.$user..."
        cyr_conn setquota "user.$user" "storage" "$quotalimit"
    }
}
```

Rename an Account

The next script, *rename*, is a Tcl script that renames a user's mailboxes. Cyradm has a built-in *rename* command, but the command works only on top-level mailboxes—it does not rename mailboxes lower in the hierarchy. The *rename* script in Example 9-2 renames the top-level mailbox and all mailboxes below it in the user's mailbox hierarchy.

You will often find it necessary to rename a user's mailbox if her name is reflected in her username and her full name changes. In the examples provided in this section, user *anndoe* (Ann Doe) married and changed her last name to Smith, and she asked the system administrator to change her Cyrus username to *annsmith*.

First, in *cyradm*, list the user's mailboxes, excluding the top-level mailbox. Save the mailbox names in a text file—you will use it later as input to the script that renames the account:

```
localhost> lm user.anndoe.*
user.anndoe.networker.bootstrap
user.anndoe.networker
user.anndoe.saved-messages
user.anndoe.sent-mail
```

Suppose we saved the *lm* output in a file called *lm.out*. To rename *anndoe*'s account to *annsmith*, you would run the command:

```
$ rename lm.out anndoe annsmith
```

Example 9-2. The rename Script

```
#!/usr/local/bin/cyradm -file
#
#     Usage: rename filename olduser newuser
#
set inputfile [lindex $argv 0]
set oldmb [lindex $argv 1]
set newmb [lindex $argv 2]
set mailstore "/var/spool/imap/user"

eval cyradm connect cyr_conn localhost 143
puts stdout "Connected to IMAP server. Authenticating..."

if [catch {eval cyr_conn authenticate -pwcommand {{
    set hostname "localhost"
    set adminid "cyrus"
    set adminpw "XXXXXXXX"
    list $adminid $adminpw
}} } result ] {
    puts stderr "$result (cleartext)"
    return -code error $result
} else {
    puts "Authentication successful."
}
##
## Open the file containing mailbox names, and create the
## top-level mailbox.
##
if [catch {open $inputfile r} fileId] {
    puts stderr "Error: cannot open $inputfile"
} else {

    ## Create the toplevel mailbox

    if [catch {cyr_conn createmailbox user.$newmb} result] {
        puts stderr $result
    } else {
        puts "Created mailbox user.$newmb"
    }
```

Example 9-2. The rename Script (continued)

```
while {[gets $fileId line] >= 0} {

    ## Build the new mailbox name from the old one
    set newf [join [lreplace [split $line .] 1 1 $newmb] . ]

    ## Create the mailbox
    if [catch {cyr_conn createmailbox $newf} result] {
        puts stderr $result
    } else {
        puts "Created sub-mailbox $newf"
    }
}

file delete -force /var/spool/cyrus/user/$newmb
file copy $mailstore/$oldmb $mailstore/$newmb
{exec /usr/bin/chown -R cyrus:mail $mailstore/$newmb}

## Delete the old account
if [catch {cyr_conn setaclmailbox user.$oldmb cyrusadm d} \
    result] {
    puts stderr $result
} else {
    puts "setaclmailbox user.$oldmb cyrusadm d"
}

if [catch {cyr_conn deletemailbox user.$oldmb} result] {
    puts stderr $result
} else {
    puts "Deleted mailbox user.$oldmb"
}
}

puts "Please run \'reconstruct user.$newmb\' as cyrus."
```

After renaming the mailboxes, run *reconstruct* as the *cyrus* user, before doing anything else. Until you have run *reconstruct*, the account is not fully active:

```
$ reconstruct -r user.annsmith
```

Shared Folders and Bulletin Boards

The Cyrus IMAP server is unique in its capability to make a mailing list available to many users via the IMAP protocol alone. Cyrus accomplishes that feat with shared folders and bulletin boards.

Shared folders and bulletin boards are ordinary Cyrus mailboxes with ACLs that allow more than one user access to the mailbox. There is really not much difference between shared folders and bulletin boards: they are both Cyrus mailboxes, and both allow users other than the mailbox owner to access the mailbox with the permissions defined in the mailbox's ACL.

When a Cyrus mailbox is referred to as a *shared folder*, it generally means that it is a mailbox owned by an individual user who wants to allow other users access to the mailbox. An additional feature of a shared folder is that, other than the "read" flag, it does not retain message state information that is unique per user. Message information like *deleted* or *important* is global to all users. That feature could be useful if it is desirable to preserve state information across accesses by different users. If you use a shared folder for a group of users, such as a Helpdesk, chances are you will want to preserve the *seen* and *answered* states across sessions, to provide a sort of work flow for the Helpdesk employees.

A *bulletin board* is a Cyrus mailbox that is owned by the system, rather than by an individual user. Bulletin boards are generally used when it is desirable to maintain a per-user *seen* state. Good uses for bulletin boards are forums such as Usenet groups and Internet mailing lists.

There are no fixed rules, only guidelines, about whether to use a shared folder or bulletin board for your particular application.

Implementing Shared Folders

When creating a shared folder, the first step is to create the mailbox that will be shared. Because clients handle mailbox names differently, make the mailbox name as descriptive as possible. Remember that with Unix authentication, the mailbox name is actually the name of a user in the password file. That limits the mailbox name to eight characters or less. A good guideline to follow when creating the top-level mailbox is to configure for the lowest common denominator. Don't use more than eight characters in the top-level mailbox name—anticipate a migration to another mail system or authentication system someday in the future. There is also the issue of MUAs—some clients can get confused by long usernames. If there are to be sub-folders in the hierarchy, you need not be as strict with naming them.

After creating the mailboxes, set the ACL to allow the appropriate users access. For example, suppose we need a shared mailbox called *announce*, with sub-folders called *events*, *for_sale*, and *official_notices*. The user *announce* has all permissions on all the mailboxes in the hierarchy. We also want the sub-folders to be readable by everyone on the Cyrus system, and we want only two users, *johndoe* and *msmith*, to append messages to the sub-folders. To allow those two users to post messages to the sub-folders, the ACLs on the sub-folders should look like:

```
localhost> lam user.announce.events
announce lrswipcda
msmith p
johndoe p
anyone lr
```

johndoe and *msmith* can append mail directly to any of the mailboxes in the hierarchy via IMAP by using the "+" notation. For example, to post a message directly to the *events* mailbox, *johndoe* or *msmith* would send a message to:

```
announce+events@yourdomain.com
```

The *deliver* program would append the message to the *events* folder in the *announce* mailbox. If any other user attempts to append mail directly to one of the shared folders, it will end up in *announce*'s inbox, where only *announce* can see it.

In order for a user to post mail to a mailbox using the + notation, that user must have *p* access rights on the mailbox.

That implies that the ACL on the top-level mailbox must be set more strictly than the *events, for_sale,* and *official_notices*. First, we create the top-level mailboxes and the sub-folders:

```
localhost> createmailbox user.announce
```

By default, the *user.announce* mailbox is created with an ACL that grants all rights to the mailbox owner, *announce*. Because we don't want other users to view the mailbox, no change in the ACL is necessary on the top-level mailbox:

```
localhost> createmailbox user.announce.events
localhost> createmailbox user.announce.for_sale
localhost> createmailbox user.announce.official_notices
```

Finally, set the ACL on each sub-folder to allow everyone read and list access, and *msmith* and *johndoe* permission to post messages to the mailboxes (repeat the last three commands for *msmith*):

```
localhost> setaclmailbox user.announce.events anyone lr
localhost> setaclmailbox user.announce.for_sale anyone lr
localhost> setaclmailbox user.announce.official_notices anyone lr
localhost> setaclmailbox user.announce.events johndoe p
localhost> setaclmailbox user.announce.for_sale johndoe p
localhost> setaclmailbox user.announce.official_notices johndoe p
```

If you use a shared folder to provide a group of staff members with a forum, distribute your workload—delegate someone as the shared folder or bulletin board owner. Give that person *all* access rights, so that person can manage the mailbox's ACL and its permissions as changes in staff occur.

Implementing Bulletin Boards

As with shared folders, the first step in creating a bulletin board is to create a mailbox that will be used as the bulletin board. After creating the mailbox, set the ACL—the ACL should have the *l* and *r* bits set so that the users can see and read the mailbox. If users are allowed to post to the bulletin board, then the *p* bit should also be set. If they are allowed to store messages they have seen in the bulletin board, then the *s* bit should be set.

If your installation's *sendmail* configuration was built using the *cyrus-proto.mc* M4 file that came with the *sendmail* distribution, mail sent to *bb+mailboxname* will be delivered to the bulletin board.

Sites that use some MTA other than *sendmail* should take a look at the *deliver*(8) manpage for details on how to invoke *deliver* to allow postings to the bulletin board.

A Word of Warning . . .

d (delete) rights should be used on bulletin boards and shared folders with caution. While *d* rights may be granted with the intention of allowing a user to delete messages in the folder or bulletin board, *d* rights also enable the user to delete the folder or bulletin board itself. When the folder or bulletin board is deleted, incoming mail bounces. The problem has been known for some time and is fixed in Cyrus Version 2.0, due to be released soon. Although the problem cannot necessarily be considered a bug, a fix exists that can be applied to versions of the source code prior to 2.0 to allow *d* rights yet prevent users from deleting the folder itself.

The fix involves changing code that checks the user's ACL in *imap/mailboxlist.c* in the *mboxlist_deletemailbox* function. The code provided in the Cyrus distribution checks the user's ACL for *d* rights before allowing him to delete a mailbox. By changing the code to test for *a* rights instead of *d* rights, a user can still be allowed to delete messages in the folder, but must have administrative rights added to his ACL before he can delete the folder. There are two ACL tests in *mboxlist_delete-mailbox*, shown in Example 9-3.

Example 9-3. The Offending Code from mboxlist.c (Cyrus IMAP Version 1.5.19)

```
mboxlist_deletemailbox(name, isadmin, userid, auth_state, checkacl)
char *name;
int isadmin;
char *userid;
struct auth_state *auth_state;
int checkacl;
{
```

Example 9-3. The Offending Code from mboxlist.c (Cyrus IMAP Version 1.5.19) (continued)

(Lines deleted for brevity...)

```
        /* Check ACL before doing anything stupid
         * We don't have to lie about the error code since we know
         * the user is an admin.
         */
        if (!(acl_myrights(auth_state, acl) & ACL_DELETE)) {
            return IMAP_PERMISSION_DENIED;
        }
```

(More lines of code deleted...)

```
    access = acl_myrights(auth_state, acl);
    if (checkacl && !(access & ACL_DELETE)) {
        mboxlist_unlock();
```

The same code, with the fix applied (in boldface type), is shown in Example 9-4.

Example 9-4. Fixed mailboxlist.c

```
mboxlist_deletemailbox(name, isadmin, userid, auth_state, checkacl)
char *name;
int isadmin;
char *userid;
struct auth_state *auth_state;
int checkacl;
{
```

(Lines deleted for brevity...)

```
        /* Check ACL before doing anything stupid
         * We don't have to lie about the error code since we know
         * the user is an admin.
         */
        if (!(acl_myrights(auth_state, acl) & ACL_ADMIN)) {
            return IMAP_PERMISSION_DENIED;
        }
```

(More lines of code deleted...)

```
    access = acl_myrights(auth_state, acl);
    if (checkacl && !(access & ACL_ADMIN)) {
        mboxlist_unlock();
```

Mailstore Partitioning

Cyrus scales well as your storage requirements grow. Scaling is accomplished by spreading the mailstore across filesystems. New partitions can be added to the mailstore at any time without requiring downtime,* copying of files, or even the users' knowledge.

The default Cyrus configuration requires two properties related to mailstore partitioning in */etc/imapd.conf*:

```
partition-default: /var/spool/cyrus
defaultpartition: default
```

Under this default configuration, when a new mailbox is created, it inherits the partition of its parent mailbox. If the new mailbox does not have a parent mailbox, then the mailbox is placed on the default partition *partition-default*.

Depending on the specifics of the hardware configuration, the system administrator may want to distribute the mailstore across several disks. Suppose, for example, a system with a single disk for its mailstore reached 90% of its disk capacity, and the administrator added two disks and a new disk controller. In this case, the system administrator would probably decide to keep her mailstore partitioning as simple as possible and add a new partition for each new disk.† After adding the new hardware to the system, formatting the disks, and mounting the new partitions, the administrator would create a *user* subdirectory under each new partition and change */etc/imapd.conf* to look like:

```
partition-default: /var/spool/cyrus
partition-1: /var/spool/cyrus1
partition-2: /var/spool/cyrus2
defaultpartition: default
```

To add new accounts to one of the new partitions, the administrator would need to specify the partition name as an argument to the *createmailbox* command. If she does not specify the partition, the mailbox is created on the default partition. For example, using *cyradm* interactively, give the command:

```
localhost> createmailbox user.marydoe 1
```

The *createmailbox* command creates a new account for *marydoe* and, because `partition-1` is located on the filesystem */var/spool/cyrus1*, places *marydoe*'s mailbox in */var/spool/cyrus1/user/marydoe/*.

To move existing accounts to other partitions, the rename script (Example 9-2) could be used. There is also a very useful public domain IMAP tool, *fast.imap* (see Chapter 18, *IMAP Tools*), which can be used to manually move or automatically balance mailboxes across partitions.

---

* This is assuming the partitions are being added, not moved. Downtime may, of course, be required to add new disk hardware to a system, but that downtime would be required regardless of the mail server software.

† While simple, the configuration takes maximum advantage of the hardware by spreading I/O requests across the two controllers.

A common partitioning scheme that is used at many sites involves dividing the mailstore into 26 partitions, one for each letter in the alphabet. Users are then assigned to the partition that corresponds to the first letter of their last name. Although many sites do this to make the system more scalable or to work around filesystem limits, we don't recommend it. The problem with the alphabet partitioning scheme is that you're likely to get an uneven distribution of mailboxes across partitions; e.g., your "m" partition might fill up before your "z" partition. Additionally, having a large number of small partitions makes the system more complex and difficult to manage. Careful configuration of the system makes this sort of partitioning scheme unnecessary. Keeping a smaller number of partitions keeps the system scalable without making it more complex than it has to be.

Quota Maintenance

On occasion, quotas will get horked. A common corrupted quota scenario goes like this: a user receives alerts from his client that he cannot save mail to his folders.* You use *cyradm* to check his quota, and everything looks fine—he has plenty of space. However, you check a little deeper and you see that his mail is being deferred to the queue and is not being delivered to his mailbox, which usually happens when a user is over quota. A quick way to determine whether the problem is quota-related is to use the *quota* command to fix the user's quota root (run the command as *user cyrus* from the shell prompt):

```
$ quota user.username
```

After running *quota*, run *cyradm* and check the quota again. Chances are that it will report the user as being over quota when you run it this time.

The *quota* command, when run with no command-line arguments, can also be used to report quota limits and usage on your entire user base:

```
$ quota
Quota  % Used    Used Root
15360       0       0 user.aa0002
15360       0       0 user.aa0006
15360       0     137 user.aa0008
15360       0       0 user.aa0009
```

If quotas become corrupted, all that is required to fix the problem is to run the *quota* command with the *–f* switch:

```
$ quota -f
```

---

* The errors depend on the client and can range from "permission denied" to "cannot save to mailbox."

The command may require several minutes to complete, depending on the number of users your system supports. More information on quota subsystem maintenance is provided in later in the chapter.

Disaster Recovery

Anticipate disaster! The best approach you can take is a proactive approach. Here are some things you can do to be prepared.

Checkpoint Your mailboxes File

Reconstructing the *mailboxes* file is time-consuming, but you can avoid reconstructing that file from scratch. Save a history of past versions of the *mailboxes* file periodically on disk so that you can go back in small increments of time to the last good copy of the *mailboxes* file. True, it may be a few minutes too old to bring your system back to its exact state before the problems started, but in most cases that is better than bringing the system down for several hours to reconstruct the *mailboxes* file. Saving one copy of the file is not useful—suppose the corruption in the *mailboxes* surfaced hours ago, and you've been backing up the corrupt file every five minutes since then? To be on the safe side, save each set of files on a separate physical disk. Even better yet, save *two* copies in two different physical locations. Save as often as possible, as often as every few minutes. A script for rotating the *mailboxes* file is given in Example 9-5 later in this chapter.

Back Up Your Data

Have a good backup strategy. While reliable backups are essential, the ability to recover files on demand is equally important. Are you prepared to restore any part of your system right now? If so, document where the data is kept and how to recover it.

Be Prepared for More than One Disaster

Disasters can happen simultaneously at more than one level in your infrastructure. What would you do if you lost both your tape backup system and your mail server at the same time? Document your infrastructure—what systems and services does Cyrus depend on? Include one or more extra Cyrus servers that can take over while the primary server is being recovered.

Keep Hard Copies of Your Configuration

If a disk containing part of your Cyrus system is lost, you must be prepared to install a new disk, rebuild the filesystem on the new disk, and restore data. To rebuild the disk, you need to know how the filesystems were laid out on the disk and how much space was allocated to each partition. Keeping hard copies of configuration data, such as your IMAP server configuration file or your MTA configuration, can make recovery of the server much easier if for some reason you must install it from scratch. Useful information to keep in hard copy includes:

- Partition tables from the format command

- Output of the *df* command

- */etc/vfstab* or */etc/fstab*

- */etc/imapd.conf*

- *sendmail.mc*

- RAID configuration files

- Automounter configuration files

Disasters and Recovery Strategies

In this section, we'll look at some common disasters and how to recover from those disasters.

Corruption or inconsistency in the mailboxes file

As we learned in Chapter 7, *Installing the Cyrus IMAP Server*, the */var/imap/ mailboxes* file is critical to the operation of the Cyrus system. Fortunately, Cyrus comes with a utility, *reconstruct*, that can be used to rebuild the *mailboxes* file in case of loss or corruption.

The *reconstruct* utility must always run as user *cyrus*! If run as *root* or another user, it will reset the ownership of the mailbox and the mailboxes will no longer be accessible.

Shut down *imapd* before running *reconstruct*. Comment out the *imapd* entry in */etc/inetd.conf*, and send a HUP signal to the *inetd* process to turn off *imapd*. Then, as user *cyrus*, run the *reconstruct* utility with the *−m* switch:

```
$ reconstruct -m
```

The *−m* argument tells *reconstruct* to correct the system-wide *mailboxes* file, if possible. After correcting *mailboxes*, *reconstruct* checks each partition defined in */etc/imapd.conf* for mailboxes, and adds them to *mailboxes* if necessary. When *reconstruct* finishes its work, uncomment *imapd* in */etc/inetd.conf* and send another HUP signal to *inetd* to turn *imapd* back on.

Be aware that on a system with a large number of users, *reconstruct* can take quite some time to run.* It is strongly recommended that on all Cyrus systems, but especially on large systems, you checkpoint your *mailboxes* file to an alternate disk periodically throughout the day and that you keep copies going several hours back. The *mailboxes* file changes when:

- A new user account is created

- A mailbox is created or deleted

- A quota root changes

- A mailbox's ACL changes

If your system has a large number of users, or your users are very active, your *mailboxes* file changes often. For systems with an active *mailboxes* file, checkpointing the *mailboxes* file every 5 or 10 minutes is recommended. Having a good copy of *mailboxes* around will help you avoid taking time to recover the file from tape and will save hours of downtime by making a *reconstruct* of the complete *mailboxes* file unnecessary. Always try replacing the corrupted *mailboxes* file with the backed-up copy before running *reconstruct*. If the file is current enough, chances are that it will suffice and the entire file will not need to be rebuilt. Example 9-5 shows a script for rotating the *mailboxes* file.

Example 9-5. Script to Rotate the mailboxes File

```perl
#!/usr/local/bin/perl

$file   = "/var/cyrus/mailboxes";
$gzip   = "/usr/local/bin/gzip";
$maxrot = 60;
$suffix = "gz";

if (! -e $file) { print "$file does not exist! exiting.\n"; exit; }

$rot = $maxrot;
while ($rot >= 0) {

    $rotn = $rot + 1;
    if (-e "$file.$rot.$suffix") {
        rename "$file.$rot.$suffix", "$file.$rotn.$suffix";
    }
    $rot = $rot - 1;
}

`cp $file $file.0`;
`$gzip $file.0`;
```

---

* On a Sun Enterprise 3500 with the *mailboxes* file on local disk, *reconstruct* took 7 hours to rebuild a *mailboxes* file containing 60,000 entries.

On less active systems, backing up *mailboxes* once per hour should be sufficient. If you have a very small number of users, *reconstruct* runs quickly and it's not really necessary to checkpoint your mailboxes file.

reconstruct does not adjust the quota usage recorded in the quota root files. After reconstructing or recovering the *mailboxes* file, it's always necessary to rebuild the quota subsystem using the *quota –f* command.

Corruption in a user's mailbox

On occasion, you will encounter inconsistencies in individual mailbox directories. *reconstruct* can also be used to recover from inconsistencies in mailboxes and mailbox hierarchies. To rebuild a single mailbox without affecting any other mailboxes in the same hierarchy, run *reconstruct* with the mailbox name as an argument. Remember, *reconstruct* must be run as the *cyrus* user:

```
$ reconstruct user.johndoe
user.johndoe
```

To rebuild a mailbox and all mailboxes below it in its local hierarchy, use the *–r* argument to *reconstruct*:

```
$ reconstruct -r user.johndoe
user.johndoe
user.johndoe.Trash
user.johndoe.work
user.johndoe.work.projects
```

reconstruct first checks the mailbox for *cyrus.header* and *cyrus.index* files. If the files exist, then *reconstruct* recovers information from those files that it cannot gather from the message files, such as the date stamp and flag names and states. *reconstruct* recovers information from the message files themselves that it cannot find in the header and cache files.

Inconsistency in quotas

On rare occasions, a mailbox will wind up with the wrong quota root. When this happens, the *cyradm listquota* command will report an incorrect quota usage. A good indication that something in the quota system has gone haywire is when a user's mail is bouncing with "Deferred—quota exceeded" errors, but *listquota* reports that the usage is below the limit. The Cyrus distribution includes a tool, *quota*(8), for maintaining the consistency of the quota subsystem.

You may recall from Chapter 6 that the Cyrus quota subsystem is comprised of a directory in the Cyrus configuration area that contains a set of text files, one file per quota root. The association between a mailbox and a quota root is not made in the quota subsystem—that information is maintained in the *mailboxes* file. Each quota file, which is named after the quota root, contains the quota root's quota usage (in bytes) and quota limit (in kilobytes). Here is an example of a quota file:

```
$ cd /var/imap/quota
$ cat user.aa0006
4052251
15360
```

The first line of *user.aa0006* is the quota usage, in bytes; the second line is the quota limit, in kilobytes.

If we go to the *mailboxes* file and look for the quota root *user.aa0006*, we can find all mailboxes that it applies to. Here is an excerpt from the *mailboxes* file. The first field in the line is the mailbox name, the second is the partition on which the mailbox resides, the third field is the quota root (sans the "user." prefix), and the last field is the mailbox's ACL:

```
user.aa0006              default aa0006   lrswipcda
user.aa0006.Drafts      default aa0006   lrswipcda
user.aa0006.Trash       default aa0006   lrswipcda
user.aa0006.sent-mail   default aa0006   lrswipcda
```

The *quota* program, when run with the *–f* option, fixes inconsistencies in the quota subsystem by recalculating the quota root of each mailbox and the quota usage of each quota root:

```
$ quota -f
```

The *quota* command first repairs the quota subsystem, then reports its results after all repairs have been made. The results include the quota root, its usage before the consistency check, and its usage after the repairs:

```
user.aa0002: usage was 0, now 307223
user.aa0006: usage was 5181, now 4052251
user.aa0030: usage was 105945, now 5446403
user.aad0006: usage was 0, now 6261
user.aadavis: usage was 0, now 8239
```

The Cyrus distribution does not include a tool for removing a quota root. To remove a quota root without removing the mailbox it is associated with, you must remove the quota root's file from the */var/imap/quota* directory, then run the *quota* command to make the quota subsystem consistent:

```
$ rm /var/imap/quota/user.aa0002
$ quota -f
```

It is advisable to run the *quota* command periodically (e.g., once per week) out of *cron* to keep the quota subsystem in a consistent state.

Loss of a disk

You heeded our advice and saved copies of your disk configurations, so you know how the partitions were laid out on the disk and what each one is used for. Here are the steps to follow:

1. Replace the disk.

2. Boot your system to single-user mode.

3. Rebuild the filesystem on the new disk and determine that you can mount each partition on its usual mount point.

4. Restore data to the new filesystem.

5. Arrange your startup scripts so that *sendmail* does not start up when the system boots, and comment out the entry for *imapd* in */etc/inetd.conf.*

6. If you recovered data that included the *mailboxes* file or any part of a mailbox, then run *reconstruct.*

7. Reboot the system. If the system comes up with all partitions mounted, then start *sendmail* and uncomment the entry for *imapd* in */etc/inetd.conf.*

Migration from Berkeley (Unix) Mailbox Format to Cyrus

Unix systems and the out-of-the-box UW IMAP server both store mail messages in Berkeley mail format (also referred to as *mbox, Unix,* or */var/mail* format) mail folders. Many sites that use Berkeley format move their users onto a Cyrus server to take advantage of the quota and ACL support that Cyrus offers. In this section, we'll walk though the steps involved in such a migration. Source code for the tools we used to accomplish the migration are provided in Appendix A.

How Do I Know My Mail Is Berkeley Format?

If your mail setup matches six out of seven of the criteria below, then you're storing mail in Berkeley format:

- There is no mail server—users log on to a Unix machine and run a mail program to read their mail.

- There *is* a mail server, but it's the UW IMAP server, running out-of-the-box with no special site configuration.

- Each user's incoming mail is stored in a spool directory, such as */var/mail* or */var/spool/mail.*

- Each user's incoming mail is stored within a single file, named after the user.

- Mail folders are stored in the user's home directory.

- Mail reading is done with programs such as Elm, PINE, *mail*(1), *rmail*(1), or *mailx*(1).

- Each mail folder contains a header, blank line, and message body, and delimits messages with the From header line.*

Issues

When converting a production mail system to Cyrus, several issues need to be taken into consideration to make the conversion go smoothly.

User-driven versus batch conversion

Will you take responsibility for moving your users over to the Cyrus server, or will you put some utility in place to allow them to do it on their own? If moving to Cyrus is optional, it might be easier on you if the users migrate their own mail to the new server. A one-time, all-or-none conversion might be optional in your circumstances. If you don't have another immediate need for the old machine and can keep both the old and new machines running simultaneously, then you could take advantage of a user-driven conversion. The size of your user base plays a role, too—user-driven conversion is much easier to manage in a small user base. In a larger user base, it becomes difficult to get everyone to move their mail before your deadline.

If you are constrained to providing mail service on the new Cyrus server immediately, then you will need to move all your users at one time in batch mode.

Downtime

Downtime is a serious consideration for sites that depend on Cyrus as a production mail server. You may decide to bypass the issue of downtime completely and move one or two users at a time over a period of months until everyone has been moved to the Cyrus server. Some sites do not have the infrastructure or hardware to support that strategy. Those sites will need to move all users from the old system to Cyrus in one fell swoop.

Downtime can be considerable if the migration is not planned carefully. If downtime is a serious issue, then a dry run of your migration plan is advisable.

---

* The From and From: header lines are not the same.

It's all or nothing!

Once you've migrated users to your Cyrus system and start delivering mail to the system, it is possible, but time-consuming, to revert to Berkeley mail. Be prepared to revert to your old system if something goes terribly wrong mid-migration. Tools for backing out of a conversion are provided later in this chapter.

Tools

Unfortunately, there are no generic migration tools good for both large and small user bases. Mark Crispin at the University of Washington developed a set of tools that includes mailbox conversion programs (see Chapter 18). The UW tools can be used to migrate a small number of mailboxes. However, those tools use the IMAP protocol to move mail around and require authentication for each user being converted, making them unsuitable for a mass migration. Those tools are somewhat problematic to use for conversion to Cyrus, and after a few days of working with them unsuccessfully, we found it easier to write our own tools. In this chapter, we provide generic tools that are good for user-driven and both large and small batch conversions.

Backward compatibility

You may be supporting features that could become problematic on a Cyrus server, such as server-side mail filtering or *.forward* files. Keep those features in mind when you're drawing up your migration plans.

User-Driven Conversion

Users can copy their own Berkeley-format incoming mailbox and mail folders into a Cyrus mailbox using the Perl script, *user2cyrus*, shown in Example 9-6. The script makes the transfer using IMAP, so the Berkeley folder and Cyrus server need not reside on the same machine. The script does assume that each user already has an account on the Cyrus server.

 If the user runs *user2cyrus* while she has an IMAP client open, she may need to exit and restart the client to see the new mailbox and messages.

To provide *user2cyrus* to your users, you would need to install it somewhere public, like */usr/local/bin*, on the machine where the Berkeley format folders reside. The script automatically skips the first message in the Berkeley folder to avoid copying the "FOLDER INTERNAL DATA" message. If you want to copy the message, then edit the script as you wish.

user2cyrus requires the NetxAP Perl module, which is freely available from CPAN.

Example 9-6. The user2cyrus Script

```perl
#!/usr/local/bin/perl
#
# This is a modified version of a public domain script written by
# Steve Snodgrass (ssnodgra@fore.com).
#
# user2cyrus - Dump a user's Unix mail file into a Cyrus mailbox
#
# Usage:     user2cyrus mbox
#
# Input:     Name of an RFC 822 mail folder
#
# Dependency:    NetxAP Perl module from CPAN
#
use File::Basename;
use Net::IMAP;

# Set this to the hostname of your IMAP server
$IMAPSERVER = "europa.acs.unt.edu";

$mbox = "$ARGV[0]";
if (!$mbox) { die "Usage: $0 mbox\n"; }

chop ($whoami = `/usr/ucb/whoami`);
if ($whoami eq "root" || $whoami eq "cyrus") {
    die "This script cannot be run by a privileged user!\n";
}


#
# Main Code
#

# Log in to Cyrus IMAP server
($user, $pass) = GetLogin();
$imap = new Net::IMAP($IMAPSERVER, Synchronous => 1);
$response = $imap->login($user, $pass);
print "Login: ", $response->status, "-",
    $response->status_text, "\n";

# cyrmailbox is the mailbox name on the Cyrus server
$cyrmailbox = "user." . "$user." . basename($mbox);

# Create the new mailbox. If the mailbox already exists, do not
# allow its contents to be overwritten!
$response = $imap->create($cyrmailbox);

print "Create: ", $response->status, "-",
    $response->status_text, "\n";
```

Example 9-6. The user2cyrus Script (continued)

```perl
if ($response->status eq "NO") {
    print "Mailbox $cyrmailbox already exists on Cyrus server!\n";
    print "Rename your file and try again.\n";
    $response = $imap->logout();
    print "Logout: ", $response->status, "-",
        $response->status_text, "\n";
    exit;
}


# Copy the mbox
if (-s $mbox) {
    TransferMbox($imap, $cyrmailbox, $mbox);
}


# Disconnect from IMAP server
$response = $imap->logout();
print "Logout: ", $response->status, "-",
    $response->status_text, "\n";


#
# Get username and password information
#
sub GetLogin {
    my ($username, $password);

    print "Enter your IMAP username: ";
    chop ($username = <STDIN>);
    system "stty -echo";
    print "Enter your IMAP password: ";
    chop ($password = <STDIN>);
    system "stty echo";
    print "\n";
    return ($username, $password);
}


#
# Dump a Unix-style mbox file into a Cyrus folder
#
sub TransferMbox {
    my ($imap, $mailbox, $mboxfile) = @_;

    my $blank = 1;
    my $count = 0;
    my $message = "";
    my $response;

    print "Transferring $mboxfile...\n";
    open(MBOX, $mboxfile);
    while (<MBOX>) {
    if ($blank && /^From /) {
        if ($message) {
        chop $message; # Remove extra blank line before next From
        $response = $imap->append($mailbox, $message) if $count;
        $count++;
```

Example 9-6. The user2cyrus Script (continued)

```
        }
        $message = "";
    }
    else {
        chop;
        s/$/\r\n/;              # IMAP requires CR/LF on each line
        $message .= $_;
    }
    $blank = /^\r$/ ? 1 : 0;
    }
    $response = $imap->append($mailbox, $message) if $count;
    $count++;
    close(MBOX);
    print "Transferred $count messages from $mboxfile to
        $mailbox.\n";
}
```

Batch Conversion: An Example and Tools

Batch conversion from a Berkeley system to a Cyrus system can be done in two different ways:

Extract and copy

Create the complete, empty mailbox hierarchy on the Cyrus server, then split the Berkeley-style folders into separate RFC 822 messages and copy them into the appropriate mailbox on the Cyrus system. Once all messages have been copied, reconstruct each mailbox hierarchy.

Extract and deliver

Similar to extract and copy, but instead of copying the extracted mail messages directly into the Cyrus mailboxes, they are piped into the *deliver* program. *deliver* places the messages in the appropriate mailbox and updates the mailbox header and cache files, making it unnecessary to reconstruct each mailbox hierarchy. There is overhead involved in using *deliver* (the state files must be updated with each message) that makes this method slower than extract and copy.

Batch conversions could be done using a utility similar to the *user2cyrus* utility shown in Example 9-6, but there is a drawback: it's nearly 75% slower in real time than an extract and copy. If you have more than 1,000 users to convert, you should probably rule it out.

The extract and copy method is the most direct and requires the least amount of downtime, making it the best option for large-scale migrations. It saves time by avoiding use of the protocol and a third-party delivery agent and by allowing some of the work (such as creating the mailbox hierarchies) to be done before taking the system down. Because this method directly manipulates the mailbox database, it is also a good opportunity to learn the mechanics of the Cyrus system. For those reasons, we will examine the extract and copy approach.

Procedure

The starting point for the conversion is a text file listing usernames of the accounts to be converted. The procedure for conversion from a Unix to a Cyrus system consists of the following steps:

1. Shut down *imapd* and *sendmail*.

2. Create an IMAP account for each user on the list.

3. Create an empty Cyrus mailbox on the new system for each mail folder that resides on the old system.

4. Transfer messages from the old incoming mailbox to the Cyrus incoming mailbox.

5. Transfer messages from the old mail folders into the new mailboxes on the Cyrus server.

6. Reconstruct the Cyrus *mailboxes* file.

7. Restart *imapd* and *sendmail*.

In the rest of the section, we will walk through an actual conversion, using the tools provided in Appendix A. As we go along, we'll also list the output and results of each step. For simplicity's sake, our example will move only one user. Note that the procedure is the same whether you have a few accounts or thousands (we have run this identical procedure on 20,000 accounts in one batch).

Step 1: Shut down imapd and sendmail

Chaos can result if mail is delivered to the Cyrus system while the conversion is underway. Be sure to turn off both *imapd* and *sendmail* before proceeding any further.

Step 2: Create the new accounts

Creating IMAP accounts in advance can save up to several hours of downtime.

First, save the list of usernames you're going to convert in a text file. We saved the usernames we're converting in a text file called *users.txt*, and that's the file used throughout the examples in this chapter. Once you have your text file, create a Cyrus IMAP account for each user in *users.txt*. This involves two steps:

• *Set up authentication for your users.* If you use Unix authentication, add the users (or NIS/NIS+ usernames or netgroups) to the local password file. If you plan to run your Cyrus system as a black box, assign each user a null shell, such as */bin/false*, to prevent them from logging in and snooping around. If your site authenticates using a SASL mechanism, such as Kerberos or CRAM-MD5, it's not necessary to add the users to the password file. If you use an alternative to Unix authentication, then Unix accounts are not required for your users. Chapter 8 has more information on how to set up authentication for your users.

- *Create an IMAP account for each user.* A handy Tcl script for creating new IMAP accounts, *addusers*, is given in Example 9-1. This step can be performed while both the new and the old systems are up and running:

```
# addusers users.txt
```

The result of Step 2 is that each user on the list now has a top-level mailbox (INBOX) with the default ACL or, in other words, an account on the Cyrus system.

Step 3: Create Cyrus mail folders

The next step, creating empty mailboxes that correspond to folders, is a bit more involved. To understand what the goal is here, see Figure 9-1. The figure shows how *johndoe*'s incoming mailbox and mail folders on a Berkeley mail format system map to Cyrus mailboxes.

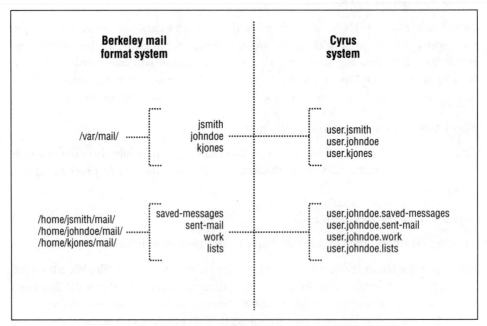

Figure 9-1. Mapping of johndoe's Berkeley mail folders to Cyrus mailboxes

As the figure shows, *johndoe*'s incoming mailbox and each of his folders must be converted into a Cyrus mailbox. The Cyrus mailbox format is different from Berkeley format in several ways. For one, it's hierarchical—the incoming mailbox is the root of the tree, and the folders and sub-folders are branches. The other difference is that Berkeley format mail folders contain many mail messages within a single file, whereas Cyrus folders store each message in a separate file. Another difference is that the Cyrus account holder does not own his own mail folders—they're owned by the Cyrus system. The details of the Cyrus mailbox format were covered in Chapter 6.

Because Cyrus mail format is so different from Berkeley format, some preparation work must be done before you actually create the empty mailboxes. First, you have to find the pathnames of all the Berkeley format folders that belong to the user and map them into mailbox names in the Cyrus namespace. Using *johndoe* as an example, we could look up his home directory in the password file and, knowing that, find all the folders in his *~/Mail* directory, then translate those folder names into Cyrus mailbox names.

The mapping from Berkeley folder names into the Cyrus namespace is accomplished using the Perl script, *bsd2cyrus. bsd2cyrus* does nothing more than formulate a list of Cyrus mailbox names—the output of *bsd2cyrus* is to be fed into another script later on to create the actual mailboxes.

To run the script and redirect its output to a file, *mailboxes.txt* (for later use in the other conversion scripts), use the command:

```
# bsd2cyrus users.txt > mailboxes.txt
```

Save the output of *bsd2cyrus* in a text file and keep it for later reference. Other conversion tools will rely on it for input, and it's the only correlation you'll have between Berkeley folder pathnames and Cyrus mailbox names.

There are several points worth noting about the *bsd2cyrus* script:

- The script expects that each user's mail folders are stored in a subdirectory off the user's home directory on the Berkeley system. In the examples in this chapter, that subdirectory is *~/mail*. The script also expects that the user's home directories will be mounted temporarily on the Cyrus machine for the duration of the conversion.

- There is always the possibility that folders on the Berkeley system may have content that is not RFC 822 compliant (e.g., they might be compressed files, executables, or subdirectories). Such folders are ignored by *bsd2cyrus*. You always have the option of going back and handling the exceptions.

- You may recall from Chapter 6 that Cyrus does not support special characters in mailbox names. *bsd2cyrus* converts all characters except alphabetic characters, digits, underscore, and dash to their ASCII representation preceded by an underscore. For example, user *diannam*'s Berkeley folder name *mail&news* would become *user.diannam.mail_046news* on the Cyrus system (046 is the ASCII representation of the character "&").

The output of the *bsd2cyrus* script will be used as input into two other scripts, which perform the following:

- Create the new, empty folders on the Cyrus system
- Convert the contents of the old BSD mail folders to Cyrus format and insert the mail into the new mailboxes

Let's look at what the *bsd2cyrus* script does. Our user, *diannam*, has several BSD mail folders on the old system:

```
% ls -aF
.                binaryfile*    how spacy    s.me
..               compressed.Z   s!me         same
.hidden          directory/     s&me         saved
Trash            gzip.gz        s*me         sent
```

After running the script, take a look at its output:

```
# cat mailboxes.txt
diannam:user.diannam.Trash:/home/jove/stu/dl0020/mail/Trash
diannam:user.diannam.s_041me:/home/jove/stu/dl0020/mail/s!me
diannam:user.diannam.s_046me:/home/jove/stu/dl0020/mail/s&me
diannam:user.diannam.s_052me:/home/jove/stu/dl0020/mail/s*me
diannam:user.diannam.s_056me:/home/jove/stu/dl0020/mail/s.me
diannam:user.diannam.same:/home/jove/stu/dl0020/mail/same
diannam:user.diannam.saved:/home/jove/stu/dl0020/mail/saved
diannam:user.diannam.sent:/home/jove/stu/dl0020/mail/sent
```

Note that the script is designed to ignore certain files, such as hidden files, directories, binary files, and empty files—that is why some files in the directory are not found in *mailboxes.txt*. As you can see in the output, the script renamed the new folders using the ASCII representation of the special characters.

Next, feed the *bsd2cyrus* output into the *createfolders* script. *createfolders* is a Tcl script that creates empty Cyrus mailboxes. This work must be done with Tcl script, because the command to create a new mailbox on a Cyrus system is a *cyradm* command—you may recall that *cyradm* is an extended Tcl interpreter. The *createfolders* script is shown in Example A-2 in Appendix A.

Here's the output of *createfolders* when we run it on the *mailboxes.txt* file that we saved earlier:

```
# createfolders mailboxes.txt
Connected to IMAP server. Authenticating...
Authentication successful.
Created mailbox user.diannam.sent-mail
Created mailbox user.diannam.saved-messages
Created mailbox user.diannam.same
Created mailbox user.diannam.s_041me
Created mailbox user.diannam.s_052me
Created mailbox user.diannam.Trash
Created mailbox user.diannam.s_046me
Created mailbox user.diannam.s_056me
```

Step 4: Transfer messages from old inbox to new inbox

Now that the framework of mailbox hierarchies is in place, the next step is to populate the top-level mailboxes with messages from the Berkeley inbox on the old system. The *inboxfer* script copies mail from the Berkeley inbox into the Cyrus INBOX. The script is shown in Example A-3. It takes the filename of your list of users (*users.txt* in our examples) as input. The usage is:

```
# inboxfer users.txt
```

Step 5: Transfer messages from old folders to Cyrus folders

Once the Berkeley inboxes have been migrated to the Cyrus system, we turn to the Berkeley-format folders. The script in Example A-5 copies the content of Berkeley-format folders on the old system, converts it to Cyrus-friendly format, and copies it into the appropriate empty Cyrus folder on the Cyrus system. The usage of the *folderxfer* script is:

```
$ folderxfer mailboxes.txt
```

Again, you use the *mailboxes.txt* file that we created with the *bsd2cyrus* script as input.

Step 6: Reconstruct the new mailboxes

The final step once everything has been copied over is to reconstruct each user's mailbox hierarchy. *reconstruct* can only be run as the *cyrus* user, so before running the *reconstruct* command, you must change the ownership of all mailboxes to user *cyrus* and group *mail*:

```
# chown -R cyrus:mail /var/spool/imap/user
```

If you have a large number of users, the *chown* command may take an hour or so to complete. Once the permissions have been changed, run the *batchreconstruct* script shown in Example A-6. The usage is:

```
$ batchreconstruct users.txt
```

Step 7: Restart imapd and sendmail

At this point, all mail has been moved to the Cyrus system. Uncomment the `imapd`
entry in */etc/inetd.conf*, restart *inetd*, and restart *sendmail*.

Backing Out

Things don't always go as planned, and so we provide you with a way to back out
of Cyrus and go back to Berkeley-format mailboxes.

We once began a conversion from the UW server to a commercial IMAP server
based on CMU Cyrus. We were concerned with the amount of time it would take
to convert our 20,000-user base to the new server. The company's technical staff
assured us that, using their conversion tools, it wouldn't take more than a day to
have our users up and running on the new server. We made the very expensive
mistake of blindly trusting their assurances and based our entire plan on their prediction of our downtime. We warned our users of the downtime, prepared our
data, and on the big day, took our old system offline and started the conversion
scripts provided to us by the developers at the company. Twelve hours later, after
only 265 users had been converted, we realized we were in deep water and
decided to back out. Example 9-7 is the script we threw together on the spot and
used to grab the converted mail and put it back where it came from.

Example 9-7. revert

```perl
#!/usr/local/bin/perl

$LOCK_EX = 2;
$LOCK_UN = 8;
$formail = "/usr/local/bin/formail";
$base    = "/var/spool/imap/user";
$spool   = "/var/mail";

open (USERLIST, "$ARGV[0]") || die "$!";

while (<USERLIST>) {

    chop;
    print "$_\n";

    opendir(DIR,"$base/$user") || die;
    @files = readdir(DIR);
    closedir DIR;

    open (BSDMAILBOX,">>$spool/$user") || next;

    foreach $file (@files) {

        next if $file eq '..';
        next if $file eq '.';
```

Example 9-7. revert (continued)

```
        flock (BSDMAILBOX,$LOCK_EX);
        if ($file =~ /\.$/) {

            open(FORMAIL,"$formail < $base/$user/$file |")
                || die;
            while (<FORMAIL>) {
                $_ =~ s/^M//g;
                print BSDMAILBOX $_;
            }
            close FORMAIL;
        }
        flock (BSDMAILBOX,$LOCK_UN);
    }
    close BSDMAILBOX;
}
close USERLIST;
```

After our horrendous experience, we attempted to develop our own conversion tools and give it another try. However, the server's value-added features and proprietary twists kept our conversion code from working as expected. We gave up and installed the open source Cyrus server instead. The tools we developed worked like a charm with Cyrus and gave us more appreciation than ever for the fruits of the open source community.

Mail Forwarding and Filtering on a Black Box

The Cyrus server is intended to run as a black box. Because users have no home directories on the Cyrus server, they cannot enable mail forwarding by creating a *.forward* file.

Forwarding

How is forwarding done without *.forward* files? You guessed it—user mail forwarding is from within the *sendmail aliases* database on a Cyrus system. To make maintenance easier, you can keep the user aliases and the system aliases in separate files:

- System aliases should be kept in the standard */etc/mail/aliases* file.

- Users' mail forwarding orders should be stored in another file (or files), defined in your local *sendmail* configuration.

Let's suppose that we will store users' forwarding orders in an alias file that's named */etc/mail/forward*. The format of the */etc/mail/forward* file is the same as the *sendmail aliases* file format. To activate the */etc/mail/forward* file, edit your M4 file (*sendmail* ships with an example, *cyrusproto.mc*, or you may have rolled your own) and add the following line:

```
define('ALIAS_FILE', '/etc/mail/aliases,/etc/mail/forward')
```

Finally, build a new *sendmail.cf* file and restart *sendmail.* If you don't use an M4 macro to build your *sendmail.cf* file, then edit your *sendmail.cf* file and look for the lines:

```
# location of alias file
O AliasFile=/etc/mail/aliases
```

Change the definition of `AliasFile` to:

```
O AliasFile=/etc/mail/aliases,/etc/mail/forward
```

Because users cannot log in and directly edit their forwarding orders, they need to be allowed to edit their forwarding orders via a web form or some other indirect method.

Migrating existing .forward files to aliases

.forward files have to be taken into account during a conversion process from a Berkeley-style mail system to Cyrus. The Perl script in Example 9-8, *fwd2alias*, finds *.forward* files for a list of users and converts the contents of the *.forward* files into an *aliases* file. Run the script on your Berkeley or UW mail system. The *aliases* file that the script produces should be moved to your Cyrus server's */etc/mail* directory and incorporated into your sendmail configuration as described earlier in this section.

Example 9-8. fwd2alias

```perl
#!/usr/local/bin/perl

open (USERS,"users.txt") || die "$!";
open (OUTFILE,">/tmp/forward") || die "$!";

while (<PR>) {

    chop;
    ($name,$pass,$uid,$gid,$quota,$comment,$gcos,$dir,$shell)
        = getpwnam($_);

    open (FW,"$dir/.forward") || warn "can't open $dir/.forward";
    chop ($address = <FW>);
    print OUTFILE "$_:$address\n";
    close FW;
}
close USERS;
close OUTFILE;
```

.forward support

If you simply must allow use of *.forward* files for one reason or another, then you can mount home directories on the Cyrus server and tweak your *sendmail* configuration to enable support for *.forward* files (*sendmail*'s *cyrusproto.mc* file comes with support for *.forward* files disabled).

To enable *.forward* support, add the users to the */etc/passwd* file, if necessary (for example, if you're using an authentication mechanism that does not require that the users have Unix accounts). *.forward* forwarding will not work unless the users have Unix logins.

Edit your *sendmail* M4 file and find the line:

```
MAILER(cyrus)
```

On the line immediately following, add the statement:

```
define('CYRUS_MAILER_FLAGS','A5@W')
```

The *w* flag tells sendmail that users exist in */etc/passwd* and that it should look for a *~/.forward* in the user's home directory.

Server-Side Mail Filtering with procmail

procmail is a popular Unix mail filtering utility used to perform server-side mail filtering. On Cyrus servers, the mail storage format makes it difficult for individual users to use *procmail* to filter and sort incoming messages into mailboxes. Traditionally, the user invokes *procmail* from their *.forward*, which doesn't exist on a black box server.

We've seen that it is indeed possible to allow users to use *.forward* files with the Cyrus IMAP server. If a user were to invoke *procmail* from a *.forward* file, he would have to use the Cyrus *deliver* program in his *procmail* rules file to deposit mail into his mailbox. In order for that to even be possible, the permissions on the *deliver* program would have to be changed to allow any user to run it (normally, it can only be run by user *cyrus*). Changing permissions in that way puts the integrity of the system at risk—we've mentioned before that the Cyrus system is finicky about ownership and permissions. It also opens a gaping security hole, essentially allowing any user to insert mail into any other user's mailbox by filtering the mail either directly or through an intermediate program.

Obviously, invoking *procmail* out of *.forward* is something to be avoided. Instead, users' mail-filtering rules could be stored centrally in a subdirectory under */var/imap* (the examples in this chapter will be stored under */var/imap/procmail*) and owned by the Cyrus system. To edit his rules, the user would log in to an authenticated CGI that runs as user *cyrus*.

The setup that is described in this section has the following essential features:

- sendmail calls *procmail,* not *deliver,* as a delivery agent.

- *procmail* reads a global *procmail* rules file and calls Cyrus *deliver* from that file to deliver mail.

- The global *procmail* rules file looks to see if the user has a personal rules file and if so, reads the rules in that file and applies them.

Figure 9-2 illustrates the three features. In the figure, the MTA passes the mail message to the delivery agent, *procmail. procmail* filters the message through the global rules file. After processing the message, the global rules file checks whether the recipient has a personal rules file and, if he does, the message is filtered through that file. Finally, the message is dropped into the user's mailbox.

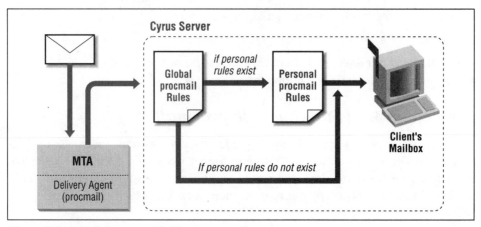

Figure 9-2. Procmail server-side filtering on a Cyrus server

The global procmail rules file

To put *procmail* to work, start by creating a global *procmail* rules file, */var/imap/procmail/procmail.global.* The global rules file contains *procmail* filtering rules that apply to every message that is received by the MTA. The rules in the global file apply to all users. Any mailbox used in a recipe in the global file must already exist—if it does not exist, *deliver* will fail and the message will bounce.

deliver is invoked in the *procmail* rules as:

```
/usr/cyrus/bin/deliver -e -a username -m user.username
```

The *−a* parameter authorizes username (the mailbox owner) to deliver mail to the specified mailbox. Why is the *−a* parameter necessary, you might ask? When *sendmail* invokes *deliver,* it runs the *deliver* process as user *cyrus.* Because *cyrus* owns every mailbox in the Cyrus system, *cyrus* can deliver to any mailbox. In fact, *cyrus* is the only user other than *root* who can deliver to a mailbox. When *deliver* is run outside of *sendmail*, it runs as the user who invoked it. Because the user is not *cyrus*, she can't deliver into any mailbox. *deliver* has to be told to grant authorization to the user to perform the delivery.

An example global rules file is given in Example 9-9. The first rule in Example 9-9 is used during testing—it saves a backup copy of every incoming message in the user's *backup* mailbox (*user.username.backup*). In order to use this rule, the *backup* mailbox *must* exist for every user on the system. Once testing is complete, the backup rule can be commented out.

The variable CYRUSUSER refers to the username of the mail recipient. CYRUSUSER is set by the MTA before *procmail* is called, so the value of CYRUSUSER is available to the filtering script.

Example 9-9. A Global procmail Rules File

```
# File: procmail.global

PATH=/usr/bin:/usr/local/bin:/usr/cyrus/bin
SHELL=/bin/sh
DELIVER=/usr/cyrus/bin/deliver
SPAM=/dev/null

# Make a backup copy of all incoming mail (comment the next entry
# out once you're finished testing procmail integration)
#:0 ic
#| $DELIVER -e -a $CYRUSUSER -m user.$CYRUSUSER.backup

# Execute CYRUSUSER's personal rules
INCLUDERC=/var/imap/procmail/user/procmail.$CYRUSUSER
```

[The user's procmail rules are included (via the INCLUDERC statement above) and executed here. Rules after this point resume after the user's personal rules have been executed.]

```
# Example recipes

# If the "To:" line doesn't exist, it's SPAM
:0:$CYRUSUSER.lock
* !^To:
| $SPAM

# Get rid of SPAM from a specific email address
:0:$CYRUSUSER.lock
* ^To:.*makemoneyfast@aol.com
| $SPAM

# All the mail that falls through to this point
# will be delivered into the user's INBOX
:0:$CYRUSUSER.lock
| $DELIVER -e -a $CYRUSUSER -m user.$CYRUSUSER
```

Personal procmail rules file

Each user has a personal *procmail* rules file. It's stored under */var/imap/procmail/ user/* in the file *procmail.username*. The personal rules file is the file each user edits when he wants to change his filtering rules. If the file exists, the INCLUDERC statement in the global *procmail* rules file runs the rules in the personal file. Example 9-10 shows a simple example of a personal *procmail* rules file.

Example 9-10. A Personal procmail Rules File

```
# File: procmail.username

MAILLISTS=user.$CYRUSUSER.Folders.Mailing_Lists
WORK=user.$CYRUSUSER.Folders.Work

# Filter mailing list messages into the appropriate mailbox

:0:$CYRUSUSER.lock
* (^Cc:|^CC:|^To:|^Sender:).*imap@cac.washington.edu
| $DELIVER -e -a $CYRUSUSER -m $MAILLISTS.imap_list

:0:$CYRUSUSER.lock
* (^Cc:|^CC:|^To:|^Sender:).*root@.*
| $DELIVER -e -a $CYRUSUSER -m $WORK
```

 Remember that mail cannot be delivered to a mailbox unless the mailbox already exists.

For the rules in the previous example to work, the mailboxes *user.username. Folders.Mailing_Lists.imap_list* and *user.username.Folders.Work* must both exist. *deliver* will fail if it cannot find the mailbox it's told to deliver to.

As with mail forwarding, the personal *procmail* files are private to the Cyrus system. In order to edit the rules, the user needs some sort of indirect method, such as a CGI form, to create or modify his rules.

Setting up the MTA

Putting it all into action involves replacing *deliver* with *procmail* as the local delivery agent. As we saw in the example *procmail* rules files, *deliver* is invoked by *procmail*, instead of directly by the MTA.

Edit */etc/sendmail.cf* and look for the section that defines the Cyrus mailer. It will look something like the lines below. If you've customized your *sendmail* configuration, it might look slightly different, but will begin with the identifier "Mcyrus".

```
Mcyrus,     P=/usr/cyrus/bin/deliver, F=lsDFMnPqA5@, S=10, R=20/40, T=X-Unix,
            U=cyrus:mail,
            A=deliver -e -m $h -- $u
```

Comment out that section and add the following lines below it:

```
Mcyrus,     P=/usr/bin/procmail, F=lsDFMnPqA5@, S=10, R=20/40, T=X-Unix,
            U=cyrus:mail,
            A=procmail -p /var/imap/procmail/procmail.global CYRUSUSER=$u
```

The *–p* argument tells *procmail* to preserve the existing environment (see the *procmail*(1) manual page for details on which environment variables are preserved). The last parameter, */var/imap/procmail/procmail.global*, tells *procmail* to use */var/imap/procmail/procmail.global* to determine its filtering behavior. The last parameter, **CYRUSUSER**, sets the CYRUSUSER variable to *username* and passes the variable to *procmail*. CYRUSUSER is used in the *procmail* rules files, as we saw in Example 9-9 and Example 9-10. Once the *sendmail* configuration changes are in place, restart *sendmail* to make the changes active.

Server-Side Filtering with CMU Sieve

CMU Sieve is a server-side mail filtering language and is described in detail in Chapter 15, *Server-Side Mail Filtering*. Sieve is supported in Cyrus releases newer than 1.6.1b and does not require any special installation. Sieve runs out of *deliver* and requires sendmail 8.9 or higher.

Usenet Integration

Cyrus IMAP supports exporting Usenet news groups as mailboxes. If you run an INN server at your site, the Cyrus distribution provides utilities that allow you to integrate Usenet news into Cyrus. INN is beyond the scope of this book—we assume that, if you attempt to integrate news with Cyrus, you have a working knowledge of the INN server.

Programs for News Integration

Four programs, *collectnews*, *rmnews*, *syncnews*, and *feedcyrus* are provided with the Cyrus distribution for managing and integrating newsgroups with Cyrus. The programs are located in */usr/cyrus/bin*. Each command, except *feedcyrus*, is further documented in section 8 of the online manual pages.

collectnews

> *collectnews* adds a list of news articles to the Cyrus auxiliary databases. When *collectnews* comes across a newsgroup that does not have a corresponding IMAP mailbox, it creates one.

rmnews

> *rmnews* removes a list of canceled, superseded, and expired news articles from the Cyrus auxiliary databases and unlinks the article files.

syncnews

> *syncnews* compares the news active file with the full list of IMAP news mailboxes and removes mailboxes that are not found in the active file. If newsgroups in the active file are found that do not have a corresponding mailbox, then the mailbox is created.

feedcyrus

> *feedcyrus* is a shell script that sends news to the Cyrus IMAP server. The script is created during the installation process if the build was configured to support news.

Configuring News

Integrating Usenet with Cyrus is simply done in two steps:

1. Create a partition for the news spool directory.

2. Set up for maintenance of the Cyrus server's auxiliary databases.

 The partition name *news* is reserved specifically for Usenet news. You must name your news partition *news*. Even if you're not integrating news with Cyrus, the partition name *news* cannot be used for any other purpose.

Create the news partition

Select a directory to use as the *news* partition. It should not be the same directory as your INN news spool. In the following example, we selected */var/spool/imap/news* to use as the news partition.

First, create the new partition directory and give ownership to the *cyrus* user:

```
# cd /var/spool/imap
# mkdir news
# chown cyrus imap-news
# chgrp mail imap-news
# chmod 750 imap-news
```

Edit your */etc/imapd.conf* and set the `newsspool` and `partition-news` options as shown in the lines below. `newsspool` is the pathname of your INN news spool directory. `newsprefix` is optional—if you want the name of the news group to appear with a prefix (e.g., "news.comp.mail" instead of "comp.mail"), then set it to your preferred prefix, followed by a ".".

```
partition-news: /var/spool/imap/news
newsprefix: news.
newsspool: /var/spool/news/articles
```

Set up auxiliary databases

The basic setup for news involves granting write access to *cyrus* on the news spool and setting up *cron* entries to feed news to the Cyrus server and synchronize the newsgroups with Cyrus mailboxes.

The Cyrus utilities run as the *cyrus* user and will write to the news spool directory. To make the news spool directory writable by user *cyrus*, add the *cyrus* user to the *news* group and make the news spool directory group writable. In */etc/group*, the line defining the *news* group should appear as follows:

```
news::13:cyrus
```

Change permissions on the news spool to allow group write access:

```
# chmod -R g+w /var/spool/news
```

Update the *newsfeeds* file by adding the following line:

```
collectnews!:*:Tf,WO:collectnews
```

Set up *cron* jobs to maintain the auxiliary databases. The jobs should run as *cyrus*, so as the *cyrus* user, add the *cron* jobs to *cyrus*'s *crontab*. *feedcyrus* should be run every ten minutes. *syncnews*, *collectnews*, and *rmnews* should be run once a day. If necessary, replace */var/news/active* with the pathname of your news active file. The crontab entries are as follows:

```
10,20,30,40,50 * * * * /usr/bin/feedcyrus
0 2 * * * /usr/cyrus/bin/syncnews /var/news/active > /dev/null 2>&1
10 * * * * /usr/cyrus/bin/collectnews
20 2 * * * /usr/cyrus/bin/rmnews </home/news/lib/expire-these.files
```

Troubleshooting

This section describes some problems commonly encountered on Cyrus systems, tells you how to diagnose them, and gives you a fix for one.

Testing the Server

From any account, telnet to the IMAP port on your Cyrus server and issue the IMAP NOOP command:

```
% telnet localhost imap
Trying 127.0.0.1...
```

```
Connected to localhost.
Escape character is '^]'.
* OK venus Cyrus IMAP4 v1.5.14 server ready
. noop
. OK Completed
```

If the server returns the message *OK Completed*, then the server is up and responding. If it returns anything other than *OK Completed*, then there is a problem—check the following:

1. Check that */etc/services* contains an entry for *imap*:

        imap   143/tcp   imap   # IMAP Server

2. Check that an entry for *imapd* exists in */etc/inetd.conf* and that *imapd* runs as the *cyrus* user:

        imap stream tcp nowait cyrus /usr/cyrus/bin/imapd imapd

3. Check the permissions on the *imapd* executable:

    ```
    $ ls -l /usr/cyrus/bin/imapd
    -rwxr-xr-x   1 cyrus    mail   303576 Apr  1 10:07 /usr/cyrus/bin/imapd*
    ```

4. Check permissions on all directories on the path to *imapd*. The *cyrus* user must be able to traverse that path.

User cannot access mailboxes

If the server is up, then the problem is most likely a client configuration. Check to make sure she used the correct syntax to define her mailboxes.

If the syntax is correct, then the user may be trying to access a mailbox for which she has no permissions. In that case, check the ACL on the mailbox.

User stops receiving mail

If the user is able to log in to the server and read his mail, but complains that he has not been receiving mail, then:

1. Make sure *sendmail* is running.

2. Check to see if the user is over quota.

3. Check to see if the user's quota is in a consistent state.

Users are unable to log in

First, determine whether the problem is authentication-related or if the server is not responding. Check the latest entries in */var/log/imapd.log*. If there are more than a few `badlogin` entries, such as this one:

```
May 13 15:21:54 venus imapd[21934]: badlogin: europa [129.120.220.72] plaintext
announce Incorrect password
May 13 15:22:02 venus last message repeated 1 time
```

then the problem is related to authentication. If it does not appear to be an authentication problem, skip this section and read on.

If you use Unix shadow passwords to authenticate users:

1. (Cyrus IMAP Version 1.5.24 and older) Check to see if the *pwcheck* daemon is running. If not, then start it (*etc/init.d/pwcheck start*).

2. Determine whether the user's password has a space character. Space characters are not supported in all IMAP clients.*

If you authenticate users using Kerberos:

1. Check that the */etc/srvtab* file exists.

2. If the file exists, check that the permissions are 0400 (`-r--------`) and that it is owned by user *cyrus* and group *mail*.

3. Run *klist –srvtab*. If either *rcmd* or *imap* are not there, restart the server.

Adding SSL Support to Cyrus

If sending passwords in cleartext across the wire makes you nervous and you don't have the infrastructure to support Kerberos or CRAM, then you can hack SSL support into IMAP as a quick workaround. To take advantage of SSL, you would of course have to use an IMAP client that supports SSL. Currently, your choices are narrow: Netscape Messenger and Outlook Express/Outlook 98. The entire procedure for adding SSL support to IMAP is covered in Appendix B, *Adding SSL Support to IMAP*.

---

* Not all IMAP clients quote the password like they should.

IV

The UW IMAP Server

10

Introduction to the UW IMAP Server

This chapter provides a high-level picture of the University of Washington IMAP server. The server is part of the IMAP4rev1/C-Client Development Environment written by Mark Crispin of the University of Washington. Crispin is also the author of the IMAP RFC itself, as well as several of the ancillary RFCs related to IMAP.

The primary strength of the UW server is its flexibility. While the Cyrus IMAP server has very specific requirements about the format of the mailstore, UW goes to great lengths to support numerous formats. If Cyrus with all its advanced administration and information-sharing features can be thought of as doing a lot with a little bit, UW is the converse, doing a little bit with a lot. UW lacks the application-layer quotas and access-control support of Cyrus, but its ability to handle many different mail formats makes it an attractive choice for sites that have a chaotic mail infrastructure. It's also the best server for sites that need to bring IMAP up in a hurry with a minimum of time spent on configuration and migration.

What Is UW IMAP?

The University of Washington IMAP server (UW IMAP) is an IMAP server that uses *inetd* or a similar Internet superdaemon to provide users IMAP access to a mailstore.

Usually when people refer to UW IMAP, they're referring specifically to the IMAP daemon component of the IMAP4rev1/C-Client Development Environment. The development environment bundle includes an IMAP test utility called *mtest* and an IMAP API library called C-Client. It also includes a couple of POP servers that offer proxy access to your IMAP server through POP, for an easier transition from legacy POP systems. The UW IMAP daemon itself is bundled with the popular PINE mail client and included with many versions of the Linux operating system.

Available in a separate package are the UW IMAP Utilities, a set of tools for managing an IMAP server. The UW IMAP utilities were developed by the University of Washington and based on the C-Client API. They're covered in Chapter 18, *IMAP Tools.*

The UW feature set and design make it well suited for an existing Unix system that wants to add IMAP. It can be used out of the box on any Unix shell user system, without modifications or special infrastructure.

It can also be used for a dedicated IMAP server; however, you may need to start thinking about modifying it if you plan on scaling it to very large user communities. How many UW IMAP users a particular system will support depends greatly on the hardware and the operating system. UW IMAP does not need much in the way of CPU resources, but it does require adequate per-process memory and disk bandwidth. You can have more UW IMAP users on a system than Unix shell users, but within reason: if a particular machine won't handle 5,000 Unix shell users well, don't expect it to handle 100,000 UW IMAP users well.

In general, scaling works better with a cluster of small systems than with a gigantic monolith. A fast CPU is much less important than lots of disk bandwidth. As simple a trick as putting sendmail's */var/spool/mqueue* directory on a different disk than IMAP mailboxes results in significant performance benefits.

The University of Washington serves its community of 80,000 users with a cluster of small, inexpensive IMAP servers, each of which is assigned a portion of the overall user space. The IMAP servers are in a special DNS domain that is tied to UW's account system. User *fred* may be moved to a different IMAP server, but *fred.deskmail.washington.edu* always points to his assigned IMAP server.

Most Unix variants, particularly the open source varieties, typically come with an unlabeled IMAP daemon (*imapd*). Chances are that the daemon is the UW IMAP server. You will probably find no obvious documentation or clues as to the daemon's origins, but if you'd like to identify it as the UW server, there are a couple of things to try. First, look at the server's capabilities:

```
% echo ". CAPABILITY" | /usr/local/sbin/imapd
* OK localhost IMAP4rev1 v12.250 server ready
* CAPABILITY IMAP4 IMAP4REV1 NAMESPACE IDLE SCAN SORT MAILBOX-REFERRALS
LOGIN-REFERRALS AUTH=LOGIN AUTH=ANONYMOUS THREAD=ORDEREDSUBJECT
. OK Completed
%
```

Most IMAP daemons answer the CAPABILITY command with the name of the company or organization that released the daemon. The UW IMAP server doesn't identify itself as belonging to any particular organization. If the server's version number is of the format "v12.NNN" (versions prior to UW IMAP 2000) or the format "v2000.NNN" (UW IMAP 2000), it's most likely the UW server. The SCAN, SORT, and THREAD capabilities are UW experimental capabilities; their presence also suggests that the server is the UW server.

You can also look for artifacts of the UW *phile* driver. The *phile* driver is likely to be found only in software based on the UW C-Client library:

```
% strings /usr/local/sbin/imapd | egrep phile
phile
phile
phile recycle stream
%
```

Be careful, though, because there are likely to be other IMAP servers out there based on the C-Client libraries.

Probably the most interesting and significant fact about the UW IMAP server is that it was written by Mark Crispin, the progenitor of IMAP itself. It's fair to say that Crispin is to the IMAP community as Linus Torvalds is to the Linux community. Crispin invented IMAP entirely on his own, when he was asked to build a distributed mail system with no guidance. He wrote the original IMAP server from scratch in DEC-20 assembly language in 1985. IMAP's early design was strongly influenced by the DEC-20 mail system, of which Crispin was also the primary developer and maintainer. The first nine years of IMAP's development can be attributed entirely to Crispin.

History

The UW IMAP server was first written in November 1990. It took Mark Crispin only a few days to write *imapd*, because he based it on the C-Client library. Quoting Crispin, "If you have the right underlying structures and tools, any project can be reduced to triviality."

imapd didn't include support for traditional Unix mailbox format in its original release. The users of legacy Unix mail programs such as */bin/mail* were clamoring for Unix mailbox support in *imapd*, though. Crispin was reluctant to add Unix mailbox support because of its limitations, such as the inability to have a mailbox open by multiple users simultaneously. He added this support to a later release, though, and support for other mailbox formats followed soon after. The current preferred mailbox format, mbx, continues this tradition.

It's interesting that, from its inception, UW *imapd* supported multiple, simultaneous access to a single mailbox using tenex format, something that was considered impossible on Unix systems.

The C-Client Library

C-Client, also written by Crispin, was originally developed while he worked at Stanford beginning in 1988. C-Client is a C port of an LISP IMAP client, hence its name—it's the C client as opposed to the LISP client.

C-Client is a C API that implements IMAP and SMTP as well as numerous mailbox driver interfaces that read and write different mailbox formats, which we'll talk about in later chapters. The UW IMAP daemon is based on C-Client. Many IMAP client programs are also based on C-Client, including the popular PINE mail client.

You'll find excellent documentation on C-Client included in the UW IMAP source distribution in the file *docs/internal.txt.*

UW's Strengths

UW *imapd* is at once both a kit of sorts and a completely self-contained IMAP server. By kit, we mean that there are adequate mechanisms built into UW IMAP to extend it to use virtually any kind of mailbox or authentication scheme, often with only a relinking required. By self-contained, we mean that it already has support for most authentication and mailbox schemes you're likely to want to use.

Flexibility

The UW server takes a very different approach than the Cyrus server to dealing with mailbox formats. Cyrus understands only one mailbox format. To access a Cyrus mailstore, you're limited to access through the Cyrus server. The UW server, on the other hand, understands many different mailbox formats. It goes to great lengths to detect the format of an existing mailbox and work with it.

The flexibility in mailbox formats can be a major selling point for the UW server. Some sites have users who demand that mail be stored in standard Unix format so that it can be directly manipulated (e.g., with Unix tools like *grep* or with Unix mail clients like *elm*) without using IMAP. With the UW server, the site administrator has the option of leaving the mailstore open to direct access or locking it down to IMAP access only.

You may come across claims that the UW server doesn't perform as well as Cyrus. Most performance comparisons of UW to Cyrus are comparing apples to oranges. The default UW IMAP installation uses traditional Unix mailbox format, where the mailbox is a single file of concatenated messages. Cyrus, on the other hand, stores the mailbox in a slightly modified form of the MH format, where each message is stored in a separate file and tracked in an index file. Cyrus does not have to share its data with legacy mail software, so it doesn't have to make the compromises that the UW server does.

In general, Cyrus is faster than the UW server. However, the UW server can do some things (notably, expunge many messages and search text) faster than Cyrus because it doesn't have to deal with multiple files. Replacing the traditional Unix mailbox format with the *mbx* format helps close the gap. A huge benefit is the support for server-based sorting in the UW server. PINE users who use sorted views will notice much better performance from the UW server than from Cyrus.

So the real answer is, "it all depends."

Modularity

UW IMAP also provides system administrators with a modular system. If you want to write code to provide a value-added service or scale not easily available elsewhere, UW IMAP may be a good choice.

UW's Limitations

All this plug-and-play ability must, of course, come at some price. With UW IMAP, that price is lack of support for some important features and a certain degree of Unix-centricity. Note that we say these are limitations, not necessarily shortcomings. Ultimately the result of the limitations is that UW IMAP is a tightly focused server.

No Support for IMAP Quotas

UW IMAP does not support the RFC 2087 quota extension. That means that, instead of application-specific IMAP quotas, UW IMAP servers must rely on the underlying OS for quotas. The effect is that, with the default Unix MDA, a message delivered to an over-quota UW INBOX is bounced back to the sender. It is not deferred and reattempted later—it bounces hard. On an RFC 2087–compliant server, the message would be held in queue for n days and delivery would be reattempted periodically, until either the usage drops below the quota limit or time runs out and the mail is bounced.[*]

Many system administrators would prefer that UW IMAP included support for IMAP quotas (RFC 2087) because such support would allow a finer degree of granularity over allocating space in the mailstore to users. A user, for example, could have numerous unrelated quotas that apply to different parts of her personal mailstore. The IMAP quota specification provides for not just one quota, but entire hierarchies of quotas. User *joebob* might have a quota of 10 MB on his INBOX, a

---

[*] Such soft bouncing assumes that the system employs a RFC 2087–cooperative Mail Delivery Agent (MDA), such as Cyrus's *deliver* program. The number of days mail is held in queue is, strictly speaking, a Mail Transport Agent (MTA) thing.

separate overall quota of 30 MB on his entire collection of mailboxes including the INBOX, and a further quota of 10 MB on his sent-mail folder.

Many sites' quota needs may be met just fine by using the standard Unix quota facility. Because incoming mailboxes are frequently on different partitions than users' personal mail folders, it's straightforward to use something like *edquota*(1) to assign users one quota for the */var/spool/* partition, which might hold the users' INBOXes, and another quota for the */export/home* partition, which might hold users' personal mailboxes.

The RFC 2087 quota behavior is kinder to the sender and the recipient at the expense of storage and processing resources used to retain and attempt redelivery of the overflow mail in local queues. The UW behavior is kinder to local system resources at the expense of message sender and recipient angst.

You may be stuck on the horns of a dilemma in which you can't do without the distinctive features of UW IMAP, but you've absolutely got to have quotas that result in Cyrus-style soft bounces. In that case, you might be able to cobble something together by chaining two MTAs together, one that houses your destination mailboxes, and the other a queuing host that initially receives all the incoming mail bound for the mailbox host. It's feasible that the MTA on the queuing host could be modified to retain quota bounces from the destination host, retaining them for later attempts. Such wizardry should only be attempted by the pure of heart and strong of spirit, preferably after massive coffee consumption.

No Support for IMAP ACLs

At the time this book was written, UW included no support for IMAP ACLs (RFC 2086). That lack of support means that, instead of using an IMAP client's built-in mechanism to grant or remove access to mailboxes, a user must rely on the operating system's access control mechanisms (e.g., change permissions on a file using *chmod*). Support for IMAP ACLs in the UW server is in the design phase now and will be included in upcoming releases.

Relies Heavily on Unix

Out of the box, UW *imapd* relies very heavily on the underlying Unix operating system structure. For example, you can't have an IMAP user that doesn't also exist in */etc/passwd*. You can't assign a quota that doesn't already exist on a Unix filesystem. And you can't create a hierarchy of mailboxes that doesn't correspond to files and directories in the underlying filesystem.

Note that everything we say about UW *imapd* applies to UW *imapd* straight out of the box unless otherwise noted. Because the server is so flexible, you can make it fit nearly any requirements it doesn't already fit, with some time and code.

UW IMAP Concepts

Black Box and Clearbox Models

We mention black box* and clearbox modes only because, once you unpack the UW IMAP development environment, you're likely to run across several references to a black box mode in the accompanying documentation. You may also see mention of it in discussion lists and, if you're so inclined, in the server source code itself. Clearbox mode, the default, is the mode in which we strongly urge you run UW IMAP. Black box mode has to be explicitly enabled.

References to black box IMAP servers usually occur in two contexts. One context refers to a machine whose mission is solely that of an IMAP server—it does not provide shell, Web, or other Internet services. In the other context, black box refers to a configuration mode and namespace intended solely for internal use at the University of Washington. It's easy to get the impression from the UW documentation that black box is a valid configuration choice for users outside the University of Washington. It's not. UW black box mode was designed for a single server at UW. It is not a general mechanism, nor is it intended as such. UW's public servers don't even use black box mode, even though they are black boxes. Later, we'll give you chapter and verse of the warning from Mark Crispin himself.

In the general context of Internet messaging, though, the black box distinction is usually loose enough to include any server that:

- Has no interactive logins (with the exception of the administrators' accounts)
- Serves up only IMAP and closely related protocols (SMTP, for example)

UW IMAP Namespace

Having hopefully scared you away from attempting to operate the UW server in black box mode, let's talk briefly about the UW IMAP namespace. In the context of IMAP, a namespace is a convention for describing the location of a mailbox in relation to other mailboxes. Some familiar namespaces in other contexts include the Usenet News newsgroup namespace and the DNS domain namespace.

IMAP4 (RFC 2060) doesn't specify a namespace. There is an IMAP Namespace document (RFC 2342) that presents two alternative approaches to the namespace: the Complete Hierarchy model and the Personal Mailbox model. The Personal Mailbox model is used by UW IMAP as the namespace that describes the location

---

* Mark Crispin mentioned these briefly in the course of a discussion on the UW IMAP mailing list concerning the IMAP server namespace in 1997. See *http://www.washington.edu/imap/listarch/ msg02743.html.*

of each individual user's mailboxes in relation to her home directory. UW IMAP uses the Complete Hierarchy model to name shared, public, and anonymous mailboxes relative to the root of the public namespace.

Issuing the IMAP NAMESPACE command to an out-of-the-box UW IMAP server results in something like the output below:

```
# telnet localhost imap
Trying 127.0.0.1...
Connected to localhost.
Escape character is '^]'.
* OK localhost IMAP4rev1 v12.250 server ready
. login kwm xxxxxxxxx
. OK Completed
. namespace
* NAMESPACE (("" "/")("#mhinbox" NIL)("#mh/" "/")) (("~" "/"))
(("#shared/" "/") ("#ftp/" "/")("#news." ".")("#public/" "/"))
. OK Completed
. logout
* BYE myhost.unt.edu IMAP4rev1 server terminating connection
. OK Completed
Connection closed by foreign host.
```

The NAMESPACE command returns a list of namespaces (e.g., ("#mh/" "/")). Each namespace consists of the namespace's name and a hierarchy separator. The hierarchy separator is a character used in a mailbox name to delimit different levels in the mailbox hierarchy. Take the "~" namespace, for example: a mailbox in that namespace would have a name like *~/mail/saved-messages*.

In the previous example, the logged-in user *kwm* has at least eight namespaces available, most of which have "/" as a hierarchy separator, but one of which uses ".". Within the context of this example, then, *#shared/yippie/tie/yie/yea/* is a syntactically valid mailbox name, whereas *#news/comp/dcom/telecom* isn't.

Onward to the individual namespaces of UW IMAP:

INBOX

The INBOX appears as the first token, ("" "/"), in the output of the NAMESPACE command. As specified in section 5.1 of RFC 2060, this special reserved name is a token that stands for "the primary mailbox for this user on this server." UW IMAP even uses some elementary heuristics to try and figure out what mailbox type (Unix, mmdf, mbx, etc.) the user is given to using so it can apply the appropriate mailbox driver.

#mhinbox

This special name tells UW IMAP to assume that the INBOX is in MH format. Because the INBOX occupies only one level of the hierarchy, there is no hierarchy separator, hence the NIL. UW IMAP includes MH implementation to support legacy mailboxes only. If you really want to use an MH format INBOX, then you have to use *#mhinbox*.

#news

> This name permits reading of a local news spool. *#news.alt.sysadmin.recovery*,
> for example, would present the contents of the *alt.sysadmin.recovery* news-
> group as if it were a read-only IMAP mail mailbox. You can also substitute the
> stock driver for one that makes UW IMAP use *#news* as a proxy NNTP server.

#ftp

> *#ftp* is a way to download files from the anonymous FTP directory using
> IMAP. The mailbox *#ftp/pub/messages* actually points to and serves up the file
> *~ftp/pub/messages*. This capability is typically used to serve up one or more
> mailboxes to users who aren't necessarily provisioned at your site.

#public

> Another anonymous login name. This is different from *#ftp* in that it serves a
> directory dedicated to IMAP. This would be good for data you want to serve
> through IMAP only, not through FTP.

#shared

> *#shared* is like *#public*, except that *anonymous* IMAP users cannot access
> *#shared*, whereas they can access *#ftp* and *#public*.

~/ (tilde expansion)

> UW IMAP supports the use of a tilde (~) to indicate files in the home direc-
> tory of the logged-in user. Ordinarily, users of multiuser systems keep their
> mailboxes in a directory somewhere south of their top-level home directory.
> Something along the lines of *~/mail/* or *~/Mail/* is probably more useful than
> browsing through the top-level files in the user's home directory.

Remote names

> Using the remote names convention, UW IMAP can be turned into an IMAP,
> POP3, or NNTP proxy. A mailbox specification like *{news.myisp.net/*
> *nntp}comp.mail.imap* can be used to present a Usenet newsgroup in the same
> way any mailbox is presented in your MUA. Likewise, you can use the same
> method to pull up your POP3 mailbox or another IMAP mailbox.

C-Client Drivers

The University of Washington IMAP can be thought of as the *emacs* of IMAP servers. *emacs*'s power lies in the fact that it knows little or nothing about individual
terminal types—instead, it interfaces to the *curses* API and the Termcap/Terminfo
capability databases, which are easy to use and know about a wide variety of ter-
minals. At its core, UW IMAP doesn't access mailboxes directly. Instead, it makes
calls to the C-Client API. C-Client is an API that uses numerous modular drivers to
perform mailbox operations (see Figure 10-1).

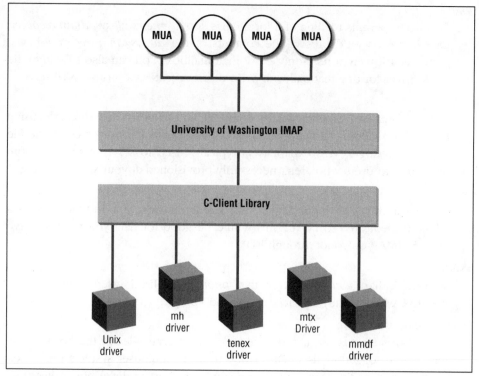

Figure 10-1. C-Client API

Modularity is one of the primary strengths of UW IMAP. In the default clearbox mode, which is the mode all but a handful of people should use, the server goes through some simple heuristics to try and match up the mailbox in question with the correct mailbox driver. In order, it tries to match the mailbox with mbox, mx, mbx, tenex, mtx, mmdf, Unix, and, finally, just plain flat file formats. One of the drivers is selected if certain expected files are present and are in the anticipated format. For example, if mbox, mx, and mbx selection fail, the server would next check to see if file ~/*mail.txt* exists and is either empty or in tenex format. If it did exist and it was empty or in tenex format, then UW IMAP would select the tenex driver and proceed.

Authentication and Authenticator Modules

Another strength of UW IMAP is its ability to use additional authenticator modules. By default, the MD5 and Unix standard authentication types are included at build time. Inclusion of Kerberos 4, OTP, S/Key, or other types of authentication schemes can be accomplished by adding a third-party authenticator module.

Your selection of an authentication method directly impacts two features of your mail service: scalability and security. It affects your scalability because different components of different authentication mechanisms begin to break down at different sizes. The flat file, */etc/passwd*, begins to become quite difficult to provision after a certain number of users. Exactly how many depends on the operating system; on some systems it is as low as 10,000 users. The kernel structure defining the number of hard links to any given directory is a fixed number of bits wide (usually 32). That places a fixed limit on the number of users you can have in a non-hashed home directory structure. Component limits like this impact your choice of what authentication mechanisms scales best for you.

The far more obvious impact of your authentication mechanism choice is on security. Depending on the scheme you use, you could be tossing a copy of your front door key into the street every time you enter your home. If you use Unix authentication, you're exposing yourself to the single biggest vulnerability on most IMAP servers: the use of cleartext passwords. More and more people are hopping on the Internet. An increasing number of those people are running mail clients to check for new mail (and sending a cleartext password over the Net in the process) every 5 or 10 minutes. The Net is becoming a gold mine for passwords.

The IETF is working to remedy the situation by refusing to standardize protocols that rely on cleartext authentication. In the meantime, you can do your part to help. If you simply must use a cleartext password, engineer a provisioning system so that it precludes reusing your mail password on any other system. Or employ a virtual private network (VPN) mechanism, such as Point-to-Point Tunneling Protocol (PPTP), Secure Shell (SSH), or Secure Socket Layer (SSL), to encrypt the path between your mail client and the mail server. Webmail is another option. You could install a web-based IMAP client (such as IMP or WING*), run the HTTP server with SSL, and keep the IMAP server and the web server on the same machine. Passwords will then travel from the web server to the IMAP server over the machine's loopback interface and will not travel the Net.

Addition of both drivers and authenticators is accomplished by including them in the EXTRAAUTHENTICATORS= or EXTRADRIVERS= lines of the top-level makefile. Some drivers or authenticators may require that you add or patch code in your build tree before rebuilding IMAP to accommodate their product.

---

* See Chapter 5, *Web-Based IMAP Clients*, for a discussion of webmail.

Logging

There are various ways to keep track of what's going on with your UW server. It's likely that you'll want to log its messages to *syslog*.

Here are the kind of *syslog* entries you can expect from UW IMAP. Typically, they're logged to facility *mail* and level *debug*.

The following entry is generally the first log entry you'll see. It means the LISTEN on the IMAP TCP port established a connection with a remote machine, in this case, 10.120.220.41:

```
Jun  9 14:55:14 nec imapd[14506]: imap service init from 10.120.220.41
```

The following sequence typifies the trail left behind by IMAP login successes and failures:

```
Jun  5 23:24:40 nec imapd[27712]: Login user=kwm host=raz.unt.edu [10.120.110.4]
Jun  9 11:33:49 nec imapd[11568]: Authenticated user=kwm host=raz.unt.edu
    [10.120.110.4]
Jun  7 22:32:36 nec imapd[5310]:  Login failure user=ANONYMOUS host=localhost
    [127.0.0.1]
Jun  5 23:19:07 nec imapd[27668]: Logout user=kwm host=grove.acad.unt.edu
    [10.120.220.41]
```

As usual, some stuff will always fall on the floor:

```
Jun  9 14:39:53 nec imapd[14429]: Autologout user=??? host=raz.unt.edu
    [10.120.110.4]
Jun  5 23:17:26 nec imapd[27652]: command stream end of file,
    while reading char user=??? host=localhost [127.0.0.1]
Jun  9 16:09:39 nec imapd[19284]: AUTHENTICATE LOGIN failure
    host=grove.acad.unt.edu [10.120.220.41]
Jun  5 23:17:24 nec imapd[27652]: Missing command before authentication
    host=localhost [127.0.0.1]
Jun 10 00:48:44 nec imapd[29142]: Connection reset by peer, while reading
    line user=kwm host=grove.acad.unt.edu [10.120.220.41]
```

Installing TCP Wrappers (*tcpd*) is also a good step. The *tcpd* wrapper daemon has a facility for variable expansion in commands given at connect time. For example, if you put an entry like the following in your */etc/hosts.allow* file:

```
ALL: ALL: (logger -p auth.debug -t "tcp_wrapper[$$]" \
"client(%a), \
client info(%c), \
daemon(%d), \
client address (%h), \
client hostname (%n), \
daemon PID (%p), \
server info (%s), \
client username (%u).\
")&
```

your *syslog* log file will then begin to accumulate log entries like the following:

```
Jun 10 23:26:45 nec tcp_wrapper[1961]: client(10.120.220.41),
     client info(grove.acad.unt.edu), daemon(imapd),
     client address (grove.acad.unt.edu), client hostname (grove.acad.unt.edu),
     daemon PID (1960), server info (imapd@raz.unt.edu),
     client username (29009).
```

Of course, there's the ultimate in logging—the protocol analyzer. One non-open source alternative that is included with every copy of Solaris is *snoop*. The following is a command line that would help watch an IMAP session between two hosts. The *−x 54* tells *snoop* to dump the contents of each packet in classical hexdump format with hex on the left and the ASCII translation on the right, but skipping the first 54 bytes of overhead. The *port imap* means "display all packets using the port assigned to 'imap' in the */etc/services* file." It's assumed that, barring the use of *−d <device>*, the primary network interface is used.

```
# snoop -x 54 port imap

grove.acad.unt.edu -> raz.unt.edu  TCP D=143 S=49462
     Ack=3848578507 Seq=3307990424 Len=17 Win=8760
          0: 3030 3030 3030 3133 204c 4f47 4f55 540d    00000013 LOGOUT.
         16: 0a                                          .

   raz.unt.edu -> grove.acad.unt.edu TCP D=49462 S=143
     Ack=3307990441 Seq=3848578507 Len=0 Win=8760

   raz.unt.edu -> grove.acad.unt.edu TCP D=49462 S=143
     Ack=3307990441 Seq=3848578507 Len=89 Win=8760

          0: 2a20 4259 4520 6e65 632e 756e 742e 6564    * BYE raz.unt.ed
         16: 7520 494d 4150 3472 6576 3120 7365 7276    u IMAP4rev1 serv
         32: 6572 2074 6572 6d69 6e61 7469 6e67 2063    er terminating c
         48: 6f6e 6e65 6374 696f 6e0d 0a30 3030 3030    onnection..00000
         64: 3031 3320 4f4b 204c 4f47 4f55 5420 636f    013 OK Co
         80: 6d70 6c65 7465 640d 0a                      mpleted..
```

A bit of street wisdom here—commercial protocol analyzers are some of your more expensive toys. You might want to exploit the full capability of things like *snoop, tcpdump, ethereal,* and other open source or easily available packages before you decide that the added bit of functionality is worth the cost.

Does UW IMAP Match Your Needs?

Many sites select UW for its simplicity. For many system administrators, the ability to just slap an entry into your *imapd.conf* file and have a functional IMAP server with literally no time spent on configuration is highly attractive.

If a large proportion of your Unix users access traditional Unix mail directly or with native mail clients, UW will allow you to gradually move the users from traditional Unix mail access methods to IMAP. UW lets you add IMAP to the mix without taking anything away. As we'll see a few chapters later, the Cyrus IMAP server requires "all or nothing." The only way to access Cyrus mailboxes is via IMAP— direct access is not possible because the mailboxes are owned by the Cyrus system and are invisible to normal users.

If you have mailstores in two or more formats or you need to have shell account access to your mailstore, UW is probably the best choice. If you have a modest number of users (under 15,000, say) and can suitably work around the lack of ACL and IMAP quota support, then UW IMAP will probably work for your site.

If you need something that scales to many users more easily, then Cyrus is the best choice. Cyrus fits better because of ACL and IMAP quota support. If you have no need for simultaneous shell account and IMAP access to the same mailboxes, then you would probably be better served by Cyrus.

A typical growth path for an email infrastructure goes something like this:

- The first email system is usually something largely proprietary, either loosely based on Internet standards or not based on Internet standards at all: Group-Wise, Notes, or Exchange.

- The day of open standards reckoning arrives, and open source Internet email systems start replacing the old proprietary ones. Until recently, this was very likely to be a POP3 server. Now, that's only somewhat likely.

- The single-mode POP3 server starts to grate on users' nerves when they have to search around for the PC they were using when they last downloaded individual pieces of mail. They will beg for IMAP as they struggle with mail in Netscape on one machine, Pegasus mail on another, and a handful of messages they accumulated during their vacation in Yahoo! Mail.

- The company has been bought out five times in as many years, with a couple of mergers thrown in for fun. UW IMAP isn't supporting the patchwork quilt mail system as well as you'd like, so you design a new system from scratch using Cyrus IMAP that should last through the next dozen mergers.

Everyone has heard the old saw: "The only hard and fast rule is that there are no hard and fast rules." It applies equally well to choosing an IMAP server. We're not just trying to play it safe by saying that. UW IMAP and Cyrus are both strong packages with a great deal of overlap and some definite cultural differences. A good way to think of it might be to see UW IMAP as being the Apache of Unix IMAP servers and Cyrus as being the Netscape. Large and small sites use each, but trying to say which is better is like choosing which of the Mac or the PC is better.

To help you decide whether you prefer UW or Cyrus, Table 10-1 gives a comparison of the features listed with the IMAP CAPABILITY command of Cyrus v1.5.14 and UW IMAP v4.7.

Table 10-1. A Comparison of Some Cyrus and UW Features

Feature	Cyrus IMAP v1.5.19	UW IMAP v4.7
Protocol Revision	IMAP4rev1	IMAP4rev1
IMAP4 ACL Extension (RFC 2086)	✓	Not supported
IMAP4 QUOTA Extension (RFC 2087)	✓	Not supported
IMAP4 IDLE Command (RFC 2177)	Not supported	✓
IMAP4 Mailbox Referrals (RFC 2193)	Not supported	✓
IMAP4 Login Referrals (RFC 2221)	Not supported	✓
IMAP4 Namespace (RFC 2342)	✓	✓
IMAP SORT Extension (Draft)	Not supported	✓
IMAP THREAD Extension (Draft)	Not supported	✓

Here's a more detailed description of the features listed in Table 10-1:

RFC 2086 (ACL Extension)
> RFC 2086 provides a system for associating access controls with users and mailboxes that are wholly separate from the rights that may be present in the underlying operating systems. Access rights such as lookup, read, keeping seen/unseen information across sessions, write, insert, post, create, delete, and administer are associated with user/mailbox pairs.

RFC 2087 (Quota)
> RFC 2087, known as the Quota Extension, permits servers to place limits on user resource usage. In theory, limits may be placed on any practical resource consumed by IMAP operations. In practice, quotas are usually limited to restrictions on disk usage. Quotas are not necessarily all encompassing, but are applied to one or more "quota roots," which are arbitrary points in a user's namespace, below which her quotas are inherited unless new quota roots with different sets of quotas are encountered.

RFC 2177 (Idle)
> RFC 2177 provides a way for the IMAP server to know that it can asynchronously give "EXISTS" responses without being periodically polled to do so (e.g., with a NOOP command). The client can go into idle mode, then after some period of time, return from idle mode by sending a DONE. After leaving idle mode, the client receives all the EXISTS responses that may have queued up during the idle interval because the size of the SELECTed or EXAMINEd mailbox changed.

RFC 2221 (Login Referral)

RFC 2221 gives an IMAP server the ability to authenticate a user, then direct him to a new mailbox, essentially saying, "Yeah, I know you're legit, but you're supposed to get your mail down the hall now." Login Referral capability is useful for sites that split their user base out over numerous mail servers, using the front-door mail processor as a kind of connection multiplexer.

RFC 2193 (Mailbox Referral)

The Mailbox Referral capability, as specified in RFC 2193, gives a kind of symbolic linking capability to individual mailboxes. Thought of another way, it does for mailboxes what RFC 2221 does for entire sessions. With this capability, users may find that their shared folders, or perhaps their personal folders over a given size threshold, have been moved to *BigMailServer@example.com* and will be automatically redirected accordingly.

RFC 2342 (Namespace)

The Namespace capability (RFC 2342) provides a method for clients to discover the symbolic descriptions of the various namespaces used on a given server. Servers that implement this command probably require less user configuration on the client end to get their users up and running.

Draft: IMAP SORT Extension

The IMAP SORT extension is a standard for sorting messages on the server instead of the client.

Draft: IMAP THREAD Extension

The IMAP THREAD extension provides for a threaded view with the server doing the threading instead of the client.

When choosing between Cyrus and UW, remember that, although Cyrus gives you one choice of mailstore format, UW gives you many choices. As you will read in the file *docs/drivers.txt,* in the UW server the various mailbox drivers vary in performance from very good to very poor and have some unique characteristics. It would be an unfair test to pit Cyrus against UW with one of its poorly performing mailbox drivers.

Unfortunately, although you might want to compare Cyrus with UW using its mh driver, the mh driver is listed as being a very poor performer. A better test would be to use the mtx or mbx driver, both of which permit concurrent read-write operations and are listed as very good performers. The University of Washington prefers mbx format.

Late-Breaking Note

When we went to press, the University of Washington was in the early stages of releasing the next major versions of their server, UW IMAP 2000. Here's a preview of the major differences between UW IMAP 2000 and the previous 4.x release:

- **Integrated SSL, TLS, and STARTTLS functionality.** SSL and TLS/STARTTLS functionality are integrated into UW IMAP 2000 by means of the OpenSSL package, available from *http://www.openssl.org/*. TLS is the next generation version of SSL. UW neither supplies nor supports the OpenSSL package, but the UW IMAP does dovetail with it to provide end-to-end encrypted IMAP service, with encryption of both authentication and data. A new document, *docs/SSLBUILD*, conveys the mechanics of how to bring up UW with this capability.

  There are two advantages to doing SSL/TLS this way rather than with *stunnel*. One of the benefits is process economy. Instead of each *imapd* process having a corresponding *stunnel* process, both the SSL/TLS and IMAP functions are carried out by the *imapd* process. Another is that instead of having only SSL functionality, the OpenSSL-enabled *imapd* has SSL and TLS functionality, which includes support for STARTTLS—which, in turn, enables a session to begin in unencrypted mode, then transition cleanly to encrypted mode.

- **Improved C++ Compatibility.** Historically, C++ developers who build their own C-Client applications and servers with the C-Client Toolkit have had a moderate amount of difficulty getting C-Client to build as well with C++ as with a standard C compiler. A new header file, *c-client. h*, greatly reduces or eliminates that problem.

- **Kerberos Version 5.** UW IMAP 2000 will support Kerberos v5 in both Unix and Win32 builds. If you build it for Windows 2000 or Windows ME, Kerberos v5 is enabled automatically. Kerberos v4 is not directly supported by UW in IMAP 2000.

- **The IMAP Administrator.** Starting in UW IMAP 2000, UW IMAP has the feature of an IMAP Administrator. By using this feature, a system administrator can log in by giving her user ID and password, but indicate a different user and actually be logged in as that user, although she is using her own password. If your site supports the "SASL authorization identity," you can use that to emulate *su* functionality in IMAP to let you troubleshoot another person's mailbox without having to know his passwords.

—Continued—

Only users who are in the Unix group *mailadm* can use this facility. If your site doesn't support the SASL authorization identity mechanism, you can separate your authorization identity from your authentication identity with an asterisk. The authorization identity is the identity of the user whose mailbox you are examining, and the authentication identity is your own user ID. The credentials would be the password you normally use to gain access to the server. For example, if you are user *helpdesk* and you are troubleshooting the mailbox for user *enduser*, you would log in as *enduser*helpdesk*. The "*" hack works for all UW IMAP authenticators, such as MD5 and Kerberos.

- **Support for the MULTIAPPEND extension.** In draft status at the time of publication, this extension permits an arbitrary number of messages to be appended to a mailbox in a single atomic action. They either all succeed or all fail uniformly. The draft is available at *http://search.ietf.org/internet-drafts/draft-crispin-imap-multiappend-01.txt.*

11

Installing UW IMAP

Installing UW IMAP is easier than installing your average MS-Windows package. If you've got a few essential skills, you should not only be able to easily pull down the current UW package, but upgrade it as frequently as you desire.

With UW, compatibility is the name of the game. Unadulterated, UW IMAP runs on a wide variety of hardware and talks to an equally wide variety of mailstores. Chances are, you can just compile the thing, slap the necessary entries into your */etc/services* and */etc/inetd.conf* files, restart *inetd,* and you're in business. On a good day you may be able to go from no IMAP to a completely installed UW IMAP server inside 15 or 20 minutes.

Where Do You Get UW IMAP?

The procedures we outline in this section are for retrieving, compiling, and installing the latest source code to UW IMAP. Before we launch into that, it bears mentioning that you *can* get prebuilt binaries of the UW server, we just don't recommend it. It's our experience that just about everything runs cleaner if you build it either on the system on which it will eventually run or on one very nearly like it.

If you insist, however, prebuilt binaries are available at *ftp://ftp.cac.washington. edu/pine/unix-bin/* as *imapd-bin.<machine_type>* (where <machine_type> is probably one of *aix, du, hpux, linux, next, sgi, solaris, sun,* or *ultrix*).

Further discussion of what kind of prebuilt binaries are available may be found at *ftp://ftp.cac.washington.edu/pine/README.*

Eager Linux types can, of course, find an appropriate RPM* file at *http://rufus.w3.org/linux/RPM/Server_Mail.html*, download it over a speedy Internet connection, and install it on their machine inside of a minute or so. Once you've gotten your sea legs with UW IMAP, however, you'll probably find it worth your while to rebuild from source.

When you do build from source, the obvious first thing you'll need will be the UW IMAP source distribution. The canonical URL for the most recent version is *ftp://ftp.cac.washington.edu/imap/imap.tar.Z*. If you find that link stale, your two next best bets are to check the UW IMAP Information Center at *http://www.washington.edu/imap/* or The IMAP Connection at *http://www.imap.org/* for pointers to the right link.

Download the latest version of the IMAP source distribution using anonymous FTP. Put the distribution *tar* file in the working directory in which you will build the software, then decompress and unpack the *tar* file:

```
% zcat imap.tar.Z|tar xvf -
```

Note that if you've got the Lynx browser installed, you can save a few steps by downloading the IMAP distribution using the *lynx −dump* command:†

```
% lynx -dump ftp://ftp.cac.washington.edu/imap/imap.tar.Z | uncompress | tar xvf -
```

In the directory where you unpacked the software, you should have a top-level directory named for the current version of the IMAP package:

```
% ls -ld imap-*
drwxr-xr-x   9 104      wheel        4096 May 23 08:35 imap-4.7c
```

Inside that directory, you'll find a README file; a documentation directory; make-files for Windows NT, Windows NT with Kerberos, Windows CE, and Unix; the source tree; and a tools directory for tools generated as part of the build process:

```
% cd imap-4.5
% ls -FaCs
total 64            4 CONTENTS     2 docs/        4 makefile.wce
   2 ./            28 Makefile     6 makefile.nt  2 src/
   2 ../            6 README       6 makefile.ntk 2 tools/
```

---

* RPM stands for Red Hat Package Manager. Like the Carnegie Mellon University *depot* system, it's a widely used method for retrieving software and other files from remote archives and installing them locally. To date, although RPM is attempting wider acceptance and is an open and flexible enough architecture to do so, its primary following is concentrated in the Linux community.

† At-length proselytization about the way-cool all-around utility of Lynx is somewhat beyond the scope of this chapter. Lynx is available from *http://lynx.browser.org/*. *lynx −dump* is rather like */usr/bin/cat* for the Web. It's a pretty groovy way of scriptifying or just simplifying downloads from remote archives like web or FTP sites.

Keeping Current

You'll want to keep current on which release and version of UW IMAP is the latest and what features it has. Before going any further, we should explain the numbering system for IMAP release and version numbers. Release numbers take the form MAJOR [.MINOR] [.STATUS], where MAJOR is the major version number, MINOR is the minor version number, and STATUS is an optional status for pre-releases. STATUS is usually either blank (meaning final), beta, or alpha. Version numbers likewise take the form MAJOR [.EDIT]. MAJOR is the major version number, and EDIT is a number that is incremented each time the *imapd.c* source file is edited. Changes in the release number indicate that a change could have taken place anywhere in the UW IMAP Toolkit. Changes in the version number indicate that a change in *imapd.c* only has taken place.

If you run across a bug, you'll probably want to check the latest release to see if the bug has been addressed. Barring bug fixes, whether or not you want to upgrade to a newer version of UW IMAP probably depends on the feature set of the revision in question. A good way to compare revisions is to check the contents of *docs/RELNOTES* in the distribution. If a change hasn't made it into that document, check the archives of the C-Client mailing list. More on that list later.

There are two ways to find out the version of a given distribution of the UW IMAP server. One is to install it, then *telnet* into the port onto which you've installed the server and see what the prompt says.

Here's an example of finding Version 12.250 on the local host:

```
% telnet localhost imap
Trying 127.0.0.1...
Connected to localhost.
Escape character is '^]'.
* OK localhost IMAP4rev1 v12.250 server ready
. logout
* BYE nec.unt.edu IMAP4rev1 server terminating connection
. OK Completed
Connection closed by foreign host.
```

and Version 10.231 on a UW host:

```
% telnet ftp.cac.washington.edu imap
Trying 140.142.4.227...
Connected to ftp.cac.washington.edu.
Escape character is '^]'.
* OK ftp2.cac.washington.edu IMAP4rev1 v10.231 server ready
. logout
* BYE ftp2.cac.washington.edu IMAP4rev1 server terminating connection
. OK Completed
Connection closed by foreign host.
```

A less strenuous method would be to search through *src/imapd/imapd.c* in your distribution and look for the line containing "*version". This line:

```
char *version = "12.250";        /* version number of this server */
```

comes from a 12.250 version.

Significant new versions are always announced to the IMAP Interest List. We'll give you various ways to participate in this list later on. First, let's get down to building some software.

What Systems Does It Support?

UW IMAP supports many platforms. With little or no modification, the UW software will build on:

A/UX

AIX (generic; 3.2; 4.1; AIX/370; 2.2.1 for RT)

Altos SVR4 (generic; with GCC)

AmigaDOS (with a 68020+; using AS225R2; with a 680x0 using "new" socket library)

AOS for RT

Atari ST Mint

BSD (generic; BSD/i386 3.0 and higher; FreeBSD; OpenBSD; NetBSD)

Bull DPX/2 B.O.S.

Convex

Data General DG/UX (up to 5.4)

Dynix, EP/IX

HP-UX (9.x with and without GCC; 10.x with and without GCC; 10.x with DCE security)

ICL DRS/NX

Interactive Systems OS

Linux (with Pluggable Authentication Modules (PAM) and with traditional passwords and crypt() in the C library)

LynxOS

MachTen, NEXTSTEP (3.x;)

OSF/1(Digital Unix) (Version 4)

PTX, Pyramid, SCO Open Server (5.0.x GCC 2.7.1*)

Solaris using GCC

Sun OS using GCC

RISC Ultrix (DEC-5000) using GCC

---

* Crispin notes in the Makefile: "(95q4 from Skunkware _not_ 98q2!)". He tells us that he doesn't know what that means, but probably it's meaningful to an SCO Open Server site.

What Hardware?

You name it! Everything from mainframes running AIX/370; PCs running all flavors of BSD, Linux, SolarisX86, NextStep, or SCO Open Server; Macintoshes running A/UX, and, of course, the large numbers of native Unix machines running
Solaris, AIX, HP/UX, Sun OS, etc. Efforts are even under way to complete a port to
Windows CE, just in case you want to run an IMAP server in your pocket!*

What Else Do You Need?

You'll need a compiler.† That's about it. Of course, your IMAP server would be
rather atypical if it didn't have a mailstore to serve, but strictly speaking, there's
nothing to keep you from using it without a mailstore. In fact, one possible configuration might be to use a single UW IMAP server as a kind of multiplexer to other
IMAP and NNTP servers. Although the UW server doesn't directly support this
functionality as distributed, as the output from the CAPABILITIES command might
lead you to believe, accommodations are made for those who want to add their
own code to provide this function. We'll discuss those a little later on in the configuration section.

What Do You Get with UW IMAP?

After building the UW IMAP server, you will find the following programs in the
source tree:

mtest

> The C-Client test bed program. This is a fairly simple command-line testing
> program for IMAP servers. We'll get into the specifics of using this utility in the
> UW system administration chapter. *mtest* is largely useful to developers using
> the C-Client library who want to test new mailbox drivers, system administra-
> tors troubleshooting an IMAP client/server issue who want an IMAP-specific
> protocol analyzer, or anyone who simply wants to learn more about what
> happens "on the wire" between an IMAP client and server.

ipop2d and ipop3d

> These are Post Office Protocol servers (Versions 2 and 3, respectively) that you
> can run on your mail server to provide POP access to any IMAP server. If a

---

* WinCE will potentially be run on desktop machines as well, but saying "I have an IMAP socket in my
 pocket 'cause I thought it was cool" just has a certain ring to it.

† If you're considering any other compiler, especially a C compiler, give GCC a shot first. It compiles programs in C, C++, Objective C, Ada 95, Fortran 77, and Pascal, and runs on a variety of systems ranging
 the vast majority of Unix and Unix-like systems to Windows NT/95 and VMS. See *http://gcc.gnu.org/* for
 more information.

given INBOX is accessed by the POP daemon before IMAP, then IMAP will access it in read-only mode. If IMAP gets to it first, POP access will fail with an access error.

imapd

The IMAP4rev1 daemon. The likely reason why you're mucking about with all this stuff in the first place. A perfectly acceptable course of action for many folks with nothing-out-of-the-ordinary Unix boxes is to build the software, throw a reference to it in */etc/inetd.conf,* and be up and running.

The C-Client library (c-client.a)

The heart of the IMAP package. All the other software in this package uses the C-Client library, and it's the API this library provides that gives UW IMAP its mailbox flexibility and extensibility.

Important Documents

The README in the top-level directory boils down the Unix install to five steps. If you've installed *inetd* services and built open source software before, you can use that quick-start list or the slightly less terse version in *docs/BUILD* to bring everything up in five minutes or so.

If you stray from the minimalist path, you're likely to find that some of the features aren't as well documented as you'd like. A post to the C-Client mailing list is likely to get a speedy answer, usually from Crispin himself. Many of the folks on C-Client like it to remain a fairly low-traffic list, however, so try to exhaust the local docs and the mailing list archives before you post. Here's an annotated list of the local docs you'll have in your archive:

CONTENTS

An overview of what you'll find where in the IMAP Toolkit tree.

README

Quick build notes and miscellaneous notes.

docs/BUILD

Notes on building the Toolkit for most major platforms.

docs/drivers.txt

Definitely one of the more valuable docs in this Toolkit. It walks you through the heuristics C-Client goes through in deciding what mailbox driver to use on any given mailbox; it also documents the UW IMAP namespace and compares the performance of each of the mailbox drivers.

docs/rfc/*

Copies of pertinent, and some impertinent, RFCs.

docs/CONFIG

> Directions on how to stray from the plug-and-play path by changing the code and adding authenticators and mailbox drivers.

docs/calendar.txt

> This is the best smart-ass answer to a naive question that we've run across. Worth stopping your installation, getting a cup of coffee or chai tea, and reading at leisure.

docs/RELNOTES

> Probable very old release notes dating back to the last incremental release, not the current version. Good for historical information, but cull through the C-Client archives for canonical information about your particular version of the UW IMAP Toolkit.

docs/bugs.txt

> Same caveat as for *RELNOTES*. Useful, but dated, information. The C-Client archives are a good source for information to augment this.

docs/naming.txt

> An overview of what you'll find where in the IMAP Toolkit tree.

docs/imaprc.txt

> Documentation on the use and dangers of the UW-specific *imaprc* file. A better name would be "Pandora's box." We advise you not to use this file, as does Mark Crispin, if you're not actually installing UW IMAP at the University of Washington. This file is reserved for the UW-specific black box mode, which makes numerous, undocumented assumptions about the character and arrangement of your mailstore. Use of this file is the easiest way to take what is essentially a plug-and-play effortless server install and turn it into a downward-spiraling conundrum of sysadmin pain.

docs/ internal.txt

> Concise and complete documentation on C-Client API internals. A great starting point if you're itching to write a mailbox driver.[*]

How Do You Install It?

The quick-start steps for the impatient are as follows. Later on, we'll cover deviations you might like to make in this routine:

1. Change directories to the top-level directory created when you untarred the distribution file. With IMAP 4.5, the directory name is *imap-4.5*.

---

[*] Actually, basing a mailbox driver on an existing, working driver is a better place to start, but you'll want to have this file handy nevertheless.

2. Select your OS/compiler combination from the list in *Makefile*. For example, *gso* is Solaris and GCC.

3. Do a *make <keyword>* where <keyword> is your OS/compiler combo. For example, *make gso*.

4. Rejoice in the wonder of compiling open source software as your IMAP Toolkit builds (alternatively, try to figure out why the compile failed or why your compiler doesn't work, etc.) Once it finishes, you'll have all the components built and ready to put into action.

5. Become *root* and copy the *imapd* binary to */usr/local/etc*. Linux admins may prefer */usr/local/sbin*.

6. Make sure you've got an entry like this in your */etc/services* file:

       imap   143/tcp

7. Make sure you've got corresponding entries in your */etc/inetd.conf* file. If you're *not* using *TCP Wrappers*:*

       imap   stream tcp   nowait root   /usr/local/etc/imapd   imapd

   If you are using *TCP Wrappers*:†

       imap   stream tcp   nowait root   /usr/local/etc/tcpd /usr/local/sbin.imapd

   It doesn't matter if you call your services *imap*, *imap4*, or even *InternetMail-AccessProtocol* as long as the name you use in */etc/services* is exactly the same as the name you use in */etc/inetd.conf*. Before you send a HUP signal to *inetd*, take a minute and make absolutely sure that the location you give for your *imapd* software is accurate and contains either symbolic links to the right binaries or the binaries themselves.

8. Finally, signal *inetd* to reread its configuration file:

       # ps -ef | grep inetd
       root   170   1 0   Sep 27 ?   0:00 /usr/sbin/inetd -s
       # kill -HUP 170

The IMAP distribution includes POP2 and POP3 daemons. If you don't intend to provide POP services, there's no need to spend time installing the IPOP2d/IPOP3D servers. If you see mention of POP in the IMAP documentation, just ignore it. POP is not required for IMAP to function. Once upon a time, it made terrific sense to provide POP3 mailbox service instead of or at least in parallel to IMAP, because few mainstream mail user agents supported IMAP. That hasn't been true for a long

---

* TCP Wrappers (*ftp://ftp.win.tue.nl/pub/security*) is a wrapper program for *inetd* that allows monitoring and filtering of *inetd* services.

† If you have inexplicable problems connecting to your IMAP server from any other machine and you're running TCP Wrappers, try removing TCP Wrappers from the equation to see if that makes any difference.

time. All major email apps now support IMAP, and POP3 is becoming a legacy protocol. If you've got some stubborn POP3 users, though, or some special need, UW IMAP's POP2 and POP3 daemons are a pretty elegant way to gateway your new mailstore using an old protocol. POP2 is such a legacy protocol, however, that unless you have clear user demand, there's little or no reason to install the POP2 daemon.

Not Leaving Well Enough Alone...

There's a small handful of things you can do to alter the baseline installation of the IMAP toolkit and accompanying servers. In most cases, you won't need to alter anything in the default installation. You might be well advised to just run it in the default configuration for a while and see what customer demands are met by modest changes in the installation, rather than trying to anticipate the demands of your users in advance.

Monkeying with the Makefiles

One way of customizing your installation is to change certain variables in the makefiles. Once you've made a backup copy of the original *Makefile* or a last-known working copy and you've changed the variables you want, go ahead and redo your "make <SystemType>" as discussed previously to build your customized version of the IMAP Toolkit.

The top-level *Makefile* has three lines of note:

```
EXTRAAUTHENTICATORS=
EXTRADRIVERS=mbox
PASSWDTYPE=std
```

As you might guess, **EXTRAAUTHENTICATORS** and **EXTRADRIVERS** are the mechanisms through which additional authentication and mailbox drivers are added into the C-Client library and, by extension, the IMAP daemon. We'll go into more detail about this in Chapter 12, *UW System Administration*. Notice also that the *mbox* driver is explicitly enabled. All other drivers are enabled by default, there's no need to list them here. These lines are primarily for implementing add-on authenticators and mailbox drivers.

The **PASSWDTYPE** variable can be set to one of a variety of plaintext password mechanisms, which are listed out in the makefile:

```
# afs   AFS authentication database
# dce   DCE authentication database
# nul   no plaintext authentication (note: this will break some secure
#         authenticators -- don't use without checking first!!)
# std   system standard (typically passwd file), determined by port
```

There are a handful of extra switches you can turn on in the top-level makefile, like Y4K (yep, Year 4000) leap-year correction to accommodate the fact that years evenly divisible by 4000 aren't leap years, or enabling British Summer Time. They're all well-documented; all you need to do is uncomment the appropriate line for each switch.

Another Makefile you may want to examine and change is the *imapd/Makefile*. There are likewise three variables you may want to customize:

```
ALERT=/etc/imapd.alert
USERALERT=.imapalert
ANO=/etc/anonymous.newsgroups
```

`ALERT` specifies the general IMAP alert file. Place a single-line message in this file, and each user should see that notification as soon as they start using the IMAP server. Different clients should use different ways of displaying the message, but all compliant clients should display the message somehow. `USERALERT` is a file you put in the user's home directory (or whatever you define their *homedir* to be in the code) to send a notification to an individual user. `ALERT` is good for such notifications as "IMAP will be going down for three hours starting 3am November 4, 2001," while `USERALERT` is good for such things as "Attention user jbk00234: Your E-Mail is obnoxious, please get a life at once!"

The `ANO` variable defines a file that, if it exists, enables anonymous mailbox access on the IMAP server. More about this in Chapter 12.

Clobbering the Code

The vast majority of code-level changes that you're likely to want to make to the way UW IMAP operates have been isolated to the file *src/osdep/unix/env_unix.c*. `env_init()` and `sysinbox()` are routines that each have a value that you may want to change to customize to your environment. The source documentation also says that `mailboxdir()` and `mailboxfile()` may also have some commonly useful things to change, but that hasn't been our experience. If you want to investigate those, the details are in *docs/CONFIG*.

env_init()

If you want the top-level mailbox directory for UW to be something other than the user's home directory, search in *env_unix.c* for this line:

```
myHomeDir = cpystr (home);/* use real home directory */
```

and change these lines to something like the following. In this example, you would change the default top-level mailbox directory to *~/mail* for any given user:

```
sprintf (tmp,"%s/mail",home);
    myHomeDir = cpystr (tmp);
```

One source of confusion for new UW IMAP users is suddenly seeing all their home directory files mixed in with their mailboxes. Setting `myHomeDir` to a different value fixes this.

`sysinbox()`

On some systems, it might be preferable to have the MTA deliver incoming mail to somewhere different from the traditional */var/spool/mail/USER* location. If you have a good reason to do this, say because you want incoming mail to be subject to the same partition quota as the stored mailboxes, make a change in the `sysinbox()` routine.

This example supposes that, instead of the traditional mailspool, you want INBOX to be physically located in *~/.mailbox* in a user's home directory. In this case, you would change:

```
sprintf (tmp,"%s/%s",MAILSPOOL,myusername ());
```

to:

```
sprintf (tmp,"%s/.mailbox",myhomedir ());
```

and your user INBOXes would be distributed across the home directory space.

Where Can You Go for Help If You Get Stuck?

Two good starting places are The IMAP Connection, at *http://www.imap.org/,* and the University of Washington IMAP Information Center, at *http://www.washington.edu/imap/.* Each site is a portal to various sites and archives. The IMAP Connection focuses primarily on the IMAP protocol and the software that uses it. Possibly its best resource is an interactive database of IMAP software: client, server, gateway, utilities, etc. The UW IMAP Information Center is primarily focused on UW IMAP software.

Speaking of archives, two mailing lists essential for getting good, up-to-date information are the IMAP mailing list and the C-Client mailing list. Instructions for joining and viewing the archives of the IMAP mailing list are at *http://www.washington.edu/imap/imap-list.html.* Information about the C-Client list and its archives is at *http://www.washington.edu/imap/c-client-list.html.*

Finally, you can use your local Usenet server or Deja News (*http://www.deja.com/*) to read the *comp.mail.imap* group for a good unbiased, or at least equally unbalanced, collective viewpoint on the state of IMAP clients and servers.

12

In this chapter:
• *General Issues*
• *Authentication*
• *Security*
• *UW IMAP Utilities*

UW System Administration

The UW IMAP server is so much of a plug-and-play package, there's not a lot of system administration to talk about. A few things should be mentioned, though, so we'll cover them before going on to bigger issues, like security.

General Issues

Some broad issues should be addressed up front. As we've mentioned several times already, you would probably have a perfectly good IMAP server setup if you just slapped the location of the prebuilt binary that probably came with your operating system into *inetd.conf* and ran it. Unix system administrators being what they are, however, we'd be remiss in our duties if we didn't give you a handful of "nerd knobs" to tweak on the UW server, so here goes.

IMAP Alerts

The UW server supports IMAP alerts, *motd* type messages that all IMAP users see in their IMAP client when a connection to the server is first established.

To set up an alert, put the alert message text in the file */etc/imapd.alert*.

Because many clients don't handle IMAP alerts perfectly, keep the alert text down to one line. Also, keep in mind that the alert message is displayed every time a user connects to the server, so it's best to use alerts only for critical messages.

Disabling the mbox Driver

If you compiled the UW server to support the mbox driver (it's enabled by default), the server's behavior when an INBOX is opened may not be what you expect or desire. With mbox support, when INBOX is opened, the server checks the user's home directory for a Unix mailbox format file called *mbox*. If it exists, the server selects that file as the INBOX and transfers all mail from the user's mail spool file to the *mbox* file.

The mbox driver can be disabled by editing the top-level Makefile and removing mbox from the **EXTRADRIVERS** list and rebuilding the UW server. Rebuilding and reinstalling the server will not take care of messages that were already transferred from the mail spool file to the *mbox* file. Those messages have to be moved back to the spool file by hand, or the user will not be able to read them unless she explicitly opens *mbox*.

Alternative Default Subdirectory for User Mailboxes

Many users of host-based mail programs will find their mailboxes sitting under ~/ *mail/*. If you want UW to default to that directory and have it appear as "~/" to IMAP clients, go to the file *src/osdep/unix/env_unix.c* in your source distribution, change some code in the function **env_init()**, and rebuild the server.

In the function **env_init()** in *env_unix.c*, you'll find the following line assigning a value to **myHomeDir**:

```
myHomeDir = cpystr (home);        /* use real home directory   */
```

Add a line so the assignment is made to something more of your liking. Something like this would do nicely:

```
sprintf (tmp,"%s/mail",home) ;/* I'd rather have this value */
     myHomeDir = cpystr (tmp) ;/* original string copy line  */
```

Changing Location of INBOX

The only easy way to contain users' disk usage on your UW server is through OS quotas, because UW doesn't support IMAP-specific quotas. For this reason, you might want to move the default INBOX for your users to somewhere in their home directory structure so it can be contained by the same quota as the rest of their personal files.

You may, for example, want to change your delivery agent so that it delivers to *~someuser/mail/incoming* instead of */var/spool/mail/someuser*. To make that change, go to the function **sysinbox()** in *env_unix.c*:

```
/*  Return system standard INBOX
 *  Accepts: buffer string
 */
```

```
char *sysinbox ()
{
  char tmp[MAILTMPLEN];
  if (!sysInbox) {                /* initialize if first time */
    sprintf (tmp,"%s/%s",MAILSPOOL,myusername ());
    sysInbox = cpystr (tmp);    /* system inbox is from mail spool */
  }
  return sysInbox;
}
```

and change the `sprintf` line, making the assignment to `tmp` something like this:

```
sprintf ( tmp,"%s/mail/incoming",myhomedir() );
```

Permissions

/tmp must be world-writable. If it's not world-writable, the UW server will log syslog messages like this one, complaining that it cannot open mailbox lock files:

```
Apr  2 14:44:51 serverhost imapd[5759]: \
    Mailbox lock file /tmp/.80001d.29bc2 open failure: Permission denied
```

If you're using Unix mailbox format, you'll only be able to open mailboxes in read-only mode until the permissions are fixed. To correct the permissions, use the command:

```
# chmod 1777 /tmp
```

The permissions of individual lock files under */tmp* should be read-write by world (0666). If the permissions are set to something other than 0666, then they were changed either in error or with malicious intent (see the section "Security" later in this chapter).

Mailbox Formats

The question of maildir format comes up more and more often as MTA alternatives to sendmail, such as Qmail, take on more of a following. Although UW supports a variety of mailstore formats, Qmail's maildir format is not supported. There are no plans to add support for maildir.

Authentication

One of the appeals of UW IMAP is its flexibility with regard to authentication and mailbox format schemes. Here's a brief overview of some of the more common areas of concern with UW authentication.

Disabling Plaintext Passwords

It's possible to disable plaintext passwords before they disable you. Doing so involves rebuilding the server with an alternate authentication method and the password type set to nul:

```
% make lnx EXTRAAUTHENTICATORS=gss PASSWDTYPE=nul
```

At least one EXTRAAUTHENTICATOR (gss, in the previous example) must be specified, or the server will have no mechanism for users to log in.

ble anonymous login, create
that anonymous user access
:ftp/), and Public (*#public/*)

le support for PAM (Plugga-
supports PAM, then rebuild

ations that vary slightly from
passwords with PAM, Solaris

isted as comments in the top-
hapter 10, *Introduction to the*

ponse Authentication Mecha-
ls to be done is to create the

CRAM-MD5 authentication database. If the CRAM-MD5 authentication database exists, then plaintext password authentication via the IMAP LOGIN command will use the CRAM-MD5 passwords instead of Unix passwords.

The default location for the CRAM-MD5 authentication database is */etc/cram-md5. pwd*. The format of the database is shown in Example 12-1. The first field of each line is the username; the second field is the password. Fields are separated by a tab. Lines beginning with # are comments.

Example 12-1. CRAM-MD5 Authentication Database

```
# CRAM-MD5 authentication database
# Format: <username><tab><password>
johndoe234&xx7
msmithmypasswd
qpublicbad!pass
```

You may have noticed that the password appears in the authentication database unencrypted. To protect the database, the file permissions should be restricted to read and write access by root only. Use the following command to change the permissions on the database:

```
# chmod 0400 /etc/cram-md5.pwd
```

Every CRAM-MD5 database entry must correspond to an entry in */etc/passwd*. Think of *cram-md5.pwd* as a variation on */etc/shadow*. Each holds only username and password information. It is left to */etc/passwd* to hold the UID, GID, GECOS, and home directory information. It is permitted, and probably recommended in some configurations, for the user's entry in */etc/passwd* to be disabled either by locking the username in the */etc/passwd* or */etc/shadow* or by assigning the user a non-functional shell.

Kerberos

To build the UW server to support Kerberos V5, use:

```
% make systemtype EXTRAAUTHENTICATORS=gss
```

The *gss* authentication module supports Kerberos V5. Note that users will also be able to log in using plaintext Unix authentication, unless you specifically disable plaintext authentication (see earlier in this chapter). The UW server does not include support for Kerberos V4.

Security

As with any other package, there are some security housekeeping items that you ought to address when you install it.

Disabling Plaintext Passwords

It's possible to disable plaintext passwords before they disable you. Doing so involves rebuilding the server with an alternate authentication method and the password type set to nul:

```
% make lnx EXTRAAUTHENTICATORS=gss PASSWDTYPE=nul
```

At least one EXTRAAUTHENTICATOR (gss, in the previous example) must be specified, or the server will have no mechanism for users to log in.

Enabling Anonymous Login

Anonymous IMAP login is disabled by default. To enable anonymous login, create an empty file called */etc/anonymous.newsgroups*. Note that anonymous user access is limited to mailboxes in the News (*#news/*), FTP (*#ftp/*), and Public (*#public/*) namespaces.

Using PAM for Plaintext Passwords

UW includes a port for Linux distributions that include support for PAM (Pluggable Authentication Modules). If your Linux distribution supports PAM, then rebuild the UW server with the Linux-PAM (lnp) port:

```
% make lnp
```

Solaris systems prior to Solaris 8 have PAM implementations that vary slightly from the Linux PAM implementation. To support plaintext passwords with PAM, Solaris sites should rebuild UW as follows:

```
% make clean
% make sol PASSWDTYPE=pmb
```

Other systems should build with PASSWDTYPE=pam:

```
% make systemtype PASSWDTYPE=pam
```

System types are too numerous to list here. They're listed as comments in the top-level UW IMAP Makefile and discussed briefly in Chapter 10, *Introduction to the UW IMAP Server*.

CRAM-MD5

The UW server supports CRAM-MD5[*] (Challenge-Response Authentication Mechanism). To enable CRAM authentication, all that needs to be done is to create the

---

[*] *http://www.imap.org/docs/rfc2195.html*

CRAM-MD5 authentication database. If the CRAM-MD5 authentication database exists, then plaintext password authentication via the IMAP LOGIN command will use the CRAM-MD5 passwords instead of Unix passwords.

The default location for the CRAM-MD5 authentication database is */etc/cram-md5.pwd*. The format of the database is shown in Example 12-1. The first field of each line is the username; the second field is the password. Fields are separated by a tab. Lines beginning with # are comments.

Example 12-1. CRAM-MD5 Authentication Database

```
# CRAM-MD5 authentication database
# Format: <username><tab><password>
johndoe234&xx7
msmithmypasswd
qpublicbad!pass
```

You may have noticed that the password appears in the authentication database unencrypted. To protect the database, the file permissions should be restricted to read and write access by root only. Use the following command to change the permissions on the database:

```
# chmod 0400 /etc/cram-md5.pwd
```

Every CRAM-MD5 database entry must correspond to an entry in */etc/passwd*. Think of *cram-md5.pwd* as a variation on */etc/shadow*. Each holds only username and password information. It is left to */etc/passwd* to hold the UID, GID, GECOS, and home directory information. It is permitted, and probably recommended in some configurations, for the user's entry in */etc/passwd* to be disabled either by locking the username in the */etc/passwd* or */etc/shadow* or by assigning the user a non-functional shell.

Kerberos

To build the UW server to support Kerberos V5, use:

```
% make systemtype EXTRAAUTHENTICATORS=gss
```

The *gss* authentication module supports Kerberos V5. Note that users will also be able to log in using plaintext Unix authentication, unless you specifically disable plaintext authentication (see earlier in this chapter). The UW server does not include support for Kerberos V4.

Security

As with any other package, there are some security housekeeping items that you ought to address when you install it.

SSL and TLS

SSL and TLS will be supported in IMAP 2000 (due to be released during production of this book), but they are not supported in earlier versions. The University of Washington has an SSL patch kit for the UW IMAP server, which adds SSL and TLS server support to POP and IMAP. Unfortunately, UW cannot make it available even with the recently relaxed U.S. government export restrictions, because of lingering governmental restrictions with regard to which countries still may not receive encryption technology from the U.S., and certain peripheral issues, such as the distribution of crypto-binaries.

As an alternative approach using freely available open source software, IMAP can be tunneled through SSL or SSH using the techniques discussed in Appendix B, *Adding SSL Support to IMAP.*

Permissions on Files Under /tmp

As we mentioned before, in addition to */tmp* permissions needing to be set to 1777 (drwxrwxrwt), all lock files created in */tmp* by IMAPD must have the permissions of 0666 (-rw-rw-rw-). Yes, that does open up the possibility of malicious or accidental denial of service by changing or removing the lock files, but any permissions other than 0666 will keep shared mailboxes from working. On this issue, you have two choices. One, to go on living with the problem and knowing that it may be fairly easy to track down lock file vandals. Two, to use this opening as a good excuse for running a dedicated mail server without general CGI or shell access.

Mail Spool Directory Permissions

C-Client and, by extension, the UW IMAP server run completely without privileges, and thus require that the spool directory (in most cases, */var/spool/mail*) have 1777 protection (drwxrwxrwt). That enables read, write, and execute for user, group, and other, and it enables the sticky bit on the directory. That means that, although everyone can see the names of everyone else's lock files, they can't change them or otherwise mess with them. About the only lock-file-specific attack malicious users could do would be to preemptively create huge numbers of lock files in an attempt to block users' read-write access to their mailboxes.

UW IMAP Utilities

Chapter 18, *IMAP Tools*, lists a variety of tools to perform nearly every common IMAP task. The UW IMAP Utilities are available at *ftp://ftp.cac.washington.edu/imap/imap-utils.tar.Z*. Download and unpack the tools at the same level as your UW IMAP source:

```
% lynx -dump ftp://ftp.cac.washington.edu/imap/imap-utils.tar.Z | uncompress |
tar xvf -
```

You'll see several subdirectories. Each subdirectory has the source code for a separate utility. Change to the utility subdirectory and build the utility:

```
% cd chkmail
% make
```

In each utility subdirectory, you'll find a manual page describing the purpose and usage of the utility. Here's a brief description of the utilities:

chkmail

chkmail is a utility for checking how many messages in a given mailbox have the Recent flag set. Any mailbox that can be described in C-Client mailbox syntax (as in the PINE configuration) can be checked for new messages with this utility.

dmail

dmail is a drop-in replacement for *binmail*. It's intended for use as a local delivery agent in every case *except* as an MDA used by the transport agent. Essentially, *dmail* is intended for use in user processes, and *tmail* is intended for use in server processes.

icat

An IMAP version of */bin/cat*, icat can be used to display all the messages in a given folder in a single output stream. Users may also filter based on flags, dates, or other header values. *icat* is an excellent tool for migrating mailboxes away from proprietary or monolithic mailstores that happen to have marginal support for IMAP.

ifrom

ifrom gives a directory listing of the specified IMAP mailbox with message number, status, sender, date, and subject.

imapcopy

imapcopy and *imapmove* copy (or move) messages from an IMAP INBOX to an existing local mailbox.

imapxfer

The *imapxfer* utility uses IMAP to copy entire mailboxes from one host to another, creating them on the destination host if need be.

mbxcopy

> *mbxcopy* and *mbxmove* copy (or move) messages from one mailbox (IMAP or local) to another existing mailbox (IMAP or local).

mbxcreat

> *mbxcreate* creates new mailboxes on the local system.

mbxcvt

> *mbxcvt* copies messages from a mailbox (IMAP or local) to a new mailbox in any desired format.

tmail

> Whereas *dmail* is the preferred agent to use in user scripts and procmail-type applications, *tmail* is the preferred server-called delivery agent. *tmail* is a privileged program and, consequently, is very paranoid about its arguments. *dmail* is an unprivileged program and is not as paranoid.

This example shows how the *ifrom* utility can be used to list the contents of a mailbox:

```
% ./ifrom -s -n -t -l ~msmith/mail/test
John Doe <johndoe@theman.hoopie.net>   1-Feb-2000  Re: Career Option
```

The *−s* and *−n* flags omit the *Status* field and *Message* number fields from the output. Omitting those fields increases the width of the *From* and *Subject* fields. The *−t* flag omits the time from the data field, and the *−l* field tells *ifrom* not to restrict the output to 80 columns. The folder, *~msmith/mail/test*, contains a single message from John Doe.

Here's an example that shows how to use the *mbxcopy* utility to copy an entire mailbox to a new mailbox:

```
% ./mbxcopy INBOX ~johndoe/mail/saved-mail
%Mailbox vulnerable - directory /var/spool/mail must have 1777 protection
/var/spool/mail/johndoe [38 message(s)] => /home/johndoe/mail/saved-mail
[Ok]
%
```

V

Other Topics

13

Addressing IMAP Security

Keeping your IMAP server secure is no different from keeping your other resources secure. Well...let's back up for a second. You can't keep your IMAP server secure any more than you can keep anything else secure. Short of sealing your server in a block of titanium and firing it off into the sun, the best you can do is keep your server *mostly* secure. The standard test of whether you're spending too much time on security is whether you've made it more difficult to compromise your system than the rewards of doing so are worth. Of course, hell-bent, disgruntled employees probably think any level of compromise is worth any amount of effort, so we'll expend a bit more effort on their behalf.

There are three things to keep in mind:

- Stay informed!

- Stay updated!

- Stay vigilant!

The best thing you can do to stay informed is to make it a habit of reviewing online resources, such as mailing lists, Usenet newsgroups, and web sites, for information about recently discovered vulnerabilities in all the various operating systems, servers, clients, and tools you use. It's safe to say that because your professional world revolves around providing service to your users and, at best, security is a secondary concern, you'll be far from the first person to learn about vulnerabilities on your system. Hackers,* on the other hand, are likely to live in a world that revolves *entirely* around discovering vulnerabilities in your system and

---

* The popular press has narrowed common usage until crackers, phreaks, and hackers all became the same. For brevity and with the exception of this protestation, we'll acquiesce to the same usage. There's an excellent discussion of the meaning of *hack* at the Jargon File site (*http://www.tuxedo.org/~esr/jargon/html/The-Meaning-of-Hack.html*).

leaving their unauthorized handprints inside. Already, you have a scenario where your potential opponents are much more motivated than you are. Your best hope is to be more rational than they are and expend your effort in the best possible way as you shore up your system security

Perhaps the only thing worse than not knowing and not fixing the vulnerabilities in your system is knowing and not fixing. It's simply not enough to know that you have some vulnerabilities in your system and that someday you'll get around to fixing them. We're proud of our systems and want to add features to move them forward. And we know that system security is one of those jobs that are invisible when done well. It very often boils down to working on security rather than adding new wonderful features to our systems. Someday, you'll be glad you did— when one of your peers at another site has to spend a week rebuilding everything from scratch because he didn't. Don't just learn about the flaws in your system—stay ahead of the curve by updating your software regularly. Apply the necessary patches, workarounds, and updates as necessary to keep your system beyond the threshold of likely hacker attention span.

Security Resources

Online informational security resources could loosely be grouped into three categories: hacker resources, neutral resources, and security professional resources. We won't attempt to make the value judgments necessary to group each site mentioned in this chapter into the categories. We'll just say that knowing that the different categories are there might help you decide with how much gravity to take information that you find at one of the sites.

Hacker resources often present themselves as free "services," while, in actuality, they post code that many twelve-year-olds could use to take down your site. Some of the "old guard" professional sites are somewhat hypersensitive where safety is concerned. They'll only post a warning about a vulnerability after each major vendor has had an opportunity to run their "spin" through the local legal and marketing departments, making the warning only marginally helpful once the information finally gets to you.

The Computer Emergency Response Team/ Coordination Center (CERT/CC)

http://www.cert.org/

Since 1988, from its home at the Carnegie Mellon Software Engineering Institute, CERT has stood watch over security on the Internet. Although CERT is regarded as somewhat slow on the draw these days in getting the word out, they performed the difficult job of centralized security coordination back when no one else was there to do so. CERT® was formed as a response to the vulnerability pointed out by the Morris Worm attack (see *http://www.worm.net/*) that marked the first time many people ever heard of the Internet. CERT issues regular alerts in the form of advisories, summaries, and vendor-initiated bulletins, all of which are propagated through their *cert-advisory@cert.org* mailing list.

Advisories are time-sensitive notifications of events or recently discovered vulnerabilities that merit broad attention. *Summaries* are in-depth analyses of current threats on the Internet and advice on how best to address the threats. *Vendor-initiated* bulletins are postings provided by vendors who wish to send out security bulletins regarding their own products.

L0pht Heavy Industries

http://www.l0pht.com/

L0pht Heavy Industries is basically a bunch of hackers who put together a very polished full-disclosure web site that disseminates information about vulnerabilities—what systems have them, as well as how to exploit the vulnerabilities yourself. What this kind of site does is like practicing nuclear deterrence by giving everyone the missile codes and keys to the silos.

Fortunately or unfortunately, depending on your point of view, sites like this are the best source of information about newly discovered vulnerabilities. Usually, the first to discover an vulnerability will be hackers who may want to keep the vulnerability to themselves to give themselves a competitive edge over their peers. Before long, however, information about the vulnerabilities percolates out to full-disclosure sites like L0pht, RootShell, and Bugtraq, and sometime later, it eventually finds its way out to limited disclosure, industry-friendlier sites like CERT and CIAC.

Computer Incident Advisory Capability

http://ciac.llnl.gov/

The Computer Incident Advisory Capability (CIAC) is the U.S. Department of Energy's security tiger team. Their primary mission is to secure DOE facilities. Nevertheless, so much of what they do and the information they gather is of use to the general Internet community that their site has become a popular resource on the Internet over the years. One of the original security teams formed in the post–Morris Worm era, CIAC is useful to non-DOE folks mostly as a clearinghouse for warnings posted from other sites. Typically, CIAC will post CERT or vendor warnings but preface them with a sensible executive summary that boils the entire issue and its perceived urgency down to one screenful of useful information.

A couple of the more interesting features of the CIAC site are their hoaxes list (*http://ciac.llnl.gov/ciac/CIACHoaxes.html*) and chain letter list (*http://ciac.llnl.gov/ciac/CIACHoaxes.html*). CIAC collects data and stories on many Internet hoaxes and chain letters and keeps them as caveats.

RootShell

> *http://www.rootshell.com/*

RootShell is arguably the most informative, commonly known site about vulnerabilities and events on the net. This full-disclosure site has reportedly been assigned partial blame by the U.S. Department of Defense for substantial increases in hacking attempts directed against DOD resources.

RootShell is, for the most part, a very attractive and useful site. The frequency with which vulnerabilities and methods are posted will keep anyone with a morbid interest in who's gotten hacked lately coming back for more. On a more practical note, RootShell propagates more than just plain-vanilla information on IP buffer overflow attacks. There's plenty of information on the site to encourage sleeplessness among the ranks of JavaScript users, Novell IPX network managers, MS-Windows SMB/CIFS users, anyone using a certain kind of UPS, anyone using certain kinds of wireless networking, anyone using certain kinds of printers—you get the idea. RootShell is food for your to-do list.

Bugtraq and SecurityFocus.com

> *http://securityfocus.com/*

If you have time to keep up to date with only one security web site, *http://securityfocus.com* would be a good one to pick. The crown jewel of the site is the Bugtraq mailing list archives. Bugtraq content is much like RootShell, in that they're both full-disclosure sites. Bugtraq has much more of a system administrator flavor than RootShell, which is aimed more at an audience of hackers. As an interesting exercise, search the Bugtraq archive for keywords related to the systems you run (e.g., Solaris, sendmail, IMAP) and see what comes up.

Security Focus also has one of the very best archives around of security-related software. You might even consider it the Tucows or Hotfiles* of security software, with generous examples of access control, auditing, authentication, cryptography, intrusion detection, network monitoring, policy enforcement, programming, recovery, replacement, sniffers, system security, and other utilities. During our review of

---

* *http://www.tucows.com/* and *http://www.hotfiles.com/*, a couple of our favorite software archives.

this site, we found a nifty MS-Windows port of the Unix standard snooping utility, *tcpdump*, which captures and dissects just about any packet on your network.

A Handful of Security Tips

As much as we'd like to be comprehensive here, we won't. We can't. Nobody can. The nature of security is that it's always incomplete. As elusive as it is, 100% uptime is much easier to achieve than 100% security. The goal of this chapter, however, is to point you in some directions that will help you get as far above 99% secure as possible.

Having a secure site has a lot to do with not making any stupid little mistakes. A friend of ours once made the mistake of running an FTP session from a remote shell account provider to a local corporate site to get his *.cshrc* file, while under contract to a national ISP. Just that single occasion of grabbing a file turned into a situation where one of my accounts was compromised, using my password, and used to run an eggdrop* server. Those five seconds of indiscretion cost many hours of work by several people who had to pull the machine out of production, re-install the OS and all software, and put it back into production.

Assume all your unencrypted keystrokes are already in the hands of hackers. If that makes you feel uncomfortable, it ought to. Strong encryption hasn't propagated to all common applications, let alone all *uncommon* applications, yet. The best you can do sometimes is assume that you will be periodically compromised and take effective, routine protective measures.

Tripwire

A good example of one of those measures would be to run Tripwire. Tripwire, a host filesystem monitoring utility originally developed at Purdue University, retains a database of checksums and other data about files, directories, and devices throughout your system and notifies you if any of those entities you're watching changes. Free, old versions of Tripwire are available from Purdue University at *ftp://coast.cs.purdue.edu/pub/tools/unix/Tripwire/*. For-pay, commercial, new versions are available from Tripwire Security, Inc. at *http://www.tripwiresecurity.com/*.

Tripwire depends on having a reliable read-only copy of its database, usually on a write-protected floppy or a CD-ROM. Once installed on a clean system that has never been on the Net, it can be used reliably to notify you of the kinds of things a hacker might do to conceal her tracks. Some of those things might be modifying

---

* Eggdrop is a daemon used to automate maintenance of an IRC channel. In this case, it was likely being used as a file server for bootleg software and cracking information. One site with a fair amount of Eggdrop information is *http://www.roon.org/eggdrop/*.

utmp or *wtmp* databases, modifying executables like *finger, who, w,* or *ps,* or doing things like making */dev/kmem** world-readable.

Social Engineering

Another vulnerability to watch out for is social engineering. A friend of ours, also a former employee of the security group at a large ISP, called his new replacement, who didn't recognize his voice, and claimed to be the Unix system administration group leader. With polite apologies, he explained that he'd lost the slip of paper on which he had his root passwords written and asked the new guy if he would be so kind as to give him the passwords over the telephone. Not only did the former employee get the complete list of root passwords, but he also proceeded to call one of the Unix system administrators and conferenced in the new guy again to confirm the spelling of one of the passwords. It was an interesting day. Production essentially ceased while everyone scrambled to change the root passwords on all the machines immediately.

There are ways to engineer your system so that it's less vulnerable to social engineering. For example, instead of having all system administrators share the account named *root*, assign each person a root-equivalent account that could easily be turned off if an event necessitated it, without affecting root access for other system administrators.

The Man-in-the-Middle

For years, a major vulnerability that was found in most computing environments was intrinsic to the local area network itself: Ethernet. Ethernet is a broadcast network, and every station on the network can potentially see the traffic to and from every other station. That leaves the enormous potential for intermediate stations to capture copies of the traffic between legitimate hosts and use the information for illegitimate aims. A "Man in the Middle" attack refers to exploitation of information available to any intermediate point between the source and the destination of an IP packet. A passive man-in-the-middle attack might be the collection of passwords from cleartext logins. An active man-in-the-middle attack might involve active substitution of SSL or SSH encryption keys or capturing one end of a TCP session.

In fact, most cable modem arrangements and even some DSL setups are susceptible to this kind of exploit. With high-bandwidth, always-on Internet access becoming more prevalent, it's not unusual for users to find themselves the target of hack

---

* On some systems, */dev/kmem* is a file providing direct access to the entirety of virtual system memory, in which you can read and write anything in process space.

attempts within minutes of the time they first come online through their new cable modem or DSL connection. Even if you manage to successfully firewall your home network, the traffic going between your home and all the places you go on the Net may be considered fair game for hackers. It's best to assume that anything you send unencrypted on the Internet can, and will, be read by someone.

As an illustration, one of the colleges at a university where we worked recently started offering an entry-level class to train fledgling Unix system administrators. As a class exercise, everyone ran packet-gathering software to collect passwords for other users whose traffic might be passing through the network where their computer lab resides. That pretty much neutralized what little security was provided by any cleartext password scheme.

There are a few things you can do to greatly reduce the number of cleartext password transmissions on your network. One way is probably already being done at your site: using switches. With an Ethernet switch, as opposed to a hub, any given port only sees unicast* traffic that is destined for devices on that port. The closer you can get to achieving a 1:1 ratio of devices to switch ports, the more resistant your system will be to packet-capturing from intermediate systems. This doesn't reduce the damage that could be done if someone manages to capture your traffic, but it does significantly reduce the likelihood that traffic will be caught.

Even on a switched network, though, malicious users on the source or destination machine can surreptitiously obtain privileges on the host, capture all the packets sent to that host, and use them for ill gain. Overall, it's better to have numerous, modestly appointed hosts serving a single purpose than a small number of superhosts serving multiple purposes each. That is true if for no other reason than that a smaller user population for each host represents a smaller number of sources for locally based attacks.

TCP Wrappers

One way to make a substantial contribution to the security of your IMAP server is to run the TCP Wrappers package.† We'll cover a few of the more prominent applications and features of TCP Wrappers here, but you'd be well advised to read the manpages in depth for a more complete understanding.

---

* For the uninitiated, network traffic can be divided into three types: unicast, broadcast, and multicast. Unicast traffic is between one single machine and another single machine. Broadcast traffic is sent from a single machine to a group of machines on a single local area network. Multicast traffic is sent from a single machine to a group of machines that may reside on two or more geographically dispersed local area networks.

† The TCP Wrappers package is available from *ftp://coast.cs.purdue.edu/pub/tools/unix/tcp_wrappers*.

The name TCP Wrappers is actually a misnomer. The TCP Wrappers package is more of a border guard than a wrapper. TCP Wrappers monitors incoming requests for TCP services, such as Telnet, FTP, POP, and IMAP, that have a one-to-one mapping onto executable files. When *inetd* receives a request for a service, it's tricked into running the TCP Wrappers program (*tcpd*) instead of the server program (for example, */usr/cyrus/bin/imapd*). The TCP Wrappers program logs the request and checks its configuration to see whether or not it is allowed to service the request. If everything's kosher, TCP Wrappers runs the server program and disposes of itself.

The distinction between a true wrapper and a TCP Wrappers–style "border guard" is important for a couple of reasons. First, TCP Wrappers can do nothing to protect your assets once it has decided to let a service daemon start. If an incoming request meets all the criteria set forth in *hosts.allow* and *hosts.deny*, then TCP Wrappers has served its entire purpose by checking the request and starting the service.

Second, TCP Wrappers is a poor tool to improve the security of daemons that may service requests from more than one remote process during their lifetime. Some HTTPDs, for example, are fired off once in *inetd*, service their first request, and then stick around to service additional requests.

Basic installation

Once you've pulled down, compiled, and done the first rough-cut of installing the TCP Wrappers package, the next step is to configure it. There's more than one way to implement TCP Wrappers. We'll just discuss the most robust and secure way. The first step is to modify your */etc/inetd.conf* file.

First, *inetd* needs to be tricked into running *tcpd* instead of a TCP service daemon. This means changing a line in */etc/inetd.conf*. If, for example, your *imapd* looks like the following line before TCP Wrappers is installed:

```
imap4  stream tcp nowait cyrus /usr/cyrus/bin/imapd imapd
```

then the TCP wrapped version would be something like this:

```
imap4  stream tcp nowait cyrus /usr/local/etc/tcpd /usr/cyrus/bin/imapd
```

In the modified version, incoming requests for the *imap4* service are handed off to */usr/local/etc/tcpd*. If *tcpd* decides that it's okay to service the *imap4* request, it will run */usr/cyrus/bin/imapd*.

Notice we've appended the full path to the process name of the *imapd* daemon in the modified version. This may not strictly be necessary, but we don't like to rely on the daemon we need being somewhere in the system path. If the default path for root gets corrupted (e.g., someone adds "." to the path to make life easier for themselves), we want one fewer thing to chase down and fix.

Now that you've changed your *inetd.conf* file, do whatever is necessary on your system to put your new *inetd.conf* into production. On most Unix systems, that means sending a HUP signal to the *inetd* process.

Before you restart *inetd*, make sure that you don't already have files called */etc/hosts.allow* or */etc/hosts.deny* in place. If you do, make sure you know that they reflect the security policy you want to enact on that particular host. If you haven't tested the rules in those files, errors could result in essential services being denied to your users—not a good thing on a production system.

Once TCP Wrappers is in production and *tcpd* is being used to fire off your individual TCP service daemons, the lack of */etc/hosts.allow* and */etc/hosts.deny* should permit *all* traffic to continue through as if TCP Wrappers weren't installed. The only difference you should notice at this point is syslog messages from *tcpd* in the log files for various TCP processes indicating when connections have been established from remote hosts.

The access files: /etc/hosts.allow and /etc/hosts.deny

The access granted to remote processes on your machine by TCP Wrappers is controlled by two files: */etc/hosts.allow* and */etc/hosts.deny*. If they don't exist or are empty, no restrictions are applied to incoming connections. *hosts.allow* is examined before *hosts.deny*. The first time a rule matches the given circumstance of connection, *tcpd* acts and further examination is discontinued. This means that if you permit all hosts in *usnd.edu* in *hosts.allow* and deny *hoopal.usnd.edu* in *hosts.deny*, *tcpd* will never see the rule to deny *hoopal.usnd.edu*. As soon as the match is made for permitting *usnd.edu*, rule examination will cease.

This section only provides a thumbnail sketch of how to set up TCP Wrappers. The *hosts_access*(5) and *host_options*(5) manpages together provide documentation for the TCP Wrappers Host Access Control Language. We're only touching on the basic essentials here.

Both *hosts.allow* and *hosts.deny* have the same format. Each entry takes the form:

```
daemon_list : client_list : option : option ...
```

daemon_list is a list of services to which a particular rule applies. The list can consist of daemon process names listed as the right-most argument in *inetd.conf* lines (*in.telnetd, in.ftpd, imapd*) and of wildcards such as ALL.

client_list is a list of source names and/or addresses to which a particular rule applies. It can include hostnames, addresses, patterns, and wildcards. *vaxb.acs. unt.edu, .acs.unt.edu, .edu*, 10.0.1.2, 129.120.51.50/255.255.255.254, *root@ALL*, and *kwm@cray23.themullets.net* are all examples of valid entries. Fully qualified domain names, portions thereof, IP addresses, IP subnets expressed as address with netmasks, and *users@hosts* are all valid. In that last example, the username would have to be verifiable via the IDENT protocol. Please bear in mind that IDENT is not a verifiably reliable method for determining the authentic identity of the person on the other end of a communications channel. A user could be running a hacked version of IDENT or could connect using a username that commonly exists on most systems (e.g., *root*).

option is a modifier to the rule such as *allow, deny, spawn, twist,* and *severity*. *allow* and *deny*, respectively, permit or prohibit the request from being serviced by your host. *twist* permits you to hand off sessions bound for a rule match to an alternate command. This would let you hand off internal requests for your company's website to an HTTP server that defaults to the intranet site and hand off external requests to your company's external HTTP server.

severity lets you change the syslog severity with which a given event/rule match is logged. This can be used as a key in */etc/syslog.conf* to direct given types of error messages to a file by themselves.

It's interesting to note that the keywords *allow* and *deny* permit the entire set of rules to be kept in one file, so you have a choice of two configuration file approaches. To keep things simple, we'll use one file, *hosts.deny*. Suppose you wanted to configure *hosts.deny* to perform the following work:

1. Deny all *telnet* connections from all sites, and display an informational banner message to anyone who tries to *telnet* into your machine.

2. Deny *imapd* connections from *hacker.someplace.org*.

You'd add these entries to your *hosts.deny*:

```
in.telnetd: ALL: banner /etc/banners : DENY
imapd: hacker.someplace.org
```

Granted, TCP Wrappers is a somewhat narrowly focused security package, but it does everything it attempts to do very well. There's not a lot of secondary documentation out there on TCP Wrappers. Fortunately, the manpages that come with the source distribution are well written and have a very good signal-to-noise ratio.

Our verdict: all IMAP servers (and arguably all Unix hosts in general) should use the TCP Wrappers package as one component of a broad security framework.

A Word Against Cleartext Passwords

Possibly the biggest security risk on your IMAP server is the constant, unrelenting transmission of many users' passwords across the net. When the user runs an

IMAP client on her local machine, the IMAP client sends the username and password in cleartext every time it contacts the server (assuming that the client and server don't support an encrypted authentication method). The username and password could travel a long way over the Internet between client and server, leaving many chances that they might be compromised somewhere along the way. Anything you can do to reduce this risk would be good. You can protect your passwords by tunneling IMAP through SSL or SSH or by using an encrypted authentication method, such as Kerberos or CRAM.

SSL

One way to reduce the risk, especially if you have a captive customer base as in a corporate intranet, is to distribute SSL-capable clients and permit *only* SSL access to your server. In Appendix B, *Adding SSL Support to IMAP*, we cover the procedure for adding SSL support to your IMAP server. Adding SSL to your IMAP server encrypts all passwords and content between the IMAP client and the server processes as well as insulates users from the details of encryption. All they need know is that by using certain IMAP clients, their email traffic is safe from useful capture on the network.

SSH

One option for secure communication between the IMAP client and server is to tunnel the communication inside the Secure Shell protocol. The difficulty in doing so is just enough that we don't recommend it for people who either aren't wizards or don't have access to wizards. The mechanics are easy enough, but it might be necessary to call on a wizard the first time a problem crops up.

Conceptually, it works like this. First, you install an SSH client on the local machine where you run your IMAP client. You use the SSH client to establish an SSH connection to the remote host where the IMAP server is running.* You also use the SSH client to establish a "listen" on a local port for IMAP requests. Here's the cool part: when you fire up your IMAP client, it connects to the IMAP port on *localhost*—your machine—instead of connecting to port 143 on a remote server machine.

The SSH client then forwards everything it receives on the local IMAP port through the SSH session, or tunnel, to the remote SSH daemon, which then forwards the data to the IMAP port on the remote host.

---

* The SSH tunnel only encrypts from the client to the remote host. If the IMAP server is not running on the remote host, then packets from the remote host to the IMAP server will not be encrypted.

How does the SSH daemon on the receiving end know what to do with all this IMAP information coming at it? Well, the information is part of the port-forwarding arrangement you gave the daemon when you first fired up the SSH session. For example, you'd invoke SSH from your client machine like this:[*]

```
client# ssh -f -L 143:localhost:143 kwm@serverhost tail -f /dev/null
```

The command must be invoked as *root* because root privilege is required to set up port forwarding. The *–f* option tells SSH to run in the background after port forwarding has been established. *–L localport:remotehost:remoteport* specifies that the given port on the local (client) host is to be forwarded to the given host and port on the remote side. In our example, we use port 143 on both the client and the host, but that's just for simplicity. In reality, you can use any port on the client that isn't already in use. The server port must be whichever port listens for IMAP requests (143 on most systems). Depending on the SSH client, you'll either be prompted for your password to log in to the server when issuing the tunneling command, or you'll have to initiate a login manually to establish the session. In all cases, you'll have to use SSH to log in to the remote host before you can use it to "launder" your connection. The entire IMAP port-forwarding scenario is shown in Figure 13-1.

If this all seems a little obtuse, don't worry. A couple of examples should help. We'll start with a command-line example. We start by using *lsof*[†] to check for software listening at local TCP port 143. There is none. We confirm this by trying to *telnet* to localhost at port 143 without success.

```
[kwm@clienthost]% lsof -i tcp:143              Lists all activity on port 143
[kwm@clienthost]% telnet localhost 143
Trying 127.0.0.1...
telnet: Unable to connect to remote host: Connection refused
```

At this point, we're certain that there's no activity, such as a listen or an open connection, on port 143 on our local machine. That port is okay to use. Next, we set up the port forwarding by issuing an SSH command. Remember that you have to be *root* to set up port forwarding:

```
[kwm@clienthost] % su -
Password:
[root@clienthost]# ssh -f -L 143:localhost:143 kwm@serverhost tail -f /dev/null
kwm@serverhost's password:
[root@clienthost]# ^D
```

---

[*] If you use a Windows or Mac SSH client such as TeraTerm, port forwarding is done through the windows interface.

[†] *lsof* (ls Open Files), a program that tells you which open files and network connections belong to which processes, is available at *ftp://vic.cc.purdue.edu/pub/tools/unix/lsof/*.

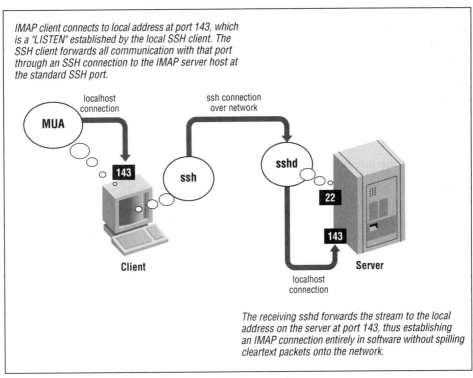

IMAP client connects to local address at port 143, which is a "LISTEN" established by the local SSH client. The SSH client forwards all communication with that port through an SSH connection to the IMAP server host at the standard SSH port.

The receiving sshd forwards the stream to the local address on the server at port 143, thus establishing an IMAP connection entirely in software without spilling cleartext packets onto the network.

Figure 13-1. IMAP port forwarding through SSH

The *tail –f /dev/null* that we tacked on to the end of the SSH command is just a low-overhead command to keep the session open. We didn't want to keep an actual shell session open and running in the background when we didn't need it, so we used the *tail* command instead.

Port forwarding is active. Now, when we look at port 143 on our local machine, it's ready to accept IMAP connections:

```
[kwm@clienthost]% lsof -i tcp:143
COMMAND  PID USER   FD    TYPE DEVICE SIZE NODE NAME
ssh     1958 root    4u  IPv4  45438       TCP localhost:imap (LISTEN)
[kwm@clienthost]% telnet localhost 143
Trying 127.0.0.1...
Connected to localhost.
Escape character is '^]'.
* OK localhost IMAP4rev1 v12.250 server ready
. capability
* CAPABILITY IMAP4 IMAP4REV1 NAMESPACE IDLE SCAN SORT MAILBOX-REFERRALS
LOGIN-REFERRALS AUTH=LOGIN AUTH=ANONYMOUS THREAD=ORDEREDSUBJECT
. OK Completed
. logout
* BYE serverhost IMAP4rev1 server terminating connection
. OK Completed
Connection closed by foreign host.
```

Although we're connected to the IMAP server port on *clienthost*, the goodbye message from the IMAP server identifies the server as *serverhost*. Users can now point their IMAP clients at port 143 on *clienthost* and have their IMAP sessions encrypted between *clienthost* and *serverhost*. If their IMAP clients are actually running on *clienthost*, their IMAP traffic is encrypted. This kind of arrangement may also be useful for remote campuses needing to participate in an enterprise's intranet by tunneling sensitive information (email over IMAP, in this case) within encrypted tunnels (SSH, here).

Encrypted authentication: Kerberos and CRAM

Another good way to provide password security is though an encryption method such as CRAM or Kerberos. CRAM encrypts the password only, and Kerberos relies on the encryption of Kerberos tickets so, strictly speaking, your password isn't going out over the Net. CRAM is less desirable than SSL because the transmission of an obviously encrypted password string amounts to hacker bait for someone with the tools to attempt cracking the encryption. Kerberos is less desirable than SSL simply because it has the added requirement of bringing up a Kerberos server.

The Core of the Problem

Some implementations of IMAP retain security information, such as passwords, in the memory space of the *imapd* process. For that reason, it's a good idea to set your maximum corefile size to zero for the *imapd* process. Because *imapd* is usually run out of *inetd*, this means setting the limit in the startup script that starts *inetd*. On a Solaris system, for example, the startup script would be found under */etc/init.d* and would be a Bourne shell script. In the Bourne shell, this is done with the command:

```
ulimit -c 0
```

Once you've done that, malicious folks can't covertly trigger a coredump in an *imapd* process and salvage password information from its contents.

Monitoring Security

We recommend a two-pronged strategy for the monitoring necessary to keep apprised of the quality of security on your network and IMAP server. First, run a variety of tools that let you observe, at a low level, the character of the traffic on your network. Second, never be in doubt about the status of your services. Know beyond any doubt if every server of yours is up or down and, by extension, if every service is up or down. Hopefully, you have the resources to engineer your Internet services so that the failure of one or two servers doesn't negatively impact the status of the service they provide.

IP Watcher

http://www.engarde.com/software/ipwatcher/

IP Watcher is a slick application that displays, in either an X or a Curses application, a list of all the current TCP-based sessions in progress and permits you to observe or disconnect them. IP Watcher is a tool you may never need. If, however, you have an incursion on your network and the hacker's already on the premises, there's a chance you might be able to gather more evidence if you have IP Watcher handy.

NetLog

http://www.net.tamu.edu/ftp/security/TAMU/netlog.README

NetLog is at the other end of the spectrum from IP Watcher. While IP Watcher excels at watching what a single person is doing on the network, right down to duplicating the contents of her Telnet session screen, NetLog lets you characterize the usage of your network over time. Think of IP Watcher as a single phone tap and NetLog as the National Security Agency.

NetLog consists of four packages, *tcplogger, udplogger, extract,* and *NetWatch.* *tcplogger* and *udplogger* log TCP and UDP sessions on the locally visible network. *extract* pulls information out of the logs they produce, and *NetWatch* is a real-time monitor: a more statistically oriented version of IP Watcher.

Using the information from *tcplogger* and a log-triggering package like *swatch* (see the next section), you can send yourself a page if a port scan starts or other weird traffic starts developing against your hosts.

swatch

ftp://coast.cs.purdue.edu/pub/tools/unix/swatch/

swatch is one of those packages that ought to be on every Unix box. If you've administered a host for any length of time, you've been there. The log files, extracts from log files, and renamed log files are slowly taking over your disk space. They're full of good information about system events, but more often than not, you find out on Monday that something went wrong on Friday at 5:30. *swatch* observes your log files, watches for regular expressions you define, and notifies you in one of about a zillion ways without getting carried away. If a given event causes 50 log messages, you can choose to be notified only once. Not surprisingly, *swatch* is written in Perl.

Network Operations Center On-Line (NOCOL)

http://www.netplex-tech.com/software/nocol/

If you ply your trade at a site of any decent size, you probably have a fair amount of resources dedicated to high-end network management packages like HP Openview, SunNet Manager, and Cabletron Spectrum. All those things are fine and dandy for configuring or pulling statistics from your various devices. If what you really want, though, is a status screen for you and your operators to tell at a glance what's running and what's not, NOCOL is very likely just the ticket.

NOCOL consists of command-line, Curses, Web, and multiple API interfaces into a single state engine. That state engine comes with monitors for ICMP ping, RPC portmapper, OSI ping, Ethernet load, TCP ports, nameserver, radius server, syslog messages, mail queue, NTP, UPS (APC) battery, Unix host performance, BGP peers, SNMP variables, and overall host data throughput. Additional probes are easily written. Rather than be in binary UP or DOWN states, each monitored service can be in info (up), warning, error, or critical states that are definable for each service.

Boiling It All Down

Essentially, in order to care for the security of your hosts and the services, you have to be both a psychologist and a sociologist. That applies to your hosts, their users, and the abusers as well. Knowing how all the processes and resources within a host interact is as important as knowing how the host interacts with other hosts on the network. Anticipating what your users are going to do next has to be balanced with time spent trying to second-guess the next hacker with too much spare time.

You're probably going to spend either too much or too little time on security. There's no way of knowing ahead of time if the risks merit the effort—that's the nature of insurance policies.

14

Running a Dedicated Server

In this chapter, we'll discuss some of the motivations and challenges associated with running a dedicated IMAP server.

What's a Dedicated Server?

One of Unix's greatest strengths can also turn into a weakness. Just because you can provide a multitude of dissimilar services on a single server doesn't mean you should. Reduce the total number of services you offer on one server to one or two, and you may increase manageability, robustness, and security several-fold. On your mail server, this could directly translate to happier end users.

The goal of a dedicated server is to minimize administration and maintenance overhead while maximizing the performance of the service to which the server is dedicated. Then what is a dedicated server? It's a host tuned to provide a single service. A dedicated IMAP server, for example, would provide only IMAP services. It would not provide shell accounts (other than accounts required for system maintenance), IRC, Usenet, or any other service that is not directly required to provide IMAP service. Simply put, a dedicated IMAP server receives mail, deposits it in the mailstore, and provides access to the mailstore exclusively by way of IMAP.

Account Provisioning

Without shell accounts on a dedicated server, how does a user perform routine tasks such as changing her password or setting up mail forwarding? Dedicated servers, by definition, have no non-administrative shell accounts. Once you've done away with shell accounts, you're presented with the challenge of finding a way to provide the shell services by other means. Your solution should be both user-friendly and ubiquitous, and it should use your available resources responsibly.

If you're confident that all your users are on the same platform, you could employ various platform-specific provisioning solutions, such as an X-based or Windows application, Microsoft Exchange form, or your own home-brew application. Trust us, though—long-term maintenance costs of those solutions far outweigh the immediate gratification you'll receive.

A Web Solution

A good way to handle provisioning on a dedicated server is to bring up a provisioning web site.

There is a web of distractions out there, ranging from reliance on browser-specific features to various early attempts at standardized client-side scripting. Administrators should remain vigilant against developing a provisioning site that becomes arcane and proprietary. Stick to your guns and develop a straightforward, simple site that permits the user to perform simple actions (e.g., a password change or quota check). Even with such a simple web site, you'll find that you've eliminated nearly all of the need for users to have shell accounts. The remainder of your reasons for having user shell accounts, assuming those reasons are not IMAP related, could subsequently be addressed by bringing up a modest shell account host, such as a commodity PC running Linux.

There are five issues at the core of any provisioning web site: security, authentication, ease of use, system load, and permanence.

Security

You are your own best judge of what security issues are relevant to your particular provisioning site. Common critical issues include security of the data stream between the browser and server, security of the data on the provisioning system itself, and the security of the implementation.

Right now, the most practical way to secure your data stream is by using SSL (Secure Sockets Layer). If you require all users to use an SSL-enabled browser with encryption using 128-bit or larger keys, you've secured your data stream sufficiently. The Herculean effort required to compromise your data stream outweighs the value of the information reward to be gained. By using SSL you have the added benefit of encrypting password strings sent from the browser to the server. If you opt not to use SSL, your users should be appropriately warned that their passwords will be transmitted over the network in cleartext.

With all the secure plumbing in place, it's equally important that the provisioning data on your server be secure as well. One well-known national ISP gained notoriety a few years ago when a hacker was able to retrieve a cleartext file containing hundreds of customer names and credit card numbers.

When developing HTML forms, something you'll want to be attentive to is using the POST instead of GET method in your forms. The GET method conveys form variables on the URL command line, making them easy to retrieve by paging through the browser's URL history. The POST method, on the other hand, conveys those variables in the input stream to the server. If you use the POST method, subsequent users of the customer's machine can't go through the browser history and collect information useful in gaining access to the customer's account.

Some sites may decide to use HTTP cookies to allow a user to log in to the provisioning system and perform tasks without having to authenticate for each task. If you employ HTTP cookies, the cookie should expire after a brief period. Although it's possible to do so, subsequent users of a workstation will find it more difficult to masquerade as a user using someone else's cookie if that cookie has expired. HTTP cookies have a secure flag that, when set, will send the cookie to the server only if the CGI request is occurring on an SSL channel. You'll probably want to set the cookie's secure flag, although it's not necessary if your provisioning system is exclusively available via SSL.

We advise that you try to have as many levels of security as practical. It's always a good thing, in the planning, to assume that one or two levels of your security will be compromised. Ask yourself "what if" questions. If you don't have any shell accounts on your standalone server, but someone manages to get shell access anyway, are the permissions on critical directories and files closed down far enough that someone with non-root access would find such access useless?

Authentication

A provisioning web site must be able to authenticate its users. There are numerous ways to authenticate users of web sites, such as HTTP cookies, HTML form variables, or truly distasteful methods like assuming a user always logs in from a particular IP address. Ultimately, the correct method of authentication for your site would be the one that provides you with the most security and is most consistent with your existing authentication environment. What we're trying to get at here is that users are most likely to embrace an interface that's easy for them to use. With regard to authentication, that frequently means avoiding multiple passwords per user whenever possible.

CGI Scripts for Common Tasks

As a starting point, here are some Perl CGI scripts that will do some of the tasks we've mentioned. The examples in this section require you to install a web server, Perl 5 (*http://www.perl.com/*), and the CGI.pm Perl module (*http://www.cpan.org/ modules/by-module/CGI/CGI.pm-2.56.tar.gz*). CGI.pm is a Perl library used to make writing CGI scripts easier. You'll find documentation on CGI.pm at *http:// stein.cshl.org/WWW/software/CGI/*.

It's highly recommended that the web server be SSL-enabled. Details on how to set up an SSL-enabled web server are beyond the scope of this book, but a quick, simple, and free way is to use Apache-SSL (*http://www.apache-ssl.org/*) and OpenSSL (*http://www.openssl.org/*).

Changing a password

The password change utility described in this section uses a freely available password-changing CGI program called *chpasswd*. *chpasswd* is available for download from the *chpasswd* author's site (*http://sic.popnet.pl/~mlody/chpasswd/chpasswd-1. 3.tar.gz*) or from FreshMeat (*http://freshmeat.net/appindex/web/tools.html*).

There is a multitude of free web-based password-changing utilities available on the Net. *chpasswd* is mentioned here because it's a utility that's used to change standard Unix and shadow passwords, and thus it fills the needs of sites that rely on Unix authentication. Many of the utilities we found employ a *setuid* Perl or shell script to perform the password change. *chpasswd*, on the other hand, is a compiled executable. Although the executable is *setuid*, *setuid* executables don't pose as many risks as *suid* scripts because scripts depend on external programs that can be replaced, for example, with copies of *bash* to provide easy root access to malevolent users. *chpasswd* has the added security of consulting a *deny* file (*/etc/www.deny*) before processing any request. Users listed in the */etc/www.deny* (*root*, for example) are not allowed to change their password using the CGI. *chpasswd* logs the results of every password change request to syslog.

chpasswd was written for Linux, but we installed it and ran it successfully under Solaris with no problems. Since the *chpasswd* program uses the operating system's native *crypt* function, it should work equally well with other flavors of Unix. Keep in mind that *crypt* supports weak cryptography and thus provides only minimal security.

To build *chpasswd*, download and unpack the source distribution and run the *configure.sh* script. The script will ask you for the path to your *cgi-bin* directory and the HTTP path to the *chpasswd* CGI script. After running the *configure.sh* script, run *make* and *make install*. *make install* will copy the *chpasswd.cgi* program into your *cgi-bin* directory and will install in the source directory a rudimentary password change HTML form that submits input to the CGI. Example 14-1 is a slightly modified version of that form.

Example 14-1. Change Password Form

```
<HTML>
<BODY>
<TITLE>Password Change</TITLE>

<H1>Change Your Password</H1>

<form method="POST" action="https://themullets.net/cgi-bin/chpasswd.cgi">

<PRE>
Username:               <input type="text" name="login">
Current password:       <input type="password" name="password">
New password:           <input type="password" name="newpassword">
Confirm new password: <input type="password" name="newpassword2">
<PRE>

<P>
<input type="submit" value="OK"> <input type="reset" value="RESET"><BR>
</FORM>
</BODY>
</HTML>
```

Checking disk quota

Sites that run the UW IMAP server often configure the server to store personal mail folders under a user's home directory. Because UW doesn't explicitly support the IMAP quota extension, UW sites usually fall back on operating-system disk quotas. In those circumstances, it's frequently handy to give the user a tool to check his quota. Example 14-2 and Example 14-3 are a CGI form and handler that allow the user to check his disk quota.

Example 14-2. Quota Check CGI Form

```
#!/usr/local/bin/perl

use CGI;

$query = new CGI;

print $query->header;
print $query->start_html(-title=>'Check Quota');
print $query->startform(-action=>"quota_results.cgi");

print $query->h1($query->center("Check Quota"));
print $query->hr;
print <<EOM;
<p>Enter your username and password and click the Check Quota button.<p>
EOM
```

Example 14-2. Quota Check CGI Form (continued)

```
print "Username: ", $query->textfield(-name=>'user'),          $query->br;
print "Password: ", $query->password_field(-name=>'password'), $query->p;
print $query->center($query->submit('action','Check Quota'));
print $query->hr;

print $query->endform;
print $query->end_html;
```

Example 14-3, the form handler, authenticates the user based on the username and password entered on the previous form, then calls an external program to get the user's quota information. We leave out the details of the password authentication for the sake of generality.

Example 14-3. Quota Check CGI Form Handler

```
#!/usr/local/bin/perl

use CGI qw(:standard);

$query = new CGI;
$user     = $query->param('user');
$password = $query->param('password');

print $query->header;
print $query->start_html(-title=>'Check Quota');
print $query->center($query->h1("Disk Quota Results"));
print $query->hr;

if (correct_pass("$user","$password") == 1) {

    $quota = `/opt/apache/cgi-bin/quota $user`;

    print <<EOF;
    Disk quota and usage for $user:<p>

    <pre>$quota</pre>
EOF
} else {
    print "Login incorrect. Go back and try again."
}

print $query->p,$query->hr;
print $query->end_html;
```

The program that does the actual quota check within the CGI is a compiled C *setuid* program that calls the Unix *quota* command. CGI scripts run as the owner of the web server process, typically the user *nobody*. *nobody* is an unprivileged user and, as such, cannot gather data on other users using Unix commands like *quota*. The *setuid* program, referred to as a wrapper, changes its process ownership to a privileged user before executing the Unix command, then switches its ownership back to the original owner once the work is done.

There are other solutions to the challenges that arise from running your web server as an unprivileged user, some of them acceptable (carefully written setuid wrappers) and some truly dangerous (giving up and running the web server as *root*). Setuid programs have their own set of security problems, but the dangers are limited compared to other solutions. The GNU C Library documentation (*http://www.gnu.org/manual/glibc-2.0.6/html_mono/libc.html*) has an excellent set of guidelines for writing good setuid programs, with examples.

quota.c, the setuid wrapper source code, is shown in Example 14-4. It's important to note that the permissions on the compiled executable must have the setuid bit set, and the executable must be owned by *root*. If both conditions are not met, the program will not be able to change ownership of the process to the root and will not have sufficient permissions to run the *quota* command:

```
# gcc -o quota quota.c
# chown root:other quota
# chmod 4755 quota
# ls -l quota
-rwsr-xr-x  1 root      other         8660 Jan  2 20:54 quota*
```

Example 14-4. Quota Command Setuid Wrapper Program

```c
#include <stdio.h>
#include <sys/types.h>
#include <unistd.h>
#include <stdlib.h>

static uid_t euid, ruid;

/* Restore the effective UID to its original value. */

void
do_setuid (void)
{
  int status;

  status = setreuid (ruid, euid);
  if (status < 0) {
    fprintf (stderr, "Couldn't set uid.\n");
    exit (status);
    }
}

/* Set the effective UID to the real UID. */

void
undo_setuid (void)
{
```

Example 14-4. Quota Command Setuid Wrapper Program (continued)

```
    int status;

    status = setreuid (euid, ruid);
    if (status < 0) {
      fprintf (stderr, "Couldn't set uid.\n");
      exit (status);
      }
}


/* Main program. */

int
main(int argc, char **argv)
{
    FILE *fp;
    int pid, pipefds[2];
    char *user = argv[1];
    static uid_t euid, ruid;

    if (argc != 2) { printf("Usage: %s user\n", *argv); exit(1); }

    /* Save the real and effective user IDs.  */
    ruid = getuid ();  euid = geteuid ();

    if (pipe(pipefds) < 0) {
        perror("pipe"); exit(1);
        }

    if ((pid = fork()) < 0) {
        perror("fork"); exit(1);
        }

    if (pid == 0) {
        close(0);
        dup(pipefds[0]);
        close(pipefds[0]);
        close(pipefds[1]);

        /* Set user to real userid (file owner) */

        do_setuid();
        execl("/usr/sbin/quota", "quota", "-v", user, (char *) 0);

        perror("exec");
        exit(1);
    }

    close (pipefds[0]);
    exit(0);
}
```

Figure 14-1 and Figure 14-2 are screen shots of the CGI form and handler results.

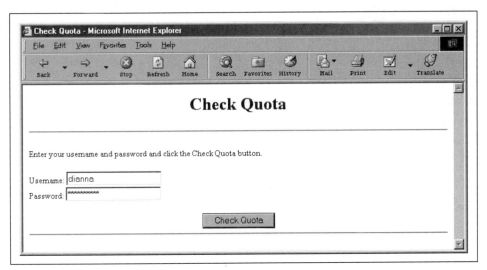

Figure 14-1. Quota CGI form

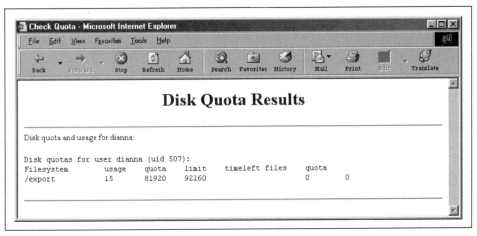

Figure 14-2. Quota CGI form handler results

Checking IMAP quotas

Sites that run the Cyrus IMAP server use quotas specific to the IMAP server, not the Unix operating system. Those sites will use either IMAP itself or the *cyradm* administration utility to report quotas. The next examples show how to check a user's quota using IMAP. The CGI form is shown in Example 14-5.

Example 14-5. CGI Form to Check IMAP Quota

```perl
#!/usr/local/bin/perl

use CGI;

$query = new CGI;

print $query->header;
print $query->start_html(-title=>'Check IMAP Quota');
print $query->startform(-action=>"imapquota_results.cgi");

print $query->h1($query->center("Check IMAP Quota"));
print $query->hr;
print <<EOM;
<p>Enter your username and password and click the Check Quota button.<p>
EOM
print "Username: ", $query->textfield(-name=>'user'),          $query->br;
print "Password: ", $query->password_field(-name=>'password'), $query->p;
print $query->center($query->submit('action','Check Quota'));
print $query->hr;

print $query->endform;
print $query->end_html;
```

Example 14-6 is the CGI form handler. After authenticating the user, the CGI script connects the user to the IMAP port and issues the IMAP *getquotaroot* directive to get the user's quota. Note that the handler relies on the Telnet.pm module; you may need to install the Net::Telnet module because it is not included with the standard Perl distribution.*

Example 14-6. CGI Form Handler to Check IMAP Quota

```perl
#!/usr/local/bin/perl

use CGI qw(:standard);
unshift (@INC, '/usr/local/lib/perl5/site_perl/5.005/Net');
use Telnet;

$query = new CGI;
$user     = $query->param('user');
$password = $query->param('password');

print $query->header;
print $query->start_html(-title=>'Check IMAP Quota');
print $query->center($query->h1("IMAP Quota Results"));
print $query->hr;

if (correct_pass("$user","$password") == 1) {

    $quotainfo = check_quota($user,$password);
```

---

* As of Perl 5.005_03.

Example 14-6. CGI Form Handler to Check IMAP Quota (continued)

```
    print <<EOF;
    IMAP quota and usage for $user:<p>

    <pre>$quotainfo</pre>
EOF
} else {
    print "Login incorrect. Go back and try again."
}

print $query->p,$query->hr;
print $query->end_html;
## Function:    check_quota
##
## Purpose:     Logs user in to IMAP, runs GETQUOTAROOT,
##              returns usage and limit
##
sub check_quota {

    my ($username, $passwd) = @_;
    my $hostname = "imap.unt.edu";

    my $imap = new Net::Telnet (Telnetmode => 0);
    $imap->open(Host => $hostname, Port => 143);

    ## Read the connection message for status

    $line = $imap->getline;
    die $line unless $line =~ /OK/;

    ## Log the user in

    $imap->print("0 login $username $passwd");
    $line = $imap->getline;
    die $line unless $line =~ /OK/;

    ## Get the quota and usage

    $imap->print("0 getquotaroot inbox");
    @lines = $imap->getlines (Timeout => 30);

    foreach $line (@lines) {
        chop $line;

        if ($line =~ /STORAGE/) {
            ($junk, $remainder) = split (/\(/, $line);
            $remainder = substr ($remainder, 0, -1);
            ($resource, $usage, $quota) = split (' ', $remainder);
            last;
        }
    }

    return "Your IMAP quota is $quota Kbytes: usage is $usage Kbytes.\n";
    exit;
}
```

Figure 14-3 and Figure 14-4 are screen shots of the IMAP quota check form and handler results.

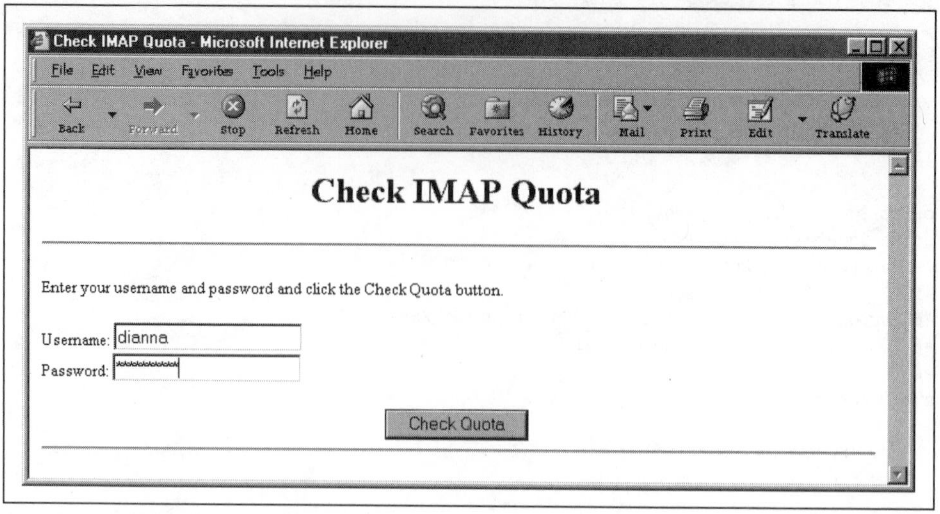

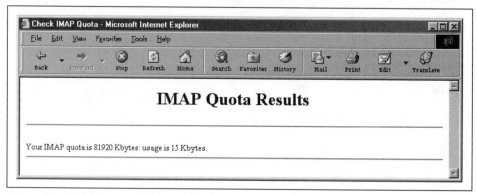

Figure 14-3. IMAP quota CGI form

Figure 14-4. IMAP quota CGI form handler results

Mission Restriction

If you decide to bring up dedicated IMAP servers, there's a short list of things you can do to help prepare your host and help focus its activities on the task at hand: IMAP. Primarily, these activities can be grouped together as limiting the number of server processes, eliminating or restricting non-administrative accounts, and reducing non-essential workload on the host.

Reducing Server Processes

Out of the box, your operating system probably supports a variety of services through the *inetd* superserver. None of those services is essential to the IMAP mission. In most cases, you can reduce your *inetd* services down to a single line in your configuration file that supports your particular IMAP service. If non-privileged users never log on to your mail host, you are somewhat freer to make assumptions about what kind of client software those users have. For example, assuming that:

- Interactive logins, if allowed, are done via Secure Shell (SSH), and SSH runs as a standalone daemon, and

- The MTA runs as standalone daemon, as does sendmail

then there's little reason to have anything but a one-line *inetd.conf* file.

Once you've shaved down your *inetd.conf* file, send a HUP signal to it to refresh the active configuration. Then, use *netstat* to get a picture of what kinds of "listens" are still active on your machine. Here's an example from a machine that hasn't completely reduced its *inetd.conf* file yet (the output has been trimmed down with some filtering from *egrep*):

```
% netstat -a | egrep -i '(tcp|udp|listen|\*|local)'

UDP
    Local Address       State
        *.sunrpc        Idle
        *.*             Unbound
        *.32771         Idle
        *.32773         Idle
        *.32774         Idle
        *.tftp          Idle
        *.32776         Idle
        *.lockd         Idle
        *.32779         Idle
        *.syslog        Idle
        *.22370         Idle
        *.nfsd          Idle
        *.32800         Idle
        *.32801         Idle
        *.snmp          Idle
        *.*             Unbound
        *.erpc          Idle
        *.37407         Idle
        *.36161         Idle
        *.36629         Idle
        *.36798         Idle
        *.36799         Idle
        *.36805         Idle
        *.762           Idle
```

```
TCP
   Local Address         Remote Address     Swind Send-Q Rwind Recv-Q  State
      *.sunrpc              *.*                  0     0     0      0 LISTEN
      *.32771              *.*                  0     0     0      0 LISTEN
      *.imap               *.*                  0     0     0      0 LISTEN
      *.cyrus              *.*                  0     0     0      0 LISTEN
      *.ftp                *.*                  0     0     0      0 LISTEN
      *.echo               *.*                  0     0     0      0 LISTEN
      *.lockd              *.*                  0     0     0      0 LISTEN
      *.32772              *.*                  0     0     0      0 LISTEN
      *.22370              *.*                  0     0     0      0 LISTEN
      *.nfsd               *.*                  0     0     0      0 LISTEN
      *.32774              *.*                  0     0     0      0 LISTEN
      *.32775              *.*                  0     0     0      0 LISTEN
      *.pop-3              *.*                  0     0     0      0 LISTEN
      *.7937               *.*                  0     0     0      0 LISTEN
      *.3306               *.*                  0     0     0      0 LISTEN
      *.80                 *.*                  0     0     0      0 LISTEN
      *.smtp               *.*                  0     0     0      0 LISTEN
      *.22                 *.*                  0     0     0      0 LISTEN
```

Notice that although several of the services are named using the tags from the */etc/ services* file, several are not. Also note that *netstat* doesn't tell you which process (for example, *httpd* or *inetd*) is acting as a server in each case.

A much better tool for generating a comprehensive list of services and associated processes running on your host is the *lsof* (list open files) utility. If you've ever used IRIX, you're probably familiar with a similar utility called *fuser*, which has much the same functionality as *lsof*. In addition to showing you the processes that have a given file open, *lsof* can also show you which processes have given TCP and UDP sockets open. The following command produces a comprehensive list of services running on the host, as did the previous *netstat* command, but it also identifies the process and user associated with each service:

```
% lsof -i | egrep -i '(command|listen|idle)' | sort

COMMAND      PID USER    FD   TYPE     DEVICE SIZE/OFF NODE NAME
automount    162 root     9u  inet 0xf5c4e968      0t0  UDP *:762 (Idle)
erpcd        284 root     3u  inet 0xf5f5e650      0t0  UDP *:erpc (Idle)
hpnpd        227 root     3u  inet 0xf5e0f1a0      0t0  UDP *:22370 (Idle)
hpnpd        227 root     4u  inet 0xf5e0f130      0t0  TCP *:22370 (LISTEN)
httpd       2934 root    20u  inet 0xf5e0f2f0      0t0  TCP *:80 (LISTEN)
httpd       4136 www     20u  inet 0xf5e0f2f0      0t0  TCP *:80 (LISTEN)
httpd      17981 www      5u  inet 0xf5e0f280   0t4051  TCP *:57651 (IDLE)
httpd      17981 www     20u  inet 0xf5e0f2f0      0t0  TCP *:80 (LISTEN)
httpd      21277 www     20u  inet 0xf5e0f2f0      0t0  TCP *:80 (LISTEN)
httpd      21425 www     20u  inet 0xf5e0f2f0      0t0  TCP *:80 (LISTEN)
httpd      23094 www     20u  inet 0xf5e0f2f0      0t0  TCP *:80 (LISTEN)
httpd      25665 www     20u  inet 0xf5e0f2f0      0t0  TCP *:80 (LISTEN)
httpd      26498 www     20u  inet 0xf5e0f2f0      0t0  TCP *:80 (LISTEN)
imapd      19062 kwm      6u  inet 0xf5f5e3b0      0t0  UDP *:36798 (Idle)
imapd      19069 kwm      6u  inet 0xf5f5e030      0t0  UDP *:36799 (Idle)
```

```
inetd       136 root    5u   inet 0xf5b302e8     0t0       TCP *:imap (LISTEN)
inetd       136 root    6u   inet 0xf5b30278     0t0       TCP *:cyrus (LISTEN)
inetd       136 root    7u   inet 0xf5b30208     0t0       TCP *:ftp (LISTEN)
inetd       136 root    8u   inet 0xf5b30198     0t0       UDP *:tftp (Idle)
inetd       136 root   12u   inet 0xf5b300b8     0t0       TCP *:echo (LISTEN)
inetd       136 root   21u   inet 0xf5e0f7c0     0t0       TCP *:pop-3 (LISTEN)
lockd       141 root    4u   inet 0xf5e0fc90     0t0       UDP *:lockd (Idle)
lockd       141 root    5u   inet 0xf5e0fc20     0t0       TCP *:lockd (LISTEN)
micq      17882 kwm     5u   inet 0xf5f5e1f0     0t81531   UDP *:36629 (Idle)
mountd      271 root    4u   inet 0xf5f5eb90     0t0       UDP *:32800 (Idle)
mountd      271 root    6u   inet 0xf5f5eab0     0t0       TCP *:32774 (LISTEN)
mysqld     8265 root    3u   inet 0xf5f5e500     0t0       TCP *:3306 (LISTEN)
nfsd        269 root    4u   inet 0xf5f5ed50     0t0       UDP *:nfsd (Idle)
nfsd        269 root    5u   inet 0xf5f5ece0     0t0       TCP *:nfsd (LISTEN)
nscd       5334 root   10u   inet 0xf5e0f3d0     0t0       UDP *:36161 (Idle)
nsrexecd   1377 root    3u   inet 0xf5f5ef10     0t0       TCP *:7937 (LISTEN)
rpc.bootp   276 root    0u   inet 0xf5f5e960     0t0       UDP *:32801 (Idle)
rpc.bootp   276 root    1u   inet 0xf5f5e8f0     0t0       TCP *:32775 (LISTEN)
rpcbind     112 root    3u   inet 0xf5b30d68     0t0       UDP *:sunrpc (Idle)
rpcbind     112 root    5u   inet 0xf5b30c88     0t0       UDP *:32771 (Idle)
rpcbind     112 root    6u   inet 0xf5b30c18     0t0       TCP *:sunrpc (LISTEN)
rpcbind     112 root    7u   inet 0xf5b30ba8     0t0       TCP *:61409 (IDLE)
sendmail  22010 root    7u   inet 0xf5e0f440     0t0       TCP *:smtp (LISTEN)
snmpd       279 root    0u   inet 0xf5f5e730     0t0       UDP *:snmp (Idle)
sshd        370 root    3u   inet 0xf5c4e658     0t0       TCP *:22 (LISTEN)
sshd      19112 root    8u   inet 0xf5f5e180     0t0       UDP *:36805 (Idle)
statd       139 root    3u   inet 0xf5e0fe50     0t0       UDP *:32776 (Idle)
statd       139 root    4u   inet 0xf5e0fd00     0t0       TCP *:32772 (LISTEN)
statd       139 root    9u   inet 0xf5e0f670     0t0       UDP *:32779 (Idle)
statd       139 root   10u   inet 0xf5c4ef18     0t0       UDP *:37407 (Idle)
syslogd     166 root    4u   inet 0xf5e0f4b0     0t0       UDP *:syslog (Idle)
ypbind      120 root    4u   inet 0xf5b30518     0t0       UDP *:32773 (Idle)
ypbind      120 root    6u   inet 0xf5b30588     0t0       UDP *:32774 (Idle)
ypbind      120 root   10u   inet 0xf5b304a8     0t0       TCP *:32771 (LISTEN)
```

This listing shows the actual command, process ID, user, and TCP or UDP port associated with each service running on the current host. Once you have the actual command and user name, you can find out how the service gets started and whom to contact about moving a service to another machine, if necessary.

The next order of business would be to examine the users on your host and eliminate as many as possible, or at least remove the ability to log in interactively. With the increasing popularity of NIS, Kerberos, and the variety of authentication methods usable with the PAM interface, it's possible that there are many more users of your mail host than those explicitly listed in your */etc/passwd* file. Users may be listed in a number of places, including a NIS password map or a CRAM password database. PAM configuration files (on many systems, under */etc/pam.d/*) may also have clues as to where authentication credentials are defined for your users.

Finally, run the *ps* command on your machine, audit the *crontabs*, *at* queues (usually in */var/spool/cron*), and */etc/rc?.d/** files to get a good handle on not only what is currently running on your host, but what is likely to run each time you start it and at any arbitrary point in the future. Your first reaction to this recommendation might be to dismiss it because, after all, you're the system administrator of your mail server and you ought to know everything that goes on. If more than one person has root access to your server, however, no matter how finely tuned your workflow is, you're likely to find at least a few subtle surprises when you do an audit of your host.

The Ultimate in Dedicated Servers

We want to briefly mention the concept of separating SMTP from IMAP; that is, using separate machines to perform IMAP access to the mailstore and SMTP routing. In this separate server scheme, the SMTP router uses Local Mail Transport Protocol (LMTP) to talk to the IMAP server, as shown in Figure 14-5.

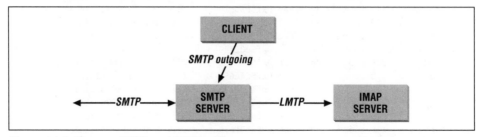

Figure 14-5. Separate SMTP and IMAP servers

That way, the IMAP server doesn't spend cycles and I/O bandwidth on managing an SMTP queue. This scheme is already being used successfully by a few early adopters and is beginning to be used more widely.

In this chapter:
• *Why Filter on the
  Server?*
• *Procmail*
• *Sieve*
• *To Filter or Not to
  Filter...*

15

*Server-Side Mail
Filtering*

Why Filter on the Server?

An old saying that rings true to email is "less is more." If you subscribe to mailing lists, post to Usenet, or frequent web sites that require your email address as part of the registration process, the character and volume of your incoming email can easily become unmanageable. You may wish to eliminate certain kinds of mail, such as SPAM (unsolicited commercial email), before you ever see it. In the case of quasi-unsolicited mail, or some mailing list traffic, you may wish to file it in a specific mailbox to keep it organized.

Many users manage their email using client-side filters. With client-side filtering, filtering can only take place while the client is running on your workstation. The mail must be downloaded before it can be filtered. Server-side filtering, however, makes downloading the mail unnecessary. The filtering occurs on the server, leaving scarce client resources free for other tasks. If you turn your workstation off and go on vacation for a week, filtering continues. All your incoming mail is organized for your return.

Procmail and Sieve are a couple of popular approaches to user-initiated server-side filtering. Procmail is the granddaddy of mail filtering software. It's the more powerful of the two, probably the most difficult to use, and is the best supported by ISPs, and it has the largest following. Procmail has a larger following primarily because it's been around longer. It's also more flexible, because it permits piping of messages into any arbitrary command or script you can dream up. Sieve is the alternative; it embraces prototypical standards being defined through various Internet drafts, listed at *http://www.cyrusoft.com/sieve/*. Sieve is the new kid on the block, is undoubtedly the most standards-based and the most secure, and has the potential to be the most appealing to end users. Sieve is more secure than Procmail, because it's more narrowly focused on specific filtering tasks.

Let's take a closer look at each approach.

Procmail

Every type of software, whether it's client software, server software, or software for personal productivity, has implementations that are available free or nearly so. Interestingly, the free implementation is sometimes the best and most popular implementation. Take sendmail, for example—it's the most well known MTA out there. Another good example is Procmail. For nearly a decade, Procmail has been used by email wizards and by the users who depend on their skills. A straightforward but powerful mechanism for flexible mail handling, Procmail does more than just filter incoming email. Depending on a variety of attributes, it can file, forward, respond to, delete, or perform any action that can be described in software, such as shell or Perl scripts.

If sendmail is the universal tool for getting mail from MTA to MTA, Procmail is the universal tool of MDAs. For the most part, anyone who's been exposed to Procmail fits into one of two classes: those who are wildly enthusiastic about Procmail and those who will be once they find the time to learn it.

Procmail was developed by Stephen R. van den Berg in 1990. In recent years, a complement of volunteers have joined forces to help Procmail evolve from a set of useful utilities written by one person to an ongoing effort that could very well outlast any given person working on it.

To use Procmail, you define, refine, and enshrine a series of Procmail filtering rules, which typically use regular expressions to describe common factors in the headers of email messages to which you want to apply some action.* For those who are so inclined, Procmail is a spectacular way to automate the tasks associated with culling through your email, filing the mail you want to keep in folders, and discarding the junk mail you don't want to keep.

One of the appeals of Procmail is that you can pipe the message header, the body, or the entire message into an external process. Once you can pipe email into a script, the actions you can take on the email are limited only by your imagination.

---

* The Unix equivalent of speaking in tongues, regular expressions (or *regex*) are the art of tersely describing text patterns using a variety of tokens and substitution rules. */aeiou/{2,3}$*, for example, becomes any two- or three-letter word consisting of all vowels. More germane to the topic, however, would be a regex like "*^Subject:\ .*(M\|m)ake\ (M\|m)oney\ (F\|f)ast*", which would catch many of the MMF messages bound for your mailbox. For more information, see *Mastering Regular Expressions* by Jeffrey E. F. Friedl (O'Reilly) or the *egrep*(1) or *regexp*(5) manpages.

Procmail comes with special-purpose facilities that will handle 99% of everything you might want to do with your email, so it's not always necessary to pipe email into a script. If, however, you want to set up a rule that auto-replies to mail by returning the day's C-SPAN television schedule to the sender, Procmail's just the ticket.

How Do You Install It?

There are two ways to run Procmail: either as the system-wide delivery agent or on a per-user basis. Let's assume here that, for whatever reason, it's impractical to use Procmail as your default MDA, so users are left to their own devices to use it.

There are a variety of mirrors for the current version of Procmail. Two sources of information are the Procmail Home Page (*http://www.procmail.org/*) and Infinite Ink's Processing Mail with Procmail site (*http://www.ii.com/internet/robots/ procmail/*).

The *procmail.org* site maintains a pointer to the latest stable version of Procmail at *ftp://ftp.procmail.org/pub/procmail/procmail.tar.gz*. Once you download and unpack it, you'll find an INSTALL file in the top-level directory that encourages you to edit the *config.h* and *Makefile*, then do a conventional build.

You can probably get away without editing anything in *config.h* and *Makefile*. On one of our test systems, a modestly loaded Sun SPARC 10 running *gcc* under Solaris 2.5.1, we ran *make* on the unadulterated source and got an error-free build in just under two minutes, forty seconds. The Procmail developers have integrated many of the tasks found in a *configure* script into the Makefile, so building Procmail leaves you with precious little to do but twiddle your thumbs and contemplate the fact that the spammers will soon be washed right out of your hair.

Building Procmail gets you the following programs:

Formail

Formail is very nearly as useful as Procmail. Not only can you use it within your Procmail recipes, but you can use it in scripts that "munge" incoming mail, or reformat into a different mail storage format. Formail can take a message on standard input and swap the *To:* and *From:* addresses around to produce a return header; it can be used to escape old headers with an "X-" or to add entirely new header fields. It is frequently used at the top of a Procmail recipe file to load the important fields of the current message into variables that might be used in a later recipe.

Lockfile

Internet messaging can sometimes be a mess of multiple processes all trying to read and write the same files at the same time. File-locking problems have become the bane of anyone with a vested interest in Internet email. The Lock-file utility is a bullet-resistant* utility for use in mail processing scripts. It's not likely to be needed inside Procmail recipes themselves. However, the odd script you might find yourself writing to convert someone's 10-year-old VMS mail file into a Unix mail file on an active NFS-mounted filesystem could bene-fit from a good application of Lockfile.

Procmail

The Leatherman Tool of email processing, Procmail takes mail messages one at a time from standard input and processes them according to a file of "reci-pes." These recipes can, based on a variety of factors, delete messages, file them in flat files or MH-style folders, bounce them to other addresses, or pipe them into other software. The factors on which the actions are based are nearly endless and include such things as header content and message size or external factors like the date, system load, or other random thing,

Mailstats

Mailstats is a nifty little shell script that reduces your Procmail log file down to statistics regarding how many messages and number of bytes (total and aver-age) went to various destinations.

How Does It Work?

Procmail, when run in "per-user" mode, is invoked from the *.forward* file. Proc-mail first sets environment variables to their default values, reads the incoming mail message to the EOF marker, separates the body from the header, and then, if no command-line arguments are present, looks for a file named *.procmailrc* in the user's home directory ($HOME). The filtering rules in *.procmailrc* determine where to distribute the mail message—usually a folder, but sometimes the message is bounced elsewhere or banished to */dev/null*.

If no *.procmailrc* file is found, or if there is no rule in the *.procmailrc* file that applies to the message, then Procmail stores the message in the user's incoming mail folder.

Simple Examples

Let's cut to the chase. We could fill a book with good ways to put Procmail to work. Our goal here, though, is just to give you some initial suggestions and point you in a useful direction. Let's jump into a sample *.procmailrc* file.

---

* It's always good to be dubious when it comes to file-locking schemes, no matter how good they are.

In Example 15-1, we give three recipes: one effectively deletes messages, one files them in a folder, and one bounces them to another email address.

Example 15-1. Example Procmail Rules File

```
MAILDIR=$HOME/mail                  # This directory must exist!
PATH=$HOME/bin:/usr/local/bin:/usr/bin:/usr/sbin
MYADDR=johndoe@imap.unt.edu
LOGFILE=$MAILDIR/procmail.log    # Keep a logfile to aid in debugging

#  RECIPE 1: Filter out annoying SPAM and drop it in the bit bucket
:0 w:
* ^Subject: .*((M|m)(AKE|ake)) ((M|m)(oney|ONEY)) ((F|f)(AST|ast)).*
/dev/null

#  RECIPE 2: Filter mailing list messages into a folder
#
:0 w:                            # Use a lockfile with personal mail folders!
* ^(To|Cc): .*info-cyrus.*
info-cyrus

#  RECIPE 3: Bounce urgent messages to my text pager
:0 c
* ^Priority: Urgent
! mypager@myhost.mydomain
```

Note that the syntax for mailbox and folder names on Cyrus servers is slightly different. Examples of Procmail rules files specific to Cyrus servers are shown in Chapter 9, *Cyrus System Administration*. For brevity, we're assuming the system here uses standard Unix format mail folders in *$HOME/mail* and that the user's incoming mail goes into */var/spool/mail/$LOGNAME*.

Example 15-2 shows a handful of mail messages and descriptions of how our procmail rules would act on them.

Example 15-2. Spam Mail

```
Date: Mon, 23 Mar 1998 05:48:11 +0100
From: Spamford and Son <spamford@junk.com>
To: <kwm@kwm.net>
Reply-To: spamford@junk.com
Subject: MAKE MONEY FAST!!!!!

Our new printing presses let YOU make money three times faster
than our previous printing presses. And NOW, a special offer! Buy
three printing presses, and get a FREE, yes FREE, bail bond.
Hurry, don't wait! Limited time offer.
```

Rule 1 in the procmail rules file (Example 15-1) looks for messages with a subject line that contains the phrase "MAKE MONEY FAST." Because Example 15-2 has such a subject line, Procmail catches it and pipes it into */dev/null*, and it is not delivered.

Example 15-3 is a message posted to a mailing list. Rule 2 looks for all mail either sent directly to or carbon copied to the *info-cyrus* mailing list and files it into a folder called *~/mail/info-cyrus*. Notice that the first line of the rule contains the two flags: a "w" and a ":". The *w* tells Procmail to wait for the filter to finish and check its exit code before filtering the message. The *:* tells procmail to lock the folder until delivery of the message is complete.

Example 15-3. Mailing List Message

```
Return-Path: <owner-info-cyrus@lists.andrew.cmu.edu>
Date: Sat, 25 Sep 1999 14:13:21 +0200 (CEST)
To: info-cyrus@lists.andrew.cmu.edu
Subject: Sieve
MIME-Version: 1.0
Content-Type: TEXT/PLAIN; charset=US-ASCII
Sender: owner-info-cyrus@lists.andrew.cmu.edu
Precedence: bulk

Could somebody post a sample Sieve script?
```

Example 15-4 is an urgent warning generated by a system watcher program. Procmail can be used to bounce incoming messages to another address, including the email address of a text pager. Rule 3 in the Procmail rules looks for messages that are flagged "Urgent." Because the message in Example 15-3 is such a message, Procmail catches it and forwards it to *mypager@myhost.mydomain*, which is the email address of a text pager.

Example 15-4. Urgent Message

```
Return-Path: <root@localhost>
Date: Sun, 26 Sep 1999 18:10:21 +0200 (CEST)
To: operator@localhost
Subject:
Priority: Urgent

Warning: /var is out of bounds (usage 95%).
```

Risks

If you receive a large amount of email, test your Procmail rules carefully. If Procmail is repeatedly unable to deliver mail due to an incorrect rules file, the system mail queue could fill up and cause a system hang.* Trying out an entirely new *.procmailrc* file is a bit like the scene in the movie where the guy has to defuse the bomb by clipping the red or the green wire, only in this case, there's a built-in

---

* The authors have seen a user bring a Sun Enterprise–class machine to a grinding halt when an error in his *.procmailrc* caused a storm of redelivery attempts. You can add some insurance against this happening on your system by limiting the number of processes per user to some fixed number.

delay of a few minutes before you hear the roar of hundreds or thousands (depending on how big the mailstream or file is that you're trying to process) of messages that are misdelivered. It's par for the course that anyone who pushes the envelope with Procmail has to spend a few days explaining to everyone why they suddenly had copies of old mail redelivered to them at the rate of 20 an hour. Take our word for it, it's always best to try out new rules on two or three test messages.

This is also a good place to mention indiscriminate Procmail user empowerment. If you've got a black box mail server and you give your users unfettered access to change their *.procmailrc* files, it's the same as giving each of them a shell account. In fact, depending on how you've implemented Procmail, it could be worse. If you've got a shared-mission mail server with shell accounts and associated safeguards already in place, then it's no big deal to let users just edit the *.procmailrc* file willy-nilly. If, however, you've got a black box mail server, we strongly advise you to wrap a CGI script around your editing functions—better yet, give users a restricted set of choices regarding what they can have Procmail do, and have the script generate a *.procmailrc* from scratch.

It should be apparent at this point that, as a user-configurable filtering agent, Procmail is wizard-friendly but may not be every end user's cup of tea. That's where Sieve comes in. Granted, Sieve has greatly reduced functionality compared to Procmail, but most users are far less demanding than your average wizard.

Sieve

Sieve, described in a draft RFC, is a language that is used to filter RFC 822 mail messages at the time of final delivery. Sieve is not intended to filter or process content other than RFC 822 messages. Sieve is not dependent on any particular platform, protocol, or mail architecture.

Background

Current filtering schemes abound, each with its own syntax and functionality, none of which interoperate with one another. Much to the dismay of both users and system administrators, mail filters must be translated or ported when a user moves from one client or server to another. If you've ever moved users from a Unix mail system to a Cyrus system, chances are that you experienced problems dealing with your Procmail users. Procmail filters don't port directly from Unix mail systems to Cyrus. There are syntax differences tied to the differences in mailbox format between the two systems. If there were a standard filtering language in place, then software developers and vendors could write filtering interfaces that could use common scripts. Sieve is intended to be just that standard.

Scope

Sieve is not a complete programming language. Not much can be done with Sieve, other than writing mail filters. Sieve was designed to make filtering simple and easy to use for the end user, while protecting the server it runs on by preventing users from doing things that could be destructive, such as making shell escapes or writing loops. Sieve is also designed to be easy to incorporate into GUI email clients, and thus promotes it as a standard across vendors and platforms. In spite of its simplicity, Sieve has all the features necessary to provide the fundamental tools needed to filter RFC 822 mail messages.

To further promote interoperability, Sieve has an extension mechanism that allows "beyond basic" functionality to be added while working within an open standards framework. Several extensions have already been suggested, including:

- Regular expression matching.

- Ability to handle detailed addressing. Detailed addressing permits the sender to bypass the INBOX and send email directly to a folder in a given mailbox. For example, mail addressed to *kwm+sample@themullets.net* will be placed, if the ACLs permit, in the folder *sample* belonging to the user *kwm@themullets.net*.

- A vacation command.

- Ability to set IMAP flags on delivery (e.g., \Deleted, \Answered, or \Seen).

- An *include* command to include an external Sieve program.

Sieve Implementations

Currently, the only freely available Sieve implementation is Carnegie Mellon University Sieve (*ftp://ftp.andrew.cmu.edu/pub/cmu-sieve/*). Sieve is integrated in Versions 1.6 and later of the Cyrus IMAP server.

The current implementation looks for the user's Sieve script in his home directory. Obviously, for sites that run the Cyrus IMAP server on a black box, code would need to look somewhere else for the scripts. Cyrus 1.6 and higher look in a configurable location defined by the *sievedir* setting in the *imapd.conf* file. Developers at CMU do plan to make that change in the next release of Sieve. If you can't wait until the next release, you can do it yourself—the code modification is trivial.

Other changes in the works include support for storing Sieve scripts on a server using ACAP.

Sieve Examples

A variety of good Sieve script examples is provided in the Sieve draft. To give you an idea of what the Sieve syntax is like, here are a sample mail message and some Sieve scripts. For each script, we tell you what happens to the message when the Sieve script processes it. The sample mail message is shown in Example 15-5.

Example 15-5. Sample Mail Message

```
Date: Tue, 8 Jul 1999 19:21:56 -0800 (PST)
From: niceguy@no.shame.org
To: johndoe@work.com
Subject: Make Money Fast!!!!!!!!!!

Wanted, 30 people earn $28 to lose 29 pounds in 31 days!!!
Guaranteed 100%! Don't delay!!! Go to http://www.over-18.com
immediately!!! Limited offer!!! Act now!!!
```

The *require* action declares an extension so that it can be used in the Sieve script. One of the extensions we've already mentioned is the *vacation* extension. Another, *fileinto*, delivers a message into a specified folder. A declaration is required to use an extension. Example 15-6 delivers the message in Example 15-5 into the user's *Spam* folder.

Example 15-6. The require and fileinto Actions

```
require "fileinto";
if header :contains ["from"] "niceguy" {
    fileinto "INBOX.Spam";
}
```

The *reject* action allows you to refuse delivery of a message and return it to the sender. When the message is returned, it's enclosed in a reject form that prints an informative message indicating why the message was rejected. In Example 15-7, our sample message is returned to the sender.

Example 15-7. The reject Action

```
if header :contains "subject" "Make Money Fast" {
    reject "I do not accept spam mail. Sorry.";
}
```

discard quietly throws a message away, as shown in the script in Example 15-8.

Example 15-8. The discard Action

```
if header :contains ["from"] ["niceguy@no.shame.org"] {
    discard;
}
```

Sieve Documentation

Here are some pointers to information on Sieve, which will be useful if you're interested in learning more and watching it progress from draft to standard.

Sieve web site

The Sieve web site, maintained by Cyrusoft International, Inc. is found at *http://www.cyrusoft.com/sieve/*.

IETF drafts

The Sieve draft is available at *http://search.ietf.org/search/brokers/internet-drafts/query.html*. Search for the string "sieve" to find the latest version.

Two proposed drafts for Sieve extensions are also available at the same site. If you search on the string "sieve", you will also find drafts for the Sieve Vacation Extension and an extension to allow specification of IMAP message flags on an IMAP server.

Mailing list and archives

Sieve discussion takes place on the MTA Filters mailing list. To subscribe, send a note to *ietf-mta-filters-request@imc.org* with the word "subscribe" in the body. An archive of the MTA Filters list is available at *http://www.imc.org/ietf-mta-filters*.

To Filter or Not to Filter...

It's clear that Procmail and Sieve have two slightly different aims. Procmail is flexible enough to be used for everything from a self-modifying reactive SPAM filter to a file server, while Sieve would offer the power of server-side filtration with the mechanical ease of client-side filtering. One issue should be covered, though. That issue is whether filtering should be done at all.

There is a handful of ethical and legal gotchas involved in doing server-side filtering, especially if the filtering is managed by the service provider and not the end user. We'll leave you to sort out the various legal issues, but here are a few issues that merit consideration before you launch into providing filtering services.

Silencing the Bullhorn

Most enterprise-wide email systems have a mechanism for sending out broadcast messages to everyone in the organization. Unfortunately, these mechanisms are frequently used for trite "anyone want to buy my Beanie Baby" messages and, likewise, for firestorms of responses about such inane messages (and counter-firestorms to those responses). Ultimately, such threads serve to introduce many of the recipients to the capabilities of their MUA's client-side filtering. The obvious problem here is that broadcast messages like "There's a large noxious cloud of Benzene descending on campus" won't reach the entire audience.

Actually, for installations that can't or won't control access to such broadcast mechanisms, this could be a good argument for using server-side filtering. Most users don't want to experiment with local filtering rules. If users knew that they could just submit a web form or send an email message to their local mail administrator requesting that they only get "official" broadcast messages, those noxious Benzene clouds would be a lot easier to avoid.

With Friends Like That...

Proactive attempts to rid users of their SPAM could backfire. If you take the narrow definition of SPAM as unsolicited commercial email, there's no way to tell without contacting the user if any given piece of mail was truly unsolicited or not. True, there's a wide number of telltale signs, like message distributions in multiples of 50, message-ID tags that fit certain patterns, or lists of recipients in alphabetical order spanning only 2 or 3 letters of the alphabet. All that needs to happen, though, is to have one message administratively discarded that the user wanted to receive and all your efforts to improve the users' messaging experience will have been for naught.

Some systems are starting to gravitate toward a "spam on the side" approach, where messages that meet certain strict suspicious criteria are filed in a special folder owned by the user. Messages are purged from that folder if they're over a week old. A system like this would be of particular value on servers that implement delivery of messages to numerous local users as links to a message that is only stored once in the physical mailstore.

Loose Cannons and Processes

This issue is more a factor with Procmail than with Sieve and is actually just a warning against loosely restricted end user shell accounts. A user could quite easily cause a process to go spinning out of control and consume an unhealthy amount of system resources by fumblefingering his *.procmailrc* file or by autofiling his mailing list messages so efficiently that he completely forgets them, and they consume great amounts of server storage.

There's no easy way, short of filtering abstinence, to ensure that these problems don't crop up. The best approach for administrators who do want to engage in server-side filtering is to keep an eye on their servers and place as many reasonable restrictions as possible on what a user can cause to happen with their filtering rules.

16

*Server
Performance
Tuning*

Although you may very well want your IMAP server to appear as a black box to your users, it should never appear so to you. In this chapter, we'll focus on a few hints that pertain primarily to IMAP servers.

Platform

On what platform should you run your IMAP servers? This is indeed the sixty-four-thousand-dollar question.

Broadly speaking, IMAP servers have many of the same requirements as other server machines. An IMAP server must be robust enough to handle a large number of connections and processes. It must also be able to stay up "24-by-7" so that users have confidence in the service. It should have enough memory and disk to store and process large amounts of mail without significant variations in performance.

The type of server platform that is able to provide that level of performance depends on your user base. As we mentioned earlier, a desktop machine (e.g., an Intel Pentium II with a 9 GB disk and 64 MB of memory, running Solaris X86, Linux, or FreeBSD) works just fine in some environments—e.g., a small company with 100 to 200 employees or an ISP with 500 to 1,000 customers.

Customers of a large ISP, however, might be far less forgiving of intermittent outages for maintenance than corporate users, who may not even notice an outage at four o'clock in the morning. Unless you use some sort of high-availability scheme like IP load-balancing or server clustering, we recommend that your servers exploit server-quality (or server-class) hardware. A server-quality machine is built from components that are engineered to higher standards than the typical desktop machine. It is also built with room for expansion and includes fully redundant, hot-swappable components. While commodity hardware may be temptingly inexpensive to purchase initially, a server-quality machine could save you hours of downtime you would have spent replacing a cheap but failing power supply or disk in the cheaper machine. Going with server-class hardware doesn't mean that you have to abandon Intel-based architecture. Companies like Compaq, Dell, and HP make very respectable server machines that, with the right software and hardware, can go toe-to-toe with most Unix-only hardware like Sun SPARC. As we write this, one of the top 200 supercomputers in the world is a cluster of commodity-class PCs running Linux[*] at Sandia National Labs, all connected by fiber channel. Theoretically, you could even run Linux on a top-of-the-line server from Sun or SGI, but we're not certain doing so would put you in the best position with Sun's or SGI's customer service when it came time to ask them for support.[†]

So what broad conclusions can we come to?

Size for Twice the Expected Load

Stuff happens. That's the only bona-fide guarantee with respect to capacity planning we make in this book.

Given that, your normal workload should never exceed half the capacity of your server. Exceptional circumstances like SPAM attacks, denial of service attacks, or network failures could easily exacerbate system load.

If you want to run your 12,000-user ISP on a single Pentium I box with a 10-year old copy of Xenix and an IMAP server you wrote in Korn shell scripts, that's okay—as long as you don't mind sitting at the console constantly making judgment calls about which sessions to kill and how next to partition and re-process your mail queue. You may have achieved an IMAP server for $200 in capital expenditures since the disk was the only thing you had to buy and the rest of the system was found in an abandoned warehouse. But once you figure in your salary and the number of projects you weren't able to address because you're continuously baby-sitting your server, the cost may be the same as a high-end server—but with only a small fraction of the performance quality.

---

[*] There are known performance problems with the default Linux filesystem. Tuning or use of an alternative filesystem on Linux systems should be considered.

[†] Although a free OS on new Sun or SGI equipment may not be the best idea, it might open up interesting OS possibilities for your ancient machines that are past end-of-life and have dubious original vendor support as is, like that old NeXT cube you might have under a pile of old trade magazines in your office.

One of the benefits of going with open source software is that you can hopefully take the money you would have spent on lower performance commercial closed source software and put it into hardware where it will do more good.

Starting up a new mail server is always a bit of a crap shoot. If you're not upgrading from a legacy system, you never have any firm numbers on which to base your sizing decisions. Conventional wisdom is that it's better to overshoot than undershoot your system capacity. Obviously, it's easy to go overboard in this regard. One ISP we know of went shopping for Usenet news servers, bought a good-sized RAID array for storage, but also bought three Origin 2000 servers to use as the NNTP servers. Two ended up taking care of the workload, while a third ended up being used as a sandbox until they found a real use for it.

Redundancy, Redundancy, Redundancy...

The idea of having an array of truly redundant IMAP servers is still in its early stages. Some folks split their users up between two or more IMAP servers. Some have modified the code in their UW servers to take advantage of the hooks for mailbox and login referrals. Most of the really solid schemes for load-balancing across redundant IMAP servers seem to be implemented in closed source commercial products that have draconian control over the functions of everything from the MTA to the server-side MUA. NFS file locking is the primary deterrent to sharing a networked mailstore between IMAP servers. Doing so involves a very high risk that IMAP-related processes, such as *sendmail, /bin/mail,* Cyrus *deliver, procmail,* and *imapd,* will stomp on one other and corrupt your mailstore.* There are, however, plenty of other places to add redundancy in your mail system.

The most obvious place to add redundancy is in the media for the mailstore itself. RAID is the most cost-effective way to do this, as we'll discuss later. One technology that's attractive for large mailstores is a Storage Area Network, or SAN. On a SAN-enabled network, compute servers are almost completely divorced from their data server counterparts. Large, gigabit-networked or multigigabit-networked disks are shared by any number of servers with no common operating system. Many of the standards are still being hammered out, as are the ideas of just the right way to market such things. Many of the server-class hardware vendors have schemes where two or more servers can be locally attached to the same disk array and have it appear as local to all the attached servers. All of these schemes, with the exception of RAID, are the kind of thing that can at least double your budget trying to get from 99.9 to 99.99 or 99.999 percent uptime. Decimal places are very expensive.

---

* Qmail's (*http://www.qmail.org/*) *maildir* format is the only free mailstore format we know of that, by its design, allows writing to an NFS-mounted mailstore.

Keep the Spaghetti on Your Plate...

...not in your mail system. Strunk and White's classic guide to writing, *Elements of Style*, opens with the rule "Avoid Unnecessary Words." A similar text for disciplined system design would open with "Avoid Unnecessary Dependencies."

A good example of this would be to run a caching-only name server on each of your mail servers, especially the SMTP servers. That way, in exchange for a periodic tiny reduction in system performance, your server would be insulated from DNS interruptions of small to moderate length. Another example would be to use an authentication system that incorporates some degree of fault-tolerance or redundancy.

You're probably ready for us to get to the meat and potatoes of this chapter. Let's move on to some of the tangible variables you can examine and change on your system to get more out of what you've got.

I/O Subsystem Tuning

Disk storage requirements can grow by as much as 100% per year. The more storage grows, the more important it becomes to provide reliable access to the data. To ensure both economical and reliable access to data, it's important to consider both scalability and high availability. The section discusses factors to consider when you select a disk subsystem for your IMAP server.

Special I/O Considerations for Cyrus and UW Systems

On Cyrus servers, disk configuration is the most critical factor in system performance. The Cyrus server is I/O bound, and if the disk configuration is not tuned, the system will spend too much time in the I/O wait state. The general idea is to have the logging partition, mailstore, mailboxes file, and mail queue partition as spread out as possible over disks and controllers. Read the Performance Notes section of the Cyrus installation guide for performance tuning guidelines.

On UW servers, disk configuration is the most critical factor in system performance. The UW server is I/O bound, and if the disk configuration is not tuned, the system will spend too much time in the I/O wait state. The general idea is to have the logging partition, mailbox files, and mail queue partition as spread out as possible over disks and controllers. A secondary consideration with UW servers is memory; when in doubt, put more RAM on your UW server, but only after tuning your disk configuration first.

Disk Interface

Integrated Drive Electronics (IDE)

Avoid IDE disks. IDE disks are cheap, but not scalable—the limit on the number of IDE disks you can connect to a bus is lower than with SCSI. Additionally, their transfer rates are lower than high-end SCSI transfer rates.

Small Computer Systems Interface (SCSI)

Fast-wide and Ultra SCSI disks are affordable and offer the performance required by an IMAP server. Fast-wide and Ultra SCSI both support up to 15 devices per bus, making them scalable alternatives. Fast-wide SCSI has a transfer rate of 20 MB/s, and Ultra SCSI's transfer rate is twice that. If you run a Cyrus server and opt for a SCSI disk subsystem, the performance Ultra SCSI will buy you is especially worth the extra cost. Although SCSI is widely used and likely will stick around for quite a few more years, keep in mind that the 15-year-old SCSI disk technology has been superseded in efficiency, performance, and scalability by fibre channel technology.

Fibre Channel Arbitrated Loop (FC-AL)

Fibre channel is nothing more than a high-speed serial connection, indifferent to the format of the data. FC-AL is an enhancement to fibre channel specification that employs a simple loop topology. FC-AL disk subsystems typically transfer data using SCSI protocols, but because the data is transferred over a high-speed fibre connection, FC-AL supports transfer rates of up to 100 MB/s. Up to 126 FC-AL devices are supported per host adapter, making FC-AL far more scalable than SCSI. FC-AL disk array implementations also support hot-pluggable components and multiple host connections.

RAID versus standalone disks

Redundant Array of Inexpensive Disks (RAID) was originally intended to combine small, inexpensive drives to achieve the reliability and performance of a single large, expensive disk. However, because disk manufacturers are now shipping large (50 GB) *inexpensive* disks, capacity is no longer the primary benefit—instead, higher performance and reliability are what a RAID system buys you. RAID arrays are designed to achieve higher performance than independent disks by replicating and/or spanning data across multiple disks.

RAID subsystems can provide high performance if the right configuration is used. If the wrong configuration is used, RAID can actually impair performance. The most popular RAID levels are RAID 0, RAID 1, RAID 1+0, and RAID 5. Each RAID level is explained here and compared in Table 16-1:

RAID 0 (striping)

Striping breaks a stream of data into equally sized chunks and writes the set of chunks (also known as a stripe) sequentially to successive drives in the disk array. Each stripe spans all drives from the first drive to the last drive in the array. Because each disk in the stripe has its own independent data channel, the transfer rate of RAID 0 approaches the sum of the transfer rates of the individual drives. RAID 0 offers high transaction-based performance because the data is spread across many spindles, which balances the I/O load. RAID 0 does not offer additional fault tolerance over individual disks.

RAID 1 (mirroring)

RAID 1, or mirroring, is designed to offer data redundancy. A mirror consists of two disks. Each write operation is duplicated to both disks—each disk is an identical copy of the other. RAID 1 offers improved performance because reads are taken from only one of the mirrored disks. However, write performance is degraded because both disks are involved in a write operation. RAID 1 is expensive because 100% duplication of data is required.

RAID 1+0 (mirroring and striping)

RAID 1+0 combines mirroring and striping to provide high data redundancy and improved performance. Data is first mirrored for redundancy, then striped for performance. RAID 1+0 can tolerate multiple disk failures with little or no degradation in performance. Like RAID 1, RAID 1+0 is expensive because 100% duplication of data is required.

RAID 5 (striping and distributed parity)

RAID 5 adds fault tolerance to striping by adding error correction information to the data. Both the data and the parity are striped across disks. RAID 5 subsystems typically have good read performance and poor write performance—for each write, the system must first perform four I/O operations and two parity calculations. The main benefit of RAID5 is the cost savings. Depending on the number of disks in the RAID, the overhead is in the range of 20 to 30%, much less than mirroring.

Table 16-1. Comparison of RAID Levels

RAID Level	Strengths	Weaknesses
RAID 0	• Improved I/O performance • Inexpensive (cost = sum of costs of disks)	• No data redundancy—if one disk fails, the entire RAID fails
RAID 1	• Improved read performance in most cases • Data redundancy	• Expensive (cost = 2 × sum of costs of disks) • Decreased write performance
RAID 1+0	• High availability • No performance sacrifice	• Expensive (cost = 2 × sum of costs of disks) • Survives multiple disk failures
RAID 5	• Cheaper than mirroring • Data redundancy	• Poor write performance • Survives only one disk failure

The recommended configuration for Cyrus IMAP servers is either RAID 1+0 or hardware RAID5. For UW IMAP servers, mirroring is recommended because it writes using Berkeley format. The improved performance, especially on large systems, is a necessity.

Filesystem Tuning

If your system has large UFS filesystems, then you will get more efficient storage and improve I/O performance by adjusting UFS parameters. Filesystem parameters are set at the time the filesystem is created with the *newfs* command.

Inode density

Inode density of a filesystem is defined as the number of kilobytes allocated per inode. The inode density determines the fixed number of inodes to create on the filesystem. Another way to think of inode density is as a prediction of the average file size of the files that are stored on the filesystem—the lower the density, the more files. For example, a density of 1 KB/inode is another way of saying that the average size of files on the filesystem is around 1 KB.

It's important from a performance standpoint to make an accurate prediction of the number of inodes. It is even more important for capacity planning. If you underestimate the number and run out of inodes, the result will be the same as if a filesystem reached its capacity—processes, such as your mail delivery agent, will not be able to create new files on the filesystem. Cyrus systems and UW systems have different needs in terms of inode density:

- A Cyrus mailstore stores a large number of small files. The default UFS inode density (2 KB per inode) is sufficient for the needs of the Cyrus system.

- UW systems store a smaller number of "average" sized files, so the default UFS inode density is somewhat thick. Build UW mailstores with a density of at least 8 KB per inode.

This example builds a UFS filesystem with an inode density of 8 KB per inode:

```
# newfs -v -i 8192 /dev/rdsk/md/raid5a
```

Here's an example* of */usr/ucb/df –i* and */usr/ucb/df –lk* output for a typical Cyrus system:†

```
% /usr/ucb/df -i
Filesystem            iused   ifree  %iused  Mounted on
/dev/md/dsk/d0      2509146 3847846   39%    /var/spool/imap
```

---

* There are a couple of different varieties of *df* on your average Solaris system, and *df* is probably going to have a different syntax on other Unix dialects, so your mileage may vary. Consult the manpage for *df.*

† Output pertaining to other partitions was removed for brevity.

```
% /usr/ucb/df -lk
Filesystem              kbytes     used   avail capacity  Mounted on
/dev/md/dsk/d0        52222520 25546655 26153640    50%   /var/spool/imap
```

As you can see, the mail spool consumes about 50% of disk capacity and about 40% of the inodes. In practice, this is suitable but probably a little close for comfort. With the previous example in mind, suppose the user community changed its usage patterns suddenly, and the average message size took a dive while the average number of messages per user in the mailstore went up. That could bring the filesystem dangerously close to the inode limit. In keeping with the "engineer so that your sustained load never goes above 50% utilization" rule, it might be better to see inode consumption at around 25% here.

Minimum free space

The minimum free space is the percentage of free space to maintain in the filesystem, between 1% and 99%. Minimum free space is space reserved as working space for the operating system to use when a filesystem reaches its capacity. The free space cannot be written by normal users—once the filesystem fills, only the superuser can write to the filesystem. Although the well-known rule is to set the free space to 10% of the filesystem size, that rule applied back in the old days when filesystems were a few megabytes, not gigabytes, in size. The rule is different nowadays, when filesystems are seldom smaller than a gigabyte. Some operating systems automatically optimize minimum free space for large filesystems. If your operating system does not, set the minimum free space to 1% of the total filesystem size on filesystems larger than 2 GB to prevent wasted disk space. The following example shows how to build a filesystem with 1% free space:

```
# newfs -v -m 1 /dev/rdsk/md/raid5a
```

This example shows how to adjust the free space on an already built, not currently mounted filesystem:

```
# tunefs -m 1 /dev/rdsk/md/raid5a
```

Memory Tuning

How Much RAM Is Enough?

Figuring real memory requirements is a complex task and is somewhat platform dependent. On IMAP systems, the physical memory requirements are directly related to the number of users actively reading their mail at one time. IMAP processes are long-lived and typically inactive for long periods. For example, a user may spend 10 minutes reading and replying to a message during one connection. That being the case, there's no reason why an IMAP process should be held in physical memory for the duration of the connection—it's perfectly acceptable for the process to be swapped out to the swap space.

A survey of large sites that run UW or IMAP servers shows that an IMAP system optimally requires 1 to 2 MB of physical memory per active IMAP session. For UW servers, the 1 to 2 MB rule also applies, but it's advisable to steer towards 2 MB. A UW IMAP process will grow to accommodate the largest message in the mailbox, so a 40 MB message will result in a 40 MB or larger IMAP process. For Cyrus servers, 1 MB per active server is sufficient, provided you optimize your swap space.

Optimizing Swap Performance

Your swap configuration is every bit as important as the amount of physical memory on your system. Swapping occurs when the operating system moves an inactive process from RAM to disk, freeing up RAM for active processes. Here are some guidelines for configuring your system's swap space for ultimate performance:

- Put swap space on a separate disk partition to rule out problems with disk fragmentation, in case the disk becomes fragmented.

- Put swap partitions on separate physical disks. You get a very large performance benefit from having swap partitions on separate disks, because I/O is spread across more than one channel.

- Put swap partitions on your fastest disks on your system.

- A good guideline for figuring total swap space on your system is to make it at least twice the size of your physical memory. Never configure the system with a swap size less than the size of your physical memory—once the system has exhausted its swap space, memory is no longer available to *any* process on the system.

- If you have more than one disk per controller, don't put swap partitions on more than one of the disks on a given controller.

- Don't swap to NFS-mounted partitions.

Kernel and Network Driver Tuning

System tuning or, more specifically, kernel, driver, and filesystem tuning are "lady or tiger" propositions. The best advice is to embrace conservatism. Before you dive into any wholesale system tuning, take some snapshots of how your system is performing over the course of a week or so, make some modest changes, then watch it for another week or so. All too often, system administrators change 5 or 10 independent variables at a time, then fall prey to the fallacy of false cause, assuming that it was one particular that caused that huge increase in system performance. Of course, it might just be that it's December 20th and most of your user base just left on Christmas vacation.

Diagnose the Problem

You've got a comfortably low system load. You're barely paging at all. You've lots of disk space, and your disk channels are not I/O bound. Your IMAP server performs wonderfully when you crank up PINE on the server itself and point it to localhost as the default IMAP server. Everything ought to be great, but it isn't. You've got a steadily growing queue of users all complaining that IMAP performance has dropped to its knees. Sounds like you have a networking problem on your hands.

This sounds like a job for *netstat. netstat* is one of those gifts that come with all Unix systems. Actually, most systems with good TCP/IP support come with *netstat.* Even MS-Windows has it.

Using netstat

Provided you've got connectivity between your clients and servers,[*] *netstat* can help you characterize your host's network load and make decisions about how to tune your network drivers. Now, it's important to say here that what we're talking about here are "networking," not "network," problems. If your actual network is bogged down, there's probably not very much you can tune on your mail server to make it perform better than the network can deliver.

If you do find, however, that you're experiencing inconsistent performance on network-based activities between hosts on the same network, it's time to do a little digging with *netstat. netstat* can tell you, for example, if your IMAP server is still listening on the IMAP port. Example 16-1 shows how to confirm. We're electing to look for the numeric description of the socket address instead of the name "imap," in case there's a problem in the */etc/services* file, in which such symbolic names are stored.

Example 16-1. Checking Up on Your IMAP with Netstat (Solaris Syntax)

```
% netstat -na | egrep '(TCP|Remote|\.143\ )'
TCP
    Local Address         Remote Address       Swind Send-Q Rwind Recv-Q  State
       *.143                  *.*                  0      0     0       0 LISTEN
  129.120.210.4.32816  129.120.210.4.143      32768      0  8192       0 ESTABLISHED
  129.120.210.4.143    129.120.210.4.32816     8192      0 32768       0 ESTABLISHED
  129.120.210.4.32926  129.120.210.4.143      32768      0  8192       0 TIME_WAIT
```

---

[*] By this, we mean that you can PING each from the other (if that's normally permitted), *telnet* to the IMAP port of the server from the client, or otherwise confirm that everyone who ought to be able to get to your IMAP server(s) can probably do so.

In the example (from the workstation on one of our desks), the *.143 in the TCP section tells you that there's a LISTEN at TCP/143. We're going to presume the listen is *inetd* making that socket available to hand off to *imapd*.

If you check the righthand "State" column, you'll see that the last session in the list is in TIME_WAIT state. When a session is in TIME_WAIT, it means that the session was closed some time back, but the socket numbers associated with that session are being held in a kind of IP purgatory for a while to ensure that some other process won't come in and resume the connection before the *imapd* process has a chance to die.

On a production multiuser IMAP server, of course, your output will hopefully be many, many entries long. On our production IMAP server at this moment, for example, we have a few more connections, as the output from the pipeline command in Example 16-2 illustrates.*

Example 16-2. A Quick Way of Seeing the IMAP Connection Load on Your Server

```
imapServer% netstat -na | egrep '\.143\ ' |\
      awk '{print $7}' | sort | uniq -c | sort -rn

 128 ESTABLISHED
  61 TIME_WAIT
   5 FIN_WAIT_2
   5 FIN_WAIT_1
   1 LISTEN
   1 CLOSING
```

In this example, we see that there are:

- 128 active sessions (ESTABLISHED state)

- 61 sessions that are closed for all intents and purposes, but still in the connection table for bookkeeping purposes (TIME_WAIT state)

- 5 sessions that are shut down on the server, but awaiting closure from the client (FIN_WAIT_2)

- 5 sessions that are shut down on both ends and are transitioning to TIME_WAIT (FIN_WAIT_1)

- 1 entry that represents *inetd* waiting for incoming IMAP connections (LISTEN)

- 1 session that is in the process of closing (CLOSING).

Most of the time, you need only be concerned about the load represented by the number of connections in the ESTABLISHED state. If you have an inordinate

---

* At least on Solaris—you might have to tweak the *awk* command on other systems.

number of connections in non-established states, it might indicate one of two things. Either your network recently had an outage and many IMAP connections were left hanging, or your system could be better tuned to meet the needs of your users. If, after a couple of hours of stable network performance, you don't see an improvement in the ratio of ESTABLISHED to non-established connections, you might want to start tuning your kernel.

On Solaris, at least, *netstat* may also be used to view a bodacious amount of layer-two and lower network statistics with *netstat –k*, as illustrated in Example 16-3.

Example 16-3. The "Netstat -k" Command (Undocumented) to Display Interface Statistics

```
% netstat -k | sed -n /^hme0:/,/^nfs_client:/qfe0:
ipackets 563551 ierrors 0 opackets 15511 oerrors 0 collisions 153
 0 framing 0 crc 0 sqe 0 code_violations 0 len_errors 0
 0 buff 0 oflo 0 uflo 0 missed 0 tx_late_collisions 0
retry_error 0 first_collisions 0 nocarrier 0 inits 25 nocanput 0
allocbfail 0 runt 0 jabber 0 babble 0 tmd_error 0 tx_late_error 0
rx_late_error 0 slv_parity_error 0 tx_parity_error 0 rx_parity_error 0
slv_error_ack 0 tx_error_ack 0 rx_error_ack 0 tx_tag_error 0
rx_tag_error 0 eop_error 0 no_tmds 0 no_tbufs 0 no_rbufs 0 rx_late_collisions 0
```

Here are a couple of common network-related dilemmas and examples of things you might do to address them:

Symptom:

Long-lived IMAP sessions inexplicably die after a long interval (several hours or days) of idle time.

Resolution:

It could be that there's a stateful firewall* between your clients and servers. One way to keep TCP sessions from dying, as they might with long-idle IMAP sessions, is to enable TCP keepalives on your mail server. TCP has no built-in mechanism for "pinging" the other side of connection every so often to make sure it's alive, but some operating systems, including Solaris and Linux, have it built into the kernel. On a Solaris host, you could enable TCP keepalives to be sent once every 50 minutes by putting the command:

```
solaris# /usr/sbin/ndd –set /dev/tcp tcp_keepalive_interval 3000000
```

in an appropriate system startup script (values are given in microseconds in Solaris).

---

* Some firewalls, especially those that make use of Network Address Translation (NAT) IP Masquerading techniques, or so-called private IP address space, use state tables to keep track of who's talking to whom. Timeouts are integral to the operation of such firewalls. Without timeouts, the state table would grow until the firewall became so resource-depleted it failed.

On Linux, the value is given in seconds:

```
linux# sysctl -w net.ipv4.tcp_keepalive_time=3000
```

or:

```
linux# echo 3000 > /proc/sys/net/ipv4/tcp_keepalive_time
```

Symptom:

Connections to your IMAP server from slow (usually dial-up) devices result in an inordinate amount of traffic.

Resolution:

It could be that your TCP driver is a bit too impatient. TCP is a guaranteed delivery protocol that sits on a non-guaranteed delivery protocol (IP). One of the mechanisms for that extra bit of reliability is the TCP ACK, a kind of receipt that is sent to acknowledge each TCP segment received. Because dial-up connections are very slow compared to direct Internet connections, your TCP driver might have its timeouts set at too short an interval to be realistic. On Solaris, you may set these to a longer, say three-second, interval by issuing these commands in an appropriate system startup script:

```
solaris# /usr/sbin/ndd -set /dev/tcp tcp_keepalive_interval_min 3000
solaris# /usr/sbin/ndd -set /dev/tcp tcp_keepalive_interval_initial 3000
```

On Linux:

```
linux# sysctl -w net.ipv4.tcp_keepalive_time=3
```

Symptom:

Large numbers of connections to your IMAP server from average-to-fast devices result in inexplicable network slowdowns.

Resolution:

You may want to crank *down* your maximum TCP retransmit interval. Doing so will increase the number of connections your machine can handle at one time. Here, we're taking it down to one minute on Solaris:

```
solaris# /usr/sbin/ndd -set /dev/tcp tcp_rexmit_interval_max 60000
```

On Linux, decrease the default value of *tcp_fin_timeout* from 180 seconds to 30 seconds, and decrease the default value of *tcp_keepalive_time* from 10,800 seconds to 1,800 seconds:

```
linux# echo 30 > /proc/sys/net/ipv4/tcp_fin_timeout
linux# echo 1800 > /proc/sys/net/ipv4/tcp_keepalive_time
```

tcp_fin_timeout is the time in seconds to wait before forcibly closing a stale connection. *tcp_keepalive_time* is the time in seconds before a keepalive will be sent on a connection.

How to Know When It's Time to Scale Up

If you're reading this section, chances are that you've come across a bottleneck on your system and you need to find the cause. A good way to diagnose the problem is to check the usage levels of each of the following resources:

*   CPU usage

*   Physical memory usage

*   I/O usage

*   Networking

This section shows how to use standard Unix tools to characterize your system's performance.

CPU Usage

To check your system's CPU usage, use the *vmstat* command. An example *vmstat* command and its output are shown in Example 16-4. The argument 3 tells *vmstat* to report on system usage every 3 seconds.

Example 16-4. vmstat

```
# vmstat 3
 procs     memory            page            disk          faults      cpu
 r b w   swap  free  re  mf pi po fr de sr f0 s0 s1 s6  in   sy   cs us sy id
 0 0 0 328912 40008  0   0  0  0  0  0  0  0  0  0  0 142 40479  47 77 23  0
 0 0 0 328912 40008  0   0  0  0  0  0  0  0  0  0  0 147 40425  44 83 17  0
 0 0 0 329160 40224  0 256  0  5  5  0  0  0  3  0  0 160 38942  84 79 21  0
 0 0 0 331000 40792  0   2  0  0  0  0  0  0  1  0  0 143 40485  49 83 17  0
 0 0 0 331000 40792  0   0  0  0  0  0  0  0  0  0  0 142 40463  47 87 13  0
```

The last three columns, under the heading "cpu," report the average percentage CPU usage over all processors. The "us" column reports the percentage of processor time used by user processes, the "sy" column reports the percentage CPU used by system processes, and the "id" column reports the percentage idle time. If you have the *top* program installed on your system, you can use it to get much the same information as *vmstat* provides.

What is a heavy CPU load?

For an IMAP server, a load average greater than 1 is considered a heavy load. In that case, you need to determine whether to upgrade to a faster CPU, add another processor to your system, or tune other parts of the system.

If it seems that your CPU load is too high, it almost never means that the CPU is too slow. It's very likely that the CPU is not doing any useful work at all, but instead is thrashing because of inadequate disk bandwidth or inadequate memory. When in doubt, add another disk and move something to it from a busy disk. If that doesn't improve the situation, add more memory. Memory is cheap, and if you don't need it now, you probably will later on.

There are various ways to figure the CPU load of your machine, and many more opinions on what an acceptable upper threshold is. The *vmstat* output has the information you need to make that determination.

One number to look at is the idle time reported by *vmstat*. In the previous example, the CPU was never observed to be idle. If this machine were ideally loaded, those numbers would always be greater than zero. Fifteen percent or so is nice.

Another important number is the number of jobs in the run state. A snapshot of that number is in the "r" column under "procs" in the *vmstat* output. A more meaningful insight into these numbers is available from *uptime* or *w −u*, where you'll get 1, 5, and 15 minute averages of the run queue size. The output of both the *uptime* and the *w −u* commands is frequently the same:

```
% w -u
   10:54pm  up 4 day(s),   3:40,   1 user,   load average: 1.14, 1.16, 1.16
```

This is the load number used by *sendmail* to indicate the threshold at which to only queue mail, or shut down its listen entirely. We've seen machines function at loads of 20 or 30, but they were crawling along at a snail's pace. System loads of 3 or 4 with peaks at 6 or 7 are usually acceptable. Bear in mind, though, that with some multiprocessing operating systems, the system load is given as the total load across all processors. A load of 16 on a 4-processor system is the same effective load as a system load of 4 on a single processor machine. We've been bitten by this when we unknowingly set *sendmail's* threshold way too low on a multiprocessor server.

How does one go about lightening the load?

First, check if there are processes contending for CPU. If there are, it will show up in the "procs" column under the "r" heading. The numbers under the "r" column denote the number of processes in the run queue. If the number is 0, as in Example 16-4, then there is no process contention. If the number is greater than 0, then there is contention, and adding an additional processor will help relieve that contention.

If there is no processor contention, then upgrading to a faster CPU will improve performance.

Physical Memory Usage

If it looks like your CPU utilization is okay, then the next point to check is physical memory usage. The *vmstat* provides some clues about memory usage. In Example 16-4, the columns under the "memory" and "page" headings pertain to memory usage.

"swap" reports the kilobytes of swap space in use, and "free" reports total free physical memory. On most Unix systems, this information is ultimately not very useful in determining actual memory usage, because the *vmstat* reports memory that the kernel has reserved for the file cache as used memory. However, that memory is actually available to user applications.

You can better determine your system's memory usage by looking at its paging activity.

I/O Usage

The *iostat* command can be used to monitor how the I/O work is being distributed across your devices. In Example 16-5, the *iostat* command is being run on a system with four disks, one of which (md3) is not currently in use. The *–D* option tells *iostat* to report usage in reads per second, writes per second, and percent utilization. The *–M* option displays data throughput in MB/second (KB/second is the default), and the parameter 3 tells *iostat* to report statistics every three seconds.

Example 16-5. iostat

```
# iostat -DM 3
            md0            md1            md2            md3
    rps wps util   rps wps util   rps wps util   rps wps util
      8   9 14.7     4   9 11.6     4   9 10.7     0   0  0.0
      0   1  0.8     0   1  0.7     0   1  0.7     0   0  0.0
      5   9 17.2     3   9 14.1     3   9 11.8     0   0  0.0
      4  41 40.2     2  41 37.3     2  41 34.0     0   0  0.0
      4  11 16.2     2  11 12.7     2  11 11.6     0   0  0.0
      0   0  0.0     0   0  0.0     0   0  0.0     0   0  0.0
      2   6  7.3     1   6  5.8     1   6  5.9     0   0  0.0
^C
#
```

The two most common symptoms to look for are:

Uneven disk usage

> If the percent-utilization varies widely from one disk to another at any given time, then I/O performance can be improved by moving the data to a RAID 0 filesystem striped across several disks.

Busy disks

If a disk is constantly utilized more than 50% of the time, you can improve performance by redistributing its data across several disks.

Networking

If your server is unable to process requests as fast as your network is sending them, then packets will be dropped and will have to be retransmitted. Retransmissions eat up yet more network bandwidth and cause further congestion.

How do you tell if your network is the bottleneck?

The *netstat* command provides information on network performance. Two factors to pay attention to are the collision rate and the number of input and output errors. In Example 16-6, the "Collis" column reports the collisions, and the "Ierrs" and "Oerrs" columns report input and output errors, respectively. There should be zero collisions on a switched full-duplex line.

Example 16-6. Using the netstat Command for Simple MAC-Layer Statistics

```
% netstat -i
Name  Mtu  Net/Dest        Address      Ipkts  Ierrs Opkts Oerrs Collis Queue
lo0   8232 loopback        localhost    1570   0     1570  0     0      0
le0   1500 129.120.210.0   nec.unt.edu  13489  0     6689  1     56     0
```

The specific symptoms to look for are:

Collis/Opkts > 10%

If collision rate is more than 10% of "Opkts" (outgoing packets), that indicates that your network is congested.

Oerrs/Opkts > 0.025%

A ratio of Oerrs to Opkts that is greater than 0.025% indicates a network hardware problem.

Ierrs/Ipkts > 0.025%

A ratio of Ierrs to Ipkts in excess of 0.025% indicates that there is an insufficient number of receive buffers.

A wide variety of freely available protocol analysis packages do 90 to 95% of what the high-dollar packages do. *tcpdump* is a popular program (bundled with some flavors of Unix), as is *snoop*, which comes bundled with all Solaris installations. Using *snoop*, as in Example 16-7, you can watch all the IMAP traffic that goes in and out of your machine.

Example 16-7. The snoop Command Used to Capture Two IMAP Protocol Packets

```
# snoop -c2 -vv proto imap
Using device /dev/le (promiscuous mode)
```

```
imap.themullets.net -> nec.unt.edu  ETHER Type=0800 (IP), size = 193 bytes
imap.themullets.net -> nec.unt.edu  IP  D=129.120.210.4 S=181.100.100.101 LEN=179,
 ID=12184
imap.themullets.net -> nec.unt.edu  TCP D=32907 S=143     Ack=2835991927
Seq=2841518292 Len=139 Win=8760
```

```
 nec.unt.edu -> imap.themullets.net ETHER Type=0800 (IP), size = 85 bytes
 nec.unt.edu -> imap.themullets.net IP  D=181.100.100.101 S=129.120.210.4 LEN=71,
ID=19460
 nec.unt.edu -> imap.themullets.net TCP D=143 S=32907     Ack=2841518431
Seq=2835991927 Len=31 Win=8760
```

In this example, *snoop* was only used to capture two packets with very little detail, so little can be determined here except that one host was indeed able to connect to the IMAP server of another. *snoop* does have the capacity, however, to display a great deal of detail about the packets you snag off the network. Even more useful is its ability to capture packets to a file for later re-examination with a variety of *snoop* options.

Running imapd: inetd Versus Standalone

The question has been brought up from time to time as to whether it's better to run *imapd* standalone, particularly on heavily loaded systems, rather than have *inetd* fork the daemon process. The UW server and Cyrus server prior to the 2.0 release run under *inetd*. Version 2.0 of the Cyrus server runs as a standalone daemon.

If a daemon has to do a lot of work at startup time (e.g., processing a large amount of configuration information), then running it standalone will result in faster connect times for your users. *sendmail* is a good example of a daemon that's better suited to run standalone—its configuration file is large. *imapd* reads a very small configuration file at startup.

The life of the connection and associated *inetd* overhead are other factors to consider. If connections to a daemon are long-lived, then there are fewer startups and thus, less *inetd* overhead. That makes the daemon a good candidate to run under *inetd*. If a connection, on the other hand, is short-lived, it's better not to run the daemon under *inetd* because of the extra overhead *inetd* will concur. *imapd* is an example of a daemon with long-lived connections, compared with daemons that make many short-lived connections, such as *sendmail* and *popd*.

Even on a heavily loaded system (e.g., 1,000 active processes), each *imapd* process will start once and remain active throughout a user's IMAP session. Since the number of connections in any given time period is small, compared to daemons like *sendmail* and *popd*, no significant benefit would be gained by running *imapd* standalone.

Charting It Up for the Suits

A picture's worth a thousand words. Doubly so when doing performance analysis or workload characterization. One of the most popular packages for graphing and gathering performance statistics is the Multi Router Traffic Grapher (MRTG) by Tobias Oetiker and Dave Rand.[*] Another popular route is the combination of the Gnuplot[†] and the NetPBM packages.[‡]

The MTRG package is the better integrated and slicker of the two. MRTG is pretty much a "soup to nuts" system statistical graphing package. It will gather the stats, archive them, and generate the HTML for your system status web page and even draw the graphs for you.

If you've already got a mechanism to gather the statistics (or have one in mind), the Gnuplot/NetPBM package might be a good choice. Gnuplot is very flexible in drawing the graphs, and NetPBM is equally flexible at batch reformatting of the graphics.

---

[*] *http://ee-staff.ethz.ch/~oetiker/webtools/mrtg/mrtg.html*

[†] *http://www.cs.dartmouth.edu/gnuplot_info.html*

[‡] *http://wuarchive.wustl.edu/graphics/graphics/packages/NetPBM/*

17

Remote Configuration Storage

Two protocols that complement IMAP, both with roots in the academic world, are the Application Configuration Access Protocol (ACAP) and the Internet Message Support Protocol (IMSP). Both protocols are used for storing user preference and address book information on a remote server, encouraging Internet desktop ubiquity.

Web sites that were once search engines are now calling themselves "portals." What makes a search engine a portal is that what used to present the same resources to all users is now personalized with customized email, scheduling, remote bookmarks, and address book functions.

Remote configuration is all part of a push to make the Internet less tied to a specific physical location, whether to your desk at work, your PC at home, or the notebook in your briefcase. As personalization spreads to more Internet applications, the ponderousness of Internet software and operating systems should decrease. The piece that makes thin client computing work is the ability to do anything anywhere. Remote configuration and personalization make that possible.

Why Store Client Configurations on a Server?

Your site may benefit from centralized configuration management. It certainly makes sense for users who want to access their email from more than one place, especially those who use shared computers. Finally, because we've all learned the hard lessons of the total cost of ownership for the PC on the desktop, centralized configuration management makes fiscal sense, too.

Benefits of Centralized Configuration Storage

The lighter Internet applications become, the more likely they are to depend on having preferences stored in a central location. Here are some examples of environments that benefit from centralized user preference management:

General access computer labs

Users who read email in general access computer labs want the same email preferences regardless of which workstation they happen to be using on a given day. Those users probably don't want the hassle of carrying their email preferences around on a floppy disk.

Mobile computing environments

Mobile users have more than one computer, usually an office computer, a home computer, and a laptop. Sometimes the laptop is checked out at random from a pool of laptops. Mobile users don't have the time to change preferences every time they change computers, nor do they want to carry the preferences around on a disk and risk losing the disk.

In-house computer hardware shops and value-added resellers

Shops that distribute large numbers of machines could set up machines to grab a generic email client configuration over the network. That configuration would customize the email client for the site, cutting down on the amount of work required on the part of the end user. DHCP is used in the same way, permitting many sites to release end users from having to configure their machine for a particular set of IP parameters. ACAP and IMSP permit users to instantly become familiar and comfortable with a possibly unfamiliar MUA.

Environments that have a centralized backup strategy

By storing user preferences in a central location, it's easy to back up and restore your users' preferences without any complex changes to your infrastructure.

Environments that support use of PDAs

Users often want the same email options on their PDAs (Personal Digital Assistants) as on their full-size computers. PDAs and sub-notebooks usually have no floppy drive, and alternatives to floppies (such as flash ROM) are very small (easy to lose) and expensive. Such devices do have the ability to connect to the network and download preferences from an Internet-accessible database. The ability to download preferences is also a very attractive option, given the limited local storage on PDAs.

Essentially, remote profile storage with IMSP or ACAP adds even more value to the enterprise infrastructure than it does to an individual's productivity. The amount of individual effort saved by central profile storage is a convenience at best. The amount of effort saved by central IT support facilities is potentially huge. As the amount of hands-on support required for each machine diminishes, so does the total cost of ownership.

Much to the amusement of longtime central computing types, the desktop computer has proved to be one of the most expensive means of getting computing to the people. Although the entry cost might be low, the sluggishness of some desktop operating systems has exponentially increased the amount of legwork and end-user machine customization necessary to support each application, as well as baseline system stability.

IMSP, ACAP, or LDAP?

If centralized user preference management were thought of as a nail, not everyone would agree what kind of hammer is needed. Two come to mind: IMSP and ACAP. One doesn't: LDAP.

There are a couple of reasons why LDAP doesn't really fit here. The lesser of the two is that LDAP is tuned to perform best in a read-intensive environment. ACAP, on the other hand, is designed to work in a mixed read/write environment, such as one where users are constantly updating preferences.

But the greater of the two reasons is that the structure of a user's configuration information, such as bookmarks and addresses, is defined by the administrator under LDAP and is static. Under ACAP, the ordering is determined by the user and can be changed on the fly. LDAP is a good fit for enterprise-wide information; it's not necessarily a good fit for email preferences storage, because each user tends to cultivate a very personalized directory of their own.

Users are likely to use LDAP-based services for tasks like finding someone's email address. Once they find it, however, they're likely to want to store it in their own address book, so they can make it meaningful in ways that are not supported in LDAP, such as:

* Tying the address to an easier-to-type nickname

* Taking advantage of auto-completion in their client

* Adding additional information that wouldn't necessarily be germane to a central directory, such as notes from the last meeting, private telephone numbers, names of spouse and children, etc.

Briefly put, ACAP is remote configuration management for the people. Table 17-1 is a brief comparison of the features of IMSP, ACAP, and LDAP. The table boils down many of the issues central to choosing a user preference management protocol.

LDAP is weak in the area of per-user attribute storage and client-defined attributes, but IMSP and ACAP are strong in this regard. With its server-side searching and large datasets, ACAP seems much more scalable and flexible than its earlier counterpart, IMSP.

Table 17-1. Comparison of IMSP, ACAP, and LDAP

Feature	IMSP	ACAP	LDAP
Optimized for read and write performance	✓	✓	✗
Data can be written by the client	✓	✓	✓
Server-side searching	✗	✓	✓
Supports large datasets	✗	✓	✓
Supports disconnected use	✓	✓	✗a
Supports client-defined attributes	✓	✓	✗
Open standard (non-proprietary)	✓	✓	✓
Supports ACLs (access control lists)	✓	✓	✓
Supports per-user authentication	✓	✓	✓
Supports per-user storage of information	✓	✓	✓
Supports hierarchical organization of information by the user	✗	✓	✗

a LDAP doesn't support disconnected mode in the sense that we're using in this book, but LDAP does nicely support the multitier equivalent of disconnected mode, where subsets of a directory/database are delegated to second- or third-tier LDAP servers. If those servers become disconnected from the top-level LDAP server, they queue up their transactions until the connection is restored.

Keep in mind also that, with traditional directory services, the protocols are designed to give the administrator a great amount of control. In IMSP and ACAP, the data is usually owned by the user, and the protocol is designed to give the control to the user. Users have the freedom not only to edit their data directly via their client, but to create hierarchies and move data around in the hierarchy, much the way they do when the data is stored on the local hard drive.

To quote Matt Wall, former manager of Project Cyrus and co-founder of Cyrusoft, Inc., on IMSP and ACAP: "We believe in the concept of 'the right tool for the right job'. We have no love for reinventing the wheel, but in researching the available options in the context of Project Cyrus, we discovered this particular type of precision screwdriver. Trying to get one of these other protocols [to work for remote preference storage] is like using a heavy-duty hammer or a wrench to get this particular screw attached."

Having narrowed our choices down to IMSP and ACAP, let's look at each in more detail.

IMSP

IMSP is an Internet protocol that allows application programs to store program options and user information—such as personal and shared address books—on a remote network server. IMSP thus provides retrieval of client configuration information, which is traditionally stored on local disk, from anywhere on the network.

The original IMSP specification was written by members of the Project Cyrus team at CMU. The first IMSP server was released in 1994, also by CMU. Development of IMSP ceased in 1995, when it became evident that there was a need for a protocol to store client preferences that applied to other types of Internet applications, not just email. At that point, IMSP was reengineered and renamed Application Configuration Access Protocol (ACAP). ACAP is discussed later in this chapter. IMSP never made it into the standards track; its status is that of "experimental draft." Despite its experimental status, IMSP is still alive and well, in use in production environments at over 1,000 sites, with more than one million end users. Because there are still very few ACAP-capable MUAs and ACAP servers, IMSP is still a good option for email client configuration storage. There are both stable IMSP clients and servers, and the protocol has been proven to work.

IMSP Specification

The IMSP Internet Draft is available from CMU at *http://asg.web.cmu.edu/cyrus/rfc/ imsp.html*.

Cyrus IMSP Server

The recommended IMSP server is the CMU's freely available Cyrus IMSP server, Version 1.6a1. Despite the alpha release number, that release of the server has been tested over time and proven stable.

Where to get IMSP

The location of the server source distribution is *ftp://ftp.andrew.cmu.edu/pub/ cyrus-mail/cyrus-imspd-v1.5a6.tar.gz*.

How to install and configure IMSP

In an appropriate directory, unpack the source distribution:

```
% zcat cyrus-imspd-v1.5a6.tar.gz | tar xvf -
```

Next, compile the sources and install the software. IMSP installs under */usr/local* by default. There are configuration options, such as authentication method, that you may want to specify explicitly. To see the possible options, run *configure --help*:

```
% ./configure -with-login=unix_shadow
% make all
# make install
```

Once IMSP is built and installed, there is some post-installation configuration you'll need to complete. First, create a directory where IMSP will store its data files:

```
# mkdir /var/imsp
```

Next, edit */etc/services* and add an entry for IMSP. The line in */etc/services* should look like this:

```
imsp 406/tcp        # Internet Message Support Protocol
```

IMSP has a single global configuration file (*/var/imsp/options*) and an individual user options file for each user. User options are stored under */var/imsp/user/ username/*.

Set up a global IMSP *options* file. As a start, copy the *options.sample* that is provided with the IMSP distribution to the data directory:

```
# cp options.sample /var/imsp/options
```

IMSP options are specified as attribute-value pairs with optional flags: *attribute [flag] value*. Possible flags include:

R   Read-only attribute

N   Read-only attribute; invisible to users, and used for options that pertain to administrators only

W   Writable attribute; the value can be changed by the client and saved in the user's personal options file

Add the following line to allow users to automatically create a new personal options directory, if the directory does not already exist:

```
imsp.create.new.users N +
```

The following lines are other entries that are commonly found in the global IMSP options file:

```
common.date R                            Current date and time
common.delivery.hosts R smtp.blah.edu    Local SMTP host
common.sent.mailbox R (INBOX.sentmail)   Default sent mail folder name
common.domain R yourdomain.edu           Local mail domain
imsp.admin.all N (johndoe)               IMSP administrative user
imsp.user.quota r 2048                   Quota on user options
```

With all that done, you're now ready to run IMSP.

How to run IMSP

The Cyrus IMSP server runs as a standalone daemon and listens for requests on port 406. To start the IMSP server, type the command:

```
# ./imspd
```

To test IMSP, telnet to the IMSP port and type in the commands shown in the following example session. If you get the response OK at startup and on login, then everything's working fine:

```
% telnet localhost imsp
Trying 127.0.0.1...
Connected to localhost.
Escape character is '^]'.
* OK Cyrus IMSP version 1.5a6 ready
001 login johndoe xxxxxxxx
001 OK user johndoe logged in
001 logout
```

Getting help

The Cyrus IMSP server is supported on the *info-cyrus* mailing list. To subscribe to the list, send a message with the text "subscribe info-cyrus" to *info-cyrus-request@andrew.cmu.edu*. An archive of the *info-cyrus* list is also available, and it's a good idea to check the archive before posting questions to the list. To view the archive, point your IMAP client to *cyrus.andrew.cmu.edu*. Use anonymous as the username and your email address as your password. The name of the folder is *archive.info-cyrus*.

Cyrusoft's "The Cyrusoft Guide to IMSP" is useful to refer to when configuring IMSP options, and it has information on how to serve up global address books via IMSP. To retrieve a copy of the Guide, visit *http://www.cyrusoft.com/support/faq/mulbpapers.html*.

IMSP Clients

Two IMAP clients support IMSP: Cyrusoft's *Mulberry* and MessagingDirect's *Execmail*. Cyrusoft's *SilkyMail*, a webmail IMAP client, also supports IMSP. IMSP support is planned for a future release of MessagingDirect's Webmail client: *Execmail Web*. In fact, the combined popularity of IMSP and web-based email has driven the development of an IMSP client library to be released soon as part of the PHP distribution.*

---

* PHP (*http://www.php.net/*) is a server-side scripting language for creating dynamic web pages and is used in several popular web-based IMAP clients.

ACAP

ACAP is an Internet protocol used by client programs to store and retrieve client program information, such as bookmarks, address books, and program preferences. ACAP provides more than just access to preferences from many locations; it can also provide access from any Internet application—not just email clients.

Like IMSP, ACAP is *not* a directory service, but rather, a protocol with a different purpose. ACAP is intended to work in harmony with directory services, not in competition with them. ACAP fills the niche between a directory service, like LDAP, and a limited-service support protocol like IMSP. ACAP, in fact, offers some specialized functions that directory services do not support:

Remote storage of email account data

> It's becoming more and more common for Internet email users to have more than one mail account (e.g., an account at work and an account at home on an ISP). Users access multiple accounts from the same machine and/or access the same accounts from different machines. They may also use more than one program that requires email account configuration information. ACAP supports the storage of email account data.

Remote storage of bookmarks

> Storing bookmark URLs is common in Internet applications such as web browser and FTP clients. Users need to access the same bookmarks from different client programs and from different machines. ACAP supports synchronization of bookmarks between multiple applications and systems, and even allows sharing a single bookmarks list between users.

Remote storage of roles

> It has become common for Internet mail users to receive and compose email in the capacity of different roles, or "personalities." For example, a user might use one email personality at work to communicate with colleagues and a different identity at home to communicate with friends and family. ACAP provides a way to store email composition preferences.*

Remote storage of a common MOTD

> ACAP supports remote storage and access of a "Message of the Day" greeting, used by system administrators to communicate important information to all users when they begin to use a system. This is particularly useful to system administrators who manage black box systems where users do not log in directly to a shell account, and thus do not see the traditional Unix "motd."

---

* We've seen a case where LDAP was used to support several "roles" per user, and the workaround (or more accurately, "kludge") was to assign each user a username to go with each identity.

Remote storage of the mailboxes dataset

This use lets you separate the information about the mailboxes from the mailboxes themselves. Clients and servers that used ACAP in this manner would keep lists of mailboxes, their new message and other status, and even information about which server on which they exist in a dedicated database, wholly separate from the mailboxes themselves.

ACAP, part of CMU's Project Cyrus initiative, evolved from IMSP. IMSP is very successful in its purpose, which is to store limited email client configuration options. It became evident once IMSP achieved widespread use, however, that there was a need to apply the underlying fundamentals of IMSP to other types of Internet clients, rather than just email. More generalized Internet preference storage was an idea whose time had come. In January 1998, the ACAP RFC was published, followed quickly by the initial release of the Cyrus ACAP server two months later.

Like IMAP itself, anyone implementing ACAP will find it's quite a moving target. The Cyrus ACAP server, for example, is the grand dame of ACAP servers, and has undergone a multiplicity of face-lifts since its initial release.

ACAP Specification

The ACAP specification is available from the IETF in RFC 2244 *(http://ietf.org/rfc/rfc2244.txt)*.

ACAP-related RFCs and drafts

The strength of a good Internet protocol lies not only it its evolution as a standard, defined in an RFC, but also in its extensibility. Like Telnet, IMAP, and SNMP MIBs, ACAP is a popular standard for which to write and implement useful extensions. Here's an overview of some of the more important ones.

The ACAP Dataset Model Internet Draft *(http://ietf.org/internet-drafts/draft-ietf-acap-dataset-model-01.txt)*, primarily intended for developers of ACAP clients, provides guidelines on how to design and access ACAP datasets and explains the relationship between ACAP attributes, entries, datasets, and dataset classes.

The ACAP Bookmarks Dataset Class Internet Draft *(http://ietf.org/internet-drafts/draft-ietf-acap-book-02.txt)* defines a standard ACAP dataset class for storing bookmark URLs.

The ACAP Email Account Dataset Class Internet Draft *(http://ietf.org/internet-drafts/draft-ietf-acap-email-02.txt)* defines a standard ACAP dataset class for email accounts and a common option for indicating a default email account.

The ACAP Email Personality Dataset Class Internet Draft *(http://ietf.org/internet-drafts/draft-ietf-acap-pers-02.txt)* defines a standard ACAP dataset class for outgoing email identities (also known as roles or personalities) and a common option for indicating a default.

The ACAP Message of the Day Dataset Class (*http://ietf.org/internet-drafts/draft-ietf-acap-motd-dataset-00.txt*) describes a common format for storing MOTD information in ACAP. It explains how site administrators may configure their ACAP MOTD service to allow multiple groups within the site to provide custom MOTD information and how a client should access and use this information.

Cyrus ACAP Server

The CMU developed the first, and the first free, ACAP server. It continues to be the benchmark ACAP server and is a great choice for those who want to dive into ACAP.

Where to get ACAP

The latest version of CMU's Cyrus ACAP server is available at *ftp://ftp.andrew.cmu. edu/pub/cyrus-mail/*. At the time of this writing, the latest version is Version 0.3. Cyrus ACAP is available in both source and binary (Solaris and Linux) distributions.

Cyrus ACAP 0.3 has several dependencies:

CMU SASL

> CMU *acapd* requires CMU's SASL library (*ftp://ftp.andrew.cmu.edu/pub/cyrus-mail/cyrus-sasl-1.5.5.tar.gz*) for authentication.

SML/NJ

> The backend of the Cyrus ACAP server is written in SML, a high-level programming language. SML/NJ (Standard ML/New Jersey implementation) is Bell Labs' SML compiler. Version 110.0.6 of SML/NJ is recommended. SML/NJ is available at *ftp://ftp.research.bell-labs.com/dist/smlnj/release/110/*. Note that if you're installing a binary distribution of Cyrus ACAP, you don't have to install SML/NJ.

GNU Make

> The ACAP documentation recommends using GNU Make (*ftp://ftp.gnu.org/gnu/make/*).

How to install and configure ACAP

The instructions outlined here are for installation from the source distribution.

You should have GNU Make, SML/NJ, and SASL installed on your system before installing ACAP. Make sure the *sml* binary is in your path so that the configure script will detect it. Unpack the ACAP source distribution.

```
% zcat cyrus-sml-acapd-0.3.tar.gz | tar xvf -
```

Run the *configure* script, *make*, and *make install* to install *acapd* on your system.[*]
The default install prefix is */usr/local/*.

```
% ./configure
% make
# make install
```

If ACAP is not defined in your */etc/services* file, then add the following line:

```
acap 674/tcp          # Application Configuration Access Protocol
```

Add the following line to */etc/inetd.conf*, then restart *inetd*:

```
acap stream tcp nowait root /usr/cyrus/bin/frontend frontend
```

Create the ACAP directories:

```
# mkdir /var/acap
# mkdir /var/spool/acap
```

Then finally, start the backend ACAP process:

```
# cd backend
# backend-acapd &
```

How to use ACAP

The Cyrus ACAP server runs as a standalone daemon and listens for requests on
port 674. To start the ACAP server, type the command:

```
# cd backend
# backend-acapd &
```

To test ACAP, *telnet* to the ACAP port and type in a few commands, as shown in
the following example session. If you get the response * at startup, then everything's working fine:

```
% telnet localhost acap
Trying 127.0.0.1...
Connected to localhost.
Escape character is '^]'.
* Acap (Implementation "SML Frontend, Carnegie Mellon Project Cyrus") (Context
Limit "100") (Sasl "PLAIN" "ANONYMOUS")
0 AUTHENTICATE "ANONYMOUS" "johndoe"
0 Ok "Welcome"
1 LOGOUT
* BYE "have a nice day"
1 OK "LOGOUT completed"
Connection closed by foreign host.
```

---

[*] We found an error in the Makefile. After running configure, you may need to add the following line to
the beginning of the "install" target: `@for d in $(SUBDIRS); \`.

Where to get help

The *info-cyrus* mailing list is the best place to go for technical questions about the Cyrus ACAP server. To subscribe to the list, send a message with the text "subscribe info-cyrus" to *info-cyrus-request@andrew.cmu.edu*. An archive of the *info-cyrus* list is also available, and it's a good idea to check the archive before posting questions to the list. To view the archive, point your IMAP client to *cyrus.andrew.cmu.edu*. Use "anonymous" as the username and your email address as your password. The name of the folder is *archive.info-cyrus*.

ACAP Clients

The following clients currently include support for ACAP:

- Cyrusoft's Mulberry
- MessagingDirect's Execmail 5.0
- Qualcomm's Eudora Pro

University of Washington plans to add ACAP support to a 4.x release of the popular PINE email client, but it had not been added as of Version 4.20.

18

IMAP Tools

A great advantage of embracing open source and open standard software is that all those nagging little—and some not-so-little—features that you would like to have, but don't, can be addressed by a handful of free software tools. Some of the tools are invasive, patching the source to your server to get their work done. Others rely only on the IMAP protocol to get their work done and would work equally well with closed source IMAP servers. All of them, however, could be used to provide a bridge between the capabilities of your server and the demands of your workload.

IMAP Administration Tools

Few things can positively affect your ability to manage your mail server like a good set of administration tools. We've found a few packages that could easily be the Leatherman Tool for your IMAP server—something you keep close by so you can use it on a moment's notice to perform some random act of maintenance. We've split these tools into two types: general server administration, and those that would be used in different load-balancing schemes.

General IMAP Server Administration

Those of our readers who are transitioning from POP3 mail servers to IMAP know that there's not a whole lot to using POP3 to administer user mailboxes. Nearly anything you might want to do in POP3 is easily accomplished by telnetting to the POP3 port and issuing commands manually. Because IMAP is a much richer protocol than POP3, there's much to be gained by having an intermediate piece of software to assist you in administering your IMAP server. That's the role played by the packages in this section.

IMAP-Admin

Author

  Eric Estabrooks

URL

  http://www.cpan.org/modules/by-module/IMAP/

Major features

  Includes methods *create, delete, list, capability, get_quotaroot, get_quota, set_ quota, get_acl, set_acl, delete_acl.*

Installation

  Standard Perl module installation. See *http://www.cpan.org/modules/INSTALL. html.*

Documentation

  Documentation is included within the module and is available at *http:// theoryx5.uwinnipeg.ca/CPAN/by-name/IMAP-Admin.html.*

Status

  Current version is 1.0.1 as of February 2000.

Licensing

  Unknown (free).

IMAP-Admin is a Perl module for basic IMAP server administration, such as creating or deleting mailboxes and setting such mailbox options as ACLs and quotas. The module is RFC 2060–compliant, and thus works with both the Cyrus and UW servers. If you feel more comfortable supporting Perl than Tcl, IMAP-Admin makes a good substitute for *cyradm,* the Tcl-based system administration utility that is distributed with the Cyrus IMAP server. An example script for creating an IMAP account using the IMAP-Admin module is shown in Example 18-1.

Example 18-1. IMAP-Admin Example Script

```
#!/usr/local/bin/perl

use IMAP::Admin;

$imap = IMAP::Admin->new('Server' => 'imap.themullets.net',
                         'Port' => 143,
                         'Login' => 'admin',
                         'Password' => 'XXXXXXXX');

#  Create johndoe's mailbox
#
$rc = $imap->create("user.johndoe");
if ($rc != 0) {
  #print "$imap->{'Error'}\n";
}
```

Example 18-1. IMAP-Admin Example Script (continued)

```
#  Confirm johndoe's mailbox is there
#
@list = $imap->list("user.johndoe");

#  Set johndoe's mailbox quota to 5 MB
#
$rc =   $imap->set_quota("user.johndoe", 5120);
@quota = $imap->get_quotaroot("user.johndoe");

#  Set the ACL on johndoe's mailbox
#
$rc =   $imap->set_acl("user.johndoe", "admin", "d", "mary", "lrs");
@acl =  $imap->get_acl("user.johndoe");

print "Created user: "; print join ' ', @list, "\n";
print "Quota: ";        print join ' ', @quota, "\n";
print "ACL: ";          print join ' ', @acl, "\n";

# Close the IMAP connection
#
$imap->close;
```

The output of the example is as follows:

```
Created user: user.johndoe
Quota: user.johndoe 0 5120
ACL: johndoe lrswipcda admin d mary lrs
```

PHP Cyrus-Tools

Authors

Didi Rieder (*adrieder@sbox.tu-graz.ac.at*) and Gernot Stocker

URL

ftp://ftp.br.vc-graz.ac.at/cyrus-tools/

Major features

Performs most aspects of Cyrus IMAP server system administration on the Web.

Installation

Installation involves unpacking the distribution into your web server's document root directory, customizing a configuration file, and adding your IMAP admin username and password to the web server's authentication file.

Documentation

Documentation is contained in the *INSTALL* file included in the distribution.

Status

Current version is 1.0.1 as of February 2000.

Dependencies

PHP 3.0.11 or greater with IMAP support and a web server that supports PHP (such as Apache).

Licensing

Public domain.

PHP Cyrus Tools actually consist of two packages: *php-cyradm* and *php-mailsettings*. *php-cyradm* provides administration of a Cyrus IMAP server via a web interface. It includes the familiar *cyradm* functions that allow mailbox management (create, rename, delete mailboxes, modify ACLs) and also allows configuration of the Cyrus server by editing the *imapd.conf* file. *php-mailsettings* allows Cyrus IMAP users to set up mail forwarding and vacation auto-responses via the Web. You're advised to enable SSL on your web server to prevent your administrator password from crossing the network in cleartext.

Balancing Users Across Cyrus Partitions

move_imap_users

Author

J.T. Chiodi (*squeegy@squeegy.org*)

URL

http://www.squeegy.org/programs/move_imap_users.tar.gz

Major features

Balances Cyrus IMAP users between IMAP partitions or allows a set of users to be moved manually from one partition to another.

Installation

The package consists of two standalone scripts. No special installation is required.

Documentation

A *README* file is included with the package.

Status

Current version is 1.1 as of February 2000.

Licensing

GNU General Public License.

An absolute treasure for Cyrus administrators, the *move_imap_users* package contains a pair of tools for moving users between IMAP partitions on a Cyrus IMAP system.

balance.imap

> *balance.imap* "load balances" a set of existing user mailboxes between two Cyrus IMAP partitions based on the available space on the partitions. It moves the mailboxes from the partition with the least available space to the partition with the most available space, until a determined threshold is reached.

fast.imap

> *fast.imap* is used to move an existing mailbox or a set of user mailboxes from one partition to another, manually.

fast.imap takes three arguments: the source partition, the destination partition, and a range of usernames. Range can be either a letter (for example, "a" would be used to move all users whose usernames begin with the letter "a") or a range of letters ("[a-m]" would be used to move all users whose usernames begin with letters ranging from "a" to "m"). When using a range, be sure to escape the square brackets so that they won't be misinterpreted by the shell:

```
% cyradm -file fast.imap imap1 imap2 a
% cyradm -file fast.imap imap1 imap2 \[a-m\]
```

balance.imap could be run periodically out of *cron* to keep mailboxes evenly distributed across partitions.

Running Multiple Instances of Cyrus on a Single Machine

cyrus-imapd-configfiles

Author

> David M. Zendzian (*dmz@dmzs.com*)

URL

> *http://www.dmzs.com/~dmz/projects/cyrus-config/cyrus-config.diff*

Major features

> Allows Cyrus to support more than one configuration file.

Installation

> *cyrus-imapd-configfiles* is a patch that is applied to the Cyrus IMAP source.

Documentation

> Documentation on setting up Cyrus to use more than one configuration file is located at *http://www.dmzs.com/~dmz/projects/cyrus-config/cyrus-virtual.txt*.

Status

> Current version is 1.0 as of February 2000.

Dependencies

Depends on Cyrus 1.6.20.

Licensing

Unknown (free).

cyrus-imapd-configfiles is a patch for the Cyrus *imapd* that adds support for a command line flag that accepts an IMAP configuration file as an option, for example:

```
imapd -c /usr/local/etc/virtual/domain1.imapd.conf
imapd -c /usr/local/etc/virtual/domain2.imapd.conf
```

Being able to use multiple configuration files comes in handy when you need to run IMAP servers for more than one domain and want to keep the data for each domain separate, but on a single machine. There is some documentation on how to set up such a scheme at *http://www.dmzs.com/~dmz/projects/cyrus-config/cyrus-virtual.txt,* but it doesn't cover the bigger picture of how to map a group of users to a particular IMAP server.

Although that bigger issue is really a networking topic and beyond the scope of this book, here are a couple of quick sketches of how it can be done. Both ways require you to install a variation of *inetd* that allows binding a service to a particular IP address and allows you to restrict access to a service based on the originating IP address. There are several such programs freely available; the one used in our examples is *xinetd* (*http://www.xinetd.org/*).

Before you go any further, Figure 18-1 is a high-level illustration of the setup we're suggesting.

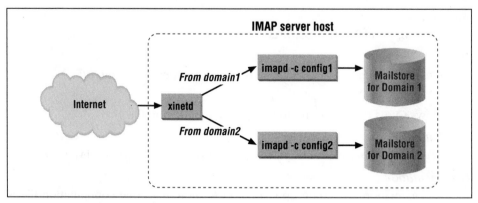

Figure 18-1. Multiple Cyrus configurations on a single host

IP traffic is filtered by *inetd* to one of two *imapd*'s based on the originating IP address. Each of the *imapd* servers operates on a separate mailstore.

Method 1: One IP, one port, multiple mailstores. Define two IMAP services in the *inetd* configuration file. Restrict one IMAP service to one domain, the other to another domain. The IP address and port are identical for the two servers. The only difference between them is that they handle IMAP requests only from a specific subnet and look at different configuration files. The configuration for *xinetd* would look something like Example 18-2.

Example 18-2. xinetd Configuration for Single Port/IP, Multiple Configurations

```
service imap
{
    socket_type     = stream
    protocol        = tcp
    wait            = no
    user            = cyrus
    only_from       = 129.120.1.0 localhost
    server          = /usr/cyrus/bin/imapd
    server_args     = -c /usr/local/etc/imap.subnet1.conf
}

service imap
{
    socket_type     = stream
    protocol        = tcp
    wait            = no
    user            = cyrus
    only_from       = 129.120.2.0 localhost
    server          = /usr/cyrus/bin/imapd
    server_args     = -c /usr/local/etc/imap.subnet2.conf
}
```

Method 2: Virtual IP per server. This method requires you to create a virtual interface for each domain for which you want to provide a separate IMAP service. Example 18-3 is the *xinetd* configuration entries for two virtual domains.

Example 18-3. xinetd Configuration for Two Virtual Domains

```
service imap
{
    socket_type     = stream
    protocol        = tcp
    wait            = no
    user            = cyrus
    only_from       = 129.120.1.0 localhost
    server          = /usr/cyrus/bin/imapd
    server_args     = -c /usr/local/etc/imap.subnet1.conf
    bind            = 129.120.1.1
}
```

Example 18-3. xinetd Configuration for Two Virtual Domains (continued)

```
service imap
{
    socket_type    = stream
    protocol       = tcp
    wait           = no
    user           = cyrus
    only_from      = 129.120.2.0 localhost
    server         = /usr/cyrus/bin/imapd
    server_args    = -c /usr/local/etc/imap.subnet2.conf
    bind           = 129.120.1.2
}
```

The abilities to balance your storage demands and customize your server-side configuraton for different classes of users are elements frequently demanded in large IMAP installations. Another element frequently stressed in large systems is user authentication. Both the performance and security of an IMAP server can be improved by moving beyond native Unix authentication.

Authentication Tools

It's becoming increasingly popular to opt out of using standard Unix authentication and to use database-based authentication instead. The advantages of alternative authentication methods are many. In many cases, you won't necessarily want your users to have regular Unix accounts on your IMAP server, and storing usernames and passwords in an alternate database allows you to get around setting up Unix accounts for everyone. Another advantage, in the case of the UW server, is that you can run your IMAP daemon as a non-privileged user. This section introduces tools that allow alternative authentication methods.

Authenticating Against a SQL Database (UW)

getpg/UW-IMAP

Author
Alex Howansky (*alex@wankwood.com*)

URL
http://www.wankwood.com/getpg/uw-imap-latest.tar.gz

Major features
Allows UW IMAP to authenticate users against a PostgreSQL database.

Installation
Involves applying a patch to the UW IMAP source distribution.

Documentation

Documentation is contained in the *README* file included in the *getpg/ UW-IMAP* package.

Status

Current version is 0.54 as of February 2000.

Dependencies

PostgreSQL, UW IMAP. Tested using *qmail* as the MTA.

Licensing

Unknown (free).

The *getpg/UW-IMAP* patch utilizes the *getpg* functions to allow the UW IMAP server to authenticate users against a PostgreSQL database. *getpg*, included in the *getpg/UW-IMAP* package, consists of a pair of C functions that are drop-in replacements for the standard `getpwnam` and `getpwuid` functions, which do Unix authentication. The replacement functions `getpgnam` and `getpguid`, authenticate users against a PostgreSQL database. The replacement functions can be used not only to patch IMAP servers, but also to patch any application that authenticates against the Unix password file. More information on the *getpg* functions can be found at *http:// www.wankwood.com/getpg/*.

Authenticating Against an SQL Database (Cyrus)

Authcheck

Author

Vladimir Ivaschenko (*vi@maks.net*)

URL

http://www.hazard.maks.net/cyrus/sql-auth.tar.gz

Major features

Tools for authenticating Cyrus users against a PostgreSQL database. Includes CGI administration tool.

Installation

Standalone Perl script. No special installation. Some IMAP configuration required.

Documentation

Documentation is contained in the *INSTALL* file included with the distribution.

Status

Current version is 0.01 as of February 2000.

Dependencies

Cyrus IMAP 1.6.20 or higher, Cyrus SASL built with *pwcheck* support, Perl modules IO::Socket, DBI, Unix::Syslog, Digest::MD5, and POSIX.

Licensing

GNU General Public License.

Authcheck is a daemon written in Perl that is used to authenticate IMAP users against an PostgreSQL database.

Authcheck requires Cyrus Version 1.6.20 or higher and Cyrus SASL Version 1.5.13 or higher built to include support for *pwcheck* authentication. Prebuilt RPMs (both source and binary) that include *pwcheck* support are available from *http://www.hazard.maks.net/cyrus/*.

Authcheck presumes that the server uses MD5 digests with its passwords. Two CGI scripts are included in the Authcheck distribution to simplify management of MD5 passwords. *imap-chpasswd.cgi.pl* is a CGI interface by which a user can change her MD5 password. *imapadmin.cgi.pl* is a CGI interface for administration of IMAP accounts that includes support for MD5 passwords. The administration CGI requires that the Cyrus admin user exist in the SQL database.

Configuring Authcheck is limited to the Authcheck daemon itself (*authcheck.pl*)— it should be modified to include your DBI DSN, database username, and password. If your Cyrus server does not use *pwcheck* authentication, then you'll have to modify */etc/imapd.conf* to include:

```
sasl_pwcheck_method: pwcheck
```

---

   authcheck.pl should be run as the *cyrus* user, never as *root*.

---

cyrus-sasl-mysql patch

Author

David M. Zendzian (*dmz@dmzs.com*)

URL

http://www.dmzs.com/~dmz/projects/cyrus-sasl-mysql/

Major features

Allows Cyrus authentication via SASL against a MySQL database.

Installation

Involves patching and rebuilding Cyrus SASL.

Documentation

> *http://www.dmzs.com/~dmz/projects/cyrus-sasl-mysql/*

Status

> Current version is 0.8.0 as of March 2000.

Dependencies

> Cyrus SASL 1.5.13 and Cyrus IMAP Version 1.6 or higher.

Licensing

> Unknown (free).

cyrus-sasl-mysql is a patch for the Cyrus SASL library that allows the Cyrus IMAP server to authenticate IMAP users against a *mysql* database. SASL authentication is supported only in Cyrus IMAP Versions 1.6 and higher. Sites running Cyrus 1.5.x wishing to use an alternative authentication method should use the *pwcheck* variant (*pwcheck_mysql*) covered in this section.

Using the *cyrus-sasl-mysql* patch involves installing the patch and rebuilding Cyrus SASL. A rebuild of Cyrus IMAP is not required, because the SASL libraries are completely separate from Cyrus IMAP and have no dependencies on Cyrus. Once you've installed the patch and rebuilt SASL, there's no going back, so it's advisable to save a copy of your original source tree before installing the patch. The author of the patch intends to add a configure option that allows SASL to be built with *mysql* support enabled or disabled.

Configuration for *mysql* authentication exists entirely in */etc/imapd.conf*. The configuration options are described at *http://www.dmzs.com/~dmz/projects/cyrus-sasl-mysql/*.

pwcheck_mysql

Author

> Aaron Newsome (*anewsome@anewsome.com*)

URL

> *http://www.mysql.com/Contrib/pwcheck_mysql-0.1.tar.gz*

Major features

> Allows IMAP users to be authenticated against a MySQL database.

Installation

> Drop a source file into the Cyrus distribution, then configure and build Cyrus.

Documentation

> Documentation is contained in the *README* file included with distribution.

Status

> Current version is 0.1 as of March 2000.

Licensing

GNU General Public License.

With *pwcheck_mysql*, you can authenticate your IMAP users against a MySQL database. Installation is not complicated. From the top level of your Cyrus source tree, copy *pwcheck_mysql.c* into the *pwcheck/* subdirectory.

Configure Cyrus IMAP as follows:

```
% ./configure --with-pwcheck=mysql --with-login=unix_pwcheck
```

Edit *pwcheck/Makefile* so that your CPPFLAGS, LIBS, and LDFLAGS definitions look something like this (the exact definitions will vary slightly by operating system):

```
CPPFLAGS = -I/usr/local/include/mysql -I. -I$(srcdir) \
    -I$(srcdir)/../lib -I$(srcdir)/../et
LIBS = -lmysqlclient -ldb -lndbm -ldl
LDFLAGS = -g -L/usr/local/lib/mysql
```

Finally:

```
% make depend
% make
# make install
```

pwcheck_pgsql

Author

Maxim Gorkov

URL

ftp://ftp.kstu.edu.ru/pub/unix/cyrus/pwcheck_pgsql-0.1.tgz

Major features

Allows Cyrus IMAP users to authenticate against a PostgreSQL database.

Installation

Copy a C source file into Cyrus source tree, edit a Makefile, then configure and rebuild Cyrus.

Documentation

README file included in package.

Status

Current version is 0.1 as of February 2000.

Dependencies

PostgreSQL, Cyrus IMAP.

Licensing

Freeware.

pwcheck_pgsql is a replacement for the Cyrus IMAP server's external authentication daemon, *pwcheck. pwcheck_pgsql* authenticates users against a PostgreSQL database instead of the Unix shadow password file.

To use *pwcheck_pgsql*, copy *pwcheck_pgsql.c* into the *pwcheck* subdirectory of the Cyrus source tree. Then, configure Cyrus:

```
% ./configure --with-pwcheck=pgsql --with-login=unix_pwcheck
```

Open *pwcheck/Makefile* and edit the definitions of `LIBS` and `LDFLAGS` to include the PostgreSQL libraries (the exact definitions will vary slightly by operating system):

```
LIBS =  -lsocket -lnsl -lcrypt -lutil -lpg
LDFLAGS = -L/usr/local/lib -R/usr/local/lib -L/usr/local/pgsql/lib -L
```

And finally, from the top level of the Cyrus source directory:

```
% make
# make install
```

Authenticating Against an LDAP Directory (Cyrus)

pwcheck_ldap

Author
> Clayton Donley (*donley@cig.mot.com*)

URL
> *http://www.linc-dev.com/Files/pwcheck_ldap.c.txt*

Major features
> Replacement for Cyrus *pwcheck* that authenticates users against an LDAP directory.

Installation
> Involves copying a C source file into the Cyrus source tree, modifying some preprocessor commands and a Makefile, and reconfiguring/rebuilding Cyrus.

Documentation
> *http://www.linc-dev.com/Files/using-pwcheck.html*

Status
> Latest version is 1.01 as of February 2000.

Licensing
> Unknown (free).

pwcheck_ldap is a replacement for the Cyrus IMAP server's external authentication daemon, *pwcheck. pwcheck_ldap* authenticates users against an LDAP directory instead of the Unix shadow password file.

To install *pwcheck_ldap*, download *pwcheck_ldap.c* and copy it into the Cyrus IMAP source tree under the *pwcheck* subdirectory.

Edit the following two lines of *pwcheck_ldap.c* to suit your site:

```
#define MY_LDAP_SERVER "localhost"
#define MY_LDAP_BASEDN "o=Motorola, c=US"
```

Find the definition of DEPLIBS in *pwcheck/Makefile.in* and change it as follows:*

```
DEPLIBS = ../lib/libcyrus.a -lldap -llber @DEPLIBS
```

Finally, configure Cyrus and rebuild it:

```
% ./configure –with-pwcheck=ldap –with-login=unix_pwcheck
% make
# make install
```

Users with *uid* and *userPassword* attributes in the LDAP directory will be able to log in to the IMAP server.

Monitoring and Testing Tools

So, now that you've brought up your load-balanced, SQL-authenticated, awesome-performing IMAP server (at least you *think* it's awesome-performing), it would probably be good if you could back up your claims of near-permanent uptime and blazing performance with more than anecdotal tales of how well it works for you and the handful of users you've polled since the last upgrade. That's where monitoring and testing tools come in. They take system performance (which you and your users understand) and turn it into numbers (which "the suits" understand) and outage notifications (which you and your operations center understand). Refer to Chapter 16, *Server Performance Tuning*, for more on performance monitoring.

SMT

Authors
    Brian Hill and Joel Loudermilk

URL
    http://www.doodlabs.com/smt/smt-1.05.tar.gz

Major features
    Monitors IMAP, POP, SMTP, DNS, and HTTP services and notifies a user if a service is down.

Installation
    Typical GNU-type software installation.

---

* If you're using the Netscape LDAP libraries, use -lldap10.

Documentation

General features are documented at *http://www.doodlabs.com/smt/*, and specifics are documented in manpages included in the SMT distribution.

Status

Current version is 1.05 as of February 2000.

Licensing

GNU General Public License.

SMT is a daemon that tests a service, such as IMAP or SMTP, by executing a test program. There are prebuilt tests included with SMT that monitor IMAP, POP3, SMTP, DNS, and HTTP. SMT can also run a user-defined test—anything goes, as long as it can be run from a shell prompt.

If the test program reports a failure, the SMT daemon executes a customized notification program to notify someone of the test failure. SMT maintains state information and makes notifications based on the change in state, not just on test failure. In other words, if a service is down, the notification will be sent out only once— the first time the service failure is detected.

SMT is light on resource utilization, using only the resources required for a test itself. Multiple tests can be executed concurrently.

To build and install SMT, unpack the distribution and from the distribution directory, type the commands:

```
% ./configure
% make
# make install
```

By default, the *smt* daemon is installed under */usr/local/bin/*, the tests under */usr/local/share/smt/*, and the manpages under */usr/local/man/*. You will have to create your own configuration file and notification script. Example 18-4 is an example configuration file for monitoring IMAP and SMTP.

Example 18-4. SMT Configuration File for IMAP and SMTP

```
logfile "/var/log/smt.log"
logdetail 4                          # Show test results in logs

test "IMAP server" {
    command "/usr/local/share/smt/imap imap.themullets.net"
    message "The IMAP server is %U"
    successcode 0
    timeout 25
}

test "SMTP" {
    command "/usr/local/share/smt/smtp mail.themullets.net"
    message "The SMTP server is %U"
```

Example 18-4. SMT Configuration File for IMAP and SMTP (continued)

```
    successcode 0
    timeout 25
}

group "Mail_Tests" {
    notification "/usr/local/etc/notify.pl dianna@pager.themullets.net"
    frequency 300
    test "SMTP"
    test "IMAP server"
}
```

Example 18-5 is the example notification script as defined in the configuration file in the previous example.

Example 18-5. SMT Notification Script

```
#!/usr/bin/perl
# Usage: notify.pl user@address messagefile
#
# messagefile is passed to the notify script by SMT as the last argument in the
# argument list.

$addressee     = "$ARGV[0]";
$messagefile   = "$ARGV[1]";

if (! $addressee && ! $messagefile) {

    print "Usage: notify user\@address messagefile\n";
    exit;
}

`/usr/bin/elm -s IMAPtest $addressee < $message`;
```

To start the SMT daemon, issue the command:

```
# smt /etc/smt.conf
```

tcpflow

Author

Jeremy Elson (*jelson@circlemud.org*)

URL

ftp://ftp.circlemud.org/pub/jelson/tcpflow/tcpflow-0.12.tar.gz

Major features

Records the conversational transactions that take place in TCP-based protocols in a format much easier to read than the default output of *snoop* or *tcpdump*. Useful only for TCP-based protocol debugging and analysis.

Installation
   Standard GNU software installation.

Documentation
   http://www.circlemud.org/~jelson/software/tcpflow/

Status
   Current version is 0.12 as of March 2000.

Dependencies
   LBL Packet Capture Library (*libpcap.a*), available from *ftp://ftp.ee.lbl.gov/libpcap.tar.Z*.

Licensing
   GNU General Public License.

An excellent tool for observing, analyzing, and troubleshooting connections between IMAP client and server, *tcpflow* captures and stores data transmitted over a TCP connection. *tcpflow* is a more narrowly focused and approachable alternative to *tcpdump*. Both programs are based on the LBL Packet Capture Library, but *tcpflow* can store captured data in separate files named for the source, TCP port, and destination IP addresses. For example, the data transmitted over an IMAP connection from a client, 129.120.156.155 port 2156, to the server, 129.120.1.1, on port 143 would be stored in the file 129.120.156.155.02156-129.120.001.001.00143.

In Example 18-6, *tcpflow* is used to observe an IMAP client (Mulberry) log in to the IMAP server running on the local host, flag a message as "important," then log out. *diannapc.themullets.net* is the hostname of the client.

Example 18-6. tcpflow

```
localhost# tcpflow 'host diannapc.themullets.net and (port imap)'
129.120.210.004.00143-129.120.217.045.02516: * OK localhost IMAP4rev1 v12.250
server ready

129.120.217.045.02516-129.120.210.004.00143: A00001 CAPABILITY

129.120.210.004.00143-129.120.217.045.02516: * CAPABILITY IMAP4 IMAP4REV1
NAMESPACE IDLE SCAN SORT MAILBOX-REFERRALS LOGIN-REFERRALS AUTH=LOGIN
AUTH=ANONYMOUS THREAD=ORDEREDSUBJECT
A00001 OK Completed

129.120.217.045.02516-129.120.210.004.00143: A00002 LOGIN johndoe "XXXXXXXX"

129.120.210.004.00143-129.120.217.045.02516: A00002 OK Completed
```

Intermediate details omitted...

```
129.120.217.045.02529-129.120.210.004.00143: A00008 STORE 1 +FLAGS (\Flagged)
```

Example 18-6. tcpflow (continued)

```
129.120.210.004.00143-129.120.217.045.02529: * 1 FETCH (FLAGS (\Seen \Flagged))
A00008 OK Completed

129.120.217.045.02529-129.120.210.004.00143: A00009 LOGOUT

129.120.210.004.00143-129.120.217.045.02529: * BYE localhost IMAP4rev1 server
terminating connection
A00009 OK Completed
```

tm: A Stress Tester

Authors

> Andrew Sutton (*Andrew.Sutton.1@ohio.edu*)
> Todd Acheson (*acheson@ohio.edu*)

URL

> *http://redbud.cats.ohiou.edu/tm/tm.tar*

Major features

> Stress-tester for Cyrus IMAP server.

Installation

> Unpack the *tar* archive and build.

Documentation

> The technical description of *tm* is at *http://redbud.cats.ohiou.edu/tm/*.

Status

> Current version is 1.1 as of March 2000.

Requirements

> Requires the *pthread** library.

Licensing

> Free, can be redistributed for non-commercial use (*http://redbud.cats.ohiou.
> edu/tm/copyright.html*).

tm is a stress tester for the Cyrus IMAP server. It's designed to test the robustness of a Cyrus system by simulating over-exaggerated use. The results of a *tm* test can be used to predict how a Cyrus system will perform under heavy loads and to identify bottlenecks on the server. Currently, *tm* has been ported only to Sun OS, IRIX and DGUX.

---

* The GNU *pthread* library is available at *ftp://ftp.cis.ohio-state.edu/mirror/gnu/pth/*.

Before attempting to run *tm* on a production system, be aware that the loads generated by *tm* are far in excess of normal system loads and could lead to downtime.

In order to simulate the effect of multiple users sharing resources, *tm* needs to perform IMAP operations asynchronously. To meet that requirement, *tm* is multithreaded and uses a separate thread for each set of write-read-verify operations. The number of threads is configured in the *tm.conf* file. A simple *tm.conf* file is shown in Example 18-7.

Example 18-7. tm.conf

```
# Example tm.conf file

{write1 read1}
{write2 read2}

# Spawn 10 noise threads
10 {noise}
```

The {writer reader} notation designates a writer-reader pair of scripts. The writer performs an operation, such as SETACL. The reader grabs the result of the operation by performing the companion operation (e.g., if the writer performs a SETACL operation, the reader would perform a GETACL). The noise thread calls another script, *noise*, which simulates work, such as users logging on to and out of the IMAP server, clients sending CAPABILITY or NOOP commands, or users fetching the contents of a mailbox.

The name of each member of the writer-reader pair corresponds to the actual name of the script that contains the IMAP commands to be executed. In the example, there are four scripts: *write1*, *write2*, *read1*, and *read2*. The *write1* and *read1* scripts are shown in Example 18-8 and Example 18-9.

Example 18-8. write1 (Example Writer Script)

```
open imap imap.themullets.net
command login testuser xxxxxxxx
loop 20
command setacl mailbox inbox johndoe lprs
command setacl mailbox inbox johndoe lwci
end
logout
```

Example 18-9. read1 (Example Reader Script)

```
open imap imap.themullets.net
command login testuser xxxxxxxx
loop 20
command getacl mailbox inbox
command getacl mailbox inbox
end
logout
```

The *tm* program compares the results of the writer and reader and logs the results of the comparison to *tm.log*. The IMAP commands and their output are written to the debug log file, *out.log*.* The test is complete when all scripts have finished running and the last operations have been logged.

Of course, having the ability to create system load is more meaningful if you also have the capacity to engineer ways to meet that load. One way to address that need is through clustering your IMAP servers.

IMAP Clustering

Unfortunately, there is no comprehensive open source package that provides IMAP server clustering. We've avoided covering commercial software tools in this chapter, but in light of the lack of free clustering software, we'll break the trend and mention one commercial product and one freely available package.

BLUETAIL Mail Robustifier

Author
    Bluetail AB

URL
    http://www.bluetail.com/products/

Major features
    Adds load balancing, scalability, and fault tolerance to IMAP services.

Installation
    http://www.bluetail.com/big/common/bmr11.pdf

Documentation
    Available at Bluetail AB's site: whitepaper (*http://www.bluetail.com/big/common/wp11.pdf*), overview (*http://www.bluetail.com/big/common/wpm.pdf*), and user manuals (*http://www.bluetail.com/big/common/bmr11.pdf*).

Status
    Current version is 1.1 as of February 2000.

---

* Use *tm*'s *−n* option to turn off debug logging to *out.log*.

Licensing

Commercial (free 30-day trial available).

BLUETAIL Mail Robustifier is a software proxy system that adds load balancing, scalability, and fault tolerance to IMAP, POP, and SMTP services running on Unix platforms. The supported platforms are Linux, Solaris, FreeBSD, and BSDi.

The software runs on a pair of dedicated proxy servers that sit between the IMAP server farm and the IMAP clients and load-balance traffic across the servers in the farm. If a proxy server dies, BLUETAIL fails over to the other node.

BLUETAIL adds scalability by allowing additional IMAP server machines to be added transparently while IMAP services are online. Likewise, machines can be removed or upgraded while IMAP is up. If an IMAP server dies, its traffic can either be routed to another server or rejected, depending on the configuration. BLUETAIL can be configured dynamically and the software can be upgraded while the system is running.

An overload control mechanism can be configured to kick in when traffic reaches a certain threshold. Once that threshold is met, any further connections will be refused. The overload control mechanism can also be used to prioritize groups of users, i.e., give premium users priority over normal users when the system begins to reach its threshold.

Additional features of BLUETAIL include RFC 2505 SPAM filtering, GUI and command-line interfaces, and monitoring and statistics gathering.

Of particular interest to Cyrus sites, BLUETAIL is capable of handling both infrastructures that share a mailstore between IMAP servers and infrastructures that have a separate mailstore per server. If the mailstore is shared, Robustifier balances the traffic between the servers. In cases where each server has a dedicated mailstore, BLUETAIL routes traffic to the appropriate server, either per-user or per-domain.

Cyrus IMAP Aggregator

Author

Project Cyrus

URL

http://asg.web.cmu.edu/cyrus/ag.html

Major features

Divides IMAP mailstore load across an arbitrary number of servers. Provides near high-availability for IMAP processing (see below).

Installation

Not released when we went to press.

Documentation

   http://asg.web.cmu.edu/cyrus/ag.html

Status

   Unreleased and pre-alpha as of June 2000.

Licensing

   Freely available.

The Cyrus IMAP Aggregator is very early into its life cycle. As we go to press, it's pre-alpha and not even released to the public. Upon release, however, the IMAP Aggregator promises to provide robust multitier reliability for IMAP systems.

An IMAP Aggregator consists of two rows of IMAP servers. A row of frontend servers take all the incoming IMAP connections from clients and act solely as proxies between the end users and the backend servers. A row of backend servers provides direct access to the mailstore. Each frontend server provides duplicate proxy services. Lose one or more of your front-row servers, and as long as some still remain, you're still completely able to provide IMAP services. Each backend server provides mailstore services for a given percentage of your users. ACAP or LDAP help the frontend servers (which act as proxies to the back servers) locate the mailbox for a particular user.

To be a true high-availability system, rather than simple multiplexing, the IMAP Aggregator would need to provide duplicate mailstore services on each of the backend servers.

IMAP APIs

You may be the type that is only be satisfied with IMAP utilities that you write yourself. Or perhaps you've got a particular need that isn't adequately met by the other packages described here. In either case, here are some IMAP APIs that might make your life a bit easier and your development time a bit shorter.

C-Client API

Author

   Mark Crispin (*mrc@cac.washington.edu*)

URL

   ftp://ftp.cac.washington.edu/imap/imap.tar.Z

Major features

   IMAP API and supporting libraries for messaging applications bundled with the UW IMAP server distribution.

Installation

   No special installation required (*make <platform>*).

Documentation

   Documentation on C-Client is included in the UW IMAP distribution, in the file *docs/internal.txt*.

Status

   Current version is 4.7a as of March 2000.

Licensing

   Free, can be redistributed, copyright restricted (see comments in source files for details).

C-Client is the granddaddy of IMAP APIs. Written by Mark Crispin, the IMAP originator, C-Client has been used at the core of many IMAP servers and clients beyond just PINE and UW-IMAP. It's probably fair to say that C-Client is a reference API for most IMAP protocol features and, as such, is more appropriate for full-scale projects than quick-and-dirty utilities.

C-Client may be found in the *src/c-client* directory of the UW-IMAP distribution, and extensive, well-written, detailed documentation on C-Client may be found in *docs/internal.txt*.

Perl APIs

Mail-IMAPClient

Author

   David J. Kernen (*kernen@erols.com*)

URL

   http://www.perl.com/CPAN/authors/id/D/DJ/DJKERNEN/Mail-IMAPClient-1.08.tar.gz

Major features

   Perl API that simplifies the conversation between a Perl script and an IMAP server.

Installation

   Standard Perl module installation. See *http://www.cpan.org/modules/INSTALL.html*.

Documentation

   http://search.cpan.org/doc/DJKERNEN/Mail-IMAPClient-1.08/README

Status

   Current version is 1.08 as of March 2000.

Dependencies

Requires Perl module IO::Socket.

Licensing

GNU General Public License.

Mail-IMAPClient (shown in Example 18-10) is an RFC 2060–compliant API that simplifies the interaction between a Perl script and an IMAP server. Virtually all client commands defined in RFC 2060 are supported. Mail-IMAPClient has been tested successfully with both the Cyrus and UW IMAP servers.

To verify that your system has IO::Socket installed, enter on the command line:

```
% perl -e 'use Socket; use IO::Socket;'
```

The module source distribution includes examples, including *imap-to-inbox.pl*, which reads a user's IMAP folders and converts them to *mbox* format. *imap-to-inbox.pl* can be used as an intermediate step converting from a proprietary IMAP server to one of the public-domain servers.

Example 18-10. Mail-IMAPClient

```perl
#!/usr/local/bin/perl

use Mail::IMAPClient;
$| = 1;

$server = "imap.themullets.net";
$port     = 143;
$user     = "johndoe";
$password = "XXXXXXXX";

&connect;
&count_messages;

sub connect {

    $imap = Mail::IMAPClient->new(
        Server      => "$server",
        User        => "$user",
        Password    => "$password",
        Port        => "$port",
    )
    || die ("Could not connect to $server:$port: $! $?");
}

sub count_messages {

    my (@folders, $folder, $count);

    @folders = $imap->folders;
```

Example 18-10. Mail-IMAPClient (continued)

```
    push(@folders, "INBOX");

    foreach $folder (@folders) {

        $count = $imap->message_count($folder);

        if (! $count) {
                print "$folder is empty.\n";
                next;
        }
        print "$count messages in $folder.\n";
    }
}
```

Net-IMAP-Simple

Author
> Joao Fonseca (*joao_g_fonseca@yahoo.com*)

URL
> *http://www.perl.com/CPAN/authors/id/J/JP/JPAF/Net-IMAP-Simple-0.93.tar.gz*

Major features
> Perl IMAP API, limited to a subset of IMAP commands.

Installation
> Standard Perl module installation. See *http://www.cpan.org/modules/INSTALL. html*.

Documentation
> *http://search.cpan.org/doc/JPAF/Net-IMAP-Simple-0.93/Simple.pm*.

Status
> Current version is 0.93 as of February, 2000.

Licensing
> Unstated (free).

This module is a simple way to access IMAP accounts. Net-IMAP-Simple is limited to the following commands:

login	*create_mailbox*
select	*rename_mailbox*
seen	*delete_mailbox*
get	*copy*
getfh	*quit*
mailboxes	

Example 18-11 is an example script using Net-IMAP-Simple.

Example 18-11. Net-IMAP-Simple Example

```perl
#!/usr/local/bin/perl

use Net::IMAP::Simple;

# Open a connection to the IMAP server
#
$server = new Net::IMAP::Simple( 'imap.unt.edu' );

# Log in to the server
#
$server->login( 'johndoe', 'XXXXXXXX' );


# Get a list of all folders
#
@folders = $server->mailboxes();

foreach $folder (@folders) {

    $number_of_messages = $server->select( $folder );

    if ($number_of_messages) {
        print "There are $number_of_messages in $folder.\n";
    } else {
        print "$folder is empty.\n";
    }
}

# close the connection
$server->quit();
```

NetxAP

Author

> Kevin Johnson (*kjj@pobox.com*)

URL

> *http://www.perl.com/CPAN/authors/id/KJOHNSON/NetxAP-0.02.tar.gz*

Major features

> Perl API featuring full set of RFC 2060 IMAP commands along with commands from many of the IMAP extensions (such as namespace, ACL, and quota).

Installation

> Standard Perl module installation. See *http://www.cpan.org/modules/INSTALL. html*.

Documentation

> *http://search.cpan.org/doc/KJOHNSON/NetxAP-0.02/Net/IMAP.pm*

Status

Current version is 0.02 as of February 2000.

Dependencies

MIME::Base64 and Digest-MD5 modules.

Licensing

Freeware.

Net::IMAP is a Perl module included in the NetxAP package. It consists of a complete set of core RFC 2060 protocol commands, with a few extras thrown in. The list is too extensive to list here, but is documented at *http://search.cpan.org/doc/ KJOHNSON/NetxAP-0.02/Net/IMAP.pm*. The NetxAP modules are still in alpha release. Although they look very promising, the author of the modules cautions against using them in production environments. Two examples that use Net::IMAP are included in the NetxAP distribution.

PHP

Author

Many contributors (*http://www.php.net/credits.php3*)

URL

http://www.php.net/

Major features

PHP IMAP API based on the C-Client library.

Installation

Standard GNU-type software installation.

Documentation

http://www.php.net/manual/ref.imap.php3

Status

Current version is 4.0 as of March 2000.

Dependencies

Requires C-Client library.

Licensing

GNU General Public License (*http://www.php.net/license.html*).

PHP includes a built-in IMAP API that's a port of the C-Client library. To use the IMAP functions, you must first install the C-Client library (refer to the section on C-Client earlier in this chapter for download information). Build the C-Client library, then copy *c-client/c-client.a* to */usr/local/lib/* (or wherever you keep your locally installed libraries). Copy *c-client/rfc822.h*, *c-client/mail.h* and *c-client/ linkage.h* to */usr/local/include* (or another directory in your include path). Once the C-Client library is installed, compile PHP with the *--with-imap* option. Complete documentation on the API functions is available in the PHP manual at *http://www.php.net/manual/ref.imap.php3*.

JavaMail

Author

Sun Microsystems

URL

http://www.javasoft.com/products/javamail/index.html

Major features

Comprehensive API for developing mail clients in Java; supports SMTP, POP, and other protocols in addition to IMAP.

Installation

Standard Java installation.

Documentation

http://www.javasoft.com/products/JavaMail-1.1.pdf (documentation also available online)

Status

Current version is 1.1.3 (February 2000); 1.2 spec draft available.

Dependencies

Requires JavaBeans Activation Framework (*javax.activation*).

Licensing

SCSL (Sun Community Source License).

VI

Appendixes

A

Conversion from Berkeley Mail Format to Cyrus: Tools

The procedure for converting a set of users from traditional Unix (Berkeley format) mail to Cyrus was outlined in Chapter 9, *Cyrus System Administration*. In this appendix, source code for the tools used in such a conversion is provided.

bsd2cyrus

bsd2cyrus is a Perl script, introduced in Chapter 9, that maps a set of users' Berkeley-format mail folders into the Cyrus namespace. The output of the *bsd2cyrus* script is used as input to other scripts that are used in converting users from a Berkeley-style mail system to a Cyrus system. *bsd2cyrus* takes as input the filename of a text file that contains a list of usernames. Example A-1 shows the *bsd2cyrus* script.

Example A-1. bsd2cyrus

```
#!/usr/local/bin/perl
    eval 'exec /usr/local/bin/perl -S $0 ${1+"$@"}'
        if $running_under_some_shell;

require "find.pl";

$inputfile  = "$ARGV[0]";
if (! $inputfile) { die "Usage: $0 inputfile\n"; }
```

For each user, get the user's home directory from the *passwd* file and search for the pathnames of all files under the user's *~/mail* directory. The **find** subroutine pushes those files onto an array. Note that the files are all pushed onto a single array, not an array per user—this is because we're assuming that you're converting a large batch of users all at one time and don't need to do anything special on a per-user basis.

```
open (DATA, $inputfile) || die "can't open $inputfile";
while (<DATA>) {
    chop;
    ($name,$pw,$uid,$gid,$quota,$cmnt,$gcos,$home) = getpwnam $_;
    next if $home eq "";
    &find("$home/mail");
}

close DATA;
```

The next lines narrow the list of files under the *~/mail* subdirectory to folders that contain mail content only. If your users store mail in directories named something other than *~/mail*, you should modify the script to look at those directories:

```
foreach (@folders) {

    ($user,$folder) = split(/:/,$_,2);
```

Before creating a mailbox on the Cyrus server, we have to check and make sure that the BSD folder on the old system has RFC 822 content. In the *bsd2cyrus* script, we assume that if the folder is any of the following:

- Directory

- Executable file

- Binary file

- Archive

- Empty file

then its content is not RFC 822. If you wish to use more or less stringent criteria—we chose to keep this example simple to illustrate the concept—in practice, you could also modify *bsd2cyrus* to log the skipped files, then go back and examine them more closely at a later time. Speaking from our own experience converting 20,000 accounts from Berkeley format on a UW IMAP system to Cyrus IMAP, the heuristic used in this example will handle 99.9% of "problem" mail folders. The more common problem we encountered was users who stored their mail folders in a non-standard *place* on the system, such as in their home directory, in system "scratch" space, or in a hidden subdirectory.

```
    if (! rfc822($folder) ) { next; }

    @tokens = split(/\//, $folder);
    $mailbox = $tokens[$#tokens];

    ## Sanity checks - earlier tests should have caught these.

    next if ($mailbox =~ /\.gz$/);        # Skip gzipped files
    next if ($mailbox =~ /\.Z$/);         # Skip compressed files
    next if ($mailbox =~ /^\./);          # Skip hidden files
```

You may recall from Chapter 6, *Introduction to the Cyrus IMAP Server*, that Cyrus IMAP does not allow special characters, such as Unix shell metacharacters and non-ASCII characters, in mailbox names. The *rm_badchars* subroutine handles special characters by converting them into their ASCII representation in the new mailbox name, preceded by an underscore:

```
    ## Replace "bad" characters with an underscore followed by
    ## the ASCII representation of the "bad" character.

    $mailbox = rm_badchars($mailbox);
    print "$user:user.$user.$mailbox:$folder\n";
}

sub wanted {
    (($dev,$ino,$mode,$nlink,$uid,$gid) = lstat($_)) &&
    -f _;
    if ($_ ne '.') { push @folders, "$user:$dir/$_"; }
}

sub rfc822 {

    my ($file) = @_;
    my ($rc) = 1;
    if (-d $file || -z $file || -B $file || -x $file) {
        $rc = 0;
    }
    return $rc;
}

sub rm_badchars {

    my ($mailbox) = @_;
    $mailbox =~ s/ /_040/g;
    $mailbox =~ s/\!/_041/g;
    $mailbox =~ s/\"/_042/g;
    $mailbox =~ s/\#/_043/g;
```

In this example, we omitted the remainder of the character translations, but in the actual script, each character that is not allowed should have a statement in the *rm_badchars* subroutine that translates it into its ASCII representation. After performing the translations, the new mailbox name is returned to the main program:

```
    return $mailbox;
}
```

createfolders

createfolders (shown in Example A-2) is a Tcl script that was used in Chapter 9 to create empty Cyrus mailboxes. It takes *bsd2cyrus*'s output as input. *bsd2cyrus*'s output contains the username, the pathname to a Berkeley-style mail folder, and its mapping into the Cyrus namespace (i.e., the Cyrus mailbox name), but *create-folders* uses only the Cyrus mailbox name.

Example A-2. createfolders

```
#!/usr/local/bin/cyradm -file
set inputfile [lindex $argv 0]

eval cyradm connect cyr_conn localhost imap
puts stdout "Connected to IMAP server. Authenticating..."

if [catch {eval cyr_conn authenticate -pwcommand {{
    set adminid cyrusadm
    set adminpw xxxxxxxx
    list $adminid $adminpw
}} } result ] {
    puts stderr "$result (cleartext)"
    return -code error $result
} else {
    puts "Authentication successful."
}

## $inputfile is a text file containing username, path to
## Berkeley format folder, and corresponding Cyrus mailbox

if [catch {open $inputfile r} fileId] {
    puts stderr "Error: cannot open $inputfile"
} else {

    while {[gets $fileId line] >= 0} {

        ## The Cyrus mailbox is the second field in the input
        ## line (arrays are indexed starting with 0).

        set mailbox [lindex [split $line ":"] 1]

        if [catch {cyr_conn createmailbox $mailbox} result] {
            puts stderr $result
        } else {
            puts "Created mailbox $mailbox"
        }
    }
}
```

inboxfer

inboxfer is a Perl script that was used in Chapter 9 to move messages from a Berkeley format inbox (e.g., */var/mail/johndoe*) into a Cyrus inbox. The script (shown in Example A-3) assumes that the Cyrus mailbox already exists and that *formail* is

available on the machine where the script runs.* *inboxfer* takes the name of the
file containing usernames, one per line, as input.

Example A-3. inboxfer

```
#!/usr/local/bin/perl

## Purpose: Extract messages from /var/mail mailbox
##          and populate the Cyrus INBOX.

$scripts   = "/home/cyrus/bin";       # Location of this script
$mailstore = "/var/spool/imap/user";  # Cyrus mailstore
$oldspool  = "/var/oldmail";          # Old mail spool

$cmd       = "/usr/local/bin/formail -n 20 -s $scripts/cpmsg";

$users = "$ARGV[0]";
if (!$users) { die "Usage: $0 $users\n"; }

open(USERS,"$users") || die "can't open $users";

while (<USERS>) {
    chop;
    $inbox = "$oldspool/$_";
    system("/usr/bin/cat $inbox | $cmd $mailstore/$_");
}
```

The system call pipes the contents of the incoming mail folder into a *formail* command. The *formail* command splits the folder up into separate mail messages and,
in turn, pipes each mail message into another Perl script, *cpmsg*, for processing.
cpmsg is the script that actually copies the message into the Cyrus mailbox. *cpmsg*
is shown in Example A-4.

formail increments an environment variable, FILENO, each time it finds a new
message in the Berkeley folder. *cpmsg* takes advantage of the FILENO variable to
come up with a unique numbering scheme for the messages within a single Berkeley mail folder. The FILENO numbers are of the format NNN, padded with leading
0's. Because Cyrus works with ordinal numbers followed by a ".", *cpmsg* must
remove leading 0's and add the "." to make a valid Cyrus message filename.

Do not use *inboxfer* to copy mail into Cyrus mailboxes that already
contain mail!

---

* *formail* is part of the *procmail* distribution, available from *http://www.procmail.org.*

inboxfer always starts its numbering with "1.". If messages in the mailboxes have numbers between "1." and the number of messages being copied, they will be overwritten.

cpmsg takes the full path of the Cyrus mailbox as an argument (for example, the full path to *johndoe*'s INBOX on most Cyrus systems would be */var/spool/imap/ user/johndoe*).

Example A-4. cpmsg

```perl
#!/usr/local/bin/perl

## This is to be called by formail. Formail calls this program
## once for each mail message when called with the -s option.
## E.g.:
##            cat mailbox.txt | formail -s thisscript.pl
##
## maildir - Directory where the mail message is to be written.

$maildir = "$ARGV[0]";
if (!$maildir) { die "Usage: $0 $maildir"; }

## Formail increments this number for each message.
## The leading "0"'s must be removed (e.g. 001 becomes 1).

$filenum = ($ENV{FILENO} - 0) + 1;

open (OUTFILE,">$maildir/$filenum.");
while (<STDIN>) {
    chop;
    print OUTFILE "$_\015\012";  ## Add CRLF to each line!
}
close OUTFILE;
```

folderxfer

folderxfer is very similar to *inboxfer* except that, instead of a list of usernames, it takes the output of *bsd2cyrus* as input and copies messages from Berkeley-format mail folders into the corresponding Cyrus mailboxes. The *folderxfer* script is shown in Example A-5.

Example A-5. folderxfer

```perl
#!/usr/local/bin/perl

## Purpose: Converts contents of Berkeley-format mail folders
##          to Cyrus mailboxes
##
## Assumptions: (1) The root mailbox and empty Cyrus folder must
##                  exist before conversion takes place.
##
```

Example A-5. folderxfer (continued)

```
##              (2) Input has been checked for illegal characters
##                  and files that do not contain mail content.
##
## Input:   A list containing the following information on each
##          line:
##
##       <username>:<cyrus-format folder name>:<BSD folder path>

$scripts     = "/home/cyrus/bin";        # Location of this script
$mailstore   = "/var/spool/imap/user";  # Cyrus mailstore
$cmd         = "/usr/local/bin/formail -n 20 -s $scripts/cpmsg";

$folders = "$ARGV[0]";
if (!$folders) { die "Usage: $0 filename"; }

open (MB,"$folders") || die "can't open $folders";
while (<MB>) {

    chop;

    ## Be careful with this split - the last token might have
    ## whitespace we want to preserve.

    ($user,$cyrusfolder,$folder) = split(/:/,$_,3);
    @fields = split(/\./,$cyrusfolder);
    $cyrfol = $fields[$#fields];

    $cat = "/usr/bin/cat \"$folder\"";
    system ("$cat | $cmd '$mailstore/$user/$cyrfol'");
}
close MB;
```

batchreconstruct

batchreconstruct is a Perl script that runs the Cyrus *reconstruct* command on each newly created Cyrus mailbox. It takes a filename or a list of usernames as input. The *batchreconstruct* script is shown in Example A-6.

Example A-6. batchreconstruct

```
#!/usr/local/bin/perl

chop ($whoami = `/usr/ucb/whoami`);
if ($whoami ne "cyrus" ) {
    die "You must be cyrus to run this script!\n";
}

$cmd   = "/usr/cyrus/bin/reconstruct -r";
$users = "$ARGV[0]";
if (!$users) { die "Usage: $0 input_file\n"; }
```

Example A-6. batchreconstruct (continued)

```perl
open(MB,"$users") || die "can't open $users";
while (<MB>) {
    chop;
    system("$cmd user.$_");
}
close MB;
```

B

Adding SSL Support to IMAP

Many users use their web browser's built-in email client to read their IMAP mail. Many browsers, such as Netscape and IE, are SSL-enabled, but because the current distribution versions of UW and Cyrus servers do not support SSL, the users can't take advantage of their browser's SSL support. There is, however, a workaround—you can use the freely available OpenSSL SSL toolkit and *stunnel*, an SSL encryption wrapper, to wrap IMAP in SSL. The procedure for adding SSL support to IMAP is documented in this appendix. It involves downloading some free software, building and installing it, generating a certificate, and modifying your *inetd* configuration.

UW 2000 and the 2.0 release of Cyrus will support native SSL and are expected to be released before this book is published.

Get the Software

The first step is to get the latest versions of the sources for OpenSSL and *stunnel.*

OpenSSL

> *http://www.openssl.org/*

OpenSSL is a free implementation of Netscape's Secure Socket Layer—the software encryption protocol behind the Netscape Secure Server and the Netscape Navigator Browser. OpenSSL implements Secure Sockets Layer *SSLv2* (Version 2) and *SSLv3* (Version 3) and Transport Layer Security (TLSv1).

Download the latest OpenSSL source distribution (Version 0.9.5a as of this writing), and unpack it where you normally build free software. The URL given at the beginning of this section is the master location for OpenSSL sources. At that URL you will also find useful documentation. A good, concise source of information is the OpenSSL FAQ, complete with instructions on generating keys, pass phrases, and certificates, that is included in the OpenSSL sources.

stunnel

> *http://mike.daewoo.com.pl/computer/stunnel*

stunnel opens an encrypted pipeline between the SSL client and the IMAP server. It decrypts the data the client sends through the pipeline and passes it over to the IMAP server in cleartext over the loopback interface, where it's safe from being snooped from the network. Download the latest version of the source distribution (which as we write this appendix, is *stunnel-2.4a.tar.gz*) to the area on your system where you normally build free software, and proceed to the next section for instructions on building *stunnel*.

Put It All Together

Now that you've got the sources, the next step is to build and install the software, create a certificate, and tweak your *inetd* configuration file.

Install OpenSSL

OpenSSL supports RSA encryption, which most web browsers use in SSL sessions. Inside the United States, however, RSA.com holds a patent on the RSA encryption algorithms, and that makes it illegal to use OpenSSL with its standard RSA support. For legal use inside the United States, OpenSSL must be built to use the RSAREF encryption libraries, which are included with the OpenSSL.* The simplest way to build OpenSSL is using the "RSAglue" method. Using this method, you'll need to build support for OpenSSL into your application, such as *stunnel*, by including the header file *RSAref.h* in your application's Makefile at build time. An example is given in the instructions for building *stunnel* a little bit later in this section.

OpenSSL installs under */usr/local/ssl* by default (not in */usr/local* as the documentation might indicate). If you don't want it installed there, then read the *INSTALL* file provided with the distribution for instructions on how to change the install location.

---

* RSAREF is no longer available for download from RSA.com's FTP site. If you want to obtain RSAREF, it
  is available from *ftp.eecs.umich.edu/pub/EECS/crypt/rsaref.tar.gz*

Unpack the distribution:

```
% zcat openssl-0.9.5a.tar.gz | tar xvf -
```

In the top level of the unpacked distribution, run the *config* script:

```
% ./config
```

Next, build OpenSSL:

```
% make
% make test
# make install
```

If you are inside the United States, there is one final step—you will need to copy the *rsaref.h* header file and *libRSAglue.a* library into */usr/local/ssl/*. Applications into which you build SSL support will reference the RSAglue library to include RSAREF support.

```
% cp rsaref/rsaref.h /usr/local/ssl/include
% cp libRSAglue.a /usr/local/ssl/lib
```

Finally, edit */usr/local/ssl/lib/openssl.cnf* as needed. Comments in that file are self-explanatory.

Install stunnel

Unpack the *stunnel* distribution:

```
% zcat stunnel-2.4a.tar.gz | tar xvf -
```

Run the configure script:

```
% ./configure
```

Edit the *Makefile*. Change the LIBS definition so that it includes the RSAglue library (RSAglue should be linked after the *ssl* library and before the *crypto* library). The following example is from a Solaris 7 system:

```
LIBS=-lpthread -lsocket -lnsl -L/usr/local/ssl/lib -lssl -lRSAglue -lcrypto
```

Then, build *stunnel*:

```
% rm config.cache
% make clean
% make
# make install
```

Note that using *stunnel* with threads has a small footprint. However, you will end up with as many IMAP sessions as you have file descriptors, so make sure to increase the number of file descriptors on a large system.

Create a Certificate

The next step is to generate a new certificate for *stunnel*. It's sufficient to build a dummy certificate for *stunnel*—private key and certificate authority are not required:

```
# cd /usr/local/ssl/certs
# ../bin/req -new -x509 -nodes -out stunnel.pem -keyout \
  stunnel.pem -days 999
# chown cyrus:mail stunnel.pem
# chmod 0600 stunnel.pem
```

On Cyrus servers, the certificate must be owned by the *cyrus* user, or the client will not be able to verify the certificate. Note also that *stunnel* might ship with a copy of *stunnel.pem*—if your *stunnel* distribution comes with a certificate, delete it and build a new one.

Modify Services

Edit */etc/services*, and add the following line:

```
simap        993/tcp        simap        # SSL enabled IMAP
```

Listen for Secure IMAP Connections

Port 993 is the standard port that listens for requests to open secure IMAP (*simap*) connections. There are two ways to listen for *simap* connections: either by running *stunnel* out of *inetd* or by running it as a standalone daemon.

Running stunnel standalone

This is the preferred method of running *stunnel*. Running *stunnel* out of *inetd* adds some overhead to your system, because SSL has to be initialized on every connection. Additionally, when you run *stunnel* out of *inetd*, *stunnel* does not support session caching and will use more memory when the system is carrying a heavy load.

To run *stunnel* standalone, run one of the following commands. For Cyrus servers:

```
# stunnel -d 993 -l /usr/cyrus/bin/imapd -r imapd
```

For UW servers:

```
# stunnel -d 993 -l /usr/local/sbin/imapd -r imapd
```

stunnel must be started as *root* in order to bind to port 993. Cyrus servers will still perform all IMAP operations as the user defined for the *imapd* service in */etc/inetd.conf* (user *cyrus* in most cases).

Running stunnel out of inetd

Edit */etc/inetd.conf*. If your server is a Cyrus server, add the line:

```
simap stream tcp nowait cyrus /usr/local/bin/stunnel stunnel -l \
    /usr/cyrus/bin/imapd imapd
```

The *–l* argument tells *stunnel* which *inetd*-type program to run.

For UW servers, use:

```
simap stream tcp nowait root /usr/local/bin/stunnel stunnel -l \
    /usr/local/sbin/imapd imapd
```

And finally, restart *inetd*:

```
# ps -ef | grep inetd
root    150    1  TS  48   Apr 21 ?     0:01 /usr/sbin/inetd -s
# kill -hup 150
```

The *stunnel* FAQ, which comes with the *stunnel* source distribution, has many suggestions for testing and troubleshooting your *stunnel* installation.

C

IMAP Commands

This appendix covers the IMAP commands as described in RFC 2060 (IMAP4rev1). Commands may only be valid in certain connection states. We'll list the commands by the state in which they're valid. Server response codes (untagged responses) are not listed here in detail, but a knowledge of the response codes is not required for general evaluation and trouble-shooting of IMAP sessions. If you require detailed knowledge of the response codes, see Section 7.1 of RFC 2060 (*http://www.ietf.org/rfc/rfc2060.txt*).

Commands Valid in Any State

CAPABILITY

The CAPABILITY command returns a list of the server's capabilities (e.g., supported authentication mechanisms and supported IMAP extensions).

Usage
> **CAPABILITY**

Arguments
> None

Untagged server response
> An untagged CAPABILITY response

Results
> OK (command completed successfully)
> BAD (invalid arguments or command unknown)

Example
A00001 CAPABILITY
```
* CAPABILITY IMAP4REV1 MAILBOX-REFERRALS LOGIN-REFERRALS AUTH=CRAM-MD5
A00001 OK Completed
```

LOGOUT

The LOGOUT command tells the server to close the network connection.

Usage
LOGOUT

Arguments
None

Untagged server responses
An untagged BYE response

Results
OK (logout completed)
BAD (command failed or invalid arguments)

Example
A00003 logout
```
* BYE localhost IMAP4rev1 server terminating connection
A00003 OK Completed
```

NOOP

The NOOP command, besides resetting the server's inactivity autologout timer, also causes a protocol round-trip, which in turn may cause an announcement of new mail. NOOP is often used to poll the status of a mailbox when the client doesn't otherwise have anything to do.

Usage
NOOP

Arguments
None

Untagged server response
None

Command result
OK (NOOP completed successfully)
BAD (invalid arguments or command unknown)

Example

```
A00002 NOOP
A00002 OK Completed
```

Commands Valid in the Non-authenticated State

AUTHENTICATE

The AUTHENTICATE command authenticates the user to the server using the specified SASL authentication mechanism.

Usage

> **AUTHENTICATE *mechanism***

Arguments

> The authentication mechanism to use

Untagged server responses

> Optional server challenge (the server sends the untagged response + and the client replies with a BASE64 encoded response that is specific to the specified authentication mechanism).

Results

> OK (successful authentication)
> NO (authentication failed)
> BAD (command unknown or invalid arguments)

Example

```
A00004 authenticate anonymous
+

A00004 OK Completed
```

LOGIN

The LOGIN command authenticates the user to the server using the plaintext password.

Usage

> **LOGIN *username password***

Arguments

> Username and password

None

Results
OK (successful login)
NO (login failed)
BAD (command unknown or invalid arguments)

Example
```
A00005 LOGIN JOHNDOE "XXXXXXXX"
A00005 NO LOGIN failed
A00006 LOGIN JOHNDOE "YYYYYYYY"
A00006 OK Completed
```

Commands Valid in the Authenticated State

APPEND

The APPEND command appends a new message to the end of the specified mailbox. If flags or a date-time string is specified as an argument, the flags and date are set accordingly in the appended message.

Usage
```
APPEND mailbox (flags) date {message-size}
```

Arguments
Mailbox name
(Optional) Parenthesized list of flags to set in the appended message
(Optional) Date/time string; the internal data of the appended message will be set to this date/time
Message size (size of the message expressed in RFC 822 octets that will follow)

Untagged server responses
No specific response

Results
OK (successfully appended)
NO (APPEND command failed due to errors in *flags, date,* or message text)
BAD (command unknown or invalid arguments)

Example
```
A00159 APPEND tmp (\Seen \Draft) {1259}
+ Ready for argument
```

```
From: "Kevin W. Mullet" <kwm@unt.edu>
To: "'kwm@unt.edu'" <kwm@unt.edu>
Subject: Case HD0000000019310, Request Urgency: Cannot access network
Message-ID: <2767191894.951954964@kwm.unt.edu>
X-Mailer: Mulberry/2.0.0b9 (Win32)
MIME-Version: 1.0
Content-Type: text/plain; charset=us-ascii; format=flowed
Content-Transfer-Encoding: 7bit

Case HD0000000019310 has been assigned to your group.  Short
Description: HD: A problem not listed here.  Open the Support Console
on remedy.unt.edu to view the case.
A00159 OK Completed
```

The APPEND command in this sample tells the server to append a message to the
tmp mailbox with the *Seen* and *Draft* flags set, and that a message 1259 octets in
size will follow. The client then sends the raw RFC 822 message text.

CREATE

The CREATE command creates a mailbox with the given name. When the mailbox name is given with a trailing hierarchy delimiter, the command creates just a
directory and not a mailbox.

Usage
> **CREATE** *mailbox*

Arguments
> Mailbox name

Untagged server responses
> None

Results
> OK (mailbox was created successfully)
> NO (mailbox could not be created)
> BAD (command unknown or invalid arguments)

Example
```
A00009 CREATE saved-messages
A00009 OK Completed
```

DELETE

The DELETE command permanently removes the specified mailbox.

Usage
> **DELETE** *mailbox*

Arguments

  Mailbox name

Untagged server responses

  None

Results

  OK (successfully deleted)
  NO (delete mailbox failed)
  BAD (command unknown or invalid arguments)

Example

```
A00004 DELETE sent-mail.old
A00004 OK Completed
```

EXAMINE

The EXAMINE command is identical to the SELECT command, except that the mailbox is selected in read-only mode.

Usage

  EXAMINE *mailbox*

Arguments

  Mailbox name

Untagged server responses

  The untagged responses FLAGS, EXISTS, and RECENT are required. The untagged responses UNSEEN and PERMANENTFLAGS are optional.

Results

  OK (EXAMINE completed successfully, mailbox is selected)
  NO (EXAMINE failed and mailbox is not selected)
  BAD (command unknown or invalid arguments)

Example

```
A00008 EXAMINE inbox
* 0 EXISTS
* 0 RECENT
* OK [UIDVALIDITY 951200840] UID validity status
* OK [UIDNEXT 26] Predicted next UID
* FLAGS (\Answered \Flagged \Deleted \Draft \Seen)
* OK [PERMANENTFLAGS ()] Permanent flags
A00008 OK Completed
```

The protocol requires the server to send the untagged responses EXISTS and RECENT before returning the OK result. The FLAGS response refers to the flags, mentioned earlier in this appendix, that are defined in the mailbox. EXISTS specifies the number of messages in the mailbox. RECENT specifies the number of messages that have the *Recent* flag set (meaning that this is the first session that has observed the message). *Recent* does not mean "unread." Not all unread messages are recent, and not all recent messages are unread. New messages are unread *and* recent. Once read, they are still recent in that session. If not read in that session, then they are unread and not recent in subsequent sessions.

Each mailbox has a UIDVALIDITY value. UIDVALIDITY is a fail-safe mechanism to permit IMAP clients to make assumptions about whether the message UID numbers in a given mailbox have changed. If they have, the UIDVALIDITY value is increased by an arbitrary value. This attribute is of particular value to clients in disconnected mode—it lets them determine if the UID numbers for the constituent messages in a given mailbox are trustworthy from one session to the next.

LIST

The LIST command returns a list of mailbox names that match the arguments given.

Usage

> **LIST *basename mailbox***

Arguments

> Base name of the part of namespace in which the *mailbox* lives
> Mailbox name (wildcards permitted)

Untagged server responses

> One or more untagged LIST responses

Results

> OK (LIST command successful)
> NO (LIST command failed)
> BAD (command unknown or invalid arguments)

Example

```
A00001 LIST "" "~/mail/*"
* LIST (\NoSelect) "/" ~/mail
* LIST (\NoInferiors) "/" ~/mail/saved-mail
* LIST (\NoInferiors) "/" ~/mail/sent-mail
A00001 OK Completed
```

Usage of the LIST command is somewhat server-implementation-specific. If the reference name argument is left empty, then the mailbox name is interpreted in the same way as it is by the SELECT command. In the previous example, taken from a UW IMAP server, mailboxes are selected relative to the user's home directory by default:

```
A00002 LIST "user.johndoe.sent-mail" "*"
* LIST () "." "user.johndoe.sent-mail"
* LIST () "." "user.johndoe.sent-mail.oldmail"
A00002 OK Completed
```

If the reference name argument contains a string, it usually specifies a level of the mailbox hierarchy. In the example above, taken from a Cyrus IMAP server, the reference argument tells the server to list all mailboxes below *user.johndoe.sent-mail* in the hierarchy.

LSUB

The LSUB command returns a list of mailbox names to which the user is subscribed.

Usage
    LSUB *basename mailbox*

Arguments
    Base name of the part of the namespace in which the *mailbox* lives
    Mailbox name (wildcards permitted)

Untagged server responses
    One or more LSUB untagged responses

Results
    OK (LSUB completed successfully)
    NO (LSUB failed)
    BAD (command unknown or invalid arguments)

Example
```
A00002 LSUB "~/mail" "*"
* LSUB () "/" ~/mail/saved-messages
A00002 OK Completed
```

RENAME

The RENAME command changes the name of the specified mailbox.

Usage
    RENAME *oldmailbox newmailbox*

Arguments
    Old mailbox name
    New mailbox name

Untagged server responses

None

Results

OK (mailbox successfully renamed)

NO (rename failed)

BAD (command unknown or invalid arguments)

Example

```
A00020 RENAME sent-mail sent-mail.old
A00020 OK Completed
```

SELECT

The SELECT command selects the specified mailbox so messages in that mailbox can be accessed. SELECT attempts to acquire read-write access but will succeed even if it can only get read-only access.

Usage

SELECT *mailbox*

Arguments

Mailbox name

Untagged server responses

The untagged responses FLAGS, EXISTS, and RECENT are required. UNSEEN and PERMANENTFLAGS are optional untagged responses.

Results

OK (SELECT completed successfully)

NO (can't access mailbox or mailbox does not exist)

BAD (command unknown or invalid arguments)

Example

```
A00003 SELECT INBOX
* 14 EXISTS
* 5 RECENT
* OK [UIDVALIDITY 951200840] UID validity status
* OK [UIDNEXT 22] Predicted next UID
* FLAGS (\Answered \Flagged \Deleted \Draft \Seen)
* OK [PERMANENTFLAGS (\Answered \Flagged \Deleted \Draft \Seen)] Permanent flags
A00003 OK Completed
```

The protocol requires the server to send the untagged responses EXISTS and RECENT before returning the OK result. The FLAGS response refers to the flags, mentioned earlier in this appendix, that are defined in the mailbox. EXISTS specifies the number of messages in the mailbox. RECENT specifies the number of messages that have the *Recent* flag set (meaning that this is the first session that has observed the message). *Recent* does not mean "unread." Not all unread messages are recent, and not all recent messages are unread. New messages are unread *and* recent. Once read, they are still recent in that session. If not read in that session, then they are unread and not recent in subsequent sessions.

Each mailbox has a UIDVALIDITY value. UIDVALIDITY is a fail-safe mechanism to permit IMAP clients to make assumptions about whether the message UID numbers in a given mailbox have changed. If they have, the UIDVALIDITY value is increased by an arbitrary value. This attribute is of particular value to clients in disconnected mode—it lets them determine if the UID numbers for the constituent messages in a given mailbox are trustworthy from one session to the next.

STATUS

The STATUS command returns the requested status data items associated with the specified mailbox. The STATUS command is used to get information about a mailbox other than the currently selected mailbox, without having to select it first. Note that you never need to run a STATUS command on the currently selected mailbox because IMAP sends (and updates) that information automatically for the selected mailbox.

Usage

> **STATUS** *mailbox item*

Arguments

> Mailbox name
> Status data item names (see Table C-1)

Untagged server responses

> One or more untagged STATUS responses

Results

> OK (STATUS successfully completed)
> NO (STATUS command failed)
> BAD (command unknown or invalid arguments)

Example

```
A00004 STATUS "~/mail/sent-mail" (MESSAGES)
* STATUS ~/mail/test3 (MESSAGES 122)
A00004 OK Completed
```

Table C-1. STATUS Data Items

Item	Meaning
MESSAGES	Number of messages in the mailbox
RECENT	Number of messages that have the *Recent* flag set (i.e., new messages)
UIDNEXT	Next UID that will be assigned to a new message in the mailbox
UIDVALIDITY	Unique identifier of the mailbox
UNSEEN	Number of messages that do not have the *Seen* flag set (i.e., unread messages)

SUBSCRIBE

The SUBSCRIBE command adds the specified mailbox to the user's list of "subscribed" mailboxes. A "subscribed mailbox" is the IMAP equivalent of a bookmarked URL in a web browser.

Usage
> **SUBSCRIBE** *mailbox*

Arguments
> Mailbox name

Untagged server responses
> None

Results
> OK (successfully subscribed to mailbox)
> NO (subscribe failed)
> BAD (command unknown or invalid arguments)

Example
```
A00032 SUBSCRIBE saved-messages
A00032 OK Completed
```

UNSUBSCRIBE

The UNSUBSCRIBE command removes the specified mailbox from the user's "subscribed" list of mailboxes.

Usage
> **UNSUBSCRIBE** *mailbox*

Arguments
> Mailbox name

Untagged server responses
> None

Results
> OK (successfully unsubscribed)
> NO (unsubscribe failed)
> BAD (command unknown or invalid arguments)

Example
```
A00033 UNSUBSCRIBE saved-messages
A00033 OK Completed
```

Commands Valid in the Selected State

CHECK

The CHECK command performs server- or mailstore-dependent mailbox house-keeping not normally performed as part of each IMAP command (also known as a *checkpoint*).

Usage
> **CHECK**

Arguments
> None

Untagged server responses
> None

Results
> OK (CHECK completed)
> BAD (command unknown or invalid arguments)

Example
```
A00002 CHECK
A00002 OK Completed
```

CLOSE

The CLOSE command removes from the currently selected mailbox all messages that have the *\Deleted* flag set and returns the user from the selected state back to the authenticated state. Unlike the EXPUNGE command, no untagged EXPUNGE responses are sent for the removed messages by the CLOSE command.

Usage
> **CLOSE**

Arguments
   None

Untagged server responses
   None

Results
   OK (CLOSE completed successfully)
   NO (No mailbox selected: CLOSE command failed)
   BAD (command unknown or invalid arguments)

Example
   A00008 CLOSE
   A00008 OK Completed

COPY

The COPY command copies the specified messages from the selected mailbox into the specified mailbox.

Usage
   COPY *message-set mailbox*

Arguments
   Set of messages to copy
   Name of target mailbox

Untagged server responses
   None

Results
   OK (successfully copied)
   NO (COPY command failed)
   BAD (command unknown or invalid arguments)

Example
   A00322 COPY 1:5 saved-messages
   A00322 OK Completed

EXPUNGE

The EXPUNGE command permanently removes all messages that have the *\Deleted* flag set from the selected mailbox.

Usage
   EXPUNGE

Arguments

None

Untagged server responses

One or more untagged EXPUNGE responses

Results

OK (EXPUNGE completed successfully)

NO (EXPUNGE failed)

BAD (command unknown or invalid arguments)

Example

```
A00010 EXPUNGE
* 1 EXPUNGE
* 4 EXPUNGE
* 0 EXISTS
* 0 RECENT
A00010 OK Expunged 2 messages
```

FETCH

The FETCH command returns message data belonging to a message or set of messages. The data items defined for the FETCH command are shown in Table C-2.

Usage

FETCH *message-set data-items*

Arguments

Set of messages

Names of message data items to retrieve

Untagged server responses

One or more untagged FETCH responses

Results

OK (FETCH completed successfully)

NO (FETCH command failed)

BAD (command unknown or invalid arguments)

Example

```
A00003 FETCH 2:4 (FLAGS)
* 2 FETCH (FLAGS (\Flagged))
* 3 FETCH (FLAGS (\Flagged \Seen))
* 4 FETCH (FLAGS ())
A00003 OK Completed
```

Table C-2. FETCH Data Items

Data Item	Meaning
ALL	Shortcut for specifying the data items FLAGS, ENVE-LOPE, INTERNALDATE, and RFC 822.SIZE
BODY	Older form of BODYSTRUCTURE that was not extensible
BODY [*section*] (*MIME part specifier*) <*partial*>	Text contained in *section* of the message body. <*partial*>, if specified, is the octet offset and desired octet count of a portion of the desired text
BODY.PEEK [*section*] <*partial*>	Same as BODY [section], but this command does not set the *Seen* message flag
BODYSTRUCTURE	The representation of the MIME information contained in the message
ENVELOPE	The parsed representation of the RFC 822 envelope
FAST	Shortcut for specifying the data items FLAGS, INTER-NALDATE, and RFC 822.SIZE
FLAGS	Flags that are set for the message
FULL	Shortcut for specifying the data items FLAGS, INTER-NALDATE, RFC 822.SIZE, ENVELOPE, and BODY
INTERNALDATE	Date the message was received by the IMAP server
RFC822	Fetches the entire RFC 822 message
RFC822.HEADER	Fetches the RFC 822 message header
RFC822.SIZE	Fetches the RFC 822 message size
RFC822.TEXT	Fetches the RFC 822 message body
UID	The message's unique identifier

SEARCH

The SEARCH command returns a list of the message numbers of messages that match the given search criteria. The defined search criteria are shown in Table C-3.

Usage

> **SEARCH (CHARSET) criteria**

Arguments

> (Optional) CHARSET specification
> Search criteria

Untagged server responses

> The untagged SEARCH response is required.

Results

> OK (SEARCH completed successfully)
> NO (SEARCH failed)
> BAD (command unknown or invalid arguments)

Example

```
00000007 SEARCH ALL 1:80 SUBJECT "key largo"
* SEARCH 69 70 71
00000007 OK Completed
```

Table C-3. SEARCH Criteria

SEARCH Key	Meaning
message-set (e.g., 1:5)	Message numbers in the given set of sequence numbers only
ALL	All messages in the selected mailbox
ANSWERED	Messages that have the *Answered* flag set
BCC *string*	Messages with BCC header field containing *string*
BEFORE *date*	Messages received before internal date *date*
BODY *string*	Messages that contain *string* in the message body
CC *string*	Messages that contain *string* in the CC header field
DELETED	Messages that have the *Deleted* flag set
DRAFT	Messages that have the *Draft* flag set
FLAGGED	Messages that have the *Flagged* flag set
FROM *string*	Messages that contain *string* in the FROM header field
HEADER *field-name string*	Messages that contain *string* in the *field-name* header field
KEYWORD *flag*	Messages with *flag* set
LARGER *n*	Messages larger than *n* 8-bit bytes in size
NEW	Messages that have the *Recent* but not the *Seen* flag set
NOT *searchkey*	Messages that do not match *searchkey*
OLD	Messages that do not have the *Recent* flag set
ON *date*	Messages received on internal date *date*
OR *searchkey1 searchkey2*	Messages that match either *searchkey1* or *searchkey2*
RECENT	Messages that have the /*Recent* flag set
SEEN	Messages that have the /*Seen* flag set
SENTBEFORE *date*	Messages whose RFC 822 *Date:* header is dated earlier than *date*
SENTON *date*	Messages whose RFC 822 *Date:* header matches *date*
SENTSINCE *date*	Messages whose RFC 822 *Date:* header is dated later than *date*
SINCE *date*	Messages with internal date later than *date*
SMALLER *n*	Messages smaller than *n* 8-bit bytes in size
SUBJECT *string*	Messages that contain *string* in the header's SUBJECT field
TEXT *string*	Messages that contain *string* in the message header or body

Table C-3. SEARCH Criteria (continued)

SEARCH Key	Meaning
TO *string*	Messages that contain *string* in the header's TO field
UID *message-set*	Messages whose unique identifiers match those specified in *message-set*
UNANSWERED	Messages that do not have the *Answered* flag set
UNDELETED	Messages that do not have the *Deleted* flag set
UNDRAFT	Messages that do not have the *Draft* flag set
UNFLAGGED	Messages that do not have the *Flagged* flag set
UNKEYWORD	Messages that do not have the given keyword flag set
UNSEEN	Messages that do not have the *Seen* flag set

STORE

The STORE command is used to set or unset message flags.

Usage

STORE message data

Arguments

Set of messages

Message data item name

Message data item value

Untagged server responses

One or more untagged FETCH responses

Results

OK (STORE completed successfully)

NO (STORE command failed)

BAD (command unknown or invalid arguments)

Example

```
A00009 STORE 1:3 +FLAGS (\Deleted)
* 1 FETCH (FLAGS (\Seen \Deleted \Flagged))
A00009 OK Completed
```

UID

The UID command uses UID numbers for a set of messages requested by the COPY, FETCH, STORE, or SEARCH commands. Normally those commands return message sequence numbers, not UID numbers.

Usage

UID command command-args

Arguments

Command name (may take one of the values COPY, FETCH, STORE, or SEARCH)

Command arguments (options arguments to the given command)

Untagged server responses

Server responds with the untagged responses FETCH and SEARCH

Results

OK (command successfully completed)

NO (command error)

BAD (command unknown or invalid arguments)

Example

```
A000002 UID SEARCH ALL 1:80 SUBJECT "key largo"
* SEARCH 151 152 153
A000002 OK Completed
```

Index

About the Authors

Dianna and Kevin Mullet are a husband and wife team who share their home in Carrollton, Texas, with awk and Lavender, who are cats, and Milo and Goldie, who are beagles. Dianna and Kevin met, married, and conceived this book while working at the University of North Texas.

Dianna is a senior Unix system administrator for a leading provider of flight simulation, training, and defense communication systems, where she maintains the Unix infrastructure and plays a leadership role in overall IT system design and integration.

In her previous career, Dianna was a widely published physical chemist. She lives and works on the leading edge, but keeps an eye out for technologies whose growth outstrips our ability to manage them. Dianna is a qualified scuba rescue diver and relishes opportunities to go on analog vacations with Kevin, who insists on packing a notebook PC and digital camera to maintain his umbilical cord to the Net.

Kevin is a voracious punster who got bit by the computer bug when he bought a Timex/Sinclair 1000 in 1982 and found himself chomping at the bit to change careers from photographer to computer geek. (Coincidentally, Dianna bought a TS1000 at the same time, and it was also her first computer.) One thing led to another, and he found himself working for local, regional, and national ISPs as a network analyst and Unix system administrator, and was network security manager for the University of North Texas. Kevin and Dianna have started Atomic Consulting, Inc., which does Unix and network consulting for small and medium size companies in the Dallas area. Kevin believes open source is more a religion than a license, that the Internet will supplant most national governments, that most economies will be reduced if not eliminated by nanotechnology, and that the ISO seven-layer model and the Sanskrit chakra system are essentially the same thing.

Also a certified scuba diver, and an avid photographer, Kevin lives to go on vacation with Dianna, who insists on bringing her analog camera, and no computer, and preserving the pioneering offline spirit of the family vacation, at least until the last hour or two of the day.

When they're not busy helping to make the Net a better, safer, more interesting place, Dianna and Kevin are busy networking their new home from scratch. Since they're in one of the few neighborhoods that can get really good ADSL service, they may never move.

They may be reached at *themullets@themullets.net.*

Colophon

Our look is the result of reader comments, our own experimentation, and feedback from distribution channels. Distinctive covers complement our distinctive approach to technical topics, breathing personality and life into potentially dry subjects.

The animal on the cover of *Managing IMAP* is a bushbuck (*Tragelaphus scriptus*), also known as a guib. Bushbucks are the smallest of the African spiral-horned antelopes, weighing between 50 and 180 pounds and measuring about 3 feet at the shoulder. Males have straight horns, which are usually 13 to 22 inches long. Bushbucks vary in color from reddish brown to almost black with white spots or stripes. The most brightly striped groups are the Senegal bushbuck and the Cameroon bushbuck, which have white vertical and horizontal stripes. Because of their vibrant markings, bushbucks are also called "harnessed antelopes."

Bushbucks live in the forests and brush of sub-Saharan Africa, usually near a plentiful source of water. Excellent swimmers, they have also populated islands, such as those in Lake Victoria. Bushbucks are solitary animals but are not territorial, so their ranges may overlap peacefully. They are elusive and shy; however, they often inhabit outskirts of towns and have been known to leap over 6-foot fences. Bushbucks will eat leaves, buds, shoots, fruits, herbs, and grasses. Their calls are similar to the barks of a baboon or to a series of grunts.

Melanie Wang was the production editor and proofreader, and Paulette Miley was the copyeditor for *Managing IMAP*. Lucy Muellner and James Carter provided production support. Darren Kelly and Catherine Morris provided quality control. Nancy Crumpton wrote the index.

Ellie Volckhausen designed the cover of this book, based on a series design by Edie Freedman. The cover image is an original engraving from the 19th century. Emma Colby produced the cover layout with QuarkXPress 4.1 using Adobe's ITC Garamond font.

Alicia Cech and David Futato designed the interior layout based on a series design by Nancy Priest. Mike Sierra implemented the design in FrameMaker 5.5.6. The text and heading fonts are ITC Garamond Light and Garamond Book. The illustrations that appear in the book were produced by Robert Romano using Macromedia FreeHand 8 and Adobe Photoshop 5. This colophon was written by Melanie Wang.

Whenever possible, our books use a durable and flexible lay-flat binding. If the page count exceeds this binding's limit, perfect binding is used.